D1563778

After Dark

AFTER DARK

THE NOCTURNAL URBAN LANDSCAPE
AND LIGHTSCAPE OF ANCIENT CITIES

EDITED BY

Nancy Gonlin and Meghan E. Strong

UNIVERSITY PRESS OF COLORADO
Louisville

Published by University Press of Colorado

University Press of Colorado
245 Century Circle, Suite 202
Louisville, Colorado 80027

 The University Press of Colorado is a proud member of
the Association of University Presses.

The University Press of Colorado is a cooperative publishing enterprise supported, in part, by
Adams State University, Colorado State University, Fort Lewis College, Metropolitan State
University of Denver, University of Alaska Fairbanks, University of Colorado, University of
Denver, University of Northern Colorado, University of Wyoming, Utah State University, and
Western Colorado University.

∞ This paper meets the requirements of the ANSI/NISO Z39.48–1992 (Permanence of Paper)

ISBN: 978-1-64642-259-3 (hardcover)
ISBN: 978-1-64642-260-9 (ebook)
https://doi.org/10.5876/9781646422609

Library of Congress Cataloging-in-Publication Data

Names: Gonlin, Nancy, editor. | Strong, Meghan E., editor.
Title: After dark : the nocturnal urban landscape and lightscape of ancient cities / edited by
  Nancy Gonlin, Meghan E. Strong.
Description: Louisville : University Press of Colorado ; Albany : Institute for Mesoamerican
  Studies, [2022] | Includes bibliographical references and index.
Identifiers: LCCN 2022013722 (print) | LCCN 2022013723 (ebook) | ISBN 9781646422593
  (hardcover) | ISBN 9781646422609 (epub)
Subjects: LCSH: Cities and towns, Ancient. | Municipal lighting—History. | City and town
  life—History. | Lighting—Social aspects. | Night—Social aspects. | Sociology, Urban. |
  BISAC: SOCIAL SCIENCE / Archaeology
Classification: LCC HT114 .A38 2022 (print) | LCC HT114 (ebook) | DDC
  307.7609—dc23/eng/20220504
LC record available at https://lccn.loc.gov/2022013722
LC ebook record available at https://lccn.loc.gov/2022013723

Cover illustration: "Twelve Scenes of Tokyo: Kagurazaka Street after a Night Rain (Tôkyô
jûni dai: Kagurazaka-dôri, ugo no yoru)," 1929, by Yoshida Hiroshi. Courtesy of the Cleveland
Museum of Art.

Nan:

To the Bellevue College Anthropologists, past and present, who have provided collegiality, friendship, and support through the years and great enthusiasm for my research and ideas: John Osmundson, Lawrence Epstein, Manouchehr Shiva, the late Leon Leeds, Katharine Hunt, Susan Cox, Anthony Tessandori, Erica Madeleine Aguilar-Tessandori, Christine C. Dixon-Hundredmark, Jamie Holthuysen, and Stephanie Brommer

Meghan:

For my grandparents, whom I spent many nights with chasing fireflies, playing games, eating ice cream, and laughing. They helped make the night special for me, and it is now always a reminder of them

In memory of John Wayne Janusek

Contents

FIGURES

TABLES

Preface

Nancy Gonlin

Many cities of the past are characterized by some of the same features as modern cities: large, dense, heterogeneous populations; centralized, complex social, economic, and political functions; religious centers; hubs of novel ideology; and numerous other features. But ancient cities had a major difference with the present: they were not routinely lit at night. It was not until the 1800s that electrical lighting illuminated urban areas across the world, and from then onward, there has been no retreat. Modern urban nights are profusely illuminated, so much so that archaeologists may not incorporate the facet of darkness in their reconstructions of the past.

This volume is the third book that explores a novel dimension to studying the past: the "archaeology of the night" (Gonlin and Nowell 2018; Gonlin and Reed 2021). Another perspective that is logically aligned with this orientation is lychnology, or the study of "pre-modern lighting devices" and light (International Lychnological Association 2021). While focusing on nocturnal dimensions of the urban experience, a consideration of how urbanites lit up the night is essential. Darkness comes with night as well as with natural (e.g., caves) and culturally constructed venues that are sacred and profane, such as the interiors of temples and taverns. The subjects of the night, darkness, and lighting taken together form a comprehensive framework when analyzing city life and has much to offer archaeologists in deepening our examination of complexity and

https://doi.org/10.5876/9781646422609.c000

inequality as manifested in the built environment, artifactual remains, iconography, and ancient writing.

Authors of this volume explore these themes to varying degrees and deliver innovative insights on urbanism that boost our appreciation of how ancient humans navigated the night through material and conceptual adaptations to city life. These chapters were first presented in 2019 as papers at the 84th Annual Meeting of the Society for American Archaeology in Albuquerque, New Mexico. The archaeological community was extremely saddened to learn of the demise of one of the participants, Dr. John W. Janusek, a renowned Andeanist. Dr. Anna Guengerich, remarked that the night was John's favorite time. Anna ensured that John's work on this topic was completed; so, we are quite fortunate to have a chapter on Tiwanaku and the night authored by John and Anna. Our volume is in memory of John and his fondness for the night.

Other ancient cities and cultures are featured (Cahokia, Chaco Canyon, the Classic Maya, Egypt, Mesopotamia, Samothrace, Tenochtitlan, and the Wari), though no claim is made that this volume offers a comprehensive treatment of the subject. Numerous scholars were invited to contribute, but only a few brave souls answered the call. Much work remains to be done; this volume is only a beginning.

We are grateful to Andrew Bednarski for composing the index, a detailed, demanding task that he cheerfully undertook. Many thanks are due to the University Press of Colorado, whose staff I have been privileged to work with on many projects, and our excellent anonymous reviewers who provided critical insights and constructive feedback. Our authors are to be commended for their timely response for revisions and for their patience with the publishing process.

REFERENCES

Gonlin, Nancy, and April Nowell, eds. 2018. *Archaeology of the Night: Life After Dark in the Ancient World*. Boulder: University Press of Colorado.

Gonlin, Nancy, and David M. Reed, eds. 2021. *Night and Darkness in Ancient Mesoamerica*. Louisville: University Press of Colorado.

International Lychnological Association. 2021. http://www.lychnology.org/. Accessed February 14, 2021.

After Dark

1

The night is extraordinary and ordinary, sacred and secular. It is a time of day that comes naturally, and we humans have no say in stopping it. By incorporating the dimension of the night into anthropological and archaeological analyses, scholars expand our understanding of the cultural aspects and experiences throughout the full diurnal cycle, not just "daily" life. While night and day are the result of the Earth's rotation, they are also cultural constructs worth exploring, rather than suggesting any kind of environmental determinism for humans (Wright and Garrett 2018, 287). In this volume, authors take several approaches to incorporate the dimension of the night into the study of ancient cities. By looking across cultures in time and space and from across the ancient world, a rich array of nightways (Reed and Gonlin 2021, 7) is revealed (figure 1.1). Ancient cities are notoriously difficult to excavate, given their centuries of occupation, density of remains, and chronological complexity (McAtackney and Ryzewski 2017). Their study requires many resources to tease out information about urban life in the past. But, archaeologists can obtain an even greater and livelier understanding with the inclusion of the nocturnal dimension. By embracing night as a conceptual framework, scholars discover a wealth of activities, behaviors, and beliefs that took place between dusk and dawn, and their archaeological correlates.

Following Monica L. Smith (2010a, 33), let us consider the category of time/temporality to encompass

City Nights

Archaeology of Night, Darkness, and Luminosity in Ancient Urban Environments

Nancy Gonlin and
Meghan E. Strong

https://doi.org/10.5876/9781646422609.c001

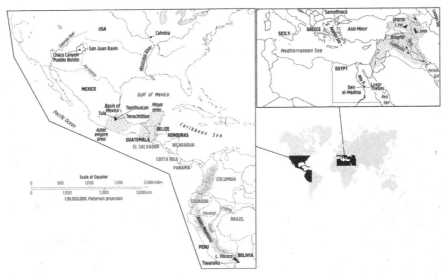

FIGURE 1.1. *World map showing locations of major urban areas discussed in the volume. Map: David M. Reed.*

the effects of the night on individuals, groups, and societies. Inspiration from her 2010 book *A Prehistory of Ordinary People* led us to further our research into the archaeology of the night (Gonlin and Nowell 2018a; Gonlin and Reed 2021). Both of us have explicitly considered the factor of night in our reconstructions of the past: Gonlin for the Classic Maya (Gonlin and Dixon-Hundredmark 2018, 2021) and Strong for the ancient Egyptians (2018, 2021). Here, we venture further by using Smith's examination of human cognitive development. We have come to understand that night and darkness are also parts of that cognitive process. Individuals and groups conquered and molded the night. Night has always influenced the human species, including our habituation to the night as part of our evolutionary development. Our deep primate roots are reflected in sleep (Nunn et al. 2010), though "comparatively, human sleep is unique in that it is shorter, deeper, and exhibits a higher proportion of rapid eye movement (REM) than expected when compared to that of other primates (Samson and Nunn 2015). Moreover, it has been hypothesized that human sleep in postindustrialized countries is vastly different from the sleep of our hominin ancestors (Worthman and Melby 2002; Worthman 2008)" (Samson et al. 2017, 91). David Samson and colleagues (2017, 97) report on their recent research of contemporary Hadza hunter-gatherers and their sleep patterns, and they find that factors affecting the duration and quality of one's sleep include the location of the sleep site (inside a hut is usually better than outside) and sound levels (less sound means better sleep). If we take these patterns to be representative of how our foraging ancestors experienced sleep, when we fast-forward to the dawn of urbanism, the noise factor and the interruption it causes in human sleep are well appreciated. Ancient city nights were both like and unlike our modern ones. The ill effects of nocturnal artificial light to humans and other species are well known (https://www.darksky.org/).

Darkness, likewise, has played a role in our evolution, though darkness is not to be equated with only the night. Both have been used as metaphors for deviance, dysfunction, and death. But darkness, like the night, is sometimes sought out, desired, or required by humans for particular purposes, such as sleeping, rituals, sorcery (e.g., Coltman and Pohl 2021), astronomy, celebrations, or photography. The criterion of darkness figures prominently in activities from foraging groups (Wiessner's 2014 study of Ju/'hoansi fireside talk), to the study of the *epeme* dance among the Hadza (Marlowe 2010), to postindustrialists who work the night shift. While humans cannot create the natural night, they can create darkness or seek out places where the absence of light is welcomed or necessary, such as the interior of caves and enclosed temples.

Whether past or present, humans handle night and darkness like no other species. Through human creativity, we modified the nocturnal urban environment, and it is the many manifestations of that modification in the archaeological record that we show here. The evidence has always been present, but archaeologists have not always viewed it from such a perspective. The specific inquiry into the night is a relatively new one in archaeology (Gonlin and Nowell 2018a; Gonlin and Reed 2021) and in the social sciences in general (Palmer 2000; Ekirch 2005; Galinier et al. 2010; Koslofsky 2011; Edensor 2017; Dunn and Edensor 2021). Here, we examine the night and use it as an interpretive lens to answer larger questions about cultural evolution and, in particular, urban transformations. The study of the dawn or sunrise also demands attention that we hope researchers will address, as Iyaxel Cojti Ren (2020) has done for the significance of the Dawn Tradition in the founding of the ancient Kaqchikel Maya polity.

Well known from ancient times is that people did not necessarily divide the day into standard twenty-four-hour segments as we moderns do with no regard for seasonality and that there were names for auspicious times of the day and night (e.g., Laurence 2007; Martínez 2012). Ray Laurence (2007, 154–166) writes about the "temporal logic of space" to describe how ancient Romans in Pompeii during the first century CE used various parts of the city from public to private at different times of the day throughout the year. Daylight and darkness determined the Roman concept of time, and even though day and night were each divided into twelve hours, the length of each hour varied considerably through the seasons (Laurence 2007, 156). For example, "At the summer solstice the day was six hours longer than at the winter solstice" (156). A firmer understanding of quotidian to state-level activities can be achieved by examining the time of day and season in which certain activities that had a definite spatial location took place. Although one's house was not explicitly sectioned into male and female divisions, men and women tended to use certain parts of a house more than others. For elites, domestic space was temporally divided, with men dominating the start and finish of the day and women dominating during the middle of the day (Laurence 2007, 162). If one were a male elite member of Pompeiian society, "this regular pattern meant that the elite were seen at a certain time and place each day" as they headed to the forum to conduct business after the morning repast (Laurence 2007, 163). This very structured use of the city by male elites contrasted sharply with the unstructured time of the rest of the population (163). The diverse jobs of such *mercennarius* were task oriented, contrasting with the modern conception of work as an eight-hour day. Placing the study of the night into this wider framework, we encourage those interested in expanding daily practices into all hours of the day.

Studies of the urban environment have an extensive history (Pirenne [1925] 1969; Childe 1950; Adams 1960; M. L. Smith 2010b; Creekmore and Fisher 2014; Hutson 2016). We social scientists discuss what it means to be urban, how the process of urbanization occurred, what constitutes a city, and how to define it (Wirth 1940), though newer interpretations do not focus on population figures alone (e.g., Alt and Pauketat 2019). Regardless, as soon as one hears the word "city," it immediately conjures up a myriad of sensorial experiences. In the hustle and bustle of humanity, the sights, sounds, and smells of urban life dominate the senses. Critically, the majority of urban environments were occupied long before the invention of electricity, adding an additional layer of darkness to the sensorial experience. Darkness evokes its own sensations and, in combination with a city's environment, creates a unique nocturnal landscape, or urban nightscape. Combining these aspects, our authors begin to build a picture of what it was like to live in an ancient city after the sun set and before bright electric lighting was commonplace.

The process of urbanization unfolded across the globe at various times and places and in drastically different environments. Numerous theories address this process, from classic writings (Childe 1950; Adams 1960) to more recent treatments (Bietak et al. 2010; Harmanşah 2013; Cowgill 2015; Moeller 2016; M. E. Smith 2019; M. L. Smith 2019). The role of the night in the urbanization process has not been routinely incorporated. However, one example from Andean archaeologists Alexei Vranich and Scott C. Smith (2018, 134) determined that "Tiwanaku's initial location and its continued success in creating a location for the interaction between pastoralists and agriculturalists can be attributed to a life cycle based on the observation of the nighttime sky." Elsewhere, the role of the moon is now a topic in Mesoamerican studies (Šprajc 2016) when considering the built environment and the skyscape.

There is abundant archaeological evidence for how ancient peoples not only coped with, but thrived, in dark urban environments. In (re)examining material culture for nighttime signatures, archaeologists can gain better insight into ancient urban environments, while advancing the archaeology of darkness and night, and lychnology—the study of ancient artificial lighting. This process contributes to sensory archaeology (e.g., Skeates and Day 2019) through a focus on the multisensual experiences of the nocturnal environment and the stimuli that the diverse population of urban inhabitants experienced at night.

Following Michael E. Smith (2007, 2011, 169, 171), middle-range theories in archaeology are critical for bridging data with grand theories. He (Smith 2011, 173) focuses on "the layout or form of cities, urban planning, and the social dynamics of urban life" in his empirical approach to the past. Archaeologists can consider how the urban environment was utilized at night, in the dark, and how aspects of the built environment relate to darkness and the night.

One might look to niche construction theory (Laland and O'Brien 2010; O'Brien and Laland 2012) to assist in our comprehension of the urban phenomenon, a situation uniquely created by humans and one in which we excel. From early on in our ancestry with the construction of shelters, we have affected our biological patterns, such as sleep (Samson et al. 2017). The urban landscape is a highly charged culturally constructed niche uniquely created by our species, and it is not likely that humans will give it up any time soon, as cities are here to stay (M. L. Smith 2019, 262). Today, for the first time in global history, there are more humans living in cities than outside them. The creation of the urban environment enticed others to join the growing number of city dwellers. The mass migration to cities that occurred throughout history was influenced by push-pull factors (Anthony 1990; Gonlin and Landau 2021) that either drew us to or repelled us from this lifestyle.

The urban environment can be considered anew with the consideration of looking at architecture and infrastructure from a nocturnal perspective. The prodigious works of Amos Rapoport are instructive at this juncture. His perspective from architecture has been gainfully employed by archaeologists studying urban environments (e.g., M. E. Smith 2007). It allows us to tease apart the components archaeologists wish to study and simultaneously retain the integrated whole. Rapoport's (1990, 15) analyses encompass four variables: "space, time, meaning, and communication." Here we quote from Rapoport to contextualize the night as one dimension of the variable of time (underline added):

> [Activities] vary and are organized in time; there is an unavoidable *temporal component*. This involves, on the one hand, the differential sequence of activities in time as well as in space, their tempos (number of activities per unit time) and rhythms (the periodicity of activities related to different cycles: lifetime, annual, seasonal, profane time/sacred time, festivals, work-day vs. weekend, day and night, etc.). On the other hand this temporal component introduces the possibility that organization in time may be *substituted* for organization in space (Rapoport 1977). (Rapoport 1990, 15)

It is through Rapoport's (1990, 13) work that we can look at the built environment as it relates to the night, using the temporal component: "It is useful to conceptualize the environment as consisting of fixed-feature elements (buildings, floors, walls, etc.), semi-fixed-feature elements ('furnishings,' interior and exterior, of all sorts), and non-fixed-feature elements (people and their activities and behaviors)." Architecture and infrastructure fall into the "fixed-feature" type of element and are the most durable, archaeologically speaking. Rapoport (1990, 13) cautions that

> the same space can then become a different setting through changes in the semi-fixed elements and varied activities of the occupants. This important role of occupants cannot be used in studies involving past environments. The inevitable absence of people makes inference from environment to activities much more difficult. It also makes analysis of semi-fixed cues critical.

The crucial semi-fixed elements rarely survive through time, barring exceptional circumstances (e.g., Sheets 2006; G. R. Storey 2018), leaving fixed-feature elements for the archaeologist to rely upon to decode ancient practices.

Architecture and infrastructure do pertain to nocturnal practices. For instance, economic pursuits, such as standing guard and conducting trade (e.g., Mexica [or Aztec] society *pochteca*, or merchants [Nichols 2013, 56]) were tied to the night through gates, roads, record keeping, and storehouses. Similarly, observations of the night sky by Egyptian priests were essential to the planning of royal burial complexes (Magli 2013). The night could be manipulated to highlight social inequalities. As some engaged in the leisure and relaxation that night brings, others spent their evenings waiting on and attending to the whims of their indulgent guests, as manifested in palaces and servant quarters. Elites used the evening to brazenly display their consumption of excess fuel and food, partying into the early hours without the concern of having to wake up with the sun to tend to essential domestic chores. Midden deposits and lighting relics attest to such activities and complement the remains of architecture and infrastructure.

In the modern world, urban humans are constantly surrounded by natural and steady artificial light that blurs day into night. As a result, the contrasts between day and night, and associated events, have been deadened in our contemporary lifestyles. Today, the normal ebb and flow of natural light levels have been replaced to the point that we endanger ourselves and other species through the alteration of natural biochemical rhythms (Chepesiuk 2009; Naiman 2014). If we were to write a book about modern city nights, we could not accurately call it "After Dark," since the lights never go out. There's a reason that Paris—one of the first European cities to embrace gas street lighting—was nicknamed La Ville Lumière. This melding of day and night has also bled over into our examination of cities of the past. Both low-density and high-density urban environments were significantly and experientially different from our modern experience, even a hundred years ago. The evolving urban nightscape can be examined from many perspectives. A focus on the archaeology of night and darkness allows us to envision dark nocturnal cityscapes that inhabitants navigated to perform particular activities, as well as the objects and meanings associated with those activities (Rapoport's "non-fixed feature" elements). Materials in the form of artifacts, features, architecture, infrastructure, and sites relate to how ancient people navigated and experienced darkness and the night in the urban landscape.

THE URBAN ENVIRONMENT AND BEHAVIORS

Night is encoded into the built environment; this study relates to environment-behavior theory as put forth in Rapoport's voluminous works (e.g., 2006; cited in M. E. Smith 2011). A consideration of the planning of urban landscapes for nocturnal activities reorients our perspective from day to night and from light to darkness, features that include the layout of space and architecture, an orientation that some researchers refer to as space syntax (Baumanova 2020) and some of which M. L. Smith (2016) and Daryl Wilkinson (2019) classify as infrastructure or "centrally sponsored construction . . . landscape connectivities" (M. L. Smith 2016, 2). Infrastructure looms large on the landscape, taking up more resources, time, and energy than that provided by a single household (2). Just as anthropologists study urbanism in a global comparative fashion, infrastructure can be studied in this manner. Here, we apply various types of infrastructure to studying the night by considering Wilkinson's (2019, 1216) classification and reimagining them in a nocturnal urban environment: (1) "static infrastructure (e.g., terraces, harbors, and storehouses), (2) circulatory infrastructure (e.g., roads, canals, aqueducts, and sewers), (3) bounding infrastructure (e.g., palisades, ditches, and corrals), and (4) signaling infrastructure (e.g., lighthouses and beacons)." Some of these examples relate more readily to night and darkness than others, such as lighthouses and beacons, which were designed to combat darkness, among other dangers. Other examples, such as palisades, may be indicative of defending one's location against raids, some of which may have taken place at night to capitalize on the element of surprise through the cover of darkness, or the period of time dedicated to sleep. All cities have infrastructure, as do all state-level societies, but infrastructure can exist without cities or states (Wilkinson 2019).

D. Wilkinson (2019, 1220–1221) enumerates how infrastructure differs from architecture. The former does not include domestic buildings, since most houses do not require large labor pools (with palaces excepted), and infrastructure is usually open construction rather than closed. Wilkinson (2019, 1222) envisions that "infrastructure often entails structures that sprawl across the landscape (roads, canals, bridges, aqueducts)" and that "infrastructure is part [of the] built environment dedicated to accommodating things, resources, and waste." Duly noted is that there is no hard-and-fast rule for distinguishing between architecture and infrastructure, and conceptual overlap is inevitable. The interconnections of architecture and infrastructure are many and extend to considerations of agency and interaction with their occupants (Müller 2015). For example, domestic compounds in the ancient city of Mohenjo-Daro relied upon the infrastructure of pipes and wells that inhabitants used to keep their places and themselves clean (Wright and Garrett 2018).

Architecture and infrastructure affect one's views at night, as stated by Monika Baumanova (2020, 137):

> It can be stated that long sightlines on one hand, and visual breaks or turns on the other, have significance for the perception of a moving observer and hence for combining with space syntax to analyze the kinaesthetic/tactile potential of the built environment. With this approach, selected aspects of visual and haptic perception can be synthesized in the study of individual buildings and entire urban settlements.

Similar observations have been made with regard to the household in ancient Egypt, for example, and how the built environment was utilized to structure encounters between residents and visitors (Spence 2004, 2015). One wonders how much ancient city planners considered nocturnal aspects of the built environment, since viewsheds (the view of an area from a location) vary considerably from day to night (e.g., Kamp and Whittaker 2018).

There are numerous examples of ancient communities with walls, from the ancient Sumerian cities of the Middle East, to the Classic Maya sites of Becan and Mayapán in Mexico, to the palisade around Cahokia in midwestern North America, to Great Zimbabwe in Zimbabwe, to Medieval European cities such as Avignon, France. City walls kept out the dangerous and unwanted, but they also functioned to keep inside the dangerous and unwanted. Walls confine and delineate boundaries of ownership and areas of control (Ekirch 2005; Koslofsky 2011). Scott Hutson (2016) speaks of "technologies of privacy," such as walls, that act as strategies for coping with the disadvantages of urbanism from "crowding, anomie, [and] health problems" (51–52). Furthermore, neighborhood formation was a way to manage crowding, and walls were built around residential units to demarcate individual house lots. Walls demarcated status, as those living within a walled city often had higher status than those living outside on the periphery. "The construction of walls and gates is an act of planning, and features like the size, exclusivity, and formality of walled compounds can suggest degrees of planning" (M. E. Smith 2007, 24).

Gates of all sizes of enclosures, from those surrounding homes to those of temples to the walls of the city itself, were carefully monitored and served as portals to safety. The form of gates themselves could relate to the interplay of day and night, as in ancient Egypt, where temple pylons symbolized the horizon, the *akhet*—the physical point in the landscape where day ended and night began (figure 1.2) (R. Wilkinson 2000, 79). Just as the horizon was a significant point of transition in the diurnal cycle, gates or doorways in sacred structures were powerful liminal spaces. Passing over these thresholds marked passage into a divine realm, leaving the secular world outside the temple walls. People who entered willingly had their senses impacted—the eyes would have to adjust to a sharp contrast from brilliant sunshine to darkness, heat levels would drop, and the heady scent of incense might permeate the air.

Roads in general have received much anthropological study (Snead et al. 2009). Widely known are the roads that drew together inhabitants of the Chaco Canyon network in Southwestern United States. Robert S. Weiner (chapter 9, this volume) considers this infrastructure and its role in nocturnal activities. In Classic Maya cities, numerous roads, or *sacbeob* (Mayan for "white

FIGURE 1.2. *The hieroglyph* akhet, *"horizon," overlaid onto the pylon entrance to Luxor Temple, Egypt. Photo: Meghan E. Strong.*

ways"), joined sacred and secular areas (Chase and Chase 2001; Keller 2009, 2010). These raised surfaces were coated with white lime plaster and would have gleamed in the night, facilitating transportation between and within urban zones. Highly prestigious temples were connected to each other through sacbeob, and fancy promenades along their courses for military processions and nocturnal ceremonies would have been facilitated (Ardren 2014). These roadways also served political, social, and economic purposes. Residents of Cobá and Yaxuna on the Yucatan Peninsula of Mexico used the causeway, the longest-known sacbe, to exchange materials items (such as Arena Red ceramics [Loya González and Stanton 2013]). Late Classic Maya peoples connected many communities along the route of this 100-kilometer-long road (Hutson et al. 2012; Loya González and Stanton 2013), linking people along the way.

Domestic architecture has been heavily analyzed by those studying urban inequality (e.g., Hutson and Welch 2019; M. E. Smith et al. 2019), and here we can examine houses anew through the lens of the night. Previously explored by Gonlin and April Nowell (2018b, 11) is the concept of nighttime household archaeology (Gonlin 2020, 398–399). For most humans, the night is private and a time for repose, making the house and its environs ideal locations for archaeologists to gather evidence for nocturnal activities. Differences in urban housing from grand palaces in city centers to those living in squalor on the edges of a city supply data upon which we can further assess socioeconomic parameters of the night. Great variation in the experience of urban residents occurred on a nightly basis.

Remains of houses also relate to "reflexive identity," according to M. L. Smith (2010a, 32), who aptly notes that "in private, material culture is used to craft expressions of self by the individual prior to the projection of that identity in public." Some of this identity may have been best expressed at night. Light emitting from a home, for example, could be a potent symbol of wealth and status, as the owners clearly had excess fuel to burn. It would be difficult to hide the bright glow emanating from one's place of residence, regardless of how one interacted with others during the day.

LYCHNOLOGY, LUMINOSITY, AND LIGHT

There is a sacredness to the night, enhanced by the interaction between darkness and flickering flames, shadow and luminosity, with many of our authors commenting on this special nocturnal ambience. The prevalence, even the overabundance, of artificial lighting in modern day has obscured our view of night and darkness. Many modern humans assume the presence or need for illumination and imagine that architecture, objects, and people were always visible in their entirety. As a result, the experience and significance of darkness and shadow, and how ancient populations perceived the visible and invisible, have been lost. The formal study of lighting technology—lychnology—has been addressed by several researchers (e.g., Parisinou 2000; Eckardt 2002; Moyes and Papadopoulos 2017; Gonlin and Dixon-Hundredmark 2021; Strong 2021).

Attention to the types of illumination in the form of candles, torches, gaslights, lamps, hearths, fireboxes, and moonlight is an essential part of analyzing nocturnal habits of ancient city dwellers. Some of these objects are openly used to interact with the night, and perhaps some of them with the supernatural, following M. L. Smith (2010a, 113). As an example of this supernatural interaction, Meghan E. Strong (chapter 2, this volume) discusses the role of light in ancient Egyptian urban rituals, especially those that honored the dead and the ancestors. In these rituals, torchlit processions through the city and the necropolis served as a means of commemorating deceased relatives. These yearly celebrations were significant means of building collective social memory and ways of displaying personal piety and identity within the community.

Lychnology brings to the fore the technology, timing, and amplitude of how early urbanites lit up their spaces to participate in nightlife, night shifts, nocturnal ceremonies, and other nightways. The types of lighting devices employed can yield insight into the cost of these implements and the social prestige that illumination imparted. M. L. Smith (2010a, 41–42) notes under the category of "technology" that "the control of even the simplest technologies is a way in which we see how individuals[,] as autonomous cognitive entities[,] make quotidian decisions to selectively modify the world around them." Remains of lighting technology are seen in humble houses and grand palaces alike, as well as in secular and religious spaces in the city, on streets, and in other infrastructure as evidence for meanings behind those usages. We should consider how shifts in resource availability affected how humans coped with the night, per M. L. Smith (2010a, 55). Estimates of the time and energy spent on procuring lighting supplies can delineate the cultural practices and the roles that artificial light played in the expression of identity.

More examples of the power of lighting technology are given in this volume, one of which dates back to at least the third millennium BCE in Mesopotamia. Tiffany Earley-Spadoni (chapter 3) utilizes archaeological and historical data to determine that the use of fire beacons and nocturnal rituals created agency for ancient Mesopotamians, who sought to ward off the perils of night, whether they were human invaders, ghosts, or witches. In ancient Greece, on the island of Samothrace in the Aegean Sea from the seventh through fourth centuries BCE, a secret cult existed in which initiates went through their rites of passage in the dark, at night. In the Sanctuary of the Great Gods, remains of artifacts, features, and architecture exist to bolster interpretations that artificial lighting played a central role in such rites. Maggie L. Popkin (chapter 4, this volume) effectively relays the sensorial experience of initiates and luminosity through her study of this mysterious cult. Weiner (chapter 9, this volume) introduces the remains of fireboxes in the Chacoan Southwest, some of which were used for signaling across many kilometers but most of which had ritual significance from placement at the consecrated intersections of roads and architecture. Without the necessary lighting, neither sacred nor profane activities could take place, realms that overlapped and intertwined with each other. In the next section, we give an overview of some of the nocturnal activities that occurred in cities across the ancient world.

URBAN NIGHTLIFE AND NIGHTWORK

Ancient cities have vastly different life at night than during the day, each with its own unique nocturnal footprint. Cities are notorious for having enriching and bawdy nightlife as well as being economically productive during the night. After dark, some urban dwellers slept while others socialized until the wee hours of the morning. Howling dogs, noisy neighbors, thugs taking advantage of darkness, partygoers stumbling home, processions promenading, scientists working their wonders into the night, holy practioners appeasing deities, sorcerers working supernatural incantations, bakers making bread, trash haulers taking it all away—these subversive, religious, and civil activities alike ensued during the dark hours of the day, sometimes with a shady cast of characters (Gonlin 2021). The unique nightscape of the urban environment presents opportunities and challenges to any city's inhabitants. It also creates a different performative space for city dwellers to use and manipulate. The human work cycle is affected by the night, and people find solutions to increase the affordances that night offers (Nowell and Gonlin 2021). The temporality of the human body and its need to sleep were and continues to be interspersed with tasks (M. L. Smith 2010a, 145). A few examples illustrate some of the vast amount of nocturnal urban work that occurred in the past.

Work at night, or in the dark, could be more dangerous, but an advantage was that darkness bestowed cover. The Mexica pochteca of Central Mexico were on the road at night to conceal their valuable cargos. Deborah Nichols (2013, 56) writes that

perhaps to conceal trading expeditions from each other as well as to hide their wealth from public view, pochteca began and ended their journeys under the cloak of darkness: "And when things had been arranged in order in their house; when all were about to go on the road, when darkness had fallen, when it was already night, then all the boats were filled." (Sahagun 1950–1982, 9:15)

During a religious ceremony, one of the many items that Mexica nobles and other merchants received was firewood, no doubt a highly prized item, and one that pertains to the night. Lacking beasts of burden in Mesoamerica, human porters would have been essential to the pochteca. M. L. Smith (2010a, 166) remarks upon the physical strength plus knowledge that porters would have required—such as the correct route, where to obtain food en route, weather prediction, and social skills. Porters and pochteca, together, moved goods along the Aztec Empire, and did so in the security of the dark.

Bread, in all its various forms, was (and is) a staple of life. In some societies, bread was made at home, while in others, bread was mass-produced in bakeries. Historian Bryan Palmer (2000, 141–142) ties in the bakery with Medieval European cities, remarking that "the classic locale of capitalist night work, however, was the bakery, a workplace that foreshadowed the rise of sweating in many industrial sectors. Bakers had a long history of honorable accomplishment, cultivated in early artisanal expressions of their guild origins and indispensable role in providing society with the staff of life."

At Chaco Canyon, a vibrant nightlife included gambling, an activity that brought together communities who used these opportunities to exchange information and goods. Weiner (chapter 9, this volume) gives details of the religious and political life of people who lived at Chaco from 800 CE to 1200 CE. He tackles the "urban" label that some may not attribute to Chaco or other ancient North American communities with low-density urbanism. Evidence for gambling abounds in the numerous bone dice and kick sticks recovered from various contexts.

An enlightening book about the transgressions of the night was written by Palmer (2000). In it, he delves into many of the dark doings in urban contexts that supply us with vivid imaginings, from witchcraft, conspiracies, and licentiousness, to pirating, socializing, sex, and more. Entire buildings may be associated with some of these behaviors, such as the *lupinares*, or brothels, of Pompeii (G. R. Storey 2018). Sacred and secular, divine and devious, were all part of cities at night. Next, we turn to an explicit consideration of the sacred.

SACRED IS THE NIGHT

Materials associated with nocturnal rituals and nightly use of the built environment furnish clues for how religious and architectural spheres differed between day and night. Many temples were found in city centers, such as the Templo Mayor in the Mexica capital of Tenochtitlan, the Karnak complex in Thebes, or the ziggurat of Ur, and some of the most significant and somber events occurred during the darkest hours of night. The time of transition from day to night and night to day was highly mythologized and ritualized. Sunset was commonly associated with the loss of life and descent into chaos, while sunrise, connected to the defeat of death and malevolent forces, was not necessarily guaranteed. As a result, these liminal times could be ominous. While night could be associated with death, it also could be associated with chthonic energies and concepts of rebirth. As a result, the experience of night was a bit of a balancing act—something to be feared and respected, embraced and kept at bay, in equal measure.

Space and spatiality, another of M. L. Smith's categories (2010a, 35–36), refers to the distinction between the age-old division of inside and outside space, and relates to the safety of being inside one's house at night versus the dangers of the outside, especially in the urban environment. Therefore, we would be remiss in our considerations of ancient urban nights if we failed to discuss the dangerous and devious aspects of the dark. For example, high in the Andes Mountains in the Lake Titicaca Basin of South America, the landscape of Tiwanaku, Bolivia, comes alive after dark. John Wayne Janusek and Anna Guengerich (chapter 5, this volume) combine ethnographic and ethnohistoric documentation with archaeology to determine that the carved monoliths occupying the center's monumental spaces, along with dangerous nonhuman beings, were awoken after dark. Additionally, those who retained astronomical knowledge of the dark skies held power over others who did not. In ancient Mesopotamia, the Assyrians and Urartians were as leery of nocturnal enemy invaders as of supernatural entities who lurked after dark, many of whom were witches and ghosts (Earley-Spadoni, chapter 3, this volume). All these dangers could be mitigated through propitiation of the dark forces.

The spatiality of work is discussed by M. L. Smith (2010a, 150), for work takes place in both spatial and temporal dimensions. There were certain spaces for night work—of special note, the practice of astronomy, which can occur in an observatory, an open area such as a plaza, a sunken court, or a field, and in the natural landscape—which was imbued with cultural significance. Martha Cabrera Romero and J. Antonio Ochatoma Cabrera (chapter 7, this volume) feature evidence for nocturnal rituals in the Wari Empire of Peru.

Wari knowledge of astronomy was extensive, indicating that there were many practitioners who worked into the dark hours at night. Nocturnal deities were part of the nightscape, and they had control over life and death. Likewise, at Chaco Canyon in the American Southwest, inhabitants constructed Great Houses, domestic architecture, roads, petroglyphs, and other features based on their astronomical knowledge (Weiner, chapter 9, this volume).

The night is gendered as well, and one's experience in urban environments is filtered through the lens of this identity, which intersects with many others. M. L. Smith (2010a, 38) observes that "ethnographic studies show that males and females often operate within different social realms and that gender configurations affect how individuals perceive even 'objective' aspects such as their physical surroundings." We apply this observation to the nocturnal urban environment and see different behaviors for different genders in the night, an "objective" aspect of the physical surroundings. In-depth research on the night and gender differences exists in many disciplines (Rotenberg et al. 2001; Meyer and Grollman 2014). Archaeologists could consider this avenue of research a productive one to expand gender studies of the past that have been impactful on our interpretations (e.g., Conkey and Spector 1984; Gero and Conkey 1991). This orientation relates to our next topic, on how power is manifested in the night.

POWER AND DARKNESS IN THE NIGHT

Powerful people manipulated the darkness to their advantage, something that is expressed in writing, architecture, and the built urban environment. Here, the Classic Maya (250–900 CE) of Mexico and Central America, and Mississippians of Cahokia, North America (800–1400 CE), are used to illustrate these points. In chapter 6 (this volume) Kristin V. Landau, Christopher Hernandez, and Nancy Gonlin conclude that Classic Maya kings timed their accession to power to coincide with either a new or full moon. Their conclusion is based on eighty-four accession dates from eleven sites across the Maya Lowlands, where inscriptions are recorded in long-lasting media, such as stone. The strong connection between moonlight and power was clearly understood by royals and followers alike. Massive pyramids and open plazas for gathering were incorporated into the landscape of Maya cities and served as areas for performance and observance. Whether the moon was in its most- or least-illuminated state, kings captured and recorded the moment for eternity.

Other urban architecture in Maya cities related to kingly power. Many Mesoamerican peoples played a ballgame with a rubber ball that one

FIGURE 1.3. *Ballcourt A-III at the Classic Maya city of Copan, Honduras. Photo: Nancy Gonlin.*

maneuvered into the end zone or between a sideways hoop (Whittington 2001); its origins span many ancient cultures and time periods (Blomster and Salazar Chávez 2020). In its most glorious fashion, the Classic Maya performed in specially constructed ballcourts in major cities (figure 1.3): "The location of the game is clearly associated with power and royal authority" (Tokovinine n.d.). Tokovinine (n.d.) notes that Maya kings were recognized for their valor in the ballgame and they often took on the guise of a deity: "The most impersonated divine ball player is the so-called 'old deer god,' recognizable for his man-deer traits. This is a god of hunting and feasting" who is "closely associated with the Underworld and such 'elder' gods as L and N." Hunting deer is an activity that was sometimes conducted at night, under the watchful eye of the Maya Moon Goddess. Conflating hunting, the dark Underworld, the old deer god, and the ballgame, one wonders whether some ballgames were intentionally played at night to bring together all these forces in an even more powerful show. An observed case of a nocturnal ballgame is by the ethnographers of the Purépecha of Michoacán, Mexico (García Mora 2016, 7), who record a type of ballgame that is played at night with a ball made from the root of a maguey plant. The ball is set on fire and slowly burns throughout the game. The two teams battle for supremacy, which represents the classic conflict between day and night, sun and moon (García Mora 2016, 27). While the deep history of this type of game is unknown, it surely had its roots in the past.

Elsewhere, Susan M. Alt (chapter 8, this volume) discusses the role that the night, the moon, and water held for Cahokia's residents (see also Alt 2018). This Indigenous urban center, the largest in North America, north of the Rio Grande, is where thousands of inhabitants made their home and built monumental earthen architecture. The widespread influence of Cahokia during its height of power in 1050 CE drew many inhabitants. Part of that attraction emanated from a new religion that held the night and the moon as critical powers, and this religion figured prominently in the urbanization process. Nighttime experiences of Cahokians were as vital as daytime ones.

Darkness in the Urban Environment

Dark nights in the city are a rarity today. Most of us cannot appreciate the glorious show put on by stars due to the huge amount of light pollution. Urban dwellers may take the drowned-out night sky for granted and may not question its nature, nor the loss of its visibility. But lighting has always had a socioeconomic element to it, and the ability to light up the ancient city at night is worthy of consideration. Firewood would be at a premium for competing uses, including lighting, cooking, lime and pottery manufacturing, smelting, and heating. Urban residents would have needed to obtain this commodity in the market or forage for it in surrounding wooded areas outside a city. The city of Teotihuacan, founded during Mesoamerica's Late Preclassic period around 100 BC (Cowgill 2015, 9), flourished in the central Mexican highlands (Manzanilla 2017) during the Early Classic period (250–600 CE). Over 100,000 residents of this great urban center commanded a substantial amount of firewood. Luis Barba Pingarrón and José Luis Córdova Frunz (2010) estimate that a total of 12.2 million square meters of wood were required to cook the limestone to produce the plaster used in Teotihuacan. In his study of fuel consumption, Randolph Widmer (2021) surmises that wealthier households had access to higher-quality and more-abundant fuel supplies.

Well over 100,000 people felt the draw of the metropolis of Teotihuacan, but not all were well. The darkness of disease is revealed through paleopathological studies. Rebecca Storey (1992) and colleagues (R. Storey et al. 2019) expose the types of stresses experienced by residents that were common to those living in preindustrial cities, such as enamel hypoplasias and porotic hyperostosis. Let us throw in the factor of the night as well, and from a sensorial perspective, our image of those suffering ill health through the night grows more vivid and dire, as darkness added to suffering. Ancient Egyptian and Mesopotamian peoples were particularly apprehensive about evil and disease sneaking in under the cover of darkness. Prayers, fire, and magical figures were used to ward off these nightly evils and ensure well-being and life (Ritner 1990, 1993, 224n1042; Wee 2014). Ancient cities across the globe had their share of disease outbreaks. The study of health and illness in the past comes through archaeological remains and textual sources; according to M. L. Smith (2010a, 27), "when writing was invented, medical subjects were one of the first things written about" (28). The tie-in with urban situations is easy enough to make, as it is well known that communicable diseases proliferate in dense concentrations of hosts, that is, city dwellers (Gibbons 2009).

People did much more than sleep at night, and even the seemingly inactive state of slumber is an activity that is culturally conditioned (Glaskin and Chenhall 2013). There are what M. L. Smith (2010a, 34) calls "acts of predictable duration," and sleep is one of them. She (2010a, 34) mentions sleeping and how "these fashions of sleep also constitute the relationship between the prevailing cultural pattern and also affirm it with each daily action of slumber. Sleep closes the daily cycle of activities." Adding this dimension to ancient cities gives us a better understanding of life in times past. The benches found within the remains of ancient Maya homes connote far more than the activity of sleep, for they are used as workbenches, temporary shelves, and places of power. Scholars of the past can reexamine reconstructions based on archaeological data, ethnohistories, and ethnographic accounts to amend how ancient nights are viewed. Urban environments afforded many opportunities and challenges to their inhabitants, some of which are similar to those city dwellers face today, and others of which are clearly associated with cities of the past.

Bringing our discussion back to time and temporality, there would have been seasonal influences on economic activities, religious rituals, social activities, and crime as a part of urban nights. Gonlin's colleague in the Criminal Justice Department at Bellevue College, Charlene Freyberg, relies on statistics from the Uniform Crime Report (2018) published by the FBI on their website. Here, we learn that most homicides are committed during the summer, in part, because days are longer and there is a greater amount of light—which can increase the time people spend away from their homes and raise the number of people in public. Evidence for ancient murders exists (e.g., Livius n.d., 18), so we surmise that perhaps more of them occurred when nights were shorter. Criminologists have found seasonal fluctuations in homicide and assault in modern American cities (McDowall and Curtis 2014).

Part of the infrastructure of cities includes the subterranean realm, which might be conceived of as a mythical or cosmological zone. Sometimes a significant building was constructed over a cave (natural or artificial) (e.g., Brown 2005, 391), confirming its existence as a portal to the underworld or tying in with creation myths. The presence of a cave could serve as the founding location for an entire city or town (Aguilar et al. 2005, 84). At Teotihuacan, Deborah Nichols (2016) evaluated the location of the grand Sun Pyramid and its placement over an artificially constructed cave that is tied in with the cosmos and the deities. More recently, electric resistivity methods have found evidence for a likely natural cave under the Moon Pyramid (Argote et al. 2020). Teotihuacanos carved up parts of their city to accommodate tunnels as well as canals to reroute streams (Nichols 2016).

In a more mundane consideration of the subterranean realm of cities, Palmer (2000, 147) writes that "the actual underground labors associated with sewers, subways, and mines came to occupy a place of prominence for such a gaze; the realities and representations of the labyrinth of tunnels and cavernous environments beneath the affluence of polite society ran through the fiction and form of class relations." Long before the construction of the sewers of Paris or New York City, urban inhabitants of the Indus civilization over 5,000 years ago dealt with the material reality of human refuse with infrastructure common to urban environments. Rita Wright and Zenobie Garrett (2018) report on the maintenance of the water and sewage systems at Mohenjo-Daro. Unrecorded in antiquity and mostly ignored by modern researchers, such workers were necessary to maintaining the sanitation of Indus cities: "That they worked at night is inferred from the types of work required, the odiferous nature of the trash pits they cleaned, and the presence of many of the amenities along the main thoroughfares" of the Indus cities (289). Access to potable water, a primary concern for any human habitation at any scale, became a necessary consideration of urban planners. Archaeological signatures for potable water included wedge-shaped bricks used in the construction of wells. Such infrastructure was shared communally or even built into individual houses (295).

One challenge facing city residents is the disposal of trash. The discard of massive amounts of organic and inorganic materials is an issue of major concern in today's world. M. L. Smith notes that (2010a, 126) "the discard of objects has temporal as well as spatial aspects" and that "the removal of objects also can occur on a massive scale associated with social and spiritual cleansing and renewal." The Aztec New Fire Ceremony is a prime example where these two observations coincide. In their contribution to this volume (chapter 10), Kirby Farah and Susan Toby Evans describe the drama of this event that occurred every fifty-two years and its ties to the empire's power. From palace inhabitants to residents of humble houses, the clearing of philosophical and physical detritus provided a clean slate upon which to begin a new cycle of life. New fire gave life for another cycle.

CONCLUSIONS

Worldwide and spread across a range of time periods, humans built and excelled in urban environments. *Homo sapiens* can now be considered an "urban" species (*Homo sapiens urbanus*, if you will), as more than half of us live in cities across the globe. For archaeologists to better understand the process of urbanization and city life, we need to incorporate the temporal aspect of the night. Nighttime was a critical time period in our evolution and development, and it continues to play a forceful role in our well-being. Without the night, we end up with a partial explanation and an incomplete understanding of the past. Nocturnal events structured city dwellers' days and nights, and planning and preparation for dark hours was integral to the built environment.

Some settlements, such as Tiwanaku and Chaco Canyon, were planned around the night. Certain constellations had great impact on the layout, design, and navigation of these places. Darkness enhanced the realms of the supernatural. The night was sacred to many, whether living in rural or urban areas. Some rituals were specific to the night and were performed only after darkness rose. The power of the night is unmistakable. Classic Maya rulers heightened their supremacy by carefully timing their ascension to the throne to coincide with ominous phases of the moon. The political theater that ensued against the backdrop of the night was dramatic.

The architecture, infrastructure, features, and artifacts of cities reflect the night, a fact well studied by cultural astronomers (Aveni 2008). Urban planners needed to consider aspects of the built environment from a nocturnal lens to ensure the safety and functioning of the city during the dark hours. Some preferred to labor at night, such as astronomers, bakers, and maintenance workers. Some counted on darkness to mask their activities or to enhance them, such as sorcerers, while others relied upon artificial lighting to brighten the night and accomplish their goals.

The role of the night and darkness in emerging social complexity and urbanism has been understudied and undertheorized by archaeologists, as is the twenty-four-hour rhythm of a city into which night studies can be subsumed. The chapters in this volume make strides by incorporating dimensions of darkness. Inequality was expressed in both the night and day, through places, objects, and performances. Urban nocturnal rhythms of life were affected in a myriad of ways that are just beginning to be recognized and appreciated. We look forward to seeing more archaeologists and other researchers undertake the study of the night, incorporate a twenty-four-hour dimension to quotidian practices, and consider the dawn and dusk as critical liminal times. Our journey has only begun to address these times of the day that were momentous in our ancestors' lives and continue to affect our well-being in modern times.

Acknowledgments. The inspiration for this chapter came from working with many archaeologists who have incorporated the night into their research, foremost among them, April Nowell and David M. Reed, and from Monica L. Smith's 2010 book *A Prehistory of Ordinary People.* David kindly critiqued an earlier version of this manuscript and greatly improved it with his keen editing, insights, and references; he furnished figure 1.1 for us. Monica Smith provided constructive edits and insights that clarified our thoughts. Her voluminous work on ancient cities and ordinary people served as a starting point for this chapter. Monica pointed out relevant sources, word-smithed where needed, and nudged us in the right direction, for all of which we are sincerely grateful. Jerry Moore generously provided feedback that was most welcome and we sincerely thank him. Anonymous reviewers likewise weighed in with constructive comments that assisted us in producing a better-considered chapter; in particular, we appreciate the reference to Ray Laurence's work.

REFERENCES

Adams, Robert McCormick. 1960. "The Origin of Cities." *Scientific American*, September, 3–10.

Aguilar, Manuel, Miguel Medina Jaen, Tim M. Tucker, and James E. Brady. 2005. "Constructing Mythic Space: The Significance of a Chicomoztoc Complex at Acatzingo Viejo." In *In the Maw of the Earth Monster: Mesoamerican Ritual Cave Use*, edited by James E. Brady and Keith M. Prufer, 69–87. Austin: University of Texas Press.

Alt, Susan M. 2018. "The Emerald Site, Mississippian Women, and the Moon." In *Archaeology of the Night: Life after Dark in the Ancient World*, edited by Nancy Gonlin and April Nowell, 223–246. Boulder: University Press of Colorado.

Alt, Susan M., and Timothy R. Pauketat, eds. 2019. *New Materialisms, Ancient Urbanisms*. New York: Routledge.

Anthony, David. 1990. "Migration in Archaeology: The Baby and the Bath Water." *American Anthropologist* 92 (4): 895–914.

Ardren, Traci. 2014. "Sacbe Processions and Classic Maya Urban Culture." In *Processions in the Ancient Americas; Approaches and Perspectives*. A symposium presented at Dumbarton Oaks, Pre-Columbian Studies, Washington, DC.

Argote, Denisse L., Andrés Tejero-Andrade, Martín Cárdenas-Soto, Gerardo Cifuentes-Nava, René E. Chávez, Esteban Hernández-Quintero, Alejandro García-Serrano, and Verónica Ortega. 2020. "Designing the Underworld in Teotihuacan: Cave Detection beneath the Moon Pyramid by ERT and ANT Surveys." *Journal of Archaeological Science* 118: 1–9.

Aveni, Anthony F., ed. 2008. *Foundations of New World Cultural Astronomy*. Boulder: University Press of Colorado.

Barba Pingarrón, Luis, and José Luis Córdova Frunz. 2010. *Materiales y energía en la arquitectura de Teotihuacan*. Mexico City: UNAM, Instituto de Investigaciones Antropológicas.

Baumanova, Monika. 2020. "Sensory Synaesthesia: Combined Analyses Based on Space Syntax in African Urban Contexts." *African Archaeological Review* 37 (1): 125–141.

Bietak, Manfred, Ernst Czerny, and Irene Forstner-Müller, eds. 2010. *Cities and Urbanism in Ancient Egypt: Papers from a Workshop in November 2006 at the Austrian Academy of Sciences*. Vienna: Verlag der Österreichischen Akademie der Wissenschaften.

Blomster, Jeffrey P., and Victor E. Salazar Chávez. 2020. "Origins of the Mesoamerican Ballgame: Earliest Ballcourt from the Highlands Found at Etlatongo, Oaxaca, Mexico." *Science Advances* 6 (11): 1–9.

Brown, Clifford. 2005. "Caves, Karst, and Settlement in Mayapán, Yucatán." In *In the Maw of the Earth Monster: Mesoamerican Ritual Cave Use*, edited by James E. Brady and Keith M. Prufer, 373–402. Austin: University of Texas Press.

Chase, Arlen F., and Diane Z. Chase. 2001. "Ancient Maya Causeways and Site Organization at Caracol, Belize." *Ancient Mesoamerica* 12 (2): 273–281.

Chepesiuk, Ron. 2009. "Missing the Dark: Health Effects of Light Pollution." *Environmental Health Perspectives* 117 (1): A20–A27.

Childe, V. Gordon. 1950. "The Urban Revolution." *Town Planning Review* 21 (1): 3–17.

Cojti Ren, Iyaxel. 2020. "The Emergence of the Kaqquikel Polity as Explained through the Dawn Tradition of the Guatemala Highlands." *Mayanist* 2 (1): 21–38.

Coltman, Jeremy D., and John M. D. Pohl, eds. 2021. *Sorcery in Mesoamerica*. Louisville: University Press of Colorado.

Conkey, Margaret W., and Janet D. Spector. 1984. "Archaeology and the Study of Gender." *Advances in Archaeological Method and Theory* 7: 1–38.

Cowgill, George L. 2015. *Ancient Teotihuacan: Early Urbanism in Early Mexico*. New York: Cambridge University Press.

Creekmore, Andrew T., and Kevin D. Fisher, eds. 2014. *Making Ancient Cities: Space and Place in Early Urban Societies*. New York: Cambridge University Press.

Dunn, Nicholas, and Timothy Edensor, eds. 2021 *Rethinking Darkness: Histories, Cultures, Practices*. London: Taylor and Francis.

Eckardt, Hella. 2002. *Illuminating Roman Britain*. Montagnac, France: Instrumentum.

Edensor, Tim. 2017. *From Light to Dark: Daylight, Illumination, and Gloom*. Minneapolis: University of Minnesota Press.

Ekirch, A. Roger. 2005. *At Day's Close: Night in Times Past*. New York: W. W. Norton.

Galinier, Jacques, Aurore Monod Becquelin, Guy Bordin, Laurent Fontaine, Francine Fourmaux, Juliette Roullet Ponce, Piero Salzarulo, Philippe Simonnot, Michèle Therrien, and Iole Zilli. 2010. "Anthropology of the Night: Cross-Disciplinary Investigations." *Current Anthropology* 51 (6): 819–847.

García Mora, Carlos. 2016. *El Combate Purépecha con La Pelota: Raigambre Guerrera*. Mexico City: Tsimárhu Estudio de Etnólogos.

Gero, Joan J., and Margaret W. Conkey, eds. 1991. *Engendering Archaeology: Women and Prehistory*. Oxford: Basil Blackwell.

Gibbons, A. 2009. "Civilization's Cost: The Decline and Fall of Human Health." *Science* 324: 588.

Glaskin, Katie, and Richard Chenhall, eds. 2013. *Sleep around the World: Anthropological Perspectives*. New York: Palgrave MacMillan. https://doi.org/10.1057/9781137315731.

Gonlin, Nancy. 2020. "Household Archaeology of the Classic Period Lowland Maya." In *The Maya World*, edited by Scott R. Hutson and Traci Ardren, 389–406. London: Routledge.

Gonlin, Nancy. 2021. "Dangers in the Night: Archaeological Case Studies of the Ancient Mayas of Mesoamerica." *Proceedings: II International Conference on Night Studies*, edited by Manuel Garcia-Ruiz and Jordi Nofre, 170–191. Lisboa: ISCTE, Instituto Universitário de Lisboa.

Gonlin, Nancy, and Christine C. Dixon. 2018. "Classic Maya Nights at Copan, Honduras and El Cerén, El Salvador." In *Archaeology of the Night: Life after Dark in the Ancient World*, edited by Nancy Gonlin and April Nowell, 45–76. Boulder: University Press of Colorado.

Gonlin, Nancy, and Christine C. Dixon-Hundredmark. 2021. "Illuminating Darkness in the Ancient Maya World: Nocturnal Case Studies from Copan, Honduras, and Joya de Cerén, El Salvador." In *Night and Darkness in Ancient Mesoamerica*, edited by Nancy Gonlin and David M. Reed, 103–140. Louisville: University Press of Colorado.

Gonlin, Nancy, and Kristin V. Landau. 2021. "Maya on the Move: Population Mobility in the Classic Maya Kingdom of Copan, Honduras." In *Ancient Mesoamerican*

Cities: Populations on the Move, edited by M. Charlotte Arnauld, Gregory Pereira, and Christopher Beekman, 131–147. Louisville: University Press of Colorado.

Gonlin, Nancy, and April Nowell, eds. 2018a. *Archaeology of the Night: Life after Dark in the Ancient World*. Boulder: University Press of Colorado.

Gonlin, Nancy, and April Nowell. 2018b. "Introduction to the Archaeology of the Night." In *Archaeology of the Night: Life after Dark in the Ancient World*, edited by Nancy Gonlin and April Nowell, 5–24. Boulder: University Press of Colorado.

Gonlin, Nancy, and David M. Reed, eds. 2021. *Night and Darkness in Ancient Mesoamerica*. Louisville: University Press of Colorado.

Harmanşah, Omur. 2013. *Cities and the Shaping of Memory in the Ancient Near East*. New York: Cambridge University Press.

Hutson, Scott R. 2016. *The Ancient Urban Maya: Neighborhoods, Inequality, and Built Form*. Tallahassee: University Press of Florida.

Hutson, Scott R., Aline Magnoni, and Travis W. Stanton. 2012. "'All That is Solid . . .': Sacbes, Settlement, and Semiotics at Tzacauil, Yucatan." *Ancient Mesoamerica* 23 (2): 297–311.

Hutson, Scott R., and Jacob Welch. 2019. "Old Urbanites as New Urbanists? Mixing at an Ancient Maya City." *Journal of Urban History* 47 (4): 812–831.

Kamp, Kathryn, and John Whittaker. 2018. "The Night Is Different: Sensescapes and Affordances in Ancient Arizona." In *Archaeology of the Night: Life after Dark in the Ancient World*, edited by Nancy Gonlin and April Nowell, 77–94. Boulder: University Press of Colorado.

Keller, Angela H. 2009. "A Road by Any Other Name: Trails, Paths, and Roads in Maya Language and Thought." In *Landscapes of Movement: Trails, Paths, and Roads in Anthropological Perspective*, edited by James E. Snead, Clark L. Erickson, and J. Andrew Darling, 133–157. Philadelphia: University of Pennsylvania Museum of Archaeology and Anthropology.

Keller, Angela H. 2010. "The Social Construction of Roads at Xunantunich: From Design to Abandonment." In *Classic Maya Provincial Politics: Xunantunich and Its Hinterlands*, edited by Lisa J. LeCount and Jason Yaeger, 184–208. Tucson: University of Arizona Press.

Koslofsky, Craig. 2011. *Evening's Empire: A History of the Night in Early Modern Europe*. Cambridge: Cambridge University Press.

Laland, Kevin N., and Michael J. O'Brien. 2010. "Niche Construction Theory and Archaeology." *Journal of Archaeological Method and Theory* 17 (4): 303–322.

Laurence, Ray. 2007. *Roman Pompeii: Space and Society*. London: Routledge.

Livius, Titus. Benjamin Oliver Foster, ed. n.d. *The History of Rome Book 8*. Cambridge, MA: Harvard University Press.

Loya González, Tatiana, and Travis W. Stanton. 2013. "Impacts of Politics on Material Culture: Evaluating the Yaxuna-Coba Sacbe." *Ancient Mesoamerica* 24 (1): 25–42.

Magli, Giulio. 2013. *Architecture, Astronomy and Sacred Landscape in Ancient Egypt.* Cambridge: Cambridge University Press.

Manzanilla, Linda R. 2017. *Teotihuacan: Ciudad excepcional de Mesoamérica.* Serie Opúsculos. Mexico City: El Colegio Nacional.

Marlowe, Frank. 2010. *The Hadza: Hunter-Gatherers of Tanzania.* Berkeley: University of California Press.

Martínez, David Gil. 2012. "La distinta naturaleza del día y de la noche en la antigüedad, y sus divisiones en horas." *El Futuro del Pasado* 3 (3): 285–316.

McAtackney, Laura, and Krysta Ryzewski, eds. 2017. *Contemporary Archaeology and the City: Creativity, Ruination, and Political Action.* Oxford: University of Oxford Press.

McDowall, David, and Karise M. Curtis. 2014. "Seasonal Variation in Homicide and Assault Across Large U.S. Cities." *Homicide Studies* 19 (4): 303–325.

Meyer, David, and Eric Anthony Grollman. 2014. "Sexual Orientation and Fear at Night: Gender Differences among Sexual minorities and Heterosexuals." *Journal of Homosexuality* 61 (4): 453–470.

Moeller, Nadine. 2016. *The Archaeology of Urbanism in Ancient Egypt: From the Predynastic Period to the End of the Middle Kingdom.* Cambridge: Cambridge University Press.

Rotenberg Lúcia, Luciana Fernandes Portela, Willer Baumgartem Marcondes, Cláudia Moreno, and Cristiano de Paula Nascimento. 2001. "Gênero e trabalho noturno: Sono, cotidiano e vivências de quem troca a noite pelo dia" [Gender and night work: Sleep, daily life and the experiences of night shift workers]. *Cad Saúde Pública* 17 (3): 639–649. https://doi.org/10.1590/s0102-311x2001000300018.

Moyes, Holley, and Costas Papadopoulos, eds. 2017. *The Oxford Handbook of Light in Archaeology.* Oxford: Oxford University Press.

Müller, Miriam, ed. 2015. *Household Studies in Complex Societies: (Micro)Archaeological and Textual Approaches.* Chicago: University of Chicago.

Naiman, Rubin R. 2014. *Healing Night: The Science and Spirit of Sleeping, Dreaming, and Awakening.* 2nd ed. Tucson, AZ: NewMoon Media.

Nichols, Deborah L. 2013. "Merchants and Merchandise: The Archaeology of Aztec Commerce at Otumba, Mexico." In *Merchants, Markets, and Exchange in the Pre-Columbian World*, edited by Kenneth G. Hirth and Joanne Pillsbury, 49–83. Washington, DC: Dumbarton Oaks.

Nichols, Deborah L. 2016. "Teotihuacan." *Journal of Archaeological Research* 24 (1): 1–74.

Nowell, April, and Nancy Gonlin. 2021 "Affordances of the Night: Work after Dark in the Ancient World." In *Rethinking Darkness: Histories, Cultures, Practices*, edited by Nick Dunn and Tim Edensor, 27–37. London: Routledge.

Nunn, C. L., P. McNamara, I. Capellini, B. T. Preston, and R. A. Barton. 2010. "Primate Sleep in Phylogenetic Perspective." In *Evolution and Sleep: Phylogenetic and Functional Perspectives*, edited by Patrick McNamara, Robert A. Barton, and Charles L. Nunn, 123–145. New York: Cambridge University Press.

O'Brien, Michael J., and Kevin N. Laland. 2012. "Genes, Culture, and Agriculture: An Example of Human Niche Construction." *Current Anthropology* 53 (4): 434–470.

Palmer, Bryan D. 2000. *Cultures of Darkness: Night Travels in the Histories of Transgression [From Medieval to Modern]*. New York: Monthly Review Press.

Parisinou, Eva. 2000. *The Light of the Gods: The Role of Light in Archaic and Classical Greek Cult*. London: Duckworth.

Pirenne, Henri. (1925) 1969. *Medieval Cities: Their Origins and the Revival of Trade*. Princeton, NJ: Princeton University Press.

Rapoport, Amos. 1990. "Systems of Activities, Systems of Settings." In *Domestic Architecture and the Use of Space*, edited by Susan Kent, 9–20. New York: Cambridge University Press.

Rapoport, Amos. 2006. "Archaeology and Environment-Behavior Studies." In *Integrating the Diversity of Twenty-First-Century Anthropology: The Life and Intellectual Legacies of Susan Kent*, edited by Wendy Ashmore, Marcia-Ann Dobres, Sarah Milledge Nelson, and Arlene M. Rosen, 59–70. Washington, DC: American Anthropological Association.

Reed, David M., and Nancy Gonlin. 2021. "Introduction to Night and Darkness in Ancient Mesoamerica." In *Night and Darkness in Ancient Mesoamerica*, edited by Nancy Gonlin and David M. Reed, 3–38. Louisville: University Press of Colorado.

Ritner, Robert K. 1990. "O. Gardiner 363: A Spell against Night Terrors." *Journal of the American Research Center in Egypt* 27: 25–41.

Ritner, Robert K. 1993. *Mechanics of Magical Practice*. Studies in Ancient Oriental Civilization (SAOC) 54. Chicago: University of Chicago.

Samson, David R., Alyssa N. Crittenden, Ibrahim A. Mabulla, and Audax Z.P. Mabulla. 2017. "The Evolution of Human-Sleep: Technological and Cultural Innovation Associated with Sleep-Wake Regulation among Hadza Hunter-Gatherers." *Journal of Human Evolution* 113 (December): 91–102.

Samson, David R., and C. L. Nunn. 2015. "Sleep Intensity and the Evolution of Human Cognition." *Evolutionary Anthropology* 24 (6): 225–237.

Sheets, Payson. 2006. *The Cerén Site: An Ancient Village Buried by Volcanic Ash in Central America*. 2nd ed. Belmont, CA: Thomson Wadsworth.

Skeates, Robin, and Jo Day, eds. 2019. *The Routledge Handbook of Sensory Archaeology.* London: Routledge.

Smith, Michael E. 2007. "Form and Meaning in the Earliest Cities: A New Approach to Ancient Urban Planning." *Journal of Planning History* 6 (1): 3–47.

Smith, Michael E. 2011. "Empirical Urban Theory for Archaeologists." *Journal of Archaeological Method and Theory* 18: 167–192.

Smith, Michael E. 2019. "The Generative Role of Settlement Aggregation and Urbanization." In *Coming Together: Comparative Approaches to Population Aggregation and Early Urbanization*, edited by Atilla Gyucha, 37–58. Albany: State University of New York Press.

Smith, Michael E., Abhishek Chatterjee, Angela C. Huster, Sierra Stewart, and Marion Forest. 2019. "Apartment Compounds, Households, and Population in the Ancient City of Teotihuacan, Mexico." *Ancient Mesoamerica* 30 (3): 399–418.

Smith, Monica L. 2010a. *A Prehistory of Ordinary People.* Tucson: University of Arizona Press.

Smith, Monica L., ed. 2010b. *The Social Construction of Ancient Cities.* Washington, DC: Smithsonian Institution Press.

Smith, Monica, L. 2016. "Urban Infrastructure as Materialized Consensus." *World Archaeology* 48 (1): 164–178. https://doi.org/10.1080/00438243.2015.1124804.

Smith, Monica L. 2019. *Cities: The First 6,000 Years.* New York: Viking.

Snead, James E., Clark L. Erickson, and J. Andrew Darling. 2009. "Making Human Space: The Archaeology of Trails, Paths, and Roads." In *Landscapes of Movement: Trails, Paths, and Roads in Anthropological Perspective*, edited by James E. Snead, Clark L. Erickson, J. Andrew Darling, 1–19. Philadelphia: University of Pennsylvania Museum of Archaeology and Anthropology.

Spence, Kate. 2004. "The Three-Dimensional Form of the Amarna house." *Journal of Egyptian Archaeology* 90: 123–152.

Spence, Kate. 2015. "Ancient Egyptian Houses and Households: Architecture, Artifacts, Conceptualization, and Interpretation." In *Household Studies in Complex Societies: (Micro)Archaeological and Textual Approaches*, edited by Miriam Müller, 83–100. Chicago: University of Chicago.

Šprajc, Ivan. 2016. "Lunar Alignments in Mesoamerican Architecture." *Anthropological Notebooks* 22 (3): 61–85.

Storey, Glenn Reed. 2018. "All Rome Is at My Bedside: Nightlife in the Roman Empire." In *Archaeology of the Night: Life after Dark in the Ancient World*, edited by Nancy Gonlin and April Nowell, 307–331. Boulder: University Press of Colorado.

Storey, Rebecca. 1992. *Life and Death in the Ancient City of Teotihuacan.* Tuscaloosa: University of Alabama Press.

Storey, Rebecca, Gina M. Buckley, and Douglass J. Kennett. 2019. "Residential Burial along the Southern Street of the Dead: Skeletons and Isotopes." *Ancient Mesoamerica* 30 (1): 147–161.

Strong, Meghan E. 2018. "A Great Secret of the West: Transformative Aspects of Artificial Light in New Kingdom, Egypt." In *Archaeology of the Night: Life after Dark in the Ancient World*, edited by Nancy Gonlin and April Nowell, 249–264. Boulder: University Press of Colorado.

Strong, Meghan E. 2021. *Sacred Flames: The Power of Artificial Light in Ancient Egypt.* Cairo: American University in Cairo Press.

Tokovinine, Alexandre. n.d. "The Royal Ball Game of the Ancient Maya." Mayavase.com Research Material. Accessed June 4, 2020. http://www.mayavase.com/alex/alexballgame.html.

Uniform Crime Report. 2018. Accessed June 4, 2020. https://www.fbi.gov/services/cjis/ucr.

Vranich, Alexei, and Scott C. Smith. 2018. "Nighttime Sky and Early Urbanism in the High Andes." In *Archaeology of the Night: Life after Dark in the Ancient World*, edited by Nancy Gonlin and April Nowell, 121–138. Boulder: University Press of Colorado.

Wee, John Z. 2014. "Lugalbanda under the Night Sky: Scenes of Celestial Healing in Ancient Mesopotamia." *Journal of Near Eastern Studies* 73 (1): 23–42.

Wiessner, Polly W. 2014. "Embers of Society: Firelight Talk among the Ju/'hoansi Bushmen." *Proceedings of the National Academy of Sciences of the United States of America* 111 (39): 14027–14035.

Whittington, E. Michael, ed. 2001. *The Sport of Life and Death: The Mesoamerican Ballgame.* London: Thames and Hudson.

Widmer, Randolph J. 2021. "Teotihuacan at Night: A Classic Period Urban Nocturnal Landscape in the Basin of Mexico." In *Night and Darkness in Ancient Mesoamerica*, edited by Nancy Gonlin and David M. Reed, 141–157. Louisville: University Press of Colorado.

Wilkinson, Darryl. 2019. "Towards an Archaeological Theory of Infrastructure." *Journal of Archaeological Method and Theory* 26: 1216–1241. https://doi.org/10.1007/s10816-018-9410-2.

Wilkinson, Richard H. 2000. *The Complete Temples of Ancient Egypt.* London: Thames and Hudson.

Wirth, Louis. 1940. "The Urban Society and Civilization." *American Journal of Sociology* 45 (5): 743–755.

Worthman, Carol M. 2008. "After Dark: The Evolutionary Ecology of Human Sleep." In *Evolutionary Medicine and Health: New Perspectives*, edited by Wenda R.

Trevathan, E. O. Smith, and James J. McKenna, 291–313. Oxford: Oxford University Press.

Worthman, Carol M., and Melissa K. Melby. 2002. "Toward a Comparative Developmental Ecology of Human Sleep." In *Adolescent Sleep Patterns: Biological, Social, and Psychological Influences*, edited by Mary A. Carskadon, 69–117. Cambridge: Cambridge University Press.

Wright, Rita P., and Zenobie S. Garrett. 2018. "Engineering Feats and Consequences: Workers in the Night and the Indus Civilization." In *Archaeology of the Night: Life after Dark in the Ancient World*, edited by Nancy Gonlin and April Nowell, 287–306. Boulder: University Press of Colorado.

2

The carpenter who wields an adze is more exhausted than a laborer; his fields are the timber, his plough the adze. Nighttime does not rescue him, he does more than his arms can do; at night he must kindle a light.

—After Lichtheim (2006) and Helck (1970)

Looking for Light in Ancient Egyptian Urban Rituals

Meghan E. Strong

In ancient Egypt, some had to work long hours and literally burn the midnight oil, even though nighttime was viewed as a period of relaxation. This quote offers an intriguing insight into the experience of night in an ancient Egyptian settlement, provoking numerous questions. Were homes lit with lamps or fires? How did the Egyptians use lighting to extend their day? Were certain activities or rituals restricted to the night? In this chapter, I explore the impact of artificial lighting on the nocturnal landscape. As with many aspects of ancient Egyptian culture, night was conceived of as having a dual nature—a potent, mythically charged time of rest and regeneration, but also a potentially dangerous period when evil forces could take advantage of those who let down their guard. It appears anyone could be impacted by the dangers of darkness: in the *Instructions of Amenemhet I*, the king is said to have been assassinated because "no one is strong at night."[1]

Although there is minimal mention of the night in the surviving literary corpus, what has survived helps us to draw basic inferences. It is known, for example, that night was divided into twelve hours, in complement to

https://doi.org/10.5876/9781646422609.c002

the *Hrw* (twelve hours of the day) (Spalinger 1992, 147). The term for night, *grH* (Erman and Grapow 1931, 183.12–185.9), is related to an end (Erman and Grapow 1931, 183.5–9) or completion (Erman and Grapow 1931, 182.4–183.3). With regards to time of day, grH may then denote the end or completion of the twelve hours of day. As in modern society, the evening in ancient Egypt was considered a time to put aside work and relax. One text, for example, states that a scribe should "spend the whole day writing, and read at night" (Blackman and Peet 1925, 285). However, not everyone had the luxury of using night as a time to recharge, and those who worked during the evening hours were surely dependent on a source of light.

While this chapter seeks to examine lighting in ancient Egyptian cities (figure 1.1), such an aim is more easily stated than accomplished. This situation is partly due to research bias, as the majority of archaeological exploration has been centered on well-preserved mortuary structures. Similarly, the social complexity and development of an urban society in ancient Egypt have been explored primarily through the lens of mortuary remains, burial practices, and cemetery analysis (Moeller 2016, 1). Despite the focus on funerary culture, the fact remains that many ancient settlements in Egypt are poorly preserved, and, as a result, few have been investigated with fewer results thoroughly published. The minimal archaeological remains for urban centers and rural villages alike are due to a number of factors (Moeller 2016, 9). Structures were generally made of mud brick and were located closer to the Nile floodplain, which has resulted in considerable loss over centuries of annual inundation. A similar situation prevails today, where approximately 95 percent of the population lives on the land close to the fertile Nile River and within the Nile Delta (figure 2.1). Additionally, the Nile appears to have shifted over time, and recent research has shown that this likely resulted in loss of settlements over the course of Egyptian civilization (Jeffreys 2008; Toonen et al. 2018). Areas that were not washed away may be buried under feet of alluvial deposits, a situation that existed before the construction of the Aswan Dam between 1960 and 1970. The gradual expansion of modern urbanism has also covered over a number of ancient settlements. Those cities and villages that are better preserved, and consequently better published—such as Lahun, Elephantine, Amarna, and Deir el-Medina—are located either outside the reach of the damaging Nile waters or isolated on islands above the worst flood levels.[2] The lack of settlement evidence is therefore understandable.

The lack of investigation into lighting, however, has proven more difficult to explain. A common perception is that modern Egyptologists have failed to recognize Egyptian lighting equipment, and, to some extent, this observation

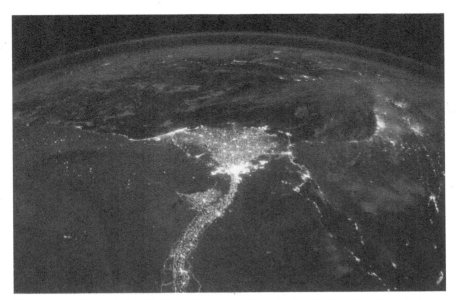

FIGURE 2.1. *View of the Nile River from space. Note the distribution of settlement along the river and throughout the delta. This pattern prevailed in the past as it does today. Photo: NASA.*

is likely correct (N. de G. Davies 1924; Robins 1939). It is also necessary to consider whether lighting was more restricted in use in comparison to other cultures of the ancient Mediterranean, such as the Greeks and Romans. Of interest, it is clear from the textual record that lighting was integral to certain nocturnal festival celebrations, one of which was a light offering ritual. If a time of day is given for the performance of a lighting ritual, the most common phrase used is *m grH*, "at night." More specifically this phrase is used to specify the night before a festival, such as *grH n wpt-rnpt*, "the night before the New Year." This time was the most prominent occasion in which lighting was presented in a nocturnal setting, an occasion that not only celebrated the death of one year and the birth of another but also commemorated the "glorified dead" throughout Egypt. Middle Kingdom (ca. 2025–1700 BCE) texts and New Kingdom (ca. 1550–1069 BCE) (table 2.1) tomb scenes indicate that the proper performance of this light offering ritual required that lights were acquired at the community temple, lit within the temple, and then carried in a procession from the temple gates out into the city or village necropolis (see chapter 10 in this volume, on the Aztec New Fire Ceremony for a comparison from the Americas). Unlike most other Egyptian rituals, which took place

TABLE 2.1. Chronology of ancient Egypt from the Early Dynastic to the Late period

Years	Periods	People/Events Relevant to This Chapter
3100–2686 BCE	Early Dynastic period	Reign of Khasekhemwy
2686–2181 BCE	Old Kingdom	Pehernefer serves as master butcher
2181–2025 BCE	First Intermediate period	
2025–1700 BCE	Middle Kingdom	Reign of Amenemhet I Reign of Senusret I Hepdjefa serves as nomarch in Asyut
1700–1550 BCE	Second Intermediate period	
1550–1069 BCE	New Kingdom	Theban tombs carved on west bank of Luxor Deir el-Medina used as home for artisans working on tombs in the Valley of the Kings
1069–664 BCE	Third Intermediate period	
664–332 BCE	Late period	

during the day, the New Year's Eve celebration took place at night in total darkness. Given the essential nature of light and nighttime in this ritual, it can be used as a case study for the utilization of artificial lighting within the urban environment through this New Year's Eve commemoration of the dead. The use of night as a performative space in an urban ritual context, as well as the role of lighting devices and luminosity in remembrance, also can be addressed.

NEW YEAR'S EVE NIGHT

The most detailed account of instructions for the New Year's Eve ritual are found in the Middle Kingdom tomb of Hepdjefa I (tomb 1) in Asyut (figure 2.2) (Griffith 1889; Reisner 1918; Kahl 2007, 2016). Hepdjefa was a nomarch and high priest of ancient Egypt's thirteenth nome centered in Asyut during the reign of the Twelfth Dynasty king Senusret I (ca.1971–1926 BCE). The most prominent feature of Hepdjefa's tomb is the extensive contracts carved into the stone walls. Within the contracts, he details how his funerary cult is meant to be maintained and the payments given to his *ka*-priest and others to ensure that his wishes are carried out. It is thanks to Hepdjefa's keen attention to detail that the necessary equipment and proper performance of the New Year's Eve rite can be reconstructed.

The first reference to the provision of light for this ritual is found in Contract 5, where it is stipulated that three *gmHt* (lighting devices) are to be provided

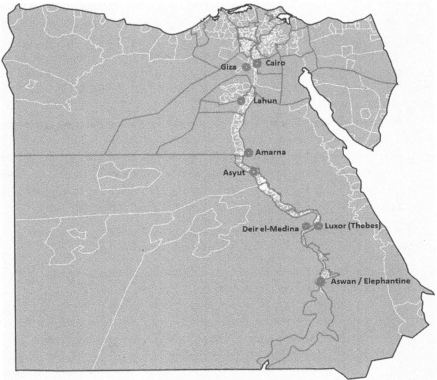

FIGURE 2.2. *Map of Egypt with locations mentioned in this chapter. Map: Meghan E. Strong*

to the ka-priest of Hepdjefa from the *SnDty*, or "keeper of the wardrobe," of the temple of Wepwawet. In Contract 9, Hepdjefa stipulates that on the night before the New Year, the cemetery overseer and his workers go to the temple of Anubis to be given two lighting implements (Griffith 1889, pl. 8, lines 312–318; Reisner 1918, 87–88):

> Causing them to go to the temple of Anubis on the 5th day of the year, New Year's eve, and on New Year's day in order to receive 2 gmHt; Contract 9, tomb of Hepdjefa

The workers are then instructed to walk in procession to the tomb of Hepdjefa as a *sAxw* (glorification) of the tomb owner (Griffith 1889, pl. 8, line 312).

> For their glorification [of Hepdjefa] as they glorify their blessed dead; Contract 9, tomb of Hepdjefa. (Griffith 1889, pl. 8, line 313)

The text also mentions that this is an act which would be performed for their own deceased family members. After the workers glorified the deceased Hepdjefa with their light offerings, they would give what was left of the lighting implement to the ka-priest. This act was apparently very significant, as Contract 9 stipulates that parcels of land and the hindquarter of a bull would be distributed to the cemetery overseer and his workers for this service (Griffith 1889, pl. 8, lines 313–314).

The practice of presenting light to the deceased continues, and in fact becomes more prominent, in the New Kingdom. Expanding on the Middle Kingdom texts referencing when the offering of light would take place, the New Kingdom texts provide much more information as to why light would be offered. One rather poetic phrase, which first appears in the early Eighteenth Dynasty (ca. 1493–1458 BCE) during the reigns of Thutmose II and Hatshepsut, states:

> May a *tkA* [lighting device] be lit for you at night until sunlight shines upon your chest; tomb of Paheri, el-Kab (Tylor and Griffith 1894, 30)

Near identical inscriptions are also found in the Eighteenth Dynasty Theban tombs of Sennefer (TT96), Senemiah (TT217) and May (TT130).[3] In addition to these inscriptions, New Kingdom tomb scenes illustrate the New Year's Eve nighttime procession described in Hepdjefa's contracts. Scenes in the tomb chapels of Amenemhet (TT82) (N. M. Davies and Gardiner 1915, pl. XXI), Senemiah (TT127), and Menkheperrasonb (TT112) (N. M. Davies 1933, pl. XXIX) depict family members offering lighting devices to their deceased relatives for each of the five Epagomenal Days at the end of the Egyptian year, as well as the New Year. The Epagomenal Days commemorated the birthdays of the gods Osiris, Isis, Horus, Seth, and Nepthys and were seen as a treacherous but crucial transitory period of the year. Immediately following these five days was the celebration of the New Year, the beginning of the Egyptian civil calendar. Later New Kingdom scenes, such as those in the chapels of Mery (TT95) and Amenmesu (TT89) (N. M. Davies and Davies 1941), suggest that commemoration of the Epagomenal Days and New Year were combined into one offering of multiple lights. However, the core element of family members processing into the tomb chapels to offer light on the night of New Year's Eve is maintained throughout.

Another noteworthy element of these scenes is the constancy of elements included, suggesting that the procession and offering of light were part of a well-established, well-understood religious tradition. Specifically, the tombs referenced above display lighting implements presented in pairs for festivals in which the deceased are commemorated. This practice correlates to Hepdjefa's tomb contracts that reference the presentation of two lighting devices for the "glorification" of the deceased on the New Year. Additionally, the context within which these scenes are presented in the tombs focuses on the celebration of yearly festivals for the dead. Unlike other common themes in the decorative program that could include scenes of fishing, harvesting, or the funeral rites, the procession with lighting devices is clearly related to events that occur after the funeral and burial.

Scholars have previously commented on this ritual procession and assumed that this ceremony was either a symbolic ritual or that it did not actually take place at night (Dümichen 1883; N. de G. Davies 1924; Gutbub 1961). The reason for this doubt centered on the lighting implements themselves. It was thought that the handheld devices would not have been suitable for a lengthy procession because (1) hot fats, oils, or pieces of fabric could have fallen onto the hands of the carriers; and (2) the lights would not have burned long enough to navigate the walk through the necropolis and maintain their brightness by the time the bearers reached the tomb (N. de G. Davies 1924, 9). However, personal experimentation with making and using replicas of the implements depicted in New Kingdom tomb scenes indicate that they burn well, produce ample light by which to navigate, and do not drip fats or oils onto the hands of the carrier (Strong 2021). Total burn time per lighting device was approximately forty-five minutes, which is more than enough time for a procession and offering ceremony. This time could have been easily extended by making a larger device or adding additional linen and illuminant to the implement.

Although the contracts of Hepdjefa and these New Kingdom tomb scenes are separated by more than 500 years, it seems that the idea of a nocturnal procession on New Year's Eve persisted from at least the Middle Kingdom to the New Kingdom. It is clear from both sources that this ceremony was a public occasion in which members of a settlement would join together to participate in a commemoration of the deceased members of their community. Less apparent is what value the light had in this ritual and why night was specifically chosen for the performance, particularly as most Egyptian rituals took place during the day. To address these issues, the production, usage, and significance of artificial lighting in Egyptian society are considered next.

THE VALUE OF ARTIFICIAL LIGHTING

The majority of evidence for economic and social value of artificial lighting comes from the workers' village of Deir el-Medina, part of the larger ancient Egyptian capital of Waset/Thebes, modern-day Luxor. The workers here were skilled craftspeople employed in constructing and decorating the elaborate royal tombs in the Valley of the Kings (Lesko and Lesko 1994; Andreu and Barbotin 2002; Gobeil 2015). Due to the prestige of their work, the villagers of Deir el-Medina were provisioned by the king with (more or less) regular deliveries of food stuffs, tools, and other raw materials in compensation for their labor, a unique situation in comparison to most Egyptian settlements. A large amount of textual material relating to the daily lives of the villagers was uncovered at the site and provides valuable evidence for the commodities and resources available.[4] Of notable relevance to this chapter is the availability of fuel sources, especially animal fats and vegetable oils. These substances would have been used for cooking, medicinal applications, and beauty products, and as illuminants for lighting devices. In addition to accounts of goods, the tombs of the individuals who lived in this village provide one of the few records of what lighting devices looked like and how they were used.

While the settlement at Deir el-Medina was exceptional in comparison to others in the Nile Valley and the workers were likely better provisioned than the average Egyptian citizen, these records provide a point of reference for examining the cost of artificial lighting. Every laborer at Deir el-Medina received rations of bread and beer, as well as some fish and vegetables (Janssen 1975, 457). They also received rations of fuel in the form of wood and dung. Villagers would have understood the value of a good, which was generally expressed as a weight of copper (in *deben*), and would barter to obtain those goods. A goose, for example, would cost about 0.25 deben; a goat 1–3 deben; and a wide range of basketry, boxes, and leather goods between 1 and 5 deben (Janssen 1975, 525–526). One of the commonly referenced commodities in the list of provisions for Deir el-Medina was a variety of vegetable oils and animal fats, all of which would have cost between 0.5 and 1 deben per jar (Keimer 1924, 18–19; Janssen 1975, 489–490). Considering a worker could obtain a living goat for 1–3 deben—which could provide a family with milk, fertilizer for fields, and serve as a waste disposal service—a jar of oil or fat was not cheap. These oils were so highly prized that they were given out as rewards or bonuses on certain occasions.

In addition to the value of fats and oil, these products seem to have held quite high social currency. This inference is chiefly evident in titles of individuals from the Old, Middle, and New Kingdoms who were associated with the production, storage, and distribution of fats, particularly beef tallow, as cattle were highly prized by the ancient Egyptians. The Old Kingdom butcher Pehernefer, well known from his statue in the Louvre (A 107), bears the titles of master butcher, overseer of butchers, and overseer of the Rendering House or overseer of the House of Beef Fat (figure 2.3). A similar title, director or

FIGURE 2.3. *Statue of Pehernefer (A 107), Musée du Louvre, Paris; Photo: Rama / CC BY-SA 3.0 FR (https://creativecommons.org/ licenses/by-sa/3.0/fr/deed.en).*

purveyor of beef fat, appears on a seal in the tomb of the Early Dynastic ruler, Khasekhemwy (ca. 2675–2650 BCE), indicating that this post was a well-established one in Egyptian society (Petrie 1901, pl. 23, no. 198). This title continues into the Middle Kingdom in variant forms including Keeper of Fat/ Pieces of Fat and Keeper of Lamp Fat, although a more accurate translation may be Keeper of Illuminant.

These titles suggest that all steps of the process of fat production were tightly controlled and prized. Presumably master butchers, such as Pehernefer, would oversee the butchery process and ensure that all usable fat was set aside and transported to the rendering house (figure 2.4). The processing of the raw fat into a rendered tallow was then closely monitored by either the overseer of the rendering house or perhaps a director/purveyor of fat. These individuals also likely presided over the pouring of the rendered tallow into jars for storage. These jars would then have passed into the care of the keeper of fat, or keeper of illuminant, who would account for their distribution to the royal household or temples. The rarity and expense of animal fat suggest that an individual with any of these titles must have held a relatively high social status. The fact that many of these individuals could afford, or were granted the resources, to make monuments bearing their titles supports this hypothesis.

Given the expense of oils and fats as described in the village records of Deir el-Medina, it seems very unlikely that they often would have been burned for lighting. Some scholars may argue that a lack of settlement evidence, where lamps would have been used in domestic spaces, could account for the scarcity

FIGURE 2.4. *Middle Kingdom model of a slaughterhouse (20.3.10) from the tomb of Meketre (TT280) depicting individuals similar to Pehernefer, who would have overseen the butchery and processing of cattle. Photo: The Metropolitan Museum of Art, New York.*

of lighting equipment in the material record. The poor preservation and resulting minimal information about settlements from ancient Egypt cannot be avoided. However, if artificial lighting was routinely utilized in domestic contexts where it could provide illumination in the evening or in darkened interior rooms, it presumably would be found in the best recorded settlements: Lahun, Amarna, and Deir el-Medina. Although few of the houses at these sites have been excavated with thorough recording, a review of the published material does not indicate that lighting was commonly used in ancient Egyptian households.

In the database of small finds from Amarna, only three lamps were found within Eighteenth Dynasty homes (Rose 2007, 211). J.D.S. Pendlebury, one of the more prominent archaeologists to work at Amarna in the early twentieth century, recorded that several ceramic saucers were found with blackened rims, indicating that they had been used as lamps (1951, 137). Unfortunately, he gives no indication of how many of these saucers were found, nor their location. Examples of blackened round-topped or rectangular niches do exist,

FIGURE 2.5. *Scene from the tomb of Nebenmaat (TT219) in which Anubis presents a lamp at the entrance to the burial chamber. Photo: Meghan E. Strong.*

primarily in interior rooms of homes in the Workmen's Village, but these are not frequent enough to indicate that interior domestic lighting was common at Amarna (Stevens 2006, 246–247). Deir el-Medina provides slightly more archaeological evidence for lighting implements, including many fragments of lampstands and an unspecified number of lamps found in the village. However, many lampstand fragments were found in the context of small devotional shrines within the houses (Bruyère 1939, 208–209, fig. 98). This distribution may indicate that the lamps associated with these lampstands were not used primarily for everyday illumination, but rather for ritual purposes.

This interpretation is supported by depictions of lamps and other lighting devices in the tombs at Deir el-Medina. Within the beautifully painted tomb chapels and burial chambers that surround the village, lighting devices are most commonly shown as being presented to the god Osiris, king of the underworld, or by a personified emblem of the West, the land of the dead (Zivie 1979, 47, pl. 18; Saleh 1984, 75). Lamps are also shown presented before the deceased's mummy (Vandier 1935, pl. VII), by the god Anubis, who would lead the dead into the underworld (tomb of Nebenmaat; TT219) (figure 2.5), and, in one instance, before the deceased on the occasion of the New Year (Bruyère 1926, fig. 87). All these scenes are related to mortuary and ritual contexts, indicating that artificial light was less connected to a secular or domestic environment.

LIGHT, NIGHT, AND CULTURAL MEMORY

It is clear from the archaeological and textual record that the provisioning of light for the nocturnal ritual on New Year's Eve was essential. Despite the cost of the illuminant and linen, families—albeit those perhaps from a higher socioeconomic class—seem to have prioritized their participation in this festival's nocturnal procession to honor their deceased family members. This begs the question as to why this ritual was significant to ancient Egyptians.

The ritual application of lighting is not something unfamiliar in modern-day ceremonies. Churches, mosques, and temples create dramatic lit environments through the utilization of stained glass or mosaics; strategically placed candles, lamps, and windows; and selective balance between light and shadow (e.g., Nesbitt 2012; Pentcheva 2010, 2017). Artificial lighting plays an integral metaphoric role in many of the world's religions and philosophies. The menorah symbolizes the divine light of God, and, as such, one is continually kept lit in synagogues. The Hindu festival of Diwali is celebrated by the lighting of *diyas*, or small clay oil lamps, to represent the triumph of good over evil, light over darkness. Lighting candles or lanterns may also symbolize the attainment of enlightenment, such as in the Buddhist celebration of Vetak, or the virtues of hope, love, joy, and peace as in the Christian Advent wreath. Artificial lights can be employed for their more practical, but no less essential, aspects of illumination as well. The evening celebrations of Ramadan would not be complete without the brightly colored *fawanees*, traditional Egyptian lanterns, hanging throughout the streets and in front of homes. Similarly, Christmas celebrations are enhanced by brightly lit trees, glowing candles, and elaborate public lighting displays. Crucially, it is the interaction between night and artificial lighting that forms a core component in the performance and the experience and atmosphere of these religious festivals and built environments (Bille and Sørensen 2007; Bille et al. 2015). While some are imbued with ritual symbolism, all contribute to the creation of a sacred space within which certain rites are properly performed.

It is outside the scope of this chapter to thoroughly explore theories of ritual and performance, but some aspects are immediately relevant to the current discussion.[5] Ritual, for example, plays a pivotal role in social structure and cohesion (Bell 2009, 15, 20). This characteristic is particularly evident in rituals that are derived from common social interactions such as animal sacrifice (or butchery) and feasting. In complement, ritual performance serves to encode cultural traditions and transmit them on special occasions, such as festivals (Bell 2009, 45). Traditions, such as the commemoration of the New Year in ancient Egypt, were a key component to the construction of cultural memory (see chapter 4 for a comparison in ancient Greece). At the same time, objects are invested with memory and are utilized in ritual performances to transfer memory across generations (Assmann 2006, 8–9). In this way, ritual performance helps to retain memory and create a connection to the past. By extension, it also helps to connect directly to memories of the deceased and, through the performance of a ritual, make them part of the present (Gillam 2009, 2).

Applying these theories to the nocturnal procession performed during New Year's Eve may help to elucidate the significance of this ritual. First, the constancy in the depictions of this annual event in New Kingdom tombs suggests that it was indeed part of a cultural tradition. Even if there was variability in the actual performance, it was perceived to be an unchanging act. This constant aspect suggests that the performance of this procession was a means of transmitting cultural information and building social cohesion within individual communities. Second, it may be that emphasis was placed on the lighting devices during this procession because these are the objects to which cultural memory was tied, a facet that would explain why artificial light sources were primarily restricted to sacred rather than domestic spaces. The sensory experience of the lighting devices—such as the scent, warm glow, flickering flame, or emitted warmth—may have contributed to the production of memory and, by extension, remembrance of the dead. The centrality of a light source as the transmitter of cultural memory clarifies why night was used as the performance space for this ritual. This period, of course, was the best time of day to display the flickering flame of the light offerings. The darkness of night would show them off to their full effect, covering cemeteries throughout Egypt in dots of light—an experience of the night well outside the norm of any other during the year, adding to its sanctity and significance. The procession would have contributed to the sense of community and tradition, as, presumably, the majority of city and village inhabitants would have participated in the festival. The remnants of burning devices across the landscape would serve as markers of piety for the families who participated in the commemoration of their ancestors.

CONCLUSIONS

The nocturnal procession on New Year's Eve was a unique event in the ancient Egyptian calendar. In contrast to other ritual occasions, the use of night for this festival was a critical component in the commemoration of the dead. The presentation of artificial lights at the tombs of deceased members of communities served to pass down traditions and contributed to the development of cultural memory and social identity. Similar to modern festivals, such as Día de los Muertos, the offering of light commemorated the past while including the dead in the present. It seems that, at least on this night, the potential for evil and death could be overcome. Instead, the ancient Egyptians harnessed the darkness of night to celebrate the possibility of rebirth through death and rejuvenation in the afterlife.

This chapter demonstrates that the intersection of night and urban archaeology in ancient Egypt is worthy of analysis. As discussed in chapter 1 of this volume, day and night equally contributed to city life and, by extension, contributed to the construction of social identity, tradition, and cultural memory. The impact of artificial light and nocturnal darkness on ritual performance opens new lines of inquiry into religious ideologies of ancient Egypt and provides a conduit for cross-cultural comparison with other ancient civilizations. Additionally, the utilization of lighting implements and their effect on the people and places within the Egyptian urban landscape would repay such analysis. Further research into the agency of artificial lighting in ancient Egyptian society will undoubtedly contribute to our understanding of the experience and construction of the built environment, as well as the people who inhabited it.

NOTES

1. For a translation and commentary on the original text in the Papyrus Millingen, see Lichtheim (2006, 135–139).
2. The categorization of ancient Egyptian settlements is difficult for a variety of reasons. Rather than use general terminology such as "city" or "town," which may fail to capture the true meaning of the Egyptian urban environment, I will primarily use the term "settlement." For a full description of these issues and parameters for urban versus nonurban sites in Egypt, see Moeller (2016, 14–26).
3. TT is the designation for "Theban Tomb," which is used for tombs on the west bank of Luxor.
4. An online bibliography of this textual record is maintained by the University of Leiden (Demarée et al. 2018).
5. For a thorough discussion see Bell (1997, 2009) and Turner (1969), and sources cited therein.

REFERENCES

Andreu, Guillemette, and Christophe Barbotin. 2002. *Les artistes de Pharaon: Deir El-Médineh et La Vallée des Rois*. Paris: Réunion des musées nationaux, Brepols.

Assmann, Jan. 2006. *Religion and Cultural Memory: Ten Studies*. Translated by Rodney Livingstone. Cultural Memory in the Present. Stanford, CA: Stanford University Press.

Bell, Catherine. 1997. *Ritual: Perspectives and Dimensions*. New York: Oxford University Press.

Bell, Catherine. 2009. *Ritual Theory, Ritual Practice*. Oxford: Oxford University Press.

Bille, Mikkel, Peter Bjerregaard, and Tim Flohr Sørensen. 2015. "Staging Atmospheres: Materiality, Culture, and the Texture of the in-Between." *Emotion, Space and Society* 15 (May): 31–38. https://doi.org/10.1016/j.emospa.2014.11.002.

Bille, Mikkel, and Tim Flohr Sørensen. 2007. "An Anthropology of Luminosity: The Agency of Light." *Journal of Material Culture* 12 (3): 263–284.

Blackman, Aylward M., and T. Eric Peet. 1925. "Papyrus Lansing: A Translation with Notes." *Journal of Egyptian Archaeology* 11 (3/4): 284–298. https://doi.org/10.2307/3854153.

Bruyère, Bernard. 1926. *Rapport sur les fouilles de Deir El Médineh, 1924–1925*. FIFAO 3. Cairo: Institut français d'archéologie orientale.

Bruyère, Bernard. 1939. *Rapport sur les fouilles de Deir El Medineh, 1934–1935: Le Village, Les Décharges publiques, La Station de Repos Du Col de La Vallée Des Rois. (3e Pt)*. FIFAO 16. Cairo: Institut français d'archéologie orientale.

Davies, N. de G. 1924. "A Peculiar Form of New Kingdom Lamp." *Journal of Egyptian Archaeology* 10 (1): 9–14. https://doi.org/10.2307/3853990.

Davies, Nina M. 1933. *The Tombs of Menkheperrasonb, Amenmose, and Another (Nos. 86, 112, 42, 226)*. Theban Tomb Series 5. London: Egypt Exploration Society.

Davies, Nina M., and N. de G. Davies. 1941. "The Tomb of Amenmosĕ (No. 89) at Thebes." *Journal of Egyptian Archaeology* 26 (1): 131–136. https://doi.org/10.2307/3854532.

Davies, Nina M., and Alan Henderson Gardiner. 1915. *The Tomb of Amenemhēt (No. 82)*. Theban Tomb Series. London: William Clowes and Sons.

Demarée, R. J., B. J. J. Haring, W. Hovestreydt, and L. M. J. Zonhoven. 2018. *A Systematic Bibliography on Deir el-Medina*. https://www.wepwawet.nl/dmd/bibliography.htm.

Dümichen, Johannes. 1883. "Die Ceremonie des Lichtanzündens." *Zeitschrift für Ägyptische Sprache und Altertumskunde* 21: 11–15.

Erman, Adolf, and Hermann Grapow. 1931. *Wörterbuch der Ägyptischen Sprache*. Vol. 5. 12 vols. Leipzig: J. C. Hinrichs.

Gillam, Robyn Adams. 2009. *Performance and Drama in Ancient Egypt*. Duckworth Egyptology. London: Duckworth.

Gobeil, Cédric. 2015. "The IFAO Excavations at Deir el-Medina." In *Oxford Handbooks Online*. Oxford University Press. https://doi.org/10.1093/oxfordhb/978019 9935413.013.32.

Griffith, Francis Llewellyn. 1889. *The Inscriptions of Siût and Dêr Rîfeh*. London: Trübner and Co.

Gutbub, Adolphe. 1961. "Un emprunt aux textes des Pyramides dans l'hymne à Hathor, Dame de l'ivresse." In *Mélanges Maspero I—Orient ancien*, 4: 31–72. MIFAO 66. Cairo: Institut français d'archéologie orientale.

Helck, Wolfgang. 1970. *Die Lehre des Dw3-ḥtjj*. Kleine ägyptische Texte. Wiesbaden, Germany: Otto Harrassowitz.

Janssen, J. J. 1975. *Commodity Prices from the Ramessid Period: An Economic Study of the Village of Necropolis Workmen at Thebes*. Leiden, Netherlands: E. J. Brill.

Jeffreys, David. 2008. "The Survey of Memphis, Capital of Ancient Egypt: Recent Developments." *Archaeology International* 11 (0): 41–44. https://doi.org/10.5334/ai.1112.

Kahl, Jochem. 2007. *Ancient Asyut: The First Synthesis after 300 Years of Research*. Asyut Project. Vol. 1. Wiesbaden: Harrassowitz Verlag.

Kahl, Jochem. 2016. *Ornamente in Bewegung: Die Deckendekoration der Grossen Querhalle i Grab von Djefai-Hapi I. in Assiut*. Asyut Project. Vol. 6. Wiesbaden, Germany: Harrassowitz Verlag.

Keimer, Ludwig. 1924. *Die Gartenpflanzen im Alten Ägypten: Ägyptologische Studien*. Berlin: Hoffmann und Campe.

Lesko, Leonard H., and Barbara S. Lesko, eds. 1994. *Pharaoh's Workers: The Villagers of Deir el Medina*. Ithaca, NY: Cornell University Press.

Lichtheim, Miriam. 2006. *Ancient Egyptian Literature: A Book of Readings*. Vol. 2. Berkeley: University of California Press.

Moeller, Nadine. 2016. *The Archaeology of Urbanism in Ancient Egypt: From the Predynastic Period to the End of the Middle Kingdom*. Cambridge: Cambridge University Press. https://doi.org/10.1017/CBO9781139942119.

Nesbitt, Claire. 2012. "Shaping the Sacred: Light and the Experience of Worship in Middle Byzantine Churches." *Byzantine and Modern Greek Studies* 36 (2): 139–160.

Pendlebury, John Devitt Stringfellow. 1951. *The City of Akhenaten. Part 3, The Central City and the Official Quarters*. Memoirs of the Egypt Exploration Society 44. London: Egypt Exploration Society.

Pentcheva, Bissera V. 2010. *The Sensual Icon: Space, Ritual and the Senses in Byzantium*. University Park: Pennsylvania State University Press.

Pentcheva, Bissera V. 2021. "Phenomenology of Light: The Glitter of Salvation in Bessarion's Cross." Edited by Costas Papadopoulos and Holly Moyes. *The Oxford Handbook of Light in Archaeology*, Oxford: Oxford University Press.

Petrie, William M. F. 1901. *The Royal Tombs of the Earliest Dynasties. Part II.* Egypt Exploration Fund Memoirs 21. London: Egypt Exploration Fund.

Reisner, George A. 1918. "The Tomb of Hepzefa, Nomarch of Siût." *Journal of Egyptian Archaeology* 5 (2): 79–98.

Robins, F. W. 1939. "The Lamps of Ancient Egypt." *Journal of Egyptian Archaeology* 25 (2): 184–187. https://doi.org/10.2307/3854653.

Rose, Pamela J. 2007. *The Eighteenth Dynasty Pottery Corpus from Amarna.* London: Egypt Exploration Society.

Saleh, Mohamed. 1984. *Das Totenbuch in den Thebanischen Beamtengräbern des Neuen Reiches: Texte und Vignetten.* Archäologische Veröffentlichungen / Deutsches Archäologisches Institut. Abteilung Kairo 46. Mainz am Rhein, Germany: von Zabern.

Spalinger, Anthony J. 1992. "Night into Day." *Zeitschrift für Ägyptische Sprache und Altertumskunde* 119 (2): 144–156.

Stevens, Anna. 2006. *Private Religion at Amarna: The Material Evidence.* BAR International Series 1587. Oxford: Archaeopress.

Strong, Meghan. 2021. *Sacred Flames: The Power of Artificial Light in Ancient Egypt.* Cairo: American University in Cairo Press.

Toonen, Willem H. J., Angus Graham, Benjamin T. Pennington, Morag A. Hunter, Kristian D. Strutt, Dominic S. Barker, Aurélia Masson-Berghoff, and Virginia L. Emery. 2018. "Holocene Fluvial History of the Nile's West Bank at Ancient Thebes, Luxor, Egypt, and Its Relation with Cultural Dynamics and Basin-wide Hydroclimatic Variability." *Geoarchaeology* 33 (3): 273–190. https://doi.org/10.1002/gea.21631.

Turner, Victor. 1969. *The Ritual Process: Structure and Anti-structure.* Ithaca, NY: Cornell University Press.

Tylor, J. J., and F. Ll. Griffith. 1894. *The Tomb of Paheri at El Kab.* Memoir of the Egypt Exploration Fund 11. London: Egypt Exploration Fund.

Vandier, Jacques. 1935. *Tombes de Deir el-Médineh: La tombe de Nefer-Abou.* MIFAO 69. Cairo: Institut français d'archéologie orientale.

Zivie, Alain-Pierre. 1979. *La tombe de Pached à Deir el-Médineh (No 3).* MIFAO 99. Cairo: Institut français d'archéologie orientale.

3

Danger in the Mesopotamian Night

Mitigating Peril in the Heartland of Cities

Tiffany Earley-Spadoni

He struck me and turned me into a dove
[He bound] my arms like the wings of a bird
To lead me captive to the house of darkness, seat of
  Irkalla:
to the house which none who enters ever leaves,
on the path that allows no journey back
to the house whose residents are deprived of light,
where soil is their sustenance and clay their food,
where they are clad like birds in coats of feathers,
and see no light and dwell in darkness.

—Tablet VII, *Gilgamesh*, from Enkidu's
death dream, translation George (2003)

The Mesopotamian night was dark and full of terrors, but people sought ways to drive out the darkness, whether it was an enemy at the city gates, a ghost, or a witch. A Neo-Assyrian *namburbi* incantation shows offerings to four household gods, when a dwelling had been disturbed by the invasion of a fungus (Caplice 1971, 140–147). One of the invoked gods, Išum, is a god associated with fire and the hearth on the lexical level (Scurlock 2003; George 2015). Išum, much like the Roman goddess Vesta, is likewise known as the "herald of the street" and the "herald of the night" (Scurlock 2003).[1] In other words, Išum is the night watcher, charged like his mortal counterparts with patrolling the dark and narrow thoroughfares of early cities. It has been argued that the god Išum is instantiated in the fiery glow of the torch that served to guide city dwellers home; he is the one, "who patrols at night, shining

https://doi.org/10.5876/9781646422609.c003

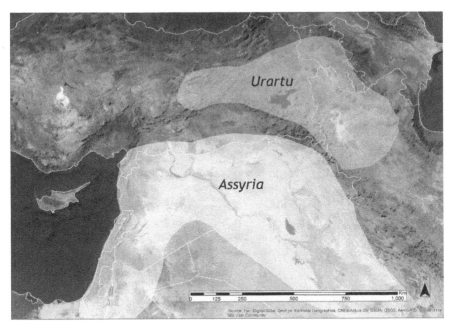

FIGURE 3.1. *The Neo-Assyrian (south) and Urartian Empires (north). The Neo-Assyrian and Urartian empires (9th to 7th centuries BCE) depicted at their respective territorial apogee. Map: Tiffany Early-Spadoni.*

a light as bright as day"[2] (George 2015, 4). Išum's association with fire lights up the nightscape of the ancient Mesopotamian city, and he was invoked for protection against nocturnal attacks such as the ones described in this chapter.

This contribution examines urban Mesopotamian nightscapes of the third through early first millennia BCE,[3] with an emphasis on the later periods. I also discuss examples from the aggressively nonurban empire of Urartu, a highland expansionary state that arose in the early first millennium BCE in modern-day Turkey, Armenia, and Iran to oppose the Neo-Assyrian state (figure 1.1; figure 3.1). In broad terms, scholars characterize the archaeological periodization of the relevant periods using subdivisions of the Bronze and Iron Ages while historical chronologies overlap these categories (table 3.1).

In this chapter, I argue that night was a dangerous, liminal time, when different kinds of enemies threatened the peace of sleep. These threats took the form of enemy invaders, ghosts, and witches. In addition to constructed landscapes, Mesopotamian imaginaries—that is, mythological realms, tales of witches, and ghost stories—offer critical insight to place and collective memory

TABLE 3.1. Archaeological and historical periods mentioned in text

Archaeological Period	Dates	Historical Correlates
Early Bronze Age (EBA)	3100–2100 BCE	Sumerian city-states (including Umma and Lagash)
Middle Bronze Age (MBA)	2100–1600 BCE	Old Babylonian city-states (including Mari)
Late Bronze Age (LBA)	1600–1200 BCE	Middle Assyrian period
Early Iron Age (EI)	1200–800 BCE	Rise of Urartian and Neo-Assyrian states

making, to the social construction of the "night." Moreover, Mesopotamian peoples devised various responses to peril and techniques to confront terror, ranging from fire beacon networks to apotropaic nocturnal rituals. The various strategies described in this chapter allowed ancient Mesopotamians to express agency over an unknown future, symbolically represented by darkness.

It is instructive to consider ideational landscapes alongside the landscapes that we might call "real" or "constructed" toward building an understanding of layered, socially constructed landscapes. Bernard Knapp and Wendy Ashmore (1999) provide a useful analytical framework in their influential treatise, which heralded a postmodern landscape archaeology. Specifically, they define three areas of inquiry: constructed, conceptualized, and ideational. Constructed landscapes are modified human landscapes built over time that reflect social belief systems. The fire beacon lightscapes described below are examples of constructed landscapes, inspired by anxiety and built by human hands. Conceptualized landscapes are, instead, primarily natural, unmodified landscapes upon which humans project belief systems, often complex. Night was a time during which Mesopotamians anxiously watched the skies for portents of the future. By the Neo-Assyrian period (ninth to seventh century BCE), astrology gained a new level of prominence in the royal court. The epistolary sources reveal scholars peering obsessively into the night sky and writing to the king of what they saw (Monroe 2019). The Mesopotamian night sky, as a backdrop in this chapter, is an excellent example of the second category. The third and final category, ideational, refers to conceptual landscapes that exist primarily in the human mind. Examples of ideational nightscapes in the form of literary descriptions of the netherworld and associated ghost stories are presented in this chapter.

THE CONSTRUCTED NIGHT

The threat of warfare was a perennial risk to the inhabitants of Mesopotamia's early city-states. Fear of uncertain futures must have conditioned the experiences

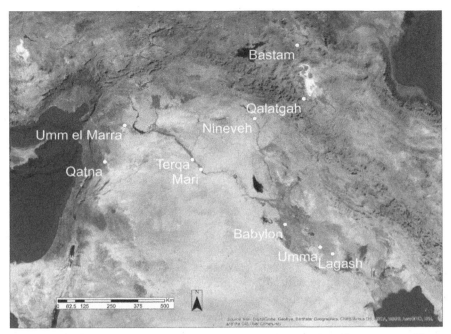

FIGURE 3.2. *Ancient places mentioned in this chapter in the modern-day countries of Syria, Iraq and Iran. Map: Tiffany Early-Spadoni.*

of early city dwellers. One perennial fear was warfare or siege of the city, a reality reflected in the world's oldest narrative texts and its city laments. When the curtain rose on the first historical narratives known in the world (ca. 2450 BCE), people were at war. Various inscribed objects describe Eannatum,[4] a ruler of the city-state of Lagash, who battled with his enemies from Umma over a choice piece of agricultural land called the Gu'edena. The inscribed monument, known as the Stele of the Vultures, a pictorial narrative of the events described in texts, memorably features vultures grasping the severed heads of enemies in their stony beaks, soaring above the military fray. While the works are highly charged pieces of state propaganda, historical content still may be derived from them (George 2013). The heaping of the dead into mass graves described in the texts may have constituted an additional humiliation or desecration, since the usual funerary rites and offerings were not administered. Arguably, deviations from normative funerary practices (see Richardson 2007) deprived the individual of peace in the afterlife, a point discussed in greater detail below.

Early city dwellers developed various techniques to respond to life's calamities, one of which was fire beacon signaling, a practice that lit up the night in times of danger (Earley-Spadoni 2015a, 2015b) (see chapter 9 in this volume on fireboxes and signaling in Chaco Canyon). The earliest historical and archaeological evidence for fire signaling in the ancient Near East comes from MBA Syria, circa 1800 BCE. Epistolary archives from the palace at Mari document the affairs of the rulers of the state and their associated functionaries.[5] Dozens of letters pertaining to fire beacons were discovered in the palace archive (Dossin 1938), and several of them are worthy of mention here. In one letter, Bannum, a high-ranking official, wrote the king that while traveling north from Mari, he saw the fire beacons being lit town by town by the Yaminites,[6] near the city of Terqa (Dossin 1938, 178). He was unsure why the beacons had been lit but promised to write back with more details. In the meantime, he recommended that the city defenses be reinforced, indicating that fire beacons were used as an early warning system. In another missive, a functionary apologized for worrying the king by lighting the beacons but explained that the Yaminites were still in a state of revolt (181). Yet another letter informed the king that an attack near Terqa was imminent, and the general Sammetar had a force assembled in the area to confront any attack. The writer reassured the king that when the fire beacon was lit at the location of attack, unknown at the moment of writing, he would come to the rescue (–183). In another letter, a certain Zindria responded to a complaint from the king about the ambiguity of a fire signal. Zindria wrote that to avoid future confusion, he would henceforth muster the troops and signal to other stations when he saw only two fires lit rather than one (183), indicating that fire communication was sometimes an imperfect system and that the meaning of signals could be contextual and agreed upon in advance. Last, the communiqués, when considered together, demonstrate that a mustering of troops was a common response to the lighting of the beacons. It is worth noting that the intended meaning of the lit fire in all instances was danger and the lighting of the beacons was meant to elicit aid from afar.

Archaeological investigations from MBA Syria also suggest the placement of sites for intentional intervisibility. The Arid Margins of Northern Syria project (Rousset et al. 2017) has cataloged more than 100 MBA sites in western Syria to investigate the observed uptick in defensive network construction during the period. They have documented a multitiered regional defense network comprising *forteresses, fortins, tors, petites tours,* and *villes fortifiées* (fortresses, forts, large towers, small towers, and fortified settlements, respectively). They conclude that regular spacing and intervisibility were key factors for the placement of structures in the study area. Not only would the regular spacing of structures (ca. twenty kilometers) have ensured safety along the road for travelers, but also it would have offered excellent visibility and intervisibility, allowing for nocturnal fire beacon signaling such as the systems described at Mari. Ethnographic research indicates that a small fire beacon can be seen from distances of more than fifty kilometers given good weather.[7] Beyond MBA Syria, there is considerable textual and archaeological evidence for the use of watchtowers and intentional intervisibility of constructed features from Levantine sites (Burke 2007), indicating that the practice was already so diffuse by the early second millennium that it may predate that era. Somewhat later than the archival documentation at Mari, a visual communication system has been documented by archaeologists at Minoan Crete (Panagiotakis et al. 2013) by the discovery of a system of intervisibile *soroi*, large stand-alone pyrotechnic installations that contained signal pyres.

One of the most vibrant examples of fire beacon use described in the textual sources from Mesopotamia comes from "The Eighth Campaign" of Sargon II, conventionally dated to 714 BCE. This complex literary text describes the progress of the Neo-Assyrian army deep into enemy territory in modern-day Iran, where they confronted their powerful enemy, Urartu. Once they arrived in the Sangibute region near Lake Urmia, the Assyrians attempted to engage the Urartians, but to no avail:

> For them to watch out for enemies (?) in the district, towers had been built on mountain peaks and provided with [stores of firewood for signals]. When they saw the (250) bonfires lit, signaling the approach of an enemy, [for which] torches [were kept ready(?)] day and night, announcing [ ], they feared my furious attack, which has no like, terror spread among them, and they were too af[raid to fight]. Without so much as a glance at their numerous possessions, they forsook their mighty fortresses and disappeared. (Foster 2005, 804)

In addition to its description of Urartu's elaborate and effective fire beacon systems, the passage implies the use of smoke signaling, since stores of fuel, presumably consisting of both green and dry wood, were kept ready for use both day and night. Fire beacons were a system to be used at night, whereas smoke signals could be used during the day.

Archaeological evidence corroborates claims made in the propagandistic Assyrian sources about Urartu's fire beacon capabilities. The EI and Urartian settlement systems of the early first millennium BCE near Lake Sevan in Armenia demonstrate intentional placement for intervisibility (Earley-Spadoni 2015b). A dense network of intervisible sites was observed south of Lake Sevan in Armenia and has been the object of systematic GIS and social network analysis studies (Earley-Spadoni 2015b). The dense interconnections of sites during the EI and subsequent Urartian annexation (figure 3.3) create

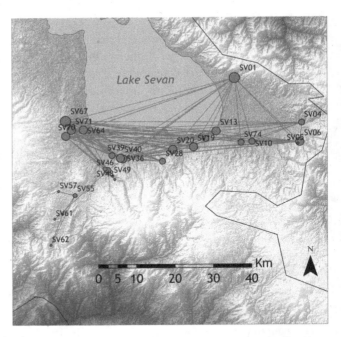

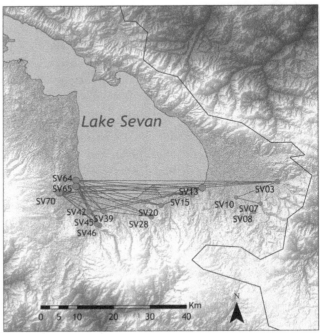

FIGURE 3.3.
Intervisibility of (a)
Early Iron Age and
(b) *Urartian sites,*
Lake Sevan, Armenia.
Maps: Tiffany
Earley-Spadoni.

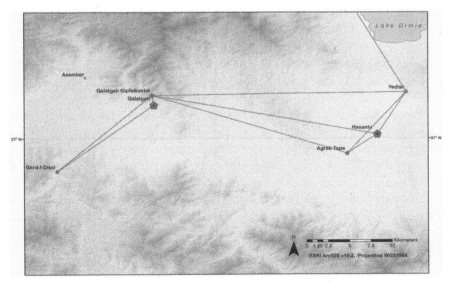

FIGURE 3.4. *Regional intervisibility permitted by the Qalatgah Watch Tower. Map: Tiffany Earley-Spadoni.*

intentionally redundant networks, meaning that if one signaling installation failed, a message could still be sent. The described networks mirror levels of redundancy found in modern telecommunications networks. Statistical verification methods applied in the study suggest that the fort and fortress networks were not the result of the organic development of the state. Instead, the sites were constructed as an integrated and intentional communications system requiring an extraordinary level of cooperation among the ancient inhabitants of the region. Some sites, for example, function as relays, or intermediate sites that forward messages from other sites in the network.

In addition to the evidence available from Armenia, there is substantial evidence for the intervisibility of fortified sites in Iran, particularly on the plain west of Lake Urmia, where stand-alone towers played a key role in intrasite communications networks. Various examples of stand-alone watchtowers are known from regional surveys performed in Iran. The investigators discovered the Qalatgah Gipfelkastel, or watchtower some 350 meters above the sizable fortress of Qalatgah at the summit of a serpentine path (Kleiss and Kroll 1977, 71). The structure boasts a view commanding the plain below, while the fortress itself has relatively poor visibility. The twenty-by-twenty-meter watchtower was an auxiliary installation whose primary function was to provide reconnaissance and to connect Qalatgah visually to other sites in its surroundings such as Hasanlu and the fort Yediar (figure 3.4). The watchtower's possible role in a regional visual communication network was noted by Wolfram Kleiss, who proposed that the site would have been an excellent relay for fire and smoke signals. A signaling tower was also documented at the major Urartian fortress of Bastam in Iran (1979, 1988), and watchtowers are certainly known from other Iron Age contexts in the ancient Near East (Edwards 2020).

In sum, fire beacon signaling was widely practiced in the Mesopotamian night. It can be argued, therefore, that fire beacon signaling was a social, collective practice by which people attempted to gain some small amount of agency in an unpredictable world. The towers, fortresses, and fire beacons, while located outside of cities, were instrumental in the defense of urban inhabitants and formed part of the infrastructure for their safety. Fire beacons fall into Darryl Wilkinson's "signaling infrastructure," discussed in chapter 1 (Wilkinson 2019). In this section, I discussed how ancient Mesopotamians utilized the darkness to warn of danger, but next I interrogate historical and archaeological evidence to understand what "night" represented to ancient Mesopotamians.

THE IDEATIONAL NIGHT

Incantation. I invoke you, Gods of the Night,
Together with you, I invoke the night, the veiled bride,
I have invoked the evening, midnight and dawn watches.
Because a witch has bewitched me,
a deceitful woman has denounced me,
caused my god and goddess to be driven from me.
I have become displeasing to those who see me,
I am afflicted by you, sleeplessness, day and night.
They filled my mouth with stupor,
which has kept food distant from my mouth,
has diminished the water at my mouth,
my song of joy has become wailing, my rejoicing mourning.
Stand by me great gods and listen to my speech.
Judge me and issue a verdict!
I made a figurine of my warlock and witch,
of my enchanter and my enchantress
I placed them at your feet and now plead:
Because they acted wickedly and yearned for ungodly things,
I pray that she die, but that I should live!
—Maqlû I, the nocturnal anti-witchcraft ritual
(see Abusch 2015 for discussion and complete translation)

To understand the Mesopotamian night, I contend that it is essential to analyze multiple lines of inquiry. Mesopotamian imaginaries—mythological realms, tales of witches, and ghost stories—offer critical insight into place and collective memory making in the past and present. The described evidence contributes to our understanding of the social construction of "night" and will therefore be considered in the section below. The examples presented constitute a rare opportunity to consider robust ideational landscapes alongside constructed ones.

The anthropology of haunting can provide additional depth to discussions of the ghosts and witches of Mesopotamia. Related to the concept of social trauma, hauntings represent, anthropologically or sociologically speaking, a refusal to forget past wrongs, and can provide a voice to the subaltern in society (González-Tennant 2018; Surface-Evans and Jones 2020). Therefore, ghosts and ghost stories function as a kind of historical memory, capable of resurrecting subversive narratives. Avery Gordon's work on haunting is applicable to the arguments presented in this chapter. Gordon asserts that taking ghosts into account as a part of fundamental belief systems of premodern and modern people can alter our very epistemologies and ontologies, both how we know and what we know (2008, 27, 64). In other words, a belief in ghosts, demons, and witches should not be trivialized by our own disbelief in them.

At the same time, I do not mean to imply a meaningful break between "ancient" and "modern" in my analysis of ghosts and witches. Historians from disparate subfields have independently challenged the long-standing sociological view that modernity is characterized by "disenchantment" (reviewed in Saler 2006), that it has been effectively sanitized of demons, ghosts, and witches.[8] Such a perspective ignores the multiplicity and multivocality of human experience and alternative forms of knowledge (Surface-Evans and Jones 2020). Ghosts, hauntings, and possessions are essential ways in which people, both ancient and modern, experience places, an idea that resonates with scholarly interest in socially constructed places (Tuan 1977, 1979).

Understanding Irkalla, the Mesopotamian netherworld, is critical for comprehending how ancient people socially constructed nightscapes. The cosmos of Mesopotamia was, arguably, organized around two poles, the heavenly court of Anu and the netherworldly court of Ereshkigal, one a land of light, the other a land of darkness. That the netherworld is a realm where light does not enter is a common understanding of that domain, the *bīt eklēti*, the house of darkness (Thavapalan 2020, 106). The Mesopotamian afterlife was not a paradise furnished with streets of gold or eternal rejoicing. Instead, its portrayal typically varied from bland to infernal. Literary texts from Mesopotamia describe Dante-esque journeys or descents into the netherworld. One such text from the first-millennium site of Sultantepe ("Nergal and Ereshkigal," STT 28[9]) describes the inmates of the netherworld, the *erṣet lā tāri*, as bird-like wraiths who dwelled in eternal night, moaned like doves, and consumed dust to sustain themselves. From the texts we learn that the arduous journey consisted of traversing a demon-filled steppe, crossing the Khubur River, and passage through seven concentric gates, each guarded by a different demon (Scurlock 1995, 1886). It was to the netherworld, the land of night, that some portion of the soul was thought to travel, and sometimes the departed souls, ghosts, could come back to afflict the land of the living.

Mesopotamian texts provide valuable interpretive frameworks for understanding ancient beliefs in ghosts, the denizens of the land of night. According to the historical sources, supernatural figures haunted the Mesopotamian night, including spirits that we might calls ghosts or demons. The Akkadian term *zāqīqu* referred to a component of the human soul that left the body at night during dreams. In fact, the gentle breezes that stirred the dust motes of long-abandoned temples or settlement mounds (tells) were thought to be residual zāqīqu spirits (Scurlock 2016, 78). The term *eṭemmu*, from the Akkadian language, can be roughly translated into English as "ghost" (Abusch 1995), though there are other constituent components of departed human souls and other ghostly spirits such as the relatively benign zāqīqu. Of the two kinds of spirits described here, the eṭemmu was by far the more dangerous, and ancient Mesopotamians developed various strategies to combat these harmful ghosts.

Ghosts could be kept safely tucked away in the netherworld by the living, but would become unruly when denied the things they needed: proper burial, mourning, or ongoing mortuary rites.[10] There is little indication that there was any final, moral judgment of the living in the land of the dead such as the weighing of the heart known from the Egyptian *Book of the Dead* (Cooper 1992). Rather, the behavior of the living made all the difference. Formalized mourning was an important way in which the living sustained the dead and constructed a collective memory of them. Mourners would sing laments, tear their garments, and eschew all finery by wearing sack cloth; professional mourners were sometimes used to create a more impressive crowd (Scurlock 1995, 1885). Grave goods were another way that the living provided for the journey that the dead must make. For the highest-status individuals, the provision of jewelry, weapons, and other forms of portable wealth is widely observable in archaeological contexts (Porter and Boutin 2014), as is the case in most of the world. However, Mesopotamian texts shed light on how these riches might have provided for the future needs of the dead. Texts such as "The Descent of Ishtar" (Lapinkivi 2010) depict the payment of jewelry to gate demons to pass through the various stages of the netherworld. Certainly, grave goods simultaneously symbolized social status and standing within the community.

Restless ghosts were known to be the cause of serious illnesses. So much so that entire corpora are dedicated to the management of ghost-induced illness (Scurlock 2006). In Mesopotamia, illness was understood to be a manifestation of evil forces, which included divine anger, demons, warlocks and witches, ghosts, and astronomical phenomena. The officials charged with healing through exorcism (āšipu/mašmaššu) and those who healed with other means such as medicines (asû) therefore had to ascertain which form of evil had befallen their patient before they could determine how to best aid the afflicted individual (Van Buylaere et al. 2018). Various techniques are known for exorcising or neutralizing malevolent ghosts,[11] particularly when they provoked illness, and these include the tying of magical knots, the production of ointments, or the burning or burying of the ghost in figurine effigy, activities that might leave material correlates (Scurlock 2006). Some textual evidence suggests that ghosts could be neutralized by a failure to respect normative burial practices such as the claims made by various Assyrian kings,[12] in which they consigned the arrogant enemies of Assyria to the grave pit and, thus, considered them the relatively harmless zāqīqu (in contrast to the more pernicious eṭemmu).

Historical sources indicate that night was a powerful and efficacious time to communicate with and confront ghosts, who were believed to dwell, ordinarily, in Irkalla, the land of darkness. Medical texts describe night terrors and nightmares as being among the various symptoms that one might suffer as the result of a ghost-induced illness, and certain antighost rituals were prescribed at sunset, a time of day when the barriers between the earthly and netherworldly planes were, arguably, more permeable (Scurlock 2006, 18–21). The nocturnal Mesopotamian kispu ritual was a rite practiced and performed to appease and neutralize potentially harmful ghosts (Tsukimoto 2010), in addition to the other social benefits of sharing a communal meal with one's ancestors. Texts indicate that the timing of the monthly kispu, the mortuary offering, was determined by lunar cycles and was performed at night during the dark of the new moon (see chapter 6 in this volume, on phases of the moon and Classic Maya kingship). The graveside ceremony was conducted at a special structure known as the bīt kispi, where food offerings were shared with ancestors (Cooper 1992, 29; Bottero 2000, 282). The nocturnal ceremony must have been illuminated by torches and lamps to facilitate its successful completion. A special, more elaborate kispu was performed in the month of Abu (July/August), a liminal time when the spirits were thought to be in flux and could travel to the world of the living (see chapter 2 for rituals honoring the dead in Egypt). Other festivals culminated with ghosts being sent home to the netherworld on boats floated on the river (Scurlock 1995, 1889). It is easy to imagine that such a spectacle occurred at night or sunset, featuring boats illuminated by torch- or lamplight. Certainly, some antighost medicines, such as salves and potions, were prescribed first thing in the morning, arguably for medical reasons (Scurlock 2006, 21), and some ghost-induced illnesses manifested symptoms both night and day.

Archaeological evidence from sites in Syria such as Umm el-Marra and Qatna point to lavish funerary rituals centered upon veneration of ancestors (Novák 2008; Schwartz 2012, 2013), which may have been performed at night. Excavations at the site of Umm el-Marra have revealed an EBA complex of elite tombs and animal interments and an MBA monumental platform and shaft containing ritually deposited human and animal bodies, features that have been interpreted by the excavators as evidence for collective burial and ancestor worship. Meanwhile, the Bronze Age evidence from the site of Qatna, including its Royal Hypogeum, has demonstrated a long history of collective versus individual burial, a trait that is more prominent at Syrian sites versus sites farther south in Iraq. Nonetheless, it is difficult to fully reconstruct the precise rituals reflected by the archaeological remains given the evidence at hand, largely to understand whether these were performed at night, though it is tempting to imagine that they were, given the association of night and mortuary rituals in the broader cultural context.

Witches lurked in the Mesopotamian night.[13] Ghosts did not always attack on their own initiative but were sometimes incited to do so by witches. A typical attack by a witch might take the form of the enchanter sending demons or ghosts to assault the patient. Witches might be human or nonhuman (Schwemer 2018), male or female. While there is some evidence for the primary practice of witchcraft or "aggressive magic" in Mesopotamia (Mertens-Wagschal 2018), antiwitchcraft rituals are relatively well attested. The sources often take the form of rites of exorcism conducted by āšipu priests—cultic officials whose purview included acts of healing (Scurlock 2006)—or, somewhat more rarely, of tablets containing performed antiwitchcraft rituals such as Maqlû (Abusch 2015). These texts, therefore, demonstrate a belief in witchcraft and attest to the practice of defensive magic against ghosts and witches.

Like ghosts, witches could be successfully opposed at night. Maqlû, "Burning," the text quoted at the beginning of this section, is an early first millennium compendium constituting a single, lengthy antiwitchcraft ceremony (Abusch 2015). Rather than invoking the gods of the sky, led by Anu, the ritual, instead, invokes the gods of night, led by Ereshkigal. Maqlû comprises eight incantation tablets, and a ninth ritual tablet. It takes place over the course of an entire night and culminates in the early dawn hours of the following morning. Like the kispu, the nocturnal ceremony must have been illuminated by torches and lamps to facilitate its successful completion vis-à-vis the reading and performing of the rites recorded upon the tablets. The goal of the ceremony was to weaken the witch and then execute her in effigy. Unlike other rituals known for the exorcism of ghosts, which required burying the figurine (Scurlock 1995, 2006), the witch in Maqlû must be burned. Like the annual, more elaborate kispu ceremony, Maqlû was performed at the end of the month of Abu (July/ August), a liminal time in which spirits were thought to move back and forth between the netherworld and the mortal realm. Witchcraft rituals were practiced to purify the afflicted person or persons and to exorcise the witch's power. Maqlû employed a nighttime ritual, indicating that it was a powerful and efficacious time to oppose evil forces; the burning of the witch in effigy must have been a true highlight of the ceremony.

DISCUSSION AND CONCLUSIONS

While uncertainty is a human universal, people confront it in culturally specific ways. Various Mesopotamian peoples discussed in this chapter viewed the future with no small amount of dread but developed techniques, some apotropaic, to confront their anxieties.

The textual references to Irkalla, the land of night, provide a rare opportunity to explore a nocturnal Mesopotamian imaginary, an ideational landscape. Here, we encounter a liminal space, a world typified by social inversion. Literary depictions of the netherworld show it as a land that brings opposites into relief. It is a place of absolute darkness, where people eat dust instead of bread. Kings serve the gods of the netherworld rather than being served. Irkalla is ruled by a queen, Ereshkigal, rather than a king, such as Anu. The fact that the netherworld is a nocturnal and liminal abode is underscored by its population of bird-like figures, which may explain how the dead might have slipped their many captors and traveled back to the world of living upon occasion. Birds, as creatures who can flit easily between here and there, are creatures that embody the notion of liminality. The land of night is the antithesis of our world and was viewed with trepidation.

Understanding the symbolic valence of "night" in Mesopotamia helps us understand and interpret how ancient people would have viewed their constructed landscapes or, more concretely, how the fire beacon systems must have represented more than a clever strategy of war. The bright flames of the beacons against the backdrop of night, arguably, symbolized safety and civilization, a point elaborated upon below. Fire beacon installations do not exist in isolation; they must be incorporated into large regional systems to work. They, therefore, became symbols of a collective, regional identity. The widespread and collaborative construction of fire beacons over time and space in Mesopotamia reflects the immediate anxieties provoked by warfare, in addition to a more diffuse anxiety about the future, as represented by the night. Fire is a bold symbol in this context, a statement about the community's ability to overcome future challenges.

Returning to Gordon's conception of haunting, ancient beliefs in ghosts and witches were an essential component of the Mesopotamian conception of "night," inseparable from the socially constructed places where they dwelled (2008). Such a perspective is critical in this context because it focuses on the power of negative or even imaginary events to create specters that cling to places and people (Surface-Evans and Jones 2020). The Assyrians, in fact, had a similar worldview, seeing abandoned and destroyed temples and tells as places haunted by ghosts of the past. Similarly, understanding the manner in which spaces are socially transformed into places is a valuable perspective (Bell 1997), one that must take hauntings and possessions into account. Ghosts and witches are a manifestation of the collective memory of past peoples and specters of social anxieties. While spirits may be disembodied, they are not intangible, and through the belief systems of ancient Mesopotamians, they became agentive forces.

While the Mesopotamian night was a place where terrors roamed the earth even more than usual, increased communication with supernatural forces was possible. The ancient people in question perceived not only danger but possibility in the sapphire ink of night. The darkest night of the new moon was a time to confront and destroy, by torch- and lamplight, various enemies: ghosts, demons, witches, or military foes. Fire beacons were means of communicating danger in the physical realm, while fire could be used to communicate with spirits, demons, and ghosts in the context of the described apotropaic rituals. It is noteworthy that the people discussed above did not resort to despair but sought various remedies in solutions as varied as fire beacon usage, the conjuring of protecting forces, and the performance of magical rituals to regain agency over the night. Thus, fire was used to communicate in more than one way and in various realms, both physical and metaphysical.

I have argued that the nighttime rituals of kispu and Maqlû were ways in which people sought to regain agency over the unpredictable and liminal, symbolically represented in their belief systems as "night." To draw a comparison to another apotropaic rite, it is valuable to consider the city laments of Mesopotamia. On a basic level, these musical compositions mourn the destruction of ancient cities. Yet, Paul Delnero (2020) has argued that Sumerian laments were much more than musical postmortems; they were enacted rituals that served to prevent the recurrence of disasters. The performance of these rites was a way in which people expressed agency in an uncertain world by endeavoring to prevent the destruction of their cities. Ancient Mesopotamians sang these hymns and performed their associated rituals not to simply bemoan their cruel fates, but, as well, to regain control over their own destinies. Rituals such as Maqlû and kispu, along with the widespread construction of fire beacon networks, can be interpreted in much the same way. Their performance did not simply reflect social anxieties but were agentive in diverting the effects of evil influences.

I conclude by returning to the image of the night watchers, officers who protected the sleeping residents of ancient cities against disaster. The night, which symbolically represented danger and the unknown, was a time when ancient Mesopotamian city dwellers confronted their fears in specific and historically contingent ways, thus regaining a sense of control over their destinies.

NOTES

1. The author would like to thank Jo Ann Scurlock, who helpfully suggested literature on the Mesopotamian night watch, and Glenn Schwartz, who provided feedback on an early draft. She also thanks Nan Gonlin, who solicited the chapter after a serendipitous meeting in virtual Orlando, and Megan Strong for her support and helpful suggestions. Some of the ideas in the chapter were originally formed in a graduate seminar on Akkadian literary texts led by Paul Delnero.

2. Quotation from George's translation of the Babylonian poem "Erra and Išum," a work first attested in Neo-Assyrian versions (see also George 2013).

3. Mesopotamia is not an emic notion, since it is a Hellenistic appellation meaning land between two rivers. This cultural concept is deceptive because it comprises many peoples who populated Iraq, Syria, and Turkey along the rivers for more than 3,000 years. Nonetheless, strong evidence for cultural continuity and the maintenance of certain traditions is an argument for considering these people and traditions together.

4. The tale is a well-attested episode inscribed in Sumerian on stone and clay objects found in excavations at the ancient city of Girsu (Cooper 1986): e.g., La 1.6, La 2.1, La 3.1, La 3.5, La 3.6, La 4.2, La 5.1, La 9.1, La 9.2, La 9.3, La 9.4, La 9.5.

5. Mari, modern Tell Hariri, was an important state in the Middle Euphrates region in the early second millennium; for a summary and additional bibliography, see Akkermans and Schwartz (2003, 313–317). The Mari Letters have been published as the result of decades of research, primarily under the auspices of the French project Archives Royal de Mari (ARM).

6. Many of the years of Zimri-Lim's reign were characterized by Yaminite revolts (Heimpel 2003).

7. Archaeologists studying intervisibility in Paquimé, Mexico were able to see a single burning yucca tree from forty-two kilometers away (Swanson 2003, 754–755, 759). A system in the American Southwest had gaps of more than seventy-two kilometers between relays (Ellis 1991).

8. Certainly, the concept of modernity may also be productively critiqued in this context (e.g., Latour 1993).

9. Cf. Tablet VII from *Gilgamesh*, Enkidu's death dream (George 2003), in which Enkidu travels as a *zāqīqu* spirit.

10. The responsibilities of the living toward the dead never ended. One's condition in the afterlife depended upon constant provision of funerary offerings, an idea reflected in the Sumerian literary text known as *Gilgamesh, Enkidu and the Nether World* (2001). The person who had no one to care for his ghost lived as a pauper, while the man with many sons to provide offerings sat in a chair listening to the judgments of the gods. Intramural burials, occurring under the floor of occupied family houses or below palaces, were common in certain Mesopotamian contexts, creating a close connection between ancestors and the living where practiced (Cooper 1992, 23). Such proximate burials provided another incentive, one imagines, to not anger the dead.

    In certain circumstances, unfinished business in the mortal plane might result in malevolent ghosts, as in the case of hapless individuals who died violent, unhappy, or untimely deaths, nearly universal tropes of ghost stories that were present in Mesopotamia too.

11. Remedies reflected the kind of demon or ghost thought to afflict the ill as represented by their symptoms.

12. See the various references from the Middle and Neo-Assyrian periods in the Chicago Assyrian Dictionary (1961) for the entry "zāqīqu," but see also Richardson (2007) for a nuanced interpretation of such claims.

13. Accusations of witchcraft, while well attested, do not appear to be overwhelmingly common in the legal proceedings of Mesopotamia, but their occasional occurrence warrants comment. Witches could be found guilty or acquitted through completion of the River Ordeal, a trial by water (see McCarter 1973, for a description). However, if exonerated, the accuser might suffer the penalty instead. The

judicial feature of punishing the accuser seems designed to suppress false or frenzied accusations of witchcraft such as those known from colonial America.

REFERENCES

Abusch, Tzvi. 1995. "Etemmu." In *Dictionary of Deities and Demons in the Bible*, edited by Karel van der Toorn, Bob Becking, and Pieter W. van der Horst, 309–312. Leiden, Netherlands: Brill.

Abusch, Tzvi. 2015. *The Witchcraft Series Maqlû*. Atlanta: SBL Press.

Akkermans, Peter M. M. G., and Glenn M. Schwartz. 2003. *The Archaeology of Syria: From Complex Hunter-Gatherers to Early Urban Societies (ca. 16,000–300 BC)*. Cambridge: Cambridge University Press.

The Assyrian Dictionary of the Oriental Institute of the University of Chicago. 1961. Volume 21, Z. Chicago: The Oriental Institute at the University of Chicago.

Bell, Michael Mayerfeld. 1997. "The Ghosts of Place." *Theory and Society* 26 (6): 813–836.

Bottero, Jean. 2000. *Mesopotamia: Writing, Reasoning, and the Gods*. Chicago: University of Chicago Press.

Burke, Aaron A. 2007. "'Magdalūma, Migdālîm, Magdoloi', and 'Majādîl': The Historical Geography and Archaeology of the 'Magdalu (Migdāl).'" *Bulletin of the American Schools of Oriental Research* 346: 29–57.

Caplice, Richard. 1971. "Namburbi Texts in the British Museum V." *Orientalia NS* 40: 133–183.

Cooper, Jerrold S. 1986. *Presargonic Inscriptions: Sumerian and Akkadian Royal Inscriptions I*. New Haven, CT: American Oriental Society.

Cooper, Jerrold S. 1992. "The Fate of Mankind: Death and Afterlife in Ancient Mesopotamia." In *Death and Afterlife: Perspectives of World Religions*, edited by Hiroshi Obayashi, 19–33. Westport, CT: Greenwood Press.

Delnero, Paul. 2020. *How to Do Things with Tears: Ritual Lamenting in Ancient Mesopotamia*. Berlin: De Gruyter.

Dossin, G. 1938. "Signaux lumineux au pays de Mari." *Revue d'Assyriologie et d'Archéologie Orientale* 35 (3/4): 174–186.

Earley-Spadoni, Tiffany. 2015a. "Envisioning Landscapes of Warfare: A Multi-regional Analysis of Early Iron Fortress-States and Biainili-Urartu." PhD diss., Johns Hopkins University, Baltimore.

Earley-Spadoni, Tiffany. 2015b. "Landscapes of Warfare: Intervisibility Analysis of Early Iron and Urartian Fire Beacon Stations (Armenia)." *Journal of Archaeological Science: Reports* 3: 22–30.

Edwards, Steven. 2020. "On the Lookout: Directional Visibility Cones and Defense in the Nebo Region, West-Central Jordan." *Open Archaeology* 6 (1): 2–18.

Ellis, Andrea. 1991. "Towers of the Gallina Area and Greater Southwest." In *Puebloan Past and Present: Papers in Honor of Stewart Peckham*, edited by Meliha S. Duran and David T. Kirkpatrick, 57–70. Albuquerque: Archaeological Society of New Mexico.

Foster, Benjamin R. 2005. *Before the Muses: An Anthology of Akkadian Literature*. 3rd ed. Bethesda: University Press of Maryland.

George, Andrew R. 2003. *The Babylonian Gilgamesh Epic: Introduction, Critical Edition, and Cuneiform Texts*. Vol. 1. Oxford: Oxford University Press.

George, Andrew R. 2013. "The Poem of Erra and Ishum: A Babylonian Poet's View of War." In *Warfare and Poetry in the Middle East*, edited by Hugh N. Kennedy, 39–71. London: IB Tauris.

George, Andrew R. 2015. "The Gods Išum and Ḫendursanga: Night Watchmen and Street-Lighting in Babylonia." *Journal of Near Eastern Studies* 74 (1): 1–8.

"Gilgamesh, Enkidu and the Nether World: Translation." 2001. The Electronic Text Corpus of Sumerian Literature. https://etcsl.orinst.ox.ac.uk/section1/tr1814.htm. Revised September 7, 2001.

González-Tennant, Edward. 2018. *The Rosewood Massacre: An Archaeology and History of Intersectional Violence*. Gainesville: University Press of Florida.

Gordon, Avery F. 2008. *Ghostly Matters: Haunting and the Sociological Imagination*. Minneapolis: University of Minnesota.

Heimpel, W. 2003. *Letters to the King of Mari: A New Translation with Historical Introduction and Commentary*. Winona Lake, IN: Eisenbrauns.

Kleiss, Wolfram. 1971. "Bericht über Erkundungsfahnen in Iran im Jahre 1970." *Archäologische Mitteilungen aus Iran* 4: 51–112.

Kleiss, Wolfram. 1979. *Bastam I: Ausgrabungen in den urartäischen Anlagen 1972–1975*. Berlin: Gebr. Mann Verlag.

Kleiss, Wolfram. 1988. *Bastam II: Ausgrabungen in den urartischen Anlagen 1977–1978*. Berlin: Gebr. Mann Verlag.

Knapp, A. Bernard, and Wendy Ashmore. 1999. "Archaeological Landscapes: Constructed, Conceptualized, Ideational." In *Archaeologies of Landscape: Contemporary Perspectives*, edited by Wendy Ashmore and A. Bernard Knapp, 1–30. Malden, MA: Blackwell.

Lapinkivi, Pirjo. 2010. *The Neo-Assyrian Myth of Ištar's Descent and Resurrection*. State Archives of Assyria VI. Helsinki: Neo-Assyrian Text Corpus Project.

Latour, Bruno. 1993. *We Have Never Been Modern*. Cambridge, MA: Harvard University Press.

McCarter, P. Kyle. 1973. "The River Ordeal in Israelite Literature." *Harvard Theological Review* 66 (4): 403–412.

Mertens-Wagschal, Avigail. 2018. "The Lion, the Witch, and the Wolf: Aggressive Magic and Witchcraft in the Old Babylonian Period." In *Sources of Evil*, edited by Greta Van Buylaere, Mikko Luukko, Daniel Schwemer, and Avigail Mertens-Wagschal, 158–169. Leiden, Netherlands: Brill.

Monroe, M. Willis. 2019. "Mesopotamian Astrology." *Religion Compass* 13 (6). John Wiley and Sons,. https://doi.org/10.1111/rec3.12318.

Novák, Mirko. 2008. "Individuum oder Kollektiv? Zur kulturgeschictlichen Stellung der Königsgruft von Qaṭna." In *Körperinszenierung–Objektsammlung–Monumentalisierung: Totenritual und Grabkult in frühen Gesellschaften: Archäologische Quellen in kulturwissenschaftlicher Perspektive*, edited by Cristoph Kümmel, Beat Schweizer, and Ulrich Veit, 207–232. Münster, Germany: Waxmann Verlag.

Panagiotakis, Nikos, Marina Panagiotaki, and Apostolos Sarris. 2013. "The Earliest Communication System in the Aegean." *Electryone* 1 (2): 13–27.

Porter, Benjamin W., and Alexis T. Boutin. 2014. "Introduction: Bringing Out the Dead in the Ancient Near East." In *Remembering the Dead in the Ancient Near East: Recent Contributions from Bioarchaeology and Mortuary Archaeology*, edited by Benjamin W. Porter and Alexis T. Boutin, 1–26. Recent Contributions from Bioarchaeology and Mortuary Archaeology. Boulder: University Press of Colorado. http://www.jstor.org/stable/j.ctt9qhksx.6.

Richardson, Seth. 2007. "Death and Dismemberment in Mesopotamia: Discorporation between the Body and Body Politic." In *Performing Death: Social Analyses of Funerary Traditions in the Ancient Near East and Mediterranean*, edited by Nicola Laneri, 189–208. Chicago: Oriental Institute of the University of Chicago.

Rousset, Marie-Odile, Bernard Geyer, Shadi Shabo, and Nazir Awad. 2017. "Un réseau défensif de l'âge du Bronze Moyen dans les marges arides de Syrie du Nord." *Paléorient* 43 (2): 115–163.

Saler, Michael. 2006. "Modernity and Enchantment: A Historiographic Review." *American Historical Review* 111 (3): 692–716. https://doi.org/10.1086/ahr.111.3.692.

Schwartz, Glenn M. 2012. "Era of the Living Dead: Funerary Praxis and Symbol in Third Millennium BC Syria." In *(Re-)Constructing Funerary Rituals in the Ancient Near East*, edited by Peter Pfälzner, Herbert Niehr, Ernst Pernicka, and Anne Wissing, 59–78. Wiesbaden, Germany: Harrassowitz Verlag.

Schwartz, Glenn M. 2013. "Memory and Its Demolition: Ancestors, Animals and Sacrifice at Umm El-Marra, Syria." *Cambridge Archaeological Journal* 23 (3): 495–522.

Schwemer, Daniel. 2018. "Evil Helpers: Instrumentalizing Agents of Evil in Anti-witchcraft Rituals." In *Sources of Evil*, edited by Greta Van Buylaere, Mikko

Luukko, Daniel Schwemer, and Avigail Mertens-Wagschal, 171–191. Leiden, Netherlands: Brill.

Scurlock, JoAnn. 1995. "Death and the Afterlife in Ancient Mesopotamian Thought." In *Civilizations of the Ancient Near East*, edited by Jack Sasson, 3:1883–1893. New York: Scribner.

Scurlock, JoAnn. 2003. "Ancient Mesopotamian House Gods." *Journal of Ancient Near Eastern Religion* 3: 99–106.

Scurlock, JoAnn. 2006. *Magico-Medical Means of Treating Ghost-Induced Illnesses in Ancient Mesopotamia*. Leiden, Netherlands: Brill.

Scurlock, JoAnn. 2016. "Mortal and Immortal Souls, Ghosts and the (Restless) Dead in Ancient Mesopotamia." *Religion Compass* 10 (4): 77–82.

Surface-Evans, Sarah L., and Sarah J Jones. 2020. "Discourses of the Haunted: An Intersubjective Approach to Archaeology at the Mount Pleasant Indian Industrial Boarding School." *Archeological Papers of the American Anthropological Association* 31 (1): 110–121.

Swanson, Steve. 2003. "Documenting Prehistoric Communication Networks: A Case Study in the Paquimé Polity." *American Antiquity* 68 (4): 753–767.

Thavapalan, Shiyanthi. 2020. *The Meaning of Color in Ancient Mesopotamia*. Leiden, Netherlands: Brill.

Tsukimoto, Akio. 2010. "Peace for the Dead, or *kispu(m)* Again." *Orient* 45: 101–109. [The Society for Near Eastern Studies in Japan.]

Tuan, Yi-Fu. 1977. *Space and Place: The Perspective of Experience*. Minneapolis: University of Minnesota.

Tuan, Yi-Fu 1979. "Space and Place: Humanistic Perspective." In *Philosophy in Geography*, edited by Stephen Gale and Gunnar Olsson, 387–427. Boston: D. Reidel Publishing.

Van Buylaere, Greta, Mikko Luukko, Daniel Schwemer, and Avigail Mertens-Wagschal. 2018. *Sources of Evil: Studies in Mesopotamian Exorcistic Lore*. Leiden, Netherlands: Brill.

Wilkinson, Darryl. 2019. "Towards an Archaeological Theory of Infrastructure." *Journal of Archaeological Method and Theory* 26: 1216–1241. https://doi.org/10.1007/s10816-018-9410-2.

4

Despite the political fragmentation of the ancient Greek world into individual *poleis*, or city-states, ancient Greeks themselves shared a common religious system (see Price 1999 for an accessible overview). Whether one lived on mainland Greece, Sicily, or Asia Minor, one worshiped a pantheon of multiple gods, communicated with those gods through sacrifice and offerings, and attended religious festivals, which took place at local as well as Panhellenic sanctuaries, of which the Sanctuary of Apollo at Delphi reigned supreme. Orthopraxis, not orthodoxy, was paramount, and religious practice, as described in literary sources and as evidenced in the archaeological and material records, united Greeks around the Mediterranean littoral up to the Black Sea. With the conquests of Alexander the Great (r. 336–323 BCE), the political preeminence of the Greek city-states was eclipsed by vast kingdoms ruled by individual monarchs. The rulers and dynasties who succeeded Alexander—the largest of which were the Seleucids in Syria and much of Asia Minor, the Ptolemies in Egypt, and the Antigonids in Macedon—vied for power and prestige, patronizing spectacular works of art and architecture not only in their capital cities but also, to varying degrees depending on the dynasty, in sanctuaries such as those of Apollo at Delphi and Delos and that of Zeus at Olympia (Constantakopoulou 2017, 87–100; see Stewart 2014 for a general overview of Hellenistic art and architecture).

Illuminating the Mysteries of the Great Gods at Samothrace, Greece

MAGGIE L. POPKIN

https://doi.org/10.5876/9781646422609.c004

While these major Panhellenic sanctuaries had enjoyed influxes of wealth and dedications for centuries, other, smaller sanctuaries found themselves invigorated in entirely new ways by the patronage of the Hellenistic kings. One such place that flourished in the Hellenistic period (ca. 323–31 BCE) was the Sanctuary of the Great Gods, or Theoi Megaloi, on the northern Aegean island of Samothrace (figure 1.1). According to ancient sources, Alexander the Great's parents, Philip II and Olympias, first met at the Sanctuary of the Great Gods (Plutarch, *Vita Alexandri* 2.2; Himerius, *Orationes* 9.12; Photius, *Bibliotheca* 243). The Samothracian sanctuary thus stood in the ancient tradition as the site that foreshadowed the birth of Alexander and a place intimately connected to the Temenid dynasty that culminated in Alexander (see Popkin 2015, 365). To link themselves with Alexander and his family and to compete with one another, Hellenistic dynasts lavished attention on the Sanctuary of the Great Gods, endowing it with magnificent marble buildings and impressive statue dedications.

Nestled at the base of the imposing Agios Giorgios ridge, the Sanctuary of the Great Gods provided an evocative home for these Hellenistic dedications. Windswept and rugged, Samothrace rises dramatically to the peak of Mount Fengari, from which Poseidon espied the plains of Troy in the *Iliad* (Homer, *Iliad* 10–18). Today, the name of Samothrace evokes the island's most famous archaeological find: the spectacular statue of the Winged Victory currently on display in the Musée du Louvre in Paris. In antiquity, however, the island's claim to fame was the cult of the Great Gods. The sanctuary housed one of the Greco-Roman world's most renowned mystery cults, second perhaps only to the Eleusinian mysteries. Open to all regardless of gender, class, or ethnicity, the Samothracian cult promised salvation at sea and a privileged position in the underworld (Cole 1984). The attraction of these promises is easy to understand, and, unsurprisingly, people from around the ancient Mediterranean traveled to the island to gain initiation into the cult of the Great Gods.

Much about the Samothracian gods and their cult remains veiled in mystery. Initiates were sworn to secrecy and seem to have upheld that vow. As a result, ancient discussions of the mystery cult often reflect hearsay rather than direct experience and contain confusing and contradictory statements about the nature of the Great Gods (Cole 1984, 1; Lewis 1959 on the ancient sources related to Samothrace). Based on surviving literary sources, epigraphy, the archaeological remains of the Sanctuary of the Great Gods, and comparison with the better documented mystery cult at Eleusis, scholars have nonetheless pieced together a view of the Samothracian mysteries, albeit a somewhat tentative one. There appear to have been two stages of initiation: an initial

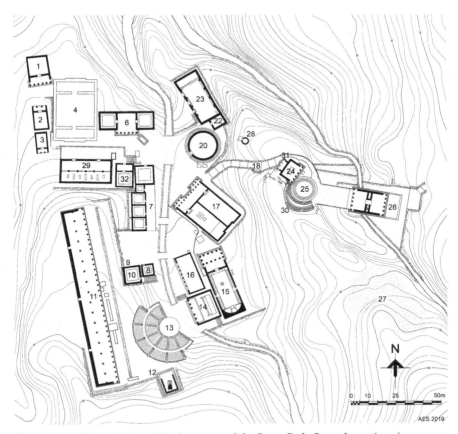

FIGURE 4.1. *Restored plan of the Sanctuary of the Great Gods, Samothrace. (1,2,3)
Unidentified Late Hellenistic buildings. (4) Unfinished early Hellenistic building. (6)
Milesian Dedication. (7,8,10) Dining rooms. (9) Faux Bronze Age niche. (11) Stoa. (12) Nike
Monument. (13) Theater. (14) Altar Court. (15) Hieron. (16) Hall of Votive Gifts. (17) Hall of
Choral Dancers. (18) Sacred Way. (20) Rotunda of Arsinoe II. (22) Sacristy. (23) Anaktoron.
(24) Dedication of Philip III and Alexander IV. (25) Theatral Circle. (26) Propylon of
Ptolemy II. (27) Southern Necropolis. (28) Doric Rotunda. (29) Neorion. (31) Ionic Porch.
(32) Hestiatorion. Drawing: American Excavations Samothrace.*

stage of *myesis* and a second stage of *epopteia*. Initiates into the first phase were
called *mystai* (those who keep silence or close their eyes), while those who had
undergone the higher order of initiation were known as *epoptai* (viewers) (see
Clinton 2003 on the terminology of the Samothracian mysteries).

The initiatory rites occurred in the Sanctuary of the Great Gods under darkness of night. Prospective initiates processed from the ancient city of Samothrace, exiting the city walls near the sanctuary and passing into the sacred temenos via the Propylon of Ptolemy II (figure 4.1, no. 26). From the Propylon of Ptolemy, visitors entered the Theatral Circle (figure 4.1, no. 25), where they may have undergone a preliminary myesis, a purificatory rite that prepared people for the coming initiation. At the Samothracian sanctuary, this preliminary rite was likely *thronosis*, in which the prospective initiates were blindfolded and sat in a chair as the cult's ministers danced, sang, and made noise around them (Clinton 2003, 62–65; Dimitrova 2008, 78, 245; Wescoat 2017a, 61–62). Once purified, prospective initiates wended down the Sacred Way (figure 4.1, no. 18) to the Central Sanctuary and the buildings that housed the main initiation rites. Scholars continue to debate the function of the Central Sanctuary's buildings. It appears likely, however, that mystai underwent initiation (i.e., into the main, not the preliminary, myesis) in the massive marble structure today known as the Hall of Choral Dancers (figure 4.1, no. 17; Clinton 2003, 61; though cf. Marconi 2010). Initiation of epoptai likely occurred in the nearby Hieron (figure 4.1, no. 15; P. W. Lehmann 1969). Following initiation, visitors gathered and dined in the Stoa and dining rooms of the sanctuary's Western Hill (figure 4.1, nos. 7, 8, 10, 11), before exiting the sanctuary along the same path on which they had entered the previous evening (see Wescoat 2017b on pilgrims' movements in the sanctuary).

Because the initiation rites in the sanctuary took place at night, artificial lighting was needed practically. Whether prospective initiates moved on their own or whether cult staff guided them as they were blindfolded, the steep terrain of the sanctuary would have been risky to navigate without the aid of lighting. Scholars have commented on the use of lamps and torches for light in the Samothracian mysteries (e.g., Nilsson 1950, 105; Wescoat 2017a, 60; Wescoat 2017b, 75), but this chapter positions luminosity—both natural and artificial—squarely at the center of visitors' phenomenological and affective experience of the sanctuary (see Bille and Sørensen 2007 on light as an active component of social life). Additionally, it considers how lighting mediated the relationship between the ancient city of Samothrace and the sanctuary itself, a relationship that scholars are only beginning to explore fully.

LIGHT AND THE GREAT GODS

People in ancient Greece often associated light with the numinousness of the gods themselves. The many images of Greek deities carrying torches, from

FIGURE 4.2. *So-called Ninnion tablet. Painted terra-cotta* pinax, *or plaque, dedicated by Ninnion to the Eleusinian divinities, ca. 370 BCE. National Archaeological Museum, Athens, no. A11036. Photo: Carole Raddato (used under Creative Commons Attribution-ShareAlike 2.0 Generic License [CC BY-SA 2.0]).*

Hecate and Dionysus to Demeter and Persephone, illustrate this association (see Parisinou 2000, 81–99). Likewise, light played a significant role in mystery cults in the ancient Greek world. The initiatory rites at the Sanctuary of Demeter at Eleusis, for example, occurred at night and involved artificial light shed by torches (Mylonas 1961, 224–285; Parisinou 2000, 64–71; Patera 2010). Aristophanes (*Frogs*, 340–350) colorfully describes the procession from Athens to Eleusis, with prospective initiates chanting and shaking flaming torches. Archaeologists have found marble torches at Eleusis that might have served as offerings (Patera 2010, 265). Of the many representations related to the Eleusinian mysteries that survive in Greek art, I mention only one of the most evocative: the Ninnion tablet, a painted terra-cotta *pinax*, or plaque, found at Eleusis and dated to circa 370 BCE. The Ninnion tablet, named after the woman who dedicated it at the Eleusinian sanctuary, depicts human initiates taking part in the initiation rites at Eleusis. The initiates carry torches, as does the figure of Demeter's daughter, Persephone (second figure from upper right) (figure 4.2) (Mylonas 1961, 213–221; Clinton 2010, 349–353). Lamps have been found at Eleusis, but their role in initiation into the Eleusinian mysteries, if any, remains unclear (Patera 2010).

We have significantly less documentary evidence for the Samothracian cult than we do for the Eleusinian mysteries, but representations in word and image related to the cult of the Great Gods indicate a close connection to artificial lighting. A relief on the lintel of the first-century CE Tomb of the Haterii is often interpreted as a depiction of the Samothracian gods Kadmilos, Axiokersa, Axiokersos, and Axieros in the guise of Hermes, Persephone, Hades, and Demeter (Pettazzoni 1908; P. W. Lehmann 1969, 1:325–327; on the identification of the Samothracian gods, see Cole 1984, 1–4). Demeter-Axieros, visible at the right edge of the relief, prominently holds a torch aloft in her left hand. Representations of torches also appear in sculpture from the sanctuary. A late Hellenistic stele from the sanctuary, now quite fragmentary but copied in the fifteenth century by Cyriacus of Ancona, records the names of initiates and is decorated with a relief showing a building (which K. Lehmann 1943 interprets as round) with a door, above which figures unfold (figure 4.3). Karl Lehmann (1943, 122) has suggested that these figures represent not statues surmounting the building, but rather a scene unfolding on a hillside behind the building. Above the doorway, bucrania and garlands extend across the building's façade. Flanking the door are two monumental torches, flames springing from their tops, around which two serpents entwine themselves (K. Lehmann 1943, 117–123; P. W. Lehmann 1969, 2:27, fig. 352).

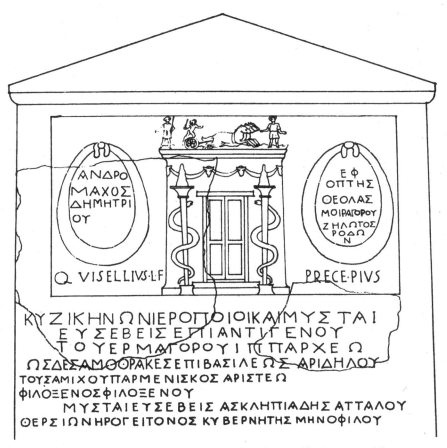

ΑΝΔΡΟ
ΜΑΧΟΣ
ΔΗΜΗΤΡΙ
ΟΥ

Ε Φ
ΟΠΤΗΣ
ΘΕΟΛΑΣ
ΜΟΙΡΑΓΟΡΟΥ
Ζ ΗΛΩΤΟΣ
ΡΟΔΩ
Ν

Q. VISELLIVS·L·F

PRECE·PIVS

ΚΥΖΙΚΗΝΩΝΙΕΡΟΠΟΙΟΙΚΑΜΥΣΤΑΙ
ΕΥΣΕΒΕΙΣΕΠΙΑΝΤΙΓΕΝΟΥ
ΤΟΥΕΡΜΑΓΟΡΟΥΙΠΠΑΡΧΕΩ
ΩΣΔΕΣΑΜΟΘΡΑΚΕΣΕΠΙΒΑΣΙΛΕΩΣ ΑΡΙΔΗΛΟΥ
ΤΟΥΣΑΜΙΧΟΥΠΑΡΜΕΝΙΣΚΟΣ ΑΡΙΣΤΕΩ
ΦΙΛΟΞΕΝΟΣΦΙΛΟΞΕΝΟΥ
ΜΥΣΤΑΙΕΥΣΕΒΕΙΣ ΑΣΚΛΗΠΙΑΔΗΣ ΑΤΤΑΛΟΥ
ΘΕΡΣΙΩΝΗΡΟΓΕΙΤΟΝΟΣ ΚΥΒΕΡΝΗΤΗΣ ΜΗΝΟΦΙΛΟΥ

FIGURE 4.3. *Restored drawing of a Samothracian stele copied by Cyriacus of Ancona.*
Drawing: American Excavations Samothrace.

The association of the Great Gods with light extended to the rites of the *mysteria*, or mysteries, themselves. An epitaph for a Samothracian initiate, an Athenian citizen named Isidoros, survives today in the Archaeological Museum of Kavala. Possibly originally erected at Amphipolis, the inscription describes "the doubly sacred light of Kabiros" (i.e., the sacred light of the two Kabiri) viewed by initiates during the rites (Dimitrova 2008, 83–90, no. 29). This fascinating inscription testifies to the central role that light and the experience of viewing it played in the Samothracian initiation rites (Dimitrova 2008, 78, 244–245). Isidoros's inscription offers the only extant epigraphic evidence that an experience of light stood at the climax of the rites. Surviving literary sources suggest that torches would have been the source of this sacred light. Nonnus, an epic Greek poet from fifth-century CE Roman Egypt, mentions "the nocturnal festive pine-torch of my mother, Hecate" (*Dionysiaca*, 4.185; Lewis 1959, 72, no. 151). He also describes the Kabiri answering "the stormy call beside the mystic torch of Samos" (*Dionysiaca* 14.18; Lewis 1959, 77, no. 166). Himerius, a Greek rhetorician of the fourth-century CE, recounts the meeting of Alexander the Great's parents in the Sanctuary of the Great Gods. When Olympias fell in love with Philip and agreed to marry him, Himerius writes, she made the "mysteries an introductory rite of the nuptial ceremony" (*Orationes* 9.12 [ed. Colonna = Photius, no. 243]; Lewis 1959, 89, no. 194). What Lewis translates as "of the nuptial ceremony" is, literally, "of the nuptial fire" (Τοῦ γαμηλίου πυρὸς), which Lewis believes evokes the torches of both the marriage ceremony and the Samothracian initiation rites. Thus, although no ancient author explicitly describes the initiation rites, the cumulative references to torches suggest strongly that torches formed part of initiation at the Sanctuary of the Great Gods.

ARCHAEOLOGICAL EVIDENCE FOR ARTIFICIAL LIGHTING IN THE SANCTUARY OF THE GREAT GODS

The archaeological record provides additional evidence for the use of torches in the Sanctuary of the Great Gods. Archaeologists have found stone blocks in the Central Sanctuary that bear cuttings to receive the bases of torches (P. W. Lehmann 1969, 2:17–18). One such block was discovered east of the Hieron's cella (figure 4.1, no. 15), where it can still be seen today (figure 4.4; P. W. Lehmann 1969, 2:55, 73). It measures 0.60 by 0.42 meters, with a height of 0.33 meters, with a central hole approximately 0.14 square meters. Excavators discovered a second torch-stone near the western corner of the Hieron's porch (height 0.22 meters, width 0.61 meters, preserved length 0.43 meters). This block had a central hole (0.16 square meters, 0.14 meters deep) that contained a lead pouring (since robbed out) to hold a beam or pole, molten lead being the material commonly used by Greek builders to surround clamps and dowels (Tucci 2015, 249). Phyllis Lehmann identified it "as a device used in the mooring of a large torch" (P. W. Lehmann 1969, 2:73; see also K. Lehmann 1952, 41, pl. 10d). K. and P. W. Lehmann also identified several marble fragments uncovered during excavations of the Hieron's apse as belonging to a marble torch that may have stood in one of the torch-stones. The fragments show the head and tail of a snake wrapping around a columnar object, a representation

FIGURE 4.4. *Extant torch-block from the vicinity of the Hieron, Sanctuary of the Great Gods, Samothrace. Photo: Maggie L. Popkin.*

that corresponds to depictions of torches on reliefs from the Samothracian sanctuary (see above on the stele drawn by Cyriacus [figure 4.3]) and to other marble torches that survive from the Greek and Roman periods (K. Lehmann 1951, 24, pl. 14b; P. W. Lehmann 1969, 1:135–137). The discoveries led P. W. Lehmann to suggest that large torches illuminated the Hieron's façade (P. W. Lehmann 1969, 2:73–74). It is not clear whether the marble fragments with

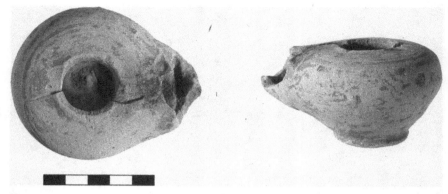

FIGURE 4.5. *Wheel-made terra-cotta lamp, of local manufacture. Found in the area of the Theatral Circle, Sanctuary of the Great Gods, Samothrace. Acc. no. 66.349c. Diam. body 0.087 m. First century BCE to first century CE. Photo: American Excavations Samothrace.*

the snake actually belong to a torch, since their shape is somewhat different than might be expected (B. D. Wescoat, personal communication, 2019). Regardless, the existence of the torch-blocks still makes it likely that sizable torches stood near the Hieron.

Monumental torches would have cast the sort of blazing light that bathed Isidoros at the culmination of his initiation. Torches, however, were not the only means of artificial lighting in the sanctuary. Lamps abound in the sanctuary's archaeological record. Terra-cotta lamps have been found in all parts of the sanctuary connected to initiation rites and postinitiation gathering and dining (e.g., K. Lehmann 1950, 14–16; K. Lehmann 1951, 30; McCredie 1965, 114; McCredie 1968, 232–233; Blevins 2017a). The manufacturing technique of lamps from the sanctuary varies; some are thrown on wheels, others are mold-made. Many of the lamps were produced locally, wheel-made of coarse clay in a standardized form consisting of a rounded body atop a string-cut base, with a broad nozzle (figure 4.5; Blevins 2017a, 387). The coarse, wheel-made lamps manufactured on Samothrace would have been inexpensive, affordable lamps. Interestingly, the manufacture of such wheel-made lamps appears to have persisted at Samothrace long after mold-made lamps had become the norm in many other regions of the Mediterranean (McCredie 1968, 233 no. 110).

Although the majority of lamps found in the sanctuary are terra-cotta, marble examples have come to light as well. Based on typological analysis, some of the marble lamps have been dated as early as the seventh century BCE (K. Lehmann 1950, 14–15, plate 10, fig. 25), others to the late fourth or early third century BCE (Oustinoff 1992, 329). The marble of the lamps has not undergone isotopic analysis, but at least several examples appear to be of Greek island marble, perhaps Thasian (Oustinoff 1992, 329–330). The marble lamps are not large (the examples from the fill of the Arsinoeion, e.g., range from 14.0 to 19.5 centimeters in diameter: Oustinoff 1992, 329–330). Residue analysis has not been performed on the terra-cotta or marble lamps at Samothrace, to my knowledge, but both types of lamps presumably burned oil as fuel. Archaeologists have found traces of beeswax in some lamps and bowls from Late Minoan Crete (Evershed et al. 1997), but oil remains the more likely substance at Samothrace.

Both marble and terra-cotta lamps found in the sanctuary frequently bear an inscription, Θ or ΘE, which clearly abbreviates the Greek name of the Great Gods (Theoi Megaloi). For example, a fragmentary lamp found in the sanctuary's Eastern Hill preserves a Θ on the top of the nozzle, inscribed in the clay as a circle with a dot in the center (Blevins 2017a, 390, no. 94). A fragmentary lamp of Thasian marble (0.178 meter in diameter), found in the fill of the Rotunda of Arsinoe II (figure 4.1, no. 20) and dated typologically to the sixth century BCE, preserves parts of an inscription on its rim: ΘE . . . Σ (figure 4.6; K. Lehmann 1950, 15, pl. 10, fig. 26). One should almost certainly reconstruct the original inscription as θεοῖς (to the gods). In the dative, this wording suggests that the lamp was dedicated by an individual to the Great Gods. Some scholars have wanted to view all the Θ and ΘE inscriptions on lamps and vessels at Samothrace as abbreviations of the dative and have consequently argued that lamps were commonly dedicated to the gods after the initiation ceremonies (Fraser 1960, 133–134). A bowl discovered in the fill of the Stoa (McCredie 1965, 115–116), however, is stamped with the full word Θεῶν, which is in the genitive (namely, *of* the gods). A fragmentary marble lamp found in the fill of the Arsinoeion preserves the ΘEΩ . . . , which should be completed as Θεῶν (Oustinoff 1992, 329, no. 321). These finds support Karl Lehmann's argument that the inscriptions abbreviate the genitive and are, in fact, marked as property of the gods (K. Lehmann 1960, 21; Blevins 2017b, 383). Terra-cotta vessels with Θ and ΘE inscriptions found in the sanctuary were incised with the letters before firing, which suggests, as Susan Blevins has noted, that sanctuary administrators were ordering them "to meet the needs of the cult" (Blevins 2017b, 383). If one considers the lamps as part of the cult and initiation practices, it seems more likely that they were property of the cult, that is, of the gods, and that we should indeed recognize the genitive in the abbreviated inscriptions.

Many of the surviving marble lamps do not preserve any signs of devices for suspension, so Lehmann has suggested that they were carried by individuals

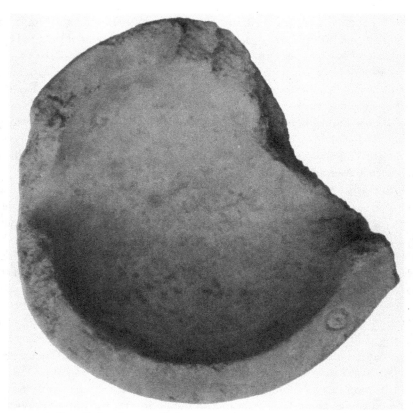

FIGURE 4.6. *Inscribed archaic marble lamp from the fill of the Rotunda of Arsinoe, Sanctuary of the Great Gods, Samothrace. Acc. no. 49.137. Note the* theta *inscribed at lower right of the image, on the lamp's rim. Photo: American Excavations Samothrace.*

during rites and then dedicated to the Great Gods (K. Lehmann 1950, 15). At the same time, marble lamps are heavier than their terra-cotta counterparts—I estimate the lamp illustrated in figure 4.6 weighs approximately five or six pounds—and might have formed part of the stationary equipment of cult buildings. The terra-cotta lamps are uniformly small and easily held. At key points in the mysteria, such as the Theatral Circle, where initiates gathered before descending into the Central Sanctuary, a place in which dozens of lamps have been found, there are no obvious locations to rest the lamps. Bonna Wescoat has argued, therefore, that at least some participants in the initiation rites held lamps as they moved throughout the sanctuary (Wescoat 2017a, 60).

If both terra-cotta and marble lamps could be purchased and carried by prospective initiates, the two materials point to the socioeconomic range of visitors to the site. As chapter 1 of this volume notes, economic and social considerations can seldom be detached from lychnological studies. Terra-cotta lamps would have been significantly cheaper than their marble counterparts. Clay was a readily available material, whereas marble, though plentiful in the Greek world, still had to be quarried and required greater skill to work. As with other types of small dedications such as figurines, which have been found in the sanctuary in terra-cotta and stone, lamps demonstrate that people of varying means participated in the cult's initiatory rites (Popkin 2017, 445).

THE EXPERIENTIAL IMPACT OF NOCTURNAL LUMINOSITY

The abundance of lamps and evidence for torches at the Sanctuary of the Great Gods is unsurprising. Artificial lighting would have been necessary for safe movement under cover of night, not only *in* the sanctuary but also *to* the sanctuary. As visitors to Samothrace today quickly experience, the island's terrain is rugged, shaped by ridges and ravines and strewn with boulders. Ongoing excavations at Samothrace will hopefully clarify the nature of a path between the ancient city walls and the entrance to the sanctuary, but even using a paved path, initiates would have moved up and down. People moving from the urban space of the city of Samothrace to the sacred space of the sanctuary would have benefited enormously from lamps to avoid stumbling, bumping into each other, and so on. Once inside the sanctuary, prospective initiates had to navigate the uneven levels of the Sacred Way and the sanctuary's tangle of monumental buildings. The Sanctuary of the Great Gods was not flat; it did not have wide open spaces connected neatly by broad spaces and paths (contrast the relatively level Sanctuary of Demeter at Eleusis). Without adequate light, visitors at night would have risked confusion at best, injury at worst.

Unlike the *sacbeob*, or roads, of Classic Maya cities (chapters 1 and 6, this volume), the surfaces of pathways in the Sanctuary of the Great Gods, at least judging from the extant Sacred Way, were not designed with nocturnal visibility in mind. The Sacred Way is lined with stone pavers, but they are not coated with plaster as one sees in some Mesoamerican contexts. Paved roads were common in Greek cities and sanctuaries, but at the Samothracian sanctuary, the choice had an added, symbolic benefit. Confusion and disorientation were desired states of mind for prospective initiates before the revelation of the mysteries. Pathways that were lit enough for safe navigation but dark enough to remain challenging to navigate could have contributed to the sensorial obscuring that preceded the clarity of initiation.

Because lighting was so obviously necessary for safe navigation of Greek sanctuaries at night, archaeologists have tended to focus on lamps and torch supports in practical terms—that is, to explain lamps in sanctuaries as necessary, without probing further their other possible meanings and functions. Eva Parisinou has argued forcefully, however, that lamps and torches had potent symbolic potential (Parisinou 1997, 2000), as they often did in other ancient societies (see, e.g., Gonlin and Dixon-Hundredmark 2021 on the Maya). Lamps and torches could serve as votive offerings to gods and illuminate nighttime sacrifices and ritual meals. Parisinou focuses on the abstract symbolism of artificial light and of flames, as symbolic of life (vs. the darkness of the underworld), (re)birth, and knowledge. More, however, can be said about the experiential and affective impact of nocturnal luminosity in the specific context of Samothrace (see Bille and Sørensen 2007 on the experiential impact of luminosity).

Artificial lighting would have brought the sanctuary's architecture to life. The Samothracian sanctuary is justly famous for its lavish marble monuments, endowed by the successors of Alexander the Great and even, perhaps, by Alexander's father, Philip, if current theories about the spectacular Hall of Choral Dancers are correct (K. Lehmann 1998, 77–78; Wescoat 2016, 430). From the Propylon of Ptolemy II (our earliest known example of the Corinthian order applied to a building's exterior) to the Rotunda of Arsinoe (the largest circular building of its kind in the Hellenistic world), Samothrace's innovative buildings were designed to dazzle and impress. Today, one can get a sense of their impressiveness from the anastylosis of the Hieron (figure 4.1, no. 15), which modern tourists encounter typically in daylight. Initiates, in contrast, would have had to wend their way among these buildings in darkness, barely able to see them, were it not for lamp- and torchlight. Yet these means of artificial lighting, if not as brightly illuminating as daylight, would have enlivened the buildings' marble façades in meaningful ways. The structures' colonnaded façades and architectural sculptures would have flickered beneath the light of torches and lamps. Whereas sunlight is steady, flames cast light that flares and recedes—that moves, in short. In the night of the sanctuary, therefore, the sources of light—lamps and torches—would have caused the architecture to appear to come almost alive. Gleams of light would have bounced off marble columns, temporarily illuminating the white shafts against the blackened porch interiors. In fact, colleagues and I have recently suggested (Wescoat et al. 2020) that the profusion of buildings in the sanctuary with prostyle façades intentionally responded to and shaped visitors' diurnal and nocturnal experiences of the site.

FIGURE 4.7. *Detail of the frieze of the Hall of Choral Dancers, ca. 340 BCE. Sanctuary of the Great Gods, Samothrace. Photo: American Excavations Samothrace.*

Architectural sculpture too would have come to life under lamp- and torchlight, as figures in pediments and on friezes would have glimmered and flashed. For example, the frieze that encircles the Hall of Choral Dancers and gives the building its modern name depicts a line of 800 maidens dancing and playing musical instruments (figure 4.7; on the frieze see P. W. Lehmann and Spittle 1982, 1:230–233; K. Lehmann 1998, 75; Marconi 2010). The chorus of maidens might have alluded to the role of chorality in the Samothracian rites, either during thronosis, the preliminary purificatory rite, or at another point during initiation (Kowalzig 2005, 62; cf. Marconi 2010). The figures are carved in an archaizing style, in poses that clearly convey the act of dancing but that do so in a stylized manner without overt dynamism. The figures' limbs are straightened, not bent, for example, and their gestures restrained. Yet any static quality the relief might have possessed would have melted under artificial lighting, as flames would have caused the figures to appear to be moving. Kevin Clinton has argued that the Hall of Choral Dancers served as the sanctuary's Telesterion, that is, the structure in which the initiation of the mystai occurred (Clinton 2003, 61, though cf. Marconi 2010). If Clinton is correct, then the animation of the hall's reliefs through flame light could have paralleled the symbolic rebirth of visitors into their new life as initiates of the cult of the Great Gods.

Nearby, the pediment of the neighboring Hieron's north façade (in front of which one of the abovementioned torch-stones was found) contained sculptures carved in the round, belonging to a scene set in a rural landscape (see P. W. Lehmann 1962 on the pedimental sculptures). Olga Palagia and colleagues have argued that the scene depicts either a local Samothracian myth presented in Ptolemaic terms or an allegory of Ptolemaic Egypt (Palagia et al. 2009). Although iconographic interpretations of the Hieron's sculptures remain open to debate, its pediments, like the frieze of the Hall of Choral

Dancers, would have presented human figures whose poses, ranging from reclining to seated and standing, and intricately carved drapery would have flickered and quickened beneath torchlight.

In addition to friezes and pedimental sculptures on buildings, life-sized or over-life-sized statue dedications in marble and bronze punctuated the space of the sanctuary. The famous Winged Victory of Samothrace (whose date, not to mention patronage, is contested, though sometime in the first half of the second century BCE seems most likely: see, e.g., Mark 1998; Palagia 2010) would have overseen visitors' movements through the Central Sanctuary, from her vantage atop the sanctuary's theater. But other statues stood closer to people as they moved through the stages of initiation. When pilgrims entered into the Theatral Circle, two concentric tiers of bronze statues, likely depicting individual benefactors, greeted them (Wescoat 2012, 76–77; Gaunt 2017; Wescoat 2017a, 255–270). Other statue dedications stood in the Central Sanctuary, and, when pilgrims retired to the Western Hill to dine and relax after initiation, marble and bronze statue monuments awaited them on the terrace in front of the Stoa (Wescoat et al. 2020). Like the frieze of the Hall of Choral Dancers and other architectural sculpture, freestanding sculptural dedications would have appeared to shudder to life, with limbs, facial features, and robes all animated by flame light. Bronze statues especially would have gleamed under firelight, their polished surfaces reflecting the glow of lamps and torches. Artificial light also would have caused statues to cast deep shadows on surrounding buildings and landscapes, heightening the statues' striking nocturnal effect. Almost no inscriptions survive that we can definitively associate with extant statue bases, so the identity of the benefactors remains largely unknown. Logically, however, most of the benefactors who erected statues in their honor were likely initiates (Susan Ludi Blevins, personal communication, 2019). If the statue dedications in the sanctuary represented primarily patrons who themselves had undergone initiation into the mysteries of the Great Gods, then their nocturnal animation through luminosity brought to life a community of initiates that pilgrims to the sanctuary would either join momentarily or have joined moments before.

The visual experience of the sanctuary at nighttime would have been fundamentally different from the experience during daytime. In part this sensation was due to the opposing directionality of pilgrims' movements: descent from the Propylon into the Central Sanctuary at night, for initiation, and ascent back to the east during daylight, as they made their way the next day back to the ancient city (Wescoat 2012; Wescoat et al. 2020). But the different lighting conditions played a role as well. Certain aspects of the sanctuary would have been shrouded in shadows, others, as just discussed, vivified by artificial light. The omnipresent oscillation between light and shadow would have evoked the contrast between ignorance and knowledge and the movement from the former to the latter that the initiation rites effectuated. Artificial light illuminated the darkness, just as initiation into the mysteria illuminated the lives, and even afterlives, of pilgrims to the sanctuary. If firelight was part of the actual initiation rites, as inscriptions and texts suggest, then the lamps that prospective initiates carried as they moved from the Propylon down the Sacred Way into the Central Sanctuary, and the torches that lit their way, would have adumbrated the climax of the initiation rites.

Artificial lighting would have impacted people's sensorial experience of the sanctuary, and of initiation, beyond the visual. The smoke emanating from lamps and torches would have curled its way to people's nostrils, creating an association between sense of smell and experiences and subsequent memories of initiation. The crackling and whooshing of torches would have contributed to initiates' auditory experience, other aspects of which would have been determined by the night. As humans have temporal biological rhythms, so too do animals. Visitors to Samothrace today hear the hum of insect life in and around the sanctuary; the cicadas, for example, can be deafening. As the moon rises, the reverberations of these diurnal insects fade beneath the stars (on the diurnal character of cicadas, see Sakis Drosopoulos and Michael Claridge 2006). The relative quiet that graces Samothrace at night would have formed the auditory backdrop (or lack thereof) for the intense experience of initiation. As Yannis Hamilakis (2013) has argued, archaeologists must interrogate the senses and their culturally and historically specific meanings. Considering how people experienced the Sanctuary of the Great Gods *at night* allows us to recognize intense sensory experiences that would have eluded visitors to the sanctuary during daytime, even though tourists' and archaeologists' experience of the sanctuary necessarily privileges a sunlit encounter with the site.

The dramatic sensorial effects of artificial lighting also surely intensified pilgrims' emotional experience of and in the Sanctuary of the Great Gods. Hamilakis (2013, 196) maintains that the main role of the senses is affective—that is, our sensorial experiences serve to move us emotionally. The play of artificial lighting in nocturnal darkness created potent sensorial experiences and, therefore, potent emotional ones as well. Light, in the words of Tim Edensor, "kindles feeling" (Edensor 2017, x). As Angelos Chaniotis has argued, nighttime, which encourages and sometimes even enforces intimacy, "plays a great part in the creation of a sense of togetherness." Precisely for this reason, he suggests, initiation rites often occur during the night, not only in antiquity but also in the present (Chaniotis 2018a, 6–7; 2018b, 197). Initiation forges an emotional community (Chaniotis 2011, 267–272), and rites that occur at night create tightly knit emotional communities even more powerfully (Chaniotis 2018a, 23–24; Dillehay 2018). As Mikkel Bille and Tim Flohr Sørensen have argued (2007, 274), light can "define sensations of intimacy and exclusion." In the Sanctuary of the Great Gods, artificial lighting helped define initiates, binding them together in the light of lamps and torches and delimiting them as a group from what existed in the dark, beyond the reach of the artificial light.

Ancient authors reliably represent the night as enhancing emotional arousal, to the extent that the night clearly served as a rhetorical emotional intensifier (Chaniotis 2018a, 8–9). Yet emotions were an inherent aspect of Greek religious practices, and "different media were applied to arouse the desired emotion(s) in and among the participants" (Chaniotis 2011, 264). Artificial lighting was, I would argue, one such technology of emotional arousal. Lamps and torches intensified the affective impact of the initiation rites at Samothrace. That Isidoros's epitaph (see above) specifically calls out "the sacred light" as the climax of initiation into the Samothracian mysteries offers evidence that, from the perspective of initiates, light was one of the most memorable, affecting, and significant elements of their initiation experience. The inscription of Isidoros is not a work of literature by an author exploiting night and artificial light for rhetorical effect. Instead, it is a primary document from an actual initiate evoking his personal experience. He equates his initiation into the mysteries of the Great Gods with the act of seeing light, and he attributes his long and healthy life to that vision of light (Dimitrova 2008, 84, lines 16–19).

SANCTUARY AND CITY: NOCTURNAL CONNECTIONS

The contrasting diurnal and nocturnal experiences extended beyond the sanctuary proper, affecting initiates' experience also of the path connecting the sanctuary to the ancient city and of the city itself. Greek colonists arrived on Samothrace around 700 BCE, probably from northwestern Anatolia or Lesbos, despite ancient authors' tendency to trace the origins of "Thracian Samos" to Samos. The city of Samothrace emerged as a thriving Greek *polis*, minting its own silver coinage as early as the sixth century BCE. Much less is known about the ancient city, however, than about the sanctuary. Surely the flourishing of the sanctuary enriched the neighboring city, as did the island's location as a natural stopping point in key Mediterranean shipping lanes (on the ancient city, see K. Lehmann 1998,19–25). American Excavations Samothrace (https://samothrace.emory.edu/) will in coming summers excavate in the area of the city walls near the Propylon of Ptolemy II (figure 4.1, no. 26). These efforts, and future excavations in the ancient city itself, will surely increase our understanding of the ancient city and its relationship to the Sanctuary of the Great Gods.

Pending further excavation, the current state of the evidence still permits several comments about the impact of luminosity on people's experience as they moved to the sanctuary for initiation and then back to the city again, and as they then moved through the metropolis after initiation. First, at the risk of stating the obvious, *nocturnal* movement served as one of the most critical connectors between city and sanctuary. People could visit the sanctuary during the day, but for prospective initiates, their most emotionally charged arrival at the sanctuary involved departing the city at night. Initiation, therefore, necessitated movement through and experience of the city at night, as people gathered and walked toward the exit in the city walls. As chapter 1 of this volume describes, urban infrastructure can take on new significance in a nocturnal context. On Samothrace, the paths within the city and linking the city to the sanctuary had to accommodate movement in daylight and in the dark—and it was the latter movement that was ritually the most significant. In fact, as excavations reveal more about the ancient city of Samothrace, archaeologists might consider more directly whether and how nocturnal ritual activity shaped urban and extraurban infrastructure on the island.

Second, Samothrace has turned up an abundance of inscriptions recording *theoroi* (sacred ambassadors) and initiates not found elsewhere in the Greek world. These inscriptions on stone—either on stelae or, often, on blocks of buildings themselves—record the names of people who underwent initiation into the mysteria of the Great Gods. The inscribed lists have been compiled and studied thoroughly by Nora Dimitrova, who has shown their inestimable value for prosopography and for understanding the cult of the Great Gods (2008). I would like to call attention here, however, to the display of the inscriptions and the impact of luminosity on how people might have interacted with them.

Several inscriptions on large stone building blocks have been found on the path between the ancient city and the Propylon of Ptolemy II and within the ancient city. Given the size of the inscriptions, they likely were found not far from their original locations. Additionally, inscriptions found inside the ancient city had been carved onto already existing monuments, suggesting that urban buildings received initiate inscriptions (Dimitrova 2008, 81). Prospective initiates moving through the city and along the path to the sanctuary at dusk would have encountered these inscribed initiate lists. Lit only by handheld lamps and perhaps torches, the inscriptions would have been difficult to read. The letters of the surviving initiate lists measure only a few centimeters in height, at most, and are shallowly carved. Reading them without daylight would have been difficult. At the same time, however, the artificial light of lamps and torches, combined with any available moonlight, would have revealed lettering, which, even in its illegibility, would have called to mind the initiates whom viewers were setting off to join.

When those same viewers—now initiates themselves—exited the sanctuary to make their way back to the ancient city, daylight would have clearly illuminated the inscribed lists. Moving along the path from the Propylon to the city and through the streets of the city itself, new initiates could now stop to read the inscriptions and consider that their names, too, might soon find a place on the stones of the city of Samothrace. With the inscribed lists, the luminosity of the night tantalized, making people aware of the inscriptions but shrouding their actual content. The luminosity of day, in contrast, revealed the full meaning of the lists, enabling people to feel themselves part of the community that the lists recorded. These sensations—of revelation and communality—affected people's experiences of the ancient city, demonstrating how, surely, the sanctuary and the city were interconnected experientially as well as politically and economically.

At the same time that the Samothracian rites of initiation created a powerful sense of community, we should remain mindful of the ways in the initiatory experience also revealed and perhaps constructed power differentials. As chapter 1 describes, people's experiences of the night are seldom equal, and people can exert control over darkness, via artificial lighting or other means, to assert and express social status. In the Sanctuary of the Great Gods, the nocturnal rites might have offered opportunities for social differentiation as well as cohesion. It is not clear whether all initiates carried terra-cotta lamps or whether some might in fact have held marble vessels. If the latter, then the material of the lamps would have visibly distinguished gradations of wealth. In either case, the sanctuary's array of monuments and dedications would have spoken to striking socioeconomic disparities. Rich and poor alike could attain initiation into the cult of the Great Gods, but only the wealthy could aspire to a life-size statue dedication in the sanctuary, and only the proverbial 1 percent would ever have been able to dedicate an entire marble building. The statues and monumental inscriptions that sprang to life under the torches and lamps of the initiation rites would have commemorated only the most elite patrons of the sanctuary. Initiates of more modest means would have struggled mightily to leave as lasting a mark of their presence.

CONCLUSIONS

The introduction to the present volume forcefully lays out the case for day and night, and light and dark, as cultural constructs as much as natural occurrences. As Tim Edensor has recently argued in his book *From Light to Dark: Daylight, Illumination, and Gloom*, "daylight, darkness, and illumination are invariably suffused with cultural values and myriad practices that solicit divergent sensory, affective, and emotional responses" (2017, 213). I have demonstrated in this chapter that the archaeology of darkness and luminosity, of artificial lighting and the spatial and temporal contexts in which people deployed it, demands our attention if we are plausibly to reconstruct the potential phenomenological and affective experiences of pilgrims to the Sanctuary of the Great Gods on Samothrace. Thinking about the Sanctuary of the Great Gods "after dark" illuminates central questions about experience, affect, and movement in the sanctuary and from the ancient city to the sanctuary. This approach, therefore, binds the ancient city to the sanctuary and brings the neighboring urban environment into closer dialogue with the sacred temenos. To understand people's experience of the Sanctuary of the Great Gods, we must better understand the archaeology of the ancient city.

This brief chapter might stand, then, as a prolegomenon of sorts to the eventual publication of broader, ongoing studies of the island of Samothrace, its city, and its sanctuary in antiquity. The American excavations in the Sanctuary of the Great Gods are currently addressing precisely the sorts of questions I have raised here, drawing on geomorphology, geology, photogrammetry, and three-dimensional digital modeling to consider visitors' phenomenological experiences of the sanctuary in antiquity. A major thrust of the research agenda is to consider how light at different times of day and night affected how visitors sensorially experienced the sanctuary. We have put forth initial observations in Wescoat et al. (2020). Here, I have argued for the affective impact that the interaction of lamplight, torchlight, and nocturnal darkness might have had on pilgrims in the context of the sanctuary's and the city's architecture, statuary, and inscriptions. Ongoing research will further elaborate these conclusions and clarify the effects of artificial lighting in the Samothracian sanctuary, just as excavation in the ancient city will surely unveil fascinating new data about how people lived in, moved through, and experienced the ancient city during day *and* night, whether en route to the sanctuary, as a final destination, or as home.

Acknowledgments. I am grateful to Nancy Gonlin and Meghan Strong for their invitation to contribute to this volume and for their helpful comments on earlier versions of this essay. I am additionally grateful to the anonymous reviewers for the University Press of Colorado for their useful feedback. Finally, I express deep thanks to Bonna Wescoat, director of American Excavations Samothrace, for welcoming me into the Samothracian family many years ago and for remaining a constant source of friendship, advice, and intellectual stimulation.

REFERENCES

Bille, Mikkel and Tim Flohr Sørensen. 2007. "An Anthropology of Luminosity: The Agency of Light." *Journal of Material Culture* 12 (3): 263–284.

Blevins, Susan Ludi. 2017a. "Lamps." In *Samothrace: Excavations Conducted by the Institute of Fine Arts of New York University*. Vol. 9, *The Monuments of the Eastern Hill*, by Bonna D. Wescoat et al., 287–394. Princeton, NJ: American School of Classical Studies at Athens.

Blevins, Susan Ludi. 2017b. "Pottery." In *Samothrace: Excavations Conducted by the Institute of Fine Arts of New York University*. Vol. 9, *The Monuments of the Eastern Hill*, by Bonna D. Wescoat et al., 359–386. Princeton, NJ: American School of Classical Studies at Athens.

Chaniotis, Angelos. 2011. "Emotional Community through Ritual: Initiates, Citizens, and Pilgrims as Emotional Communities in the Greek World." In *Ritual Dynamics in the Ancient Mediterranean: Agency, Emotion, Gender, Representation*, edited by Angelos Chaniotis, 263–290. Stuttgart: Franz Steiner Verlag.

Chaniotis, Angelos. 2018a. "Nessun Dorma! Changing Nightlife in the Hellenistic and Roman East." In *La nuit: Imaginaire et réalités nocturnes dans le monde gréco-romain*, edited by Angelos Chaniotis, 1–49. Geneva: Fondation Hardt.

Chaniotis, Angelos. 2018b. "The Polis after Sunset: What Is Hellenistic in Hellenistic Nights?" In *The Polis in the Hellenistic World*, edited by Henning Börm and Nino Luraghi, 181–208. Stuttgart: Franz Steiner Verlag.

Clinton, Kevin. 2003. "Stages of Initiation in the Eleusinian and Samothracian Mysteries." In *Greek Mysteries: The Archaeology and Ritual of Ancient Greek Secret Cults*, edited by Michael B. Cosmopoulos, 50–78. London: Routledge.

Clinton, Kevin. 2010. "The Mysteries of Demeter and Kore." In *A Companion to Greek Religion*, edited by Daniel Ogden, 342–356. Malden, MA: Blackwell.

Cole, Susan Guettel. 1984. *Theoi Megaloi: The Cult of the Great Gods at Samothrace*. Leiden, Netherlands: Brill.

Constantakopoulou, Christy. 2017. *Aegean Interactions: Delos and Its Networks in the Third Century*. Oxford: Oxford University Press.

Dillehay, Tom D. 2018. "Night Moon Rituals: The Effects of Darkness and Prolonged Ritual on Chilean Mapuche Participants." In *Archaeology of the Night: Life after Dark in the Ancient World*, edited by Nancy Gonlin and April Nowell, 179–199. Boulder, CO: University Press of Colorado.

Dimitrova, Nora M. 2008. *Theoroi and Initiates in Samothrace: The Epigraphical Evidence*. Princeton, NJ: American School of Classical Studies at Athens.

Drosopoulos, Sakis, and Michael F. Claridge, eds. 2006. *Insect Sounds and Communication: Physiology, Behaviour, Ecology, and Evolution*. Boca Raton, FL: Taylor and Francis.

Edensor, Tim. 2017. *From Light to Dark: Daylight, Illumination, and Gloom*. Minneapolis: University of Minnesota Press.

Evershed, Richard P., Sarah J. Vaughan, Stephanie N. Dudd, and Jeffrey S. Soles. 1997. "Fuel for Thought? Beeswax in Lamps and Conical Cups from Late Minoan Crete." *Antiquity* 71 (274): 979–985.

Fraser, P. M. 1960. *Samothrace: Excavations Conducted by the Institute of Fine Arts of New York University*. Vol. 2.1, *The Inscriptions on Stone*. New York: Pantheon Books.

Gaunt, Jasper. 2017. "Metal Objects." In *Samothrace: Excavations Conducted by the Institute of Fine Arts of New York University*. Vol. 9, *The Monuments of the Eastern Hill*, by Bonna D. Wescoat et al., 419–436. Princeton, NJ: American School of Classical Studies at Athens.

Gonlin, Nancy, and Christine C. Dixon-Hundredmark. 2021. "Illuminating Darkness in the Ancient Maya World: Nocturnal Case Studies from Copan, Honduras and La Joya de Cerén, El Salvador." In *Night and Darkness in Ancient Mesoamerica*, edited by Nancy Gonlin and David M. Reed, 103–140. Louisville, CO: University Press of Colorado.

Hamilakis, Yannis. 2013. *Archaeology and the Senses: Human Experience, Memory, and Affect*. New York: Cambridge University Press.

Kowalzig, Barbara. 2005. "Mapping out *Communitas*: Performances of *Theôria* in Their Sacred and Political Context." In *Pilgrimage in Graeco-Roman and Early Christian Antiquity: Seeing the Gods*, edited by Jaś Elsner and Ian Rutherford, 41–72. Oxford: Oxford University Press.

Lehmann, Karl. 1943. "Cyriacus of Ancona, Aristotle, and Teiresias in Samothrace." *Hesperia: The Journal of the American School of Classical Studies at Athens* 12 (2): 115–134.

Lehmann, Karl. 1950. "Samothrace: Third Preliminary Report." *Hesperia: The Journal of the American School of Classical Studies at Athens* 19 (1): 1–20.

Lehmann, Karl. 1951. "Samothrace: Fourth Preliminary Report." *Hesperia: The Journal of the American School of Classical Studies at Athens* 20 (1): 1–30.

Lehmann, Karl. 1952. "Samothrace: Fifth Preliminary Report." *Hesperia: The Journal of the American School of Classical Studies at Athens* 21 (1): 19–43.

Lehmann, Karl. 1960. *Samothrace: Excavations Conducted by the Institute of Fine Arts of New York University*. Vol. 2.2, *The Inscriptions on Ceramics and Minor Objects*. New York: Pantheon Books.

Lehmann, Karl. 1998. *Samothrace: A Guide to the Excavations and the Museum*. 6th ed. Rev. and enlarged. Thessaloniki: Institute of Fine Arts, New York University.

Lehmann, Phyllis Williams. 1962. *The Pedimental Sculptures of the Hieron in Samothrace*. Locust Valley, NY: Published for the Institute of Fine Arts.

Lehmann, Phyllis Williams. 1969. *Samothrace: Excavations Conducted by the Institute of Fine Arts of New York University*. Vol. 3, *The Hieron*. 3 vols. New York: Pantheon Books.

Lehmann, Phyllis Williams, and Denys Spittle. 1982. *Samothrace: Excavations Conducted by the Institute of Fine Arts of New York University*. Vol. 5, *The Temenos*. 2 vols. Princeton, NJ: Princeton University Press.

Lewis, Naphtali, ed. 1959. *Samothrace: Excavations Conducted by the Institute of Fine Arts of New York University*. Vol. 1, *The Ancient Literary Sources*. New York: Pantheon Books.

Marconi, Clemente. 2010. "*Choroi, Theoriai* and International Ambitions: The Hall of Choral Dancers and Its Frieze." In *Samothracian Connections: Essays in Honor of James R. McCredie*, edited by Olga Palagia and Bonna D. Wescoat, 106–135. Oxford: Oxbow Books.

Mark, Ira. 1998. "The Victory of Samothrace." In *Regional Schools in Hellenistic Sculpture: Proceedings of an International Conference Held at the American School of Classical Studies at Athens, March 15–17, 1996*, edited by Olga Palagia and William D. E. Coulson, 157–165. Oxford: Oxbow Books.

McCredie, James R. 1965. "Samothrace: Preliminary Report on the Campaigns of 1962–1964." *Hesperia: The Journal of the American School of Classical Studies at Athens* 34 (2): 100–124.

McCredie, James R. 1968. "Samothrace: Preliminary Report on the Campaigns of 1965–1967." *Hesperia: The Journal of the American School of Classical Studies at Athens* 37 (2): 200–234.

Mylonas, George E. 1961. *Eleusis and the Eleusinian Mysteries*. Princeton, NJ: Princeton University Press.

Nilsson, Martin P. 1950. "Lampen und Kerzen im Kult der Antike." *Opuscula Archaeologica* 6: 96–111.

Oustinoff, Elizabeth. 1992. "Marble Lamps." In *Samothrace: Excavations Conducted by the Institute of Fine Arts of New York University*. Vol. 7, *The Rotunda of Arsinoe*, by

James R. McCredie, 329–330. Princeton, NJ: American School of Classical Studies at Athens.

Palagia, Olga. 2010. "The Victory of Samothrace and the Aftermath of the Battle of Pydna." In *Samothracian Connections: Essays in Honor of James R. McCredie*, edited by Olga Palagia and Bonna D. Wescoat, 154–164. Oxford: Oxbow Books.

Palagia, Olga, Yannis Maniatis, E. Dotsika, and D. Kavoussanaki. 2009. "New Investigations on the Pedimental Sculptures of the 'Hieron' of Samothrace: A Preliminary Report." In *Asmosia VII: Actes du VIIe colloque international de l'ASMOSIA, Thasos, 15–20 septembre 2003* [Proceedings of the 7th International Conference of Association for the Study of Marble and Other Stones in Antiquity, Thassos, September 15–20, 2003], edited by Yannis Maniatis, 113–132. Athens: École française d'Athènes.

Parisinou, Eva. 1997. "Artificial Illumination in Greek Cult Practice of the Archaic and the Classical Periods: Mere Practical Necessity?" *Thetis* 4: 95–108.

Parisinou, Eva. 2000. *The Light of the Gods: The Role of Light in Archaic and Classical Greek Cult*. London: Duckworth.

Patera, Ioanna. 2010. "Light and Lighting Equipment in the Eleusinian Mysteries." In *Light and Darkness in Ancient Greek Myth and Religion*, edited by Menelaos Christopoulos, E. D. Karakantza, and Olga Levaniouk, 261–275. Lanham, MD: Lexington Books.

Pettazzoni, Raffaele. 1908. "Una rappresentazione romana dei Kabiri di Samotracia." *Ausonia* 3: 79–90.

Popkin, Maggie L. 2015. "Samothracian Influences at Rome: Cultic and Architectural Exchange in the Second Century B.C.E." *American Journal of Archaeology* 119 (3): 343–373.

Popkin, Maggie L. 2017. "Stone Objects." In *Samothrace: Excavations Conducted by the Institute of Fine Arts of New York University*. Vol. 9, *The Monuments of the Eastern Hill*, by Bonna D. Wescoat, 444–452. Princeton, NJ: American School of Classical Studies at Athens.

Price, Simon. 1999. *Religions of the Ancient Greeks*. Cambridge: Cambridge University Press.

Stewart, Andrew. 2014. *Art in the Hellenistic World: An Introduction*. New York: Cambridge University Press.

Tucci, Pier Luigi. 2015. "The Materials and Techniques of Greek and Roman Architecture." In *The Oxford Handbook of Greek and Roman Art and Architecture*, edited by Clemente Marconi, 242–265. Oxford: Oxford University Press.

Wescoat, Bonna D. 2012. "Coming and Going in the Sanctuary of the Great Gods, Samothrace." In *Architecture of the Sacred: Space, Ritual, and Experience from*

Classical Greece to Byzantium, edited by Bonna D. Wescoat and Robert G. Ouster-hout, 66–113. Cambridge: Cambridge University Press.

Wescoat, Bonna D. 2016. "New Directions in Hellenistic Sanctuaries." In *A Companion to Greek Architecture*, edited by Margaret M. Miles, 424–439. Hoboken, NJ: John Wiley and Sons, Inc.

Wescoat, Bonna D. 2017a. *Samothrace: Excavations Conducted by the Institute of Fine Arts of New York University*. Vol. 9, *The Monuments of the Eastern Hill*. Princeton, NJ: American School of Classical Studies at Athens.

Wescoat, Bonna D. 2017b. "The Pilgrim's Passage into the Sanctuary of the Great Gods, Samothrace." In *Excavating Pilgrimage: Archaeological Approaches to Sacred Travel and Movement in the Ancient World*, edited by Troels Myrup Kristensen and Wiebke Friese, 67–86. London: Routledge.

Wescoat, Bonna D., Susan Ludi Blevins, Maggie L. Popkin, Jessica Paga, Michael C. Page, William Size, and Andrew Farinholt Ward. 2020. "Interstitial Space in the Sanctuary of the Great Gods on Samothrace." In *Hellenistic Architecture, Landscape, and Human Action*, edited by Annette Haug and Asja Müller, 41–62. Leiden, Netherlands: Sidestone Press.

5

One of the main approaches that archaeologists have taken in defining and identifying "cities" in the past has been to differentiate them from their surrounding environment: the *urbs* that emerges in contradistinction to the rural surroundings. But cities possess landscapes of their own, what may be referred to as "urban ecologies"—whether the rapidly burgeoning city of Chicago emerging on the shores of Lake Michigan in the early nineteenth century, or the great capitals of pre-Columbian polities of the ancient Americas such as Cahokia, Teotihuacán, or Cusco. Research in recent decades has demonstrated that in many ancient cities, productive and agricultural infrastructure was not only present within the urban landscape but integrated into the urban fabric in both a social and material sense. The Mexica (Aztec) capital of Tenochtitlan, for instance, was constructed on an island in Lake Texcoco, and famously relied on floating raised-bed systems for the sustenance of its constituent populations (see chapter 10 by Farah and Evans, this volume). Similarly, residential patio groups of Maya cities in Mexico and Central America were interspersed with lands devoted to reservoirs (French et al. 2020) as well as extensive and intensive farming systems such as milpas and terraces (Isendahl 2012).

In this chapter, we draw inspiration from research on urban ecologies of ancient cities to consider some of the affective and experiential dimensions of an urban landscape: namely, what was it like to experience the

Living Landscapes of Night in Tiwanaku, Bolivia

John Wayne Janusek and Anna Guengerich

https://doi.org/10.5876/9781646422609.c005

pre-Columbian city of Tiwanaku after dark in the year 800 CE? In answering this question, we have had the pleasure of drawing together a number of different data sets and ideas that Janusek had been working with the last several decades since beginning work at Tiwanaku in 1987. This city rose to prominence around 500 CE on the Andean high plateau, or altiplano, of modern-day Bolivia and, until approximately 1000 CE, the monumental campuses at the heart of this urban complex served as one of the preeminent pilgrimage centers of the ancient Andes. Highly charged, evocative public ceremonies, many of which likely took place at night, were critical to the experiences of those who came to this site. Yet, despite a common emphasis on phenomenological experience in previous studies of Tiwanaku (e.g., Kolata 1993; Isbell and Vranich 2004; Janusek 2008, 2016; Vranich 2016), it is only recently that researchers have begun to explore the complementary aspects of diurnal and nocturnal experiences (Vranich and Smith 2018).

To explore the experiential dimensions of urban landscapes of night, we first provide a brief overview of the spatial and architectural organization of Tiwanaku during its heyday in 500–1000 CE, and then consider how nighttime is experienced today by Aymara residents who continue to live in the modern town of Tiahuanaco. Their modern perceptions and experiences of the happenings that take place at night provide a framework that may help conceptualize certain aspects of how nighttime was experienced in the past—underscoring its often frightening and dangerous character. We then turn to archaeological research, in which we collate three dimensions of lived practice, focusing especially on the complementary roles of fire and water. First, we consider how fire and water quite literally created the atmosphere of the outdoor spaces of the urban environment. Second, we move into the comfy adobe homes of Tiwanaku residents to provide a window into how nighttime life unfolded in those bright and warm spaces illuminated by hearths and ceramic lamps. Last, we shift to the monumental complexes that for centuries attracted pilgrims, especially in the context of nocturnal rituals of human movement, celestial rotation, and firelight that helped animate the stone sculptures that inhabited these spaces. Throughout this circuit of the urban landscape, we seek to highlight the kinds of nighttime experiences that archaeologists might observe beyond the warm and safe confines of the home space (Gonlin and Nowell 2018), and to stress how a nocturnal view of urban ecology informs a more encompassing understanding of what made ancient Tiwanaku what it was.

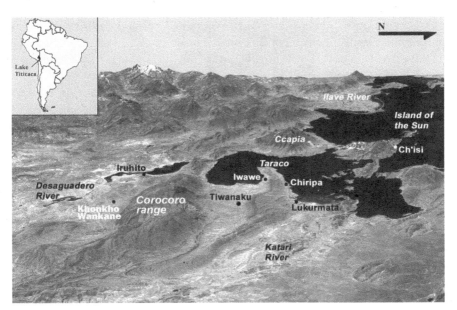

FIGURE 5.1. *View of Tiwanaku in relation to other major pre-Columbian sites. Image: Arik Ohnstad.*

THE GEOPOLITICAL AND ECOLOGICAL
CONTEXT OF TIWANAKU

Tiwanaku, located on the high plateau region or altiplano of present-day Bolivia, was one of the most prominent ceremonial-political centers of the ancient Andes (figure 1.1; figure 5.1). By 250 CE, Tiwanaku already played a prominent role in the Andean geopolitical landscape as one of a number of net-worked, interacting ceremonial centers of the Lake Titicaca Basin—including the sites of Kala Uyuni, Sonaji, Kalla Marka, and Khonkho Wankane—which shared key ritual practices, iconographic and architectural traditions, and religious communities. At some point around 500 CE, however, Tiwanaku emerged out of this geopolitical landscape as the preeminent of these centers, continuing to hold this position until the demise of its established political order after 1000 CE (Janusek 2012, 2015). The precise nature of this politi-cal formation remains a matter of debate. It is clear that secondary centers such as nearby Lukurmata formed part of the same political-religious system, supporting Tiwanaku economically (Kolata 1993; Janusek 2008), and possible colonies in far-flung areas such as the piedmont of Eastern Bolivia and the coastal foothills of Peru have been characterized as a Tiwanaku "diaspora"

(Goldstein 2000), where inhabitants maintained cultural, political, and economic links with the center. Whether Tiwanaku may be best described as a state, an empire, or its own unique political-religious phenomenon remains a matter of some debate.

Keys to Tiwanaku's geopolitical influence were the richly material ceremonial gatherings that took place in the dramaturgically elaborate spaces of its monumental center. Tiwanaku was first and foremost a pilgrimage center, which attracted adherents and participants from across the southern Andes as far as Chile and Argentina. Any experiential exploration of this urban center must therefore be grounded in the cyclical ebb and flow of pilgrims who periodically swelled the scale of the city; indeed, the same dynamics of periodic gathering continue to characterize traditional festivals among the contemporary Aymara, their descendants (Janusek 2006, 2016). As with later Andean polities, such as the Inka, some of the major features of ceremonies at the urban core of Tiwanaku were commensal gatherings, especially those focused on large-scale consumption of maize beer, or *chicha*, and of other mind-altering substances (Torres 2001; Janusek 2008; Bandy 2013).

These ceremonies took place in several monumental spaces, which were clustered in the two main "campuses" of Tiwanaku proper and its twin campus of Pumapunku, located several hundred meters to the southwest. At the campus of Tiwanaku, the three most prominent civic-religious spaces were the Kalasasaya, an elevated platform 130 by 120 meters in area; the Sunken Temple, immediately to the east of the Kalasasaya, which had functioned as the ritual center of Tiwanaku during the Late Formative Period (100 BCE–500 CE); and the Akapana, a stepped, pyramid-like platform located on the south side of the Kalasasaya and Sunken Temple and built later in Tiwanaku's history (Kolata 2003) (figure 5.2). The physical and affective experiences of space were highlighted in the design of all these features, with monumental portals placed at key points of passage to structure the movement of pilgrims through this imposing and dramatic complex (Vranich 1999, 2016; Janusek 2016). But the raison d'être and visual and spatial focus of these settings were *monoliths*: monumental, anthropomorphic stone sculptures that thought to embody powerful ancestral personages, and that presided over the ceremonies that took place there (Posnansky 1945; Janusek 2006, 2019; Bandy 2013) (figure 5.3).

These architecturally complex places must be understood within the broader ecological context of the altiplano, the materiality of which was integrated into the urban fabric of the city. At 3,800 meters above sea level, Tiwanaku ranks among the highest-altitude urban centers of the premodern world, and its distinguishing economic, architectural, and ceremonial attributes were

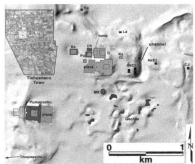

FIGURE 5.2. (left) *Organization of the two monumental campuses at Tiwanaku (Pumapunku and Tiwanaku itself) in relation to the modern town of Tiahuanaco, with major structures mentioned in text: Kalasasaya platform (Ka), Sunken Temple (ST), and Akapana platform.* (right) *Aerial view of major monumental features of the Tiwanaku campus. Photo: Johan Reinhard.*

FIGURE 5.3. *Presentation monoliths:* (a) *Bennett Monolith. Photo: John Wayne Janusek.* (b) *Ponce Monolith. Photo: John Wayne Janusek.* (c) *Fraile Monolith (adapted from nineteenth-century postcard in possession of authors).*

shaped in dialogue with this environmental setting. The large, concentrated population of the urban core was supported through vast systems of raised-field agricultural beds that abutted and drained into Lake Titicaca (Kolata and Ortloff 2003; Janusek and Kolata 2004). But productive infrastructure was similarly integrated into the urban core of Tiwanaku itself, notably in the form of wells and water features that supported llama and alpaca herds within the city environs (Flores Ochoa 1987; Janusek and Bowen 2018). Apart from subsistence activities, the expansive nighttime skies of the altiplano informed the layout of the monumental core. Key features such as the Sunken Court were designed for viewing constellations and other celestial features (Benítez 2013; Vranich 2016; Vranich and Smith 2018). Equally important were distant mountain peaks such as Kimsachata to the south, and Ccapia and Illimani to the west and east. For contemporary Aymara and for many Andean peoples of the past and present, mountains are known as *apus*, animate beings with whom human communities seek to engage to access their power. Not only were Tiwanaku's key architectural features aligned with these peaks, but the apus were materially incorporated into the site itself in the form of mono-liths, which were quarried from the sides of mountains, bringing the very sub-stance of their bodies into the city. In other words, the broader ecology within which the city of Tiwanaku was embedded was key to its experience; in turn, the experience of the city was the foundation of its geopolitical power in the southern Andean world.

NIGHT AS ALTERNATE ONTOLOGICAL DOMAIN: THE AYMARA WORLD

Today, the modern town of Tiahuanaco, founded in the sixteenth century under Spanish colonial rule, is largely made of Aymara residents whose ances-tors have lived with and near the adjacent pre-Columbian site of Tiwanaku for generations. Aymara experiences of the nighttime world, including at Tiwanaku/Tiahuanaco itself, provide a useful framework for modeling how its ancient inhabitants may have conceptualized their urban landscape at night.

For the Aymara, day and night traditionally constitute reciprocal domains, each inhabited by particular sorts of beings and characterized by specific activities. Prominent during the day is the sun's movement, and most agro-pastoral productive work takes place in daylight. More prominent at night is the movement of the moon, the Milky Way, and key constellations. For humans, night is potentially dangerous, as it is populated by a host of dread-ful nonhuman beings. These include the feared *kate*, or disembodied heads

FIGURE 5.4. *Camelid sacrifice performed as part of a nighttime ritual at Qhunqhu Liqiliqi, 2005. Photo: John Wayne Janusek.*

(Tschopik 1946); *japiñuñu*—beautiful voluptuous women who lure men and crush them between their breasts (Canessa 1993, 139); and the terrifying *condenados* (condemned)—bloodied, deteriorating Andean "zombies" who walk the earth in penance for their time on earth as selfish persons (Allen 2009). Yet night is also when solemn offerings (*muxa misa*, "sweet offering" in Aymara) of animal fat, candies, and llama fetuses are burned in offering to the apus of a given region, as well as to the earth, today often glossed as an animate female being (figure 5.4). It is the most auspicious time for communities to construct positive reciprocal relations with the vital landscapes they inhabit. Dawn and dusk, though—the moments of transition that usher in these respective domains—possess a high level of danger. In whatever activity one engages, one must be cautious at these liminal times.

Contemporary Aymara residents of Tiahuanaco are likewise familiar with another sort of nonhuman beings that may awaken at night: the anthropomorphic stone sculptures, or monoliths, that originally stood in key locations in the pre-Columbian center, such as the Sunken Court and the massive terraced platform of the Akapana (figure 5.3). While some stone sculptures still stand in the current tourist-trampled spaces they originally inhabited, most have been relocated to a recently constructed museum, and at least one other, known as the Suñawa Monolith, stands in a private house on the town square (Schaedel 1948; Guengerich and Janusek 2020). Town residents tell many narratives about having run into one of these sculptures out and about at night, or having seen one move, or heard one speak or even cry. Many residents speak about having interacted with them or know someone who has. Notably, these interactions can be dangerous: humans who are unaware that they have just

FIGURE 5.5. *Nighttime gathering of monoliths. Drawing: Adapted from sketch by Juan Rugendas (Diener Ojeda 1992).*

interacted with a monolith-being may fall into a hypnotic-like state, become ill, and, if left untreated, die. Since monoliths often appear to people in human form, interactions are difficult to comprehend for those who experience them, especially when the person who observes them is in a weakened, altered state—usually, when drunk. Whenever monoliths awaken, they awaken at night, for night is their domain, too.

Unlike many of the Aymara night beings, monoliths generally have specific personae. For example, the Pumapunku Monolith is sometimes apprehended as a beautiful woman who seduces, renders ill, and, ultimately, kills her victims. The monolith is likely considered female by modern viewers because its lower half takes the form of a flaring, skirt-like garment (originally intended to portray a tunic, a traditional element of men's dress) that resembles the *pollera* skirt that Aymara women wear today. One of the most storied monoliths is the Suñawa Monolith, found under a house patio on the town plaza in 1948. In interviews with Janusek, many individuals had rich stories about having encountered and interacted with this monolith at night. In some cases, it appeared as a person "looking for his feet"—since the monolith's pedestal and original feet were broken from its legs sometime in the past. In other narratives, a person witnesses the monolith "awaken" and move from its home, or even congregate in public settings with other, awakened monoliths (figure 5.5). In these cases, a bright flash of light announces the monolith's awakening.

For example, Marcelino Chura, who lived down the street from where the Suñawa Monolith stood, recounted the following narrative from when he witnessed such an awakening in the mid-twentieth century:

> As I lay in bed around midnight, a bright light flashed outside the window. It was as strong as the lights of a car, before cars existed in Tiahuanaco. I went downstairs and opened the door to the street, and saw Suñawa standing outside, bathed in light. I was terrified. Suñawa began to move. It turned into the plaza and proceeded to the front of the church. I was curious and wanted to follow, but my legs kept falling asleep. I made it around the corner to see Suñawa talking to two sculptures that stand on either side of the church entrance. They talked for a long time. What were they saying? Finally, they moved together toward Pumapunku, as dogs began to bark. I went back to bed frightened, shaking. I could not sleep. Just before dawn, I heard noise in the plaza. I went out and saw Suñawa speaking with several monoliths drawn from the ruins, more than a kilometer away. Finally, the other monoliths departed, Suñawa approached the door to its house, and the light suddenly shut off, as if a flashlight. (Chura, personal communication, 2010, translation by the authors)

For the monoliths of Tiahuanaco, as with other types of nonhuman persons in the traditional Andean world, night constitutes a reciprocal world of beings and actions in which humans are categorically not in power. For the most part, people are conducting nightly tasks or sleeping in their warm, sheltering, thatch-and-adobe homes. Being outside of the home—especially when in a susceptible, drunken state—exposes people to the dangerous beings who inhabit this domain. Of course, there are legitimate, socially acceptable reasons a person may be out of the home at night: tending herds in high-altitude pastures, early-morning fishing, late-night traveling, burning offerings to apus, or participating in calendrical festivals in celebration of a community patron saint. Yet the reciprocal danger is that people out at night for no acceptable reason are equally as dangerous as their nonhuman peers. They are potential thieves, or worse, *brujos* (witches) or *kharisiris* ("vampires") (Wachtel 1994), fat-suckers who seek to spiritually weaken and ultimately kill their victims. The potential power and danger of nefarious nighttime human actions parallel those of their nonhuman compatriots.

Nighttime for the modern Aymara, then, is not simply a period of darkness characterized by the cessation of ordinary diurnal activities. Instead, it comprises its own ontological domain into which humans may indeed enter but by metaphorically watching their step. What, then, was nighttime like for residents of pre-Columbian Tiwanaku? Were similar forces at play—of danger, of contrasts between the home and exterior, or the presence of powerful nonhuman beings? In the remainder of the chapter, we turn to three spatial contexts that may be examined archaeologically to explore answers to these questions: outdoor spaces, domestic interiors, and the heart of the monumental campus.

SMOKE AND MIST: NIGHTTIME URBAN ECOLOGY AT TIWANAKU

We turn first to the outdoor, extra-architectural spaces of Tiwanaku that were an essential part of its urban ecology. We pull together two subjects of investigation that have occupied Janusek and numerous colleagues for many years: widespread ash pits and urban canal systems. While a good deal of ink has been spilled in arguments about the function and origins of these features, here we set aside these discussions and focus instead on what they contributed to the nighttime experience of Tiwanaku's outdoor settings. In short, they made Tiwanaku a smoky and a misty place.

Today, on a clear night at Tiwanaku, the air is piercingly cold, given the site's high-altitude setting, and the stars are incredibly bright. For most of us growing up in cities, this natural nighttime light is easily forgotten. Yet beyond the reach of modern urban light pollution in the cities of El Alto or La Paz, night is not simply dark, and celestial bodies afford substantial light to the altiplano landscape. The stars alone illuminate much of the face of the landscape; and if the moon is present, the light is bright and silvery.

Yet, like all cities, ancient Tiwanaku produced its own forms of pollution and constituted its own heat island—what we refer to here as, respectively, a "smoke envelope" and a "mist envelope." The first of these phenomena, the smoke envelope, was the result of the numerous burning activities that were commonplace elements of urban life. At night, smoke would have accumulated within the city as a result of the many fires being lit for cooking and warmth in the frigid altiplano climate. Many other ordinary practices in the daily life of a pre-Columbian city also may have contributed to the smoke envelope, including open-air firings for pottery production during the daytime and certain forms of cooking, such as buried earth ovens, or *watias*. In the largely treeless setting of the altiplano, the major source of fuel for these fires was camelid dung from llamas or alpacas, which would have generated a strong smell, distinctive of nighttime fires. As Sillar (2000) notes, for Andean communities who traditionally rely on camelid dung, the smell more often

FIGURE 5.6. *Ash pits excavated in Akapana East domestic sectors at Tiwanaku. Photo: John Wayne Janusek.*

than not evokes strong connotations of security and comfort: with the combined effect of so many hearths, this aroma may have been perceived as a distinctively urban, "Tiwanaku" olfactory aesthetic. While these activities would certainly not have produced levels of smog to rival modern, industrialized cities, the urban density and clustering of population in residential sectors would certainly have generated a considerable volume of smoke, which likely lingered well into the night.

In addition to typical domestic practices shared with many ancient urban centers, Tiwanaku was associated with a culturally unique form of large-scale burning that would have contributed significantly to the smoke envelope—crystallized in a feature that Andrew Roddick and Janusek (2011) refer to as "ash pits." Tiwanaku's ash pits were immense and ubiquitous and are found not only at Tiwanaku itself but also at contemporary, culturally Tiwanaku centers throughout the South Titicaca Basin region (figure 5.6). For researchers who work in the region, their presence in the archaeological record has traditionally been more of a headache than a blessing, as they wreak havoc with stratigraphy, and, in particular, recklessly cut through pre-Tiwanaku contexts buried beneath them. These pits are found in residential sectors of the site in house interiors and exteriors. Invariably, they are filled with ash, which is generally mixed with dispersed, carbonized camelid-dung pellets indicative of the fuel that generated them. In many cases, they contained mixed strata, including burnt clay, and are characterized by high artifact densities that include botanical and faunal remains and ceramics related to a variety of food-related practices, including *ollas* (cooking vessels), jars for storage or fermentation, and serving and ceremonial vessels (Janusek 2003a; Janusek 2009; Roddick and Janusek 2011).

These ash pits exhibit a morphological variability that suggests that they served a variety of purposes. Some pits may have been generated through in situ forms of production, such as earth ovens or ceramic firing, and their initial excavation likely resulted from quarrying the clay-rich soil of the area to acquire adobe for constructing the houses and monumental architecture of the urban core. Most, however, probably served to dispose of the refuse generated by ongoing domestic and ceremonial activity in the urban center. Indeed, one might say that the Tiwanaku were distinctively anal-retentive about burning their garbage.

This form of ash pit first appears in the archaeological record around 500 CE, coinciding neatly with the emergence of a number of features characteristic of Tiwanaku hegemony in the region. Given the importance of commensal activities in the public ceremonies that made Tiwanaku into a regional political-religious powerhouse, Janusek and colleagues have argued that the majority of ash pits were generated to dispose of the vast quantities of organic garbage generated by these characteristically Tiwanaku consumption events. The scale of these events reinforced the scale of ash pits themselves: individual ash pits may extend up to several meters across and up to five meters deep, with as much as 40–50 percent of the surface area of residential sectors comprising zones of secondary deposition such as ash pits (Janusek 2003a, 2004, 2009; Roddick and Janusek 2011). In short, the smoke that resulted from the fires that produced these massive features would have indeed lingered well into the night.

At least as vital to the production of a nighttime urban ecology was the ubiquity of water in the city center, which produced what we term a "mist envelope." Like other well-known New World cities—Tenochtitlan, Cusco, Chimor—Tiwanaku prominently incorporated major water features into its urban design. Some of these features served for ritual effect, such as the booming sound of rainy-season waters rushing through the subsurface canals of the Akapana platform, replicating the sacred mountains that were the cosmic source of life-giving water (Kolata 2003). But they also served pragmatic engineering functions, such as subterranean canal systems that stabilized the ground beneath heavy monumental architecture (Ortloff and Janusek 2014).

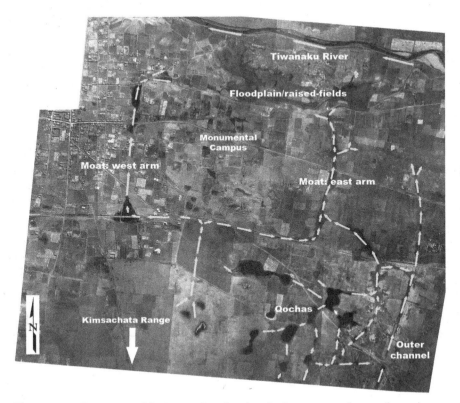

FIGURE 5.7. *Reconstructed Perimeter Canal and major interconnected water features at Tiwanaku. Image: Adapted from Janusek and Bowen (2018).*

Tiwanaku, in short, comprised a complex telluric waterscape in which the intertwined pragmatic and cosmic qualities of water underwrote the earthly prestige and power of the city (Janusek and Bowen 2018).

Here, we draw attention to open-air components of hydraulic systems that would have generated Tiwanaku's "mist envelope." Among such open-air features are *qochas*, or sunken basins, which were clustered predominantly in the residential sectors south of the northeast monumental campus. These served as sources of water for humans and camelids, especially the large flocks of llamas and alpacas that would have accompanied traders and pilgrims traveling to the city (Flores Ochoa 1987). Other features include extensive raised-field agricultural systems, including those located at the north edge of the northeast monumental campus, which pair raised agricultural beds with water-filled swales or channels. In the frigid, high-altitude climate, these water features produce misty "heat envelopes" of evaporated water that are characterized by slightly higher temperatures and serve to protect crops from frost, one of the great agricultural scourges of the altiplano (Kolata and Ortloff 2003).

A third factor contributing to nighttime mist was the massive, open water feature that surrounded the northeast monumental campus (figure 5.7). The nature of this feature has been the subject of much debate, with earlier archaeologists describing it as a defensive feature or a means to spatially demarcate elite precincts, as captured by the earlier term "moat" (Posnansky 1945; Kolata 1993). Janusek's recent research with collaborators (Ortloff and Janusek 2014; Janusek and Bowen 2018), along with complementary remote sensing studies by other teams (Lasaponara and Masini 2014), suggest that the term "perimeter canal" better conveys the principal function of this feature, which moved water slowly but methodically around the monumental complex. Intricate, interlinked canal systems, which articulated with the qochas on the south side of the city, directed water into the Perimeter Canal, which was ultimately fed by springs and streams originating in the foothills of the Kimsachata mountain range to the south. Ultimately, the Perimeter Canal channeled water into the Guaquira River along the north edge of Tiwanaku. Along the way, this system of rivers, canals, and qochas underwrote abundant urban productive systems—essentially "urban farms."

What would this system have added to nighttime ecology and experience? The amount of water moving through Tiwanaku's monumental hydraulic network, at least during the wet season (December–March), likely would have kept the city and its inhabitants several degrees warmer, as water evaporated out of the open canals, qochas, and raised fields to generate their own "mist envelopes" comparable to those produced by raised field systems. In combination with the "smoke envelope" generated at night by urban fires, the vivid celestial clarity characteristic of Tiwanaku's night sky today—and which motivated much of the design of the ceremonial core (Benítez 2013; Vranich 2016; Vranich and Smith 2018)—may have been significantly compromised by urban smoke and mist, at least at certain times of the year. At the same time, the streets and ordinary public spaces of Tiwanaku were at these times likely enriched by dense atmospheric effects that played on multiple senses—temperature, smell, sight, humidity—fluctuating temporally with the ebb and flow of the natural seasons (rainy and dry) and ritual calendars, as pilgrims periodically swelled the residential population.

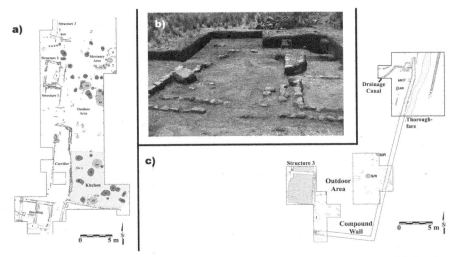

FIGURE 5.8. *Excavated household compounds in Tiwanaku's residential sectors:* (a) *South Compound of Akapana East 1;* (b) *Structure 6 in Akapana East;* (c) *Akapana East 1M. Drawing: John Wayne Janusek.*

INSIDE TIWANAKU'S DWELLING SPACES

Tiwanaku was home to a year-round population of perhaps as many as 10,000–30,000 by around 800 CE (Janusek 2009, 159), and much of the urban landscape was made up of residential sectors. In this section, we move indoors, out of the frigid altiplano air, to consider what nighttime was like in the "safe" dwelling spaces of humans that frightening and powerful nonhuman beings could not access.

Tiwanaku's monumental architectural complexes were surrounded by residential sectors that extended up to and beyond the site's Perimeter Canal and shared a common cardinal orientation across the city. The spatial organization of residential sectors varied somewhat across the city, perhaps in accordance with variation in regional or ethnic identity or by the economic focus of certain neighborhoods (Janusek 2004, 2009). At much of the site, though, residential space was organized into multi-household compounds that were bounded by small canals or large adobe walls (figure 5.8). Each compound included multiple households—comparable to residential organization in many contemporary Aymara and Quechua communities of the Andean highlands—and contained a variety of structures within the compound wall, such as kitchens, ancillary structures, patios, storage areas, wells, trash middens, and, in some cases, areas dedicated to specialized production. Compound and structure walls typically consisted of adobe bricks or *tapia* (packed-earth) blocks that rested on cobble foundations. Many of these walls were probably made out of the same clay that was quarried out of adjacent soils to form the amorphous pits that would later be filled with ashy refuse. In other words, residential space should be understood as part of Tiwanaku's broader urban ecology.

A significant conclusion of Janusek's studies of Tiwanaku housing was that most structures within these residential compounds cannot be definitely termed "dwellings" in the sense of a building dedicated to continuous habitation and daily activity (Janusek 2003a, 2004, 2009). Rather, many excavated structures in the residential compounds appear to have served as temporary residences for people who visited Tiwanaku for key ceremonial events, including family, friends, or ritual kin who came to stay there temporarily, many, perhaps, to help out during the "crunch" times that major ceremonial events would have demanded—for instance, by cooking food, brewing beer, crafting pottery vessels, and so on.

As in contemporary Aymara households, many key daily activities and specialized practices probably took place instead in the spacious outdoor patios of residential compounds. Ceramic assemblages from these spaces typically reveal high proportions of vessels for storing, fermenting, and serving food and chicha. Serving vessels invariably include Tiwanaku's iconic *keros*, or drinking goblets, along with *tazones*, shorter, concave (or hyperboloid) vessels, which were used to serve stews, soups, and other relatively solid foods. Residential structures, in contrast to shared patio spaces, were comparatively small overall, and included constricted kitchens with one or more hearths that were located next to spaces for indoor consumption and sleep. Anyone who has been inside an adobe home with a thatch roof on a brisk altiplano night, while the hearth is still burning, knows that these are warm, intimate places.

Indoor structures and nearby trash middens in residential compounds revealed remarkably high frequencies of a pottery type that remains understudied. This is the *sahumador* (or *sahumerio*), a concave vessel, often with paired handles partway down the exterior wall, which typically bears evidence for interior burning (figure 5.9). The walls of these vessels consist of a thick, soft, coarse paste that was mixed with mica and other mineral inclusions; like cooking vessels, these qualities enabled vessels to expand and contract to prevent cracking. *Sahumadores*, too, are characterized by ring-shaped raised or "false" bases that elevated the bottom interior surface of the vessel above the ground surface. This feature would have enabled the vessel to be set down on indoor surfaces such as textiles, straw, etc., without fear of flammability (Janusek 2003b). Chemical residue studies demonstrate that the interiors

FIGURE 5.9. (a) *Unburnished, undecorated sahumador.* (b) *Red-slipped, decorated sahumador.* (c) *Effigy* incensario *representing a feline.* (d) *Large* mechachua. (e, f) *Detail of raised base of unslipped sahumador and effigy incensario. Photos: John Wayne Janusek.*

of sahumadores were characterized by high lipid content indicative of some greasy substance that would have held a wick, potentially plant resins or camelid fat (Tschopik 1950; Marchbanks 1991)—either one of which would have embedded the use of sahumadores into the broader urban ecology of camelid or plant management.

Sahumadores come in two varieties in domestic contexts: an unslipped, undecorated variant with a brown to brownish-orange paste, and a decorated variant characterized by a red-slipped, burnished exterior, light brown paste, and painted designs on the exterior (figure 5.9a, b). These designs commonly comprise a ring of hollow or dotted white circles along the exterior of the false base, along with brightly colored iconography that depicts either geometric motifs or, more commonly, avian (condor or eagle) imagery, particularly focused on the wing (Janusek 2003b). It is tempting to suggest that undecorated sahumadores served largely as lamps while red-slipped vessels depicting avian wings or other iconography served largely as ritual burners. Yet such a categorization is likely too rigid, since high relative quantities of both variants are common in Tiwanaku residential compounds. This distribution suggests that both types frequently served a more mundane—what we might term "pragmatic"—purpose as lamps.

A much better-known form of burning vessel—animal-effigy *incensarios*—helps to clarify some of the interpretive differences involved here. Effigy incensarios consist of concave vessels fitted with modeled elements, usually a head and a tail on opposite sides of the rim, or in some cases a head bursting out from the side, which are in the form of camelids, felines (pumas or spotted lowland cats), or avians (eagles or condors) (Janusek 2003b) (figure 5.9c). In one variant of this form, the vessel is more extensively modeled, with the body crafted in the form of the animal's body itself, rather than the simpler concave vessel form. Like sahumadores, incensarios nearly always demonstrate clear evidence for interior burning, and they likewise share technical and formal attributes, including heat-resistant pastes and the incorporation of a false base (figure 5.9e, f). Unlike sahumadores, however, incensarios have been recovered primarily from mortuary—not residential—contexts, and most have been found at sites outside of Tiwanaku itself, especially islands in Lake Titicaca and sites adjacent to it, such as Lukurmata (Janusek 2003b, 2004).

The extreme elaboration of incensarios and their nearly exclusive association with mortuary contexts contrast with the decorative variability and the more extensive distribution of sahumadores in Tiwanaku residential contexts. Both forms of burners likely served the intertwined roles of purification and lighting in their respective contexts, but, in line with the emphasis of this volume on lychnology, we suggest that sahumadores are best characterized as lamps that were relied on to illuminate and heat Tiwanaku houses and patios at night and on a regular basis. This use does not mean they had no ritual purpose: rather, it is likely that they took on the roles of ritual purification and sensory transformation, likely when they were used to burn strong-smelling resins at notable moments in the life of the household compound. Rather than locating a ritual/quotidian divide in the distinction between sahumadores and incensarios, or between undecorated and decorated sahumadores, this form of vessel invites us to reconsider that these distinctions—like so many others commonly employed in archaeological studies of the household (public/private, male/female, production/reproduction, etc.)—are contextually generated. Indeed, it was perhaps precisely *because* sahumadores served such a central, everyday function of generating light, warmth, and domestic affect that they were able to periodically take on a more salient role in household ritual practice.

INTO TIWANAKU'S SUNKEN COURTS

Finally, we move outside the warm earthen dwelling spaces, through the smoky, misty roads that divided urban compounds, and toward Tiwanaku's inner sancta: the sunken courts associated with its well-known, monumental platform complexes such as Pumapunku, Akapana, and the Kalasasaya. Apart from constituting the center of a prestigious and potent sociopolitical center, Tiwanaku was a center of pilgrimage and social gathering. Its monumental sunken courts were central to this function, and the most prestigious events that they hosted likely took place at night.

As Alexei Vranich and Scott C. Smith (2018) discuss in their contribution to the preceding night volume (Gonlin and Nowell 2018), Tiwanaku's sunken courts were aligned to major celestial and lunar events, following traditions that had previously characterized other political-ritual centers of the South Titicaca Basin during the Late Formative Period (100 BCE–500 CE). At Tiwanaku, the Sunken Temple—located just to the east of the Kalasasaya platform (figure 5.2)—was oriented to facilitate visual linkages with the southern celestial pole rising above the sacred Mt. Kimsachata, along with the heliacal rise of night-time constellations, namely, the *yacana* constellation, comprising a llama and her calf (Benítez 2013). A similarly intensive engagement with nighttime celestial events was apparent at the nearby site of Khonkho Wankane, which constituted Tiwanaku's pair in terms of religious and political influence during the Late Formative. Khonkho Wankane was located directly south of Tiwanaku, and movement into and through its own sunken court was likewise oriented to the southern celestial pole (Vranich and Smith 2018).

In the case of Tiwanaku, the construction of the Akapana platform around 600 CE—precisely as Tiwanaku was emerging as the major political center in the South Titicaca Basin—blocked the view from the Sunken Temple to the southern celestial pole, Mt. Kimsachata, and Khonkho Wankane (Vranich and Smith 2018). The simultaneous construction of new monumental features on an east-west orientation instead fostered a new emphasis on solar movements and observations, including solstice-setting places to the west (Kolata 2003). Nevertheless, north-south celestial orientations were maintained through the construction of a new feature, the "Andesite Corridor." This corridor ran between the western face of the Kalasasaya platform and the Putuni Palace and was dramatically faced with monumental ashlars of volcanic stone. The Andesite Corridor produced a new and direct visual line of sight to Mt. Kimsachata and the southern pole, effectively reinstituting celestial orientations that had been significant during the Formative Period, and re-educating observers' attention to major components of the land- and skyscape (Janusek and Bowen 2018; Janusek 2019). Clearly, nighttime movements, rituals, and landscape engagements remained critical to Tiwanaku's program throughout its history.

The function of Tiwanaku's sunken courts as celestial and lunar viewing-theaters clearly affirms their nocturnal orientation. Yet we argue that their most dramatic function was not premised on what could be *seen from* these spaces, but rather what *took place within* them. Sunken temples were Tiwanaku's inner sancta, the places in which communal rituals occurred during major religious events. Of course, this is not to say that all pilgrims entered these spaces, and likely many remained outside due to formal proscriptions or due to fear; certainly in the case of the later pilgrimage center and oracular shrine of Pachacamac, on Peru's Central Coast, entrance required lengthy periods of fasting, offering, and preparation and was not permitted to all (Cobo 1990).

In the case of Tiwanaku's sunken courts, these enclosed spaces were rendered as highly charged sancta as a result of the objects—or, better put, the *beings*—who inhabited them. For people of ancient Tiwanaku, these beings were embodied in the massive anthropomorphic sculptures that we maintain were at the center of Tiwanaku's sociopolitical and ritual programs. It was the chance to engage these beings by rendering offerings, requesting favors, singing hymns, and, so on that ultimately brought pilgrims, diplomats, and other visitors to Tiwanaku. These are the same sculpted figures that, as described previously, are still encountered as living beings in the town of Tiahuanaco today—even as such encounters have become less common following the introduction of electric lighting. The nature of these figures as animate beings was even more central to their social role in the pre-Columbian past.

The most imposing monoliths are what we term "presentation monoliths" (Guengerich and Janusek 2020). There are five, and—unlike other types of monolith—they were all restricted in their geographical distribution to the site of Tiwanaku itself, likely to monumental structures or other key spaces key to the civic structure of the city. The Sunken Temple was home to the largest of Tiwanaku's presentation monoliths, the Bennett Monolith, a sandstone behemoth seven meters in height that, like all presentation monoliths, was entirely covered in intricate iconography. Presentation monoliths are defined by their posture, with their arms clasped tightly to their chest, in which they hold two objects that are generally interpreted as a kero, or drinking goblet, and a tablet for ingesting hallucinogenic snuff (Torres 2001) (figure 5.3). These mind-altering substances were central to the experience and the prestige of Tiwanaku, as pilgrims collectively encountered the monumental spaces of the site through different phenomenological, affective, and ontological registers (Janusek 2008, 2016; Bandy 2013). Intriguingly, presentation monoliths are consistently represented with two left hands (figure 5.3c). Following analogies with later drinking practices of the Inka nobility (Cummins 2002), who exchanged vessels with their inferiors with their left hands, and with their superiors with their right hands, this unusual depiction may indicate the nature of presentation monoliths as the ultimate hosts, whose beneficence was so all-encompassing that it rendered them categorically unable to act as inferiors to any other beings (cf. Bandy 2013). In sum, we interpret presentation

FIGURE 5.10. (a) *The Suñawa Monolith, a well-preserved extended-arm monolith.* (b) *Basalt* chachapuma *recovered at the base of the western entrance to the Akapana platform. Photos: John Wayne Janusek.*

monoliths as great ancestral personages who invited human persons to the ritual events over which they presided, guiding them to become "Tiwanaku subjects" in all the benefits and commitments that this process entailed.

Presentation monoliths were accompanied by a variety of other beings who dramaturgically complemented their leading role in the ceremonies that took place in Tiwanaku's sunken courts. At least two presentation monoliths were likely flanked by pairs of straight-armed, male-bodied guardians or attendants that we (Guengerich and Janusek 2020) refer to as "extended-arm monoliths" (figure 5.10a). These monoliths are characterized by large hands, and in one case by weapon iconography, and they hold their arms tightly clasped to their side in a disciplined posture, as if at attention and poised to act or protect. A third category of monoliths, known as *chachapumas*, was also associated with Tiwanaku's sunken courts. These figures were typically emplaced in pairs at the monumental portals through which these spaces were entered. Unlike the other monoliths, chachapumas are anthropozoomorphic and may be described as "were-felines" or "were-llamas" distinguished by their snarling expressions and menacing fangs (figure 5.10b). They are portrayed in a crouched posture, clutching an axe in one hand and a decapitated head in the other (Ponce Sanginés 1971, 81–86; Sagárnaga and Korpisaari 2007; Kolata 2003, 192–194), probably depicting the same kind of being that, in two-dimensional iconography, is commonly known as "the Decapitator" (Berenguer 2000, 32; Sagárnaga and Korpisaari 2007).

We argue that extended-arm monoliths and chachapumas were apprehended as a set of animate beings embodied in lithic form, who reinforced the proper forms of ritual action required for an encounter with the presentation monoliths who presided over the ceremonies in sunken courts (Janusek 2019; Guengerich and Janusek 2020). In other words, the presentation monoliths were not simply great ancestral hosts; they were demanding hosts. *They wanted one's subjectivity,* and the extended-arm monoliths and chachapumas may have provided the muscle, as it were, to ensure that this demand was met. Like nighttime encounters with nonhuman persons in the town of Tiahuanaco today, entry into Tiwanaku's sunken temples, especially when in a liminal, mind-altered state, would have been dramatic—in short, scary.

Archaeological assemblages provide further detail of the sensory qualities of these moments of human-nonhuman encounter. Numerous sahumadores have been recovered from sunken courtyards and their surrounding platforms; these represent a distinct subtype of sahumador, known as a *mechachua* (figure 5.9d), which is rare in residential contexts at Tiwanaku and not found outside of the city (Janusek 2003b). Unlike other types of sahumadores, mechachuas were fitted with an internal, hollow ceramic post, which in some cases formed a separate component and in other cases was fixed to the base of the vessel. These central posts served to hold a wick and the fluid or resin that fueled it. The largest mechachuas, with rims ranging from thirty to fifty centimeters in diameter, are known exclusively from Tiwanaku ceremonial contexts, primarily from Carlos Ponce Sanginés's excavations of the Kerikala area in the 1960s (Ponce 1961). Medium-sized mechachuas, with rims ranging fourteen to thirty centimeters in diameter, have been found in other Tiwanaku ceremonial contexts, as well as in nearby residential sectors such as Putuni and Akapana East (Couture and Sampeck 2003; Janusek 2003b, 70–71).

Although the archaeological methods of Ponce's excavations in the early to mid-twentieth century do not allow for precise reconstruction of their original location, the general association of large mechachuas with Tiwanaku's monumental ceremonial spaces allows us to imagine that these items were placed around the bases of the massive presentation monoliths, and of their attendants and the threatening chachapumas who guarded entrance to these spaces. The flickering flames from the massive mechachuas would have lit them up from below, affording chiaroscuro-like effects of light and animacy to the great stone ancestors. Today, in Aymara rituals celebrated at Tiwanaku and Khonkho Wankane, such as the annual June solstice or the Aymara New Year, modern burners are similarly placed around offering tables and under ancient monoliths to create analogous, dramatic ritual effects.

Tiwanaku's monoliths, which were quarried from limestone and andesite from sacred mountains—such as Ccapia and Kimsachata—semiotically indexed and materially embodied the greater Titicaca landscape. As pilgrims and devotees came into the sunken courts to engage the lithic-bodied ancestors during nighttime encounters, they formed part of a broader network of ecological relationships that expanded out far beyond the confines of the city or its ceremonial core. These spaces were exquisitely engineered to shape the experience of human participants and—through flame, shadow, and sky—to make it quite clear that, here, they were bodily encountering other types of living and powerful beings. At the same time, through celestial viewing and the lithic materiality of monoliths, they also reinforced the relationship of these spaces and these beings to Tiwanaku's surrounding landscape.

CONCLUSIONS

If dramatic encounters and embodied, sensory experiences were core to Tiwanaku's prestige and power, then it is essential to recognize the nocturnal nature of some of the most significant of these events. Although solar associations and diurnal activities gained prominence in the ceremonial life of the city after 600 CE, they never eclipsed the primacy of lunar, celestial, and nocturnal activities (cf. Vranich and Smith 2018). Principal components of the urban landscape—namely, the sunken courts at the heart of the monumental campuses—were expressly designed to facilitate nighttime experiences, and they relied on key props such as enormous mechachuas to enhance this experience. A nocturnal perspective sheds light on how other aspects of the city's urban ecology were experienced, too, especially those that were not designed with the express intent of manipulating the senses. Humble sahumadores—both homely brown ones and brightly colored, visually striking ones—brought warmth and well-being to people in their households on a nightly basis through both ordinary use and through special, ritual events. And for those who ventured outdoors at night, the watery expanses of the city and the smoke leftover from fires lit to dispose of trash altered the quality of the air, perhaps rendering slightly less visible the stars that were so central to the activities taking place in the ceremonial core nearby. All these lines of archaeological evidence—ash pits, canals, ceramics, residues, and architecture—help to clarify what dark was like for the diverse people who came together at Tiwanaku. Nighttime was full of life and activity, but—as it is now—it was also full of living beings whose presence was not always benign.

Acknowledgments (Anna Guengerich). I would like to thank volume editors Nan Gonlin and Meghan Strong for graciously working with me to make possible the publication of this chapter, which was the last that John, my spouse and colleague, drafted, and which pulls together many strands of his far-ranging and long-lasting research career at Tiwanaku. Those who knew John also knew that night was his favorite time. I am certain that he would wish to extend thanks to his Aymara collaborators and friends at Tiwanaku and at Qhunqhu Liqiliqi who introduced him over the course of his research to the events and goings-on—auspicious and otherwise—that take place on the Altiplano after dark. I would also like to thank Alexei Vranich for reading and providing feedback on this piece prior to review, as well as the anonymous reviewers who contributed during the revision process.

REFERENCES

Allen, Catherine. 2009. "Let's drink together, my dear: Persistent Ceremonies in a Changing Community." In *Drink, Power, and Society in the Andes*, edited by Justin Jennings and Brenda Bowser, 28–48. Gainesville: University of Florida Press.

Bandy, Matthew. 2013. "Tiwanaku Origins and Early Development: The Political and Moral Economy of a Hospitality State." In *Advances in Titicaca Basin Archaeology II*, edited by Alexei Vranich and Abigail Levine, 135–150. Los Angeles: Cotsen Institute of Archaeology at UCLA.

Benítez, Leonardo. 2013. "What Would Celebrants See? Sky, Landscape, and Settlement Planning in the Late Formative Southern Titicaca Basin." In *Advances in Titicaca Basin Archaeology II*, edited by Alexei Vranich and Abigail Levine, 89–104. Los Angeles: Cotsen Institute of Archaeology at UCLA.

Berenguer, José. 2000. *Tiwanaku: Lords of the Sacred Lake*. Santiago: Banco Santiago/Museo Chileno de Arte Precolombino, Santiago.

Canessa, Andrew. 1993. "The Politics of Pacha: The Conflict of Values in an Andean Community," Unpublished PhD diss., London School of Economics and Political Science, London.

Cobo, Bernabé. 1990. *Inca Religion and Customs*. Translated by R. Hamilton, foreword by J. Rowe. Austin: University of Texas Press.

Couture, N., and K. Sampeck. 2003. "Putuni: A history of Palace Architecture in Tiwanaku." In *Tiwanaku and Its Hinterland: Archaeology and Paleoecology of an Andean Civilization*. Vol. 2, edited by Alan Kolata, 226–263. Washington, DC: Smithsonian Institute.

Cummins, Tom. 2002. *Toasts with the Inca: Andean Abstraction and Colonial Images on Quero Vessels*. Ann Arbor: University of Michigan Press.

Diener Ojeda, Pablo, ed. 1992. *Rugendas: América de punto a cabo. Rugendas y la Araucanía*. Santiago: Editorial Alena.

Flores Ochoa, Jorge. 1987. "Cultivation in the Qocha of the South Andean Puna." In *Arid Land Use Strategies and Risk Management in the Andes: A Regional Anthropological Perspective*, edited by David L. Browman, 271–296. Boulder, CO: Westview Press.

French, Kirk D., Kirk D. Straight, and Elijah J. Hermitt. 2020. "Building the Environment at Palenque: The Sacred Pools of the Picota Group." *Ancient Mesoamerica* 31 (3): 409–430.

Goldstein, Paul. 2000. "Communities without Borders: The Vertical Archipelago and Diaspora Communities in the Southern Andes." In *The Archaeology of Communities: A New World Perspective*, edited by Marcello Canuto and Jason Yaeger, 182–209. Routledge: London.

Gonlin, Nancy, and April Nowell. 2018. "Introduction to the Archaeology of the Night." In *Archaeology of the Night: Life After Dark in the Ancient World*, edited by Nancy Gonlin and April Nowell, 5–24. Boulder: University Press of Colorado.

Guengerich, Anna, and John Wayne Janusek. 2020. "The Suñawa Monolith and a genre of extended-arm sculptures at Tiwanaku." *Ñawpa Pacha* 41 (1): 19–46.

Isbell, William, and Alexei Vranich. 2004. "Experiencing the Cities of Wari and Tiwanaku." In *Andean Archaeology*, edited by H. Silverman, 167–182. Malden, MA: Blackwell.

Isendahl, Christian. 2012. "Agro-urban Landscapes: The Example of Maya Lowland Cities." *Antiquity* 86 (334): 1112–1125.

Janusek, John Wayne. 2003a. "The Changing Face of Tiwanaku Residential Life: State and Social Identity in an Andean city." In *Tiwanaku and Its Hinterland: Archaeology and Paleoecology of an Andean Civilization*. Vol. 2, edited by Alan Kolata, 264–295. Washington, DC: Smithsonian Institute.

Janusek, John Wayne. 2003b. "Vessels, Time, and Society: Toward a Chronology of Ceramic Style in the Tiwanaku Heartland." In *Tiwanaku and Its Hinterland: Archaeology and Paleoecology of an Andean Civilization*. Vol. 2, edited by Alan Kolata, 30–92. Washington, DC: Smithsonian Institute.

Janusek, John Wayne. 2004. *Identity and Power in the Ancient Andes: Tiwanaku Cities through Time*. London: Routledge.

Janusek, John Wayne. 2006. "The Changing 'Nature' of Tiwanaku Religion and the Rise of an Andean state." *World Archaeology* 38 (3): 469–492.

Janusek, John Wayne. 2008. *Ancient Tiwanaku*. Cambridge: Cambridge University Press.

Janusek, John Wayne. 2009. "Residence and Ritual in Tiwanaku: Hierarchy, Specialization, Ethnicity, and Ceremony." In *Domestic Life in Prehispanic Capitals: A Study of Specialization, Hierarchy, and Ethnicity*, edited by Linda Manzanilla and Claude Chapdelaine, 149–169. Ann Arbor: Michigan Museum of Anthropology, University of Michigan.

Janusek, John Wayne. 2012. "Incipient Urbanism at the Early Andean Center of Khonkho Wankane, Bolivia." *Journal of Field Archaeology* 40 (2): 127–142.

Janusek, John Wayne. 2015. "Understanding Tiwanaku Origins: Animistic Ecology in the Andean Altiplano." In *The Past Ahead: Language, Culture, and Identity in the Neotropics*, edited by Christian Isendahl, 111–138. Uppsala, Sweden: Uppsala University Department of Archaeology and History.

Janusek, John Wayne. 2016. "Processions, Ritual Movements, and the Ongoing Production of Pre-Columbian Societies with a Perspective from Tiwanaku." In *Processions in the Ancient Americas*, edited by Susan T. Evans, 1–26. *Occasional Papers in Anthropology* 33. University Park: Pennsylvania State University.

Janusek, John Wayne. 2019. "Assembling Tiwanaku: Water and Stone, Humans and Monoliths." In *New Materialisms Ancient Urbanisms*, edited by Timothy Pauketat and Susan Alt, 94–129. London: Routledge.

Janusek, John Wayne, and Corey Bowen. 2018. "Tiwanaku as Tectonic Waterscape: Water and Stone in a Highland Andean City." In *Powerful Landscapes*, edited by Justin Jennings and Edward Swenson, 209–246. Albuquerque: University of New Mexico Press.

Janusek, John Wayne, and Alan Kolata. 2004. "Top-Down or Bottom-Up: Rural Settlement and Raised-Field Agriculture in the Lake Titicaca Basin, Bolivia." *Journal of Anthropological Archaeology* 23 (4): 404–430.

Kolata, Alan. 1993. *The Tiwanaku*. New York: Blackwell.

Kolata, Alan. 2003. "Tiwanaku Ceremonial Architecture and Urban Organization." In *Tiwanaku and Its Hinterland: Archaeology and Paleoecology of a Native Andean*

Civilization. Vol. 2, edited by Alan Kolata, 175–201. Washington, DC: Smithsonian Institution.

Kolata, Alan, and Charles Ortloff. 2003. "Tiwanaku Raised-Field Agriculture in the Lake Titicaca Basin of Bolivia." In *Tiwanaku and Its Hinterland: Archaeology and Paleoecology of a Native Andean Civilization.* Vol. 1, edited by Alan Kolata, 109–152. Washington, DC: Smithsonian Institution.

Lasaponara, Rosa, and Nicola Masini. 2014. "Beyond Modern Landscape Features: New Insights in the Archaeological Area of Tiwanaku in Bolivia from Satellite Data." *International Journal of Applied Earth Observation and Geoinformation* 26 (2014): 464–471.

Marchbanks, Michael. 1991. "Organic Residue Analysis of Tiwanaku Ceramics: Preliminary Results." Manuscript in the research archives of the Proyecto Wila Jawira, Department of Anthropology, University of Chicago.

Ortloff, Charles, and John Wayne Janusek. 2014. "Hydraulic Engineering of the Tiwanaku." In *Encyclopedia of the History of Science, Technology, and Medicine in Non-Western Cultures,* edited by Helaine Selin, 2267–2281. Heidelberg, Germany: Springer-Verlag.

Ponce Sanginés, Carlos. 1961. "Informe de labores." La Paz: Centro de Investigaciones Arqueológicas en Tiwanaku, Publicación 1.

Ponce Sanginés, Carlos. 1971. "Examen arqueológico de las ruinas precolombinas de Pumapunku." In *Procedencia de las areniscas utilizadas en el tempo precolombino de Pumapunku,* edited by Carlos Ponce Sanginés, Arturo Castaños Echazu, Waldo Ávila Salinas, and Fernando Urquidi Barrau, 13–205. La Paz: Academia Nacional de Ciencias de Bolivia.

Posnansky, Arthur. 1945. *Tiahuanacu: The Cradle of Andean Man.* New York: J. J. Agustin.

Roddick, Andrew, and John Wayne Janusek. 2011. "From Profanity to Profundity: (Grudgingly) Learning to Appreciate Tiwanaku 'Ash Pits' as Tiwanaku Cultural Practice." Paper presented at the fifty-first annual meeting of the Institute for Andean Studies, University of California-Berkeley, January 7.

Sagárnaga, Jedu, and Antti Korpisaari. 2007. "Hallazgos en la Isla de Pariti echan nuevas luces sobre los 'chachapumas' tiwanakotas." *Chachapuma: Revista de Arqueología Bolivia* 2: 5–28.

Schaedel, Richard. 1948. "Monolithic sculpture of the Southern Andes." *Archaeology* 1 (2): 66–73.

Sillar, William. 2000. "Dung by Preference: The Choice of Fuel as an Example of How Andean Pottery Production Is Embedded within Wider Technical, Social, and Economic Practices." *Archaeometry* 42 (1): 43–60.

Torres, Constantino. 2001. "Iconografía Tiwanaku en la parafernalia inhalatoria de los Andes centro-sur." *Boletín de Arqueología PUCP* 5: 427–454.

Tschopik, Harry. 1946. "The Aymara." In *The Andean Civilizations: Handbook of South American Indians*. Vol. 2, edited by Julian Stewart, 501–573. Washington, DC: Smithsonian Institution.

Tschopik, Harry. 1950. "An Andean Ceramic Tradition in Historical Perspective." *American Antiquity* 15 (3): 196–219.

Vranich, Alexei. 1999. "Interpreting the Meaning of Ritual Spaces: The Temple Complex of Pumapunku, Tiwanaku, Bolivia." Unpublished PhD diss., University of Pennsylvania, Philadelphia.

Vranich, Alexei. 2016. "Monumental Perception of the Tiwanaku Landscape." In *Political Landscapes of Capital Cities*, edited by Jessica Joyce Christie, Jelena Bogdanović, and Eulogio Guzmán, 181–211. Boulder: University Press of Colorado.

Vranich, Alexei, and Scott C. Smith. 2018. "Nighttime Sky and Early Urbanism in the High Andes: Architecture and Ritual in the Southern Lake Titicaca Basin during the Formative and Tiwanaku Periods." In *Archaeology of the Night: Life After Dark in the Ancient World*, edited by Nancy Gonlin and April Nowell, 121–138. Boulder: University Press of Colorado.

Wachtel, Nathan. 1994. *Gods and Vampires: Return to Chipaya*. Translated by C. Volk. Chicago: University of Chicago Press.

6

As the sun set on the horizon, ancient city dwellers would have felt the cooler air, heard cicadas' songs, and perhaps tasted a late-night snack (figure 6.1). Their vision, however, would have diminished as dusk turned to darkness and some form of illumination was necessary to see others, carry on activities, or get to bed. Yet once the sun fully set, nature provided other sources of light: what ancient Maya elites referred to as Uh and Ek'ob: the moon and stars (figures 6.2a, 6.2b). The ancient Mayas are well known for creating some of the most complex Indigenous societies of the Americas. Particularly during the Classic period, from 250 CE to 900 CE, large cities supporting tens of thousands of people rose and declined (figure 6.3a). The Classic Mayas (figure 1.1) inhabited the neotropics of Mexico, Guatemala, Belize, Honduras, and El Salvador, but they were never unified into a single empire or over-arching state (Sharer and Traxler 2005; Martin 2020). Maya hieroglyphs are now largely deciphered and add to the immense amount of archaeology that has taken place in this part of the world (e.g., Coe and Van Stone 2005; Martin and Grube 2008; Houston and Inomata 2009; Martin 2020). The ancient Mayas commonly recorded events relating to royal proceedings of deaths, births, marriages, period endings, and accessions to power. In combination with their elaborate calendars (Stuart 2020a), we present newly analyzed information that considers the moon and its perceived role in rulership. This study builds on previous research

Lunar Power in Ancient Maya Cities

Kristin V. Landau, Christopher Hernandez, and Nancy Gonlin

https://doi.org/10.5876/9781646422609.c006

FIGURE 6.1. *Sun setting over Laguna Tzi'bana, at Mensabak, Chiapas, Mexico. Photo: Christopher Hernandez.*

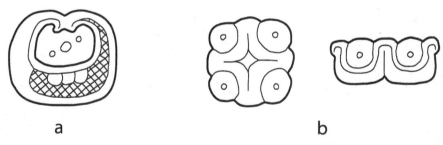

a   b

FIGURE 6.2. *Maya glyphs for* (a) *Uh (moon) and* (b) *Ek' (star). Drawings: Christopher Hernandez (after Stone and Zender 2011, 147, 151).*

that explicitly incorporates the night and darkness into archaeology to lend greater understanding of the full round of activities of everyday life (Dowd and Hensey 2016; Gonlin and Nowell 2018; Gonlin 2020a, 2020b; Gonlin and Nowell 2020; Gonlin and Reed 2021; Nowell and Gonlin 2021).

KRISTIN V. LANDAU, CHRISTOPHER HERNANDEZ, AND NANCY GONLIN

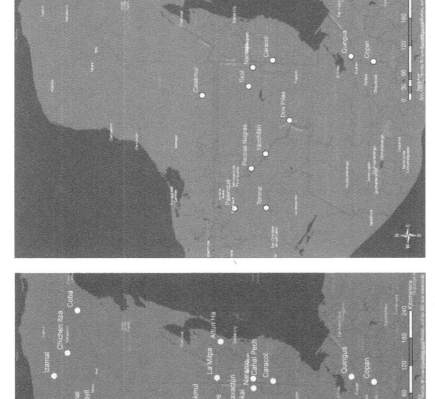

FIGURE 6.3. (a) *Map of major Classic period Maya cities.* (b) *Map of Classic period Maya cities discussed in this chapter. Maps: Kristin V. Landau.*

In this chapter, we examine how the Classic Mayas interpreted the lunar cycle. We review three models of royal authority to show how ancient rulers may have harnessed aspects of the moon to exert power. In their urban environments, these rulers performed in front of masses of followers, their contemporaries, and enemies alike to showcase their status and connection with the deities; dance was a critical part of this theatrical performance (Grube 1992; Looper 2009; Jackson 2013, 67, 74). While previous research has not identified any decisive or overriding pattern in the specific date Classic Maya rulers came to power (Martin 2020, 112), we suggest that the lunar cycle was a major consideration. Beyond the Classic period, useful information from the Postclassic period (900–1519 CE), colonial and ethnohistoric documents, and ethnographies flesh out this thesis by further contextualizing Maya practices and beliefs. Our conclusions are robustly supported by statistical analyses that complement humanistic and scientific interpretations. First, we turn to a discussion of some basic information about the moon and biological correlations that were commonly known to people in ancient times.

CLASSIC MAYA INTERPRETATIONS OF THE LUNAR CYCLE

Caught within the gravitational pull of the earth, our view of the moon is always the same side. The sunlit portion of the moon ranges from 0 percent (a "new" moon) to 100 percent (a "full" moon). As the moon waxes from new to full, it appears first as a growing crescent shape, and then as a more than half-full gibbous. At Day 15, the halfway mark, the 100 percent illuminated full moon rises just after sunset. Then it returns to gibbous form, waning into a crescent, and finally disappearing completely once again into the new moon phase (figure 6.4). This lunar cycle, called the moon's synodic period, repeats every 29.53 days, which is the same duration as the human female menstruation cycle, the fermentation period for *pulque* (a Mesoamerican alcoholic beverage made from magueys, agave plants), and the length of gestation for rabbits. The selection of these correlations is significant for understanding Mesoamerican cultures and their associations with the moon.

The ancient Mayas were one of many peoples—along with the Chinese, Japanese, various groups of Indigenous North Americans, and Mexica—who saw a "rabbit" in the moon (Aveni 2001). In the hot, humid climate of Mesoamerica, rabbits usually keep to their burrows during the daytime hours and forage at night, their daily rhythm mimicking the moon's (Milbrath 1999, 110). Producing as many as seventy-five "kittens" per year (for an average of six per litter), rabbits are one of the most fertile mammals known, an R-strategist in biological

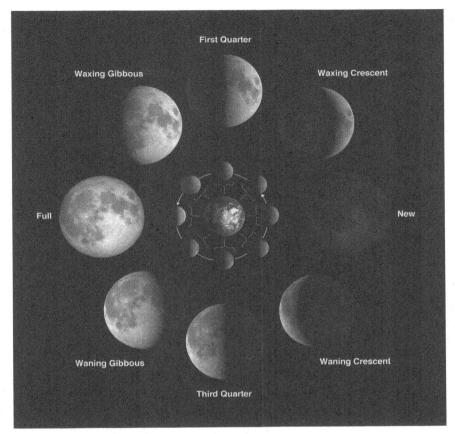

FIGURE 6.4. *The monthly lunar cycle. Photo: NASA..*

terminology. Seeing a rabbit in the moon connects astronomical and biological cycles of fertility. The three circles within the cross-hatched section of the lunar glyph (figure 6.2a) represent maize seeds, directly connecting the moon with agricultural fertility. The crescent moon was understood as a water receptacle, dumping its contents during the rainy season (Stone and Zender 2011; Hull 2020).

Many features of the Classic Maya lunar glyph derive from long-standing traditions about the Moon Goddess, who has two aspects—younger and older—representing the waxing and waning portions of the lunar cycle, respectively. She is associated with water and earth; she is considered a wife, mother, and grandmother, and is patroness of weaving, divination, pregnancy, and childbirth (Milbrath 1995; Clancy 2015). Her domain is conceived as a

FIGURE 6.5. *Copan Stela H. Line drawing. Drawing: Schele Drawing Collection at the Los Angeles County Museum of Art.*

cool, wet cave, in stark opposition to the sun, which is hot and red (Stone and Zender 2011). In Classic period monumental art, the Moon Goddess often wears a latticed or net skirt, similar to the Maize God's costume. In fact, the person represented on Stela H at the Classic city of Copan (figure 6.5) has been variously interpreted as the male Maize God, as a god or king cross-dressing, or as a female goddess (Joyce 1996; Newsome 2001; Looper 2002). The sculpture could be a merged Moon Goddess *and* Maize God, representing both female (crescent) and male (full) aspects of the moon's phases (Milbrath 1999). Lunar deities throughout Mesoamerica tended to be ambiguous in gender, perhaps mirroring the variable nature of the moon itself (Milbrath 1995). Interestingly, according to the inscription date, Stela H was erected under a full moon, when the male aspect was strongest.

Varied ideas about the moon and associated deities likely existed throughout Classic period communities. Recent advances in Maya hieroglyphic writing highlight that individual cities—such as Palenque, Mexico or La Corona, Guatemala—had their own site-specific deities that were often nuances on more widespread gods (Baron 2016). For example, Aj Kahk O' Chahk was a patron deity of Yaxchilan and a local take on Chahk, the widespread Maya rain god (Stuart 2013; Baron 2016). Understanding how deities, such as the Moon Goddess, varied across the Maya area requires further study. Nevertheless, because we are interested in how lunar power manifested across urban communities, our focus has been on establishing widespread Maya conceptions of the moon to examine how royals tapped into the urban nightscape for authority and power.

Ancient Maya scribes, priests, and rulers tracked the moon incessantly (e.g., Saturno et al. 2012). Compared to the sun, the apparent motion and cyclical changes of the moon are much more complex. Sequences of lunar cycles are helpful in predicting eclipses. The Maya dating system consists of the so-called Long Count, followed by the Calendar Round, and Lunar Series. The Long Count gives the number of days that have passed since Maya Day 0, which corresponds to the Gregorian calendar date of August 12, 3114 BCE. The Calendar Round indicates the month of the year and day of the week, just like the Gregorian calendar.

The Lunar Series consists of ten hieroglyphs recording the lunar age, how many lunar cycles already passed in the year, the number of days (twenty-nine or thirty) within the specific month, and the position of the current month within the lunar half-year or semester. Maya archaeologists and epigraphers still do not completely understand what cycle some of these glyphs are tracking or their meanings. New decipherments of glyphs associated with the Lunar Series may even provide hints on how to better correlate the Maya Long Count with our Gregorian calendar (Stuart 2020b). The Lunar Series is especially prevalent on monuments that record period endings, ruler accessions, and public rituals (Milbrath 1999, 110). It appears on media that leave open writing space, such as tall stone monuments called stelae. We consider such stone monuments as infrastructure—centrally sponsored constructions (Wilkinson 2019; chapter 1, this volume). Depending on the exact time period they were commissioned and their location throughout an ancient city, inscribed stone monuments could have functioned in any/all of Darryl Wilkinson's four categories (e.g., static, circulatory, bounding, and signaling). Since stelae are often associated with rulers and urban royal architecture, how might recording the Lunar Series relate to rulership and authority? As in other cases across the Maya area, might the association of significant political moments with astronomical events enhance meaning or the aura of power? In the following section, we consider the topic of authority and power, and its manifestation among the Classic Mayas with reference to celestial events.

MODELS OF ROYAL AUTHORITY

Returning to an anthropological classic, Max Weber (1977) classifies ruling powers into three types of authority, differentiated on the basis of legitimacy that the ruling power claims. Traditionalist authority rests in the everyday routine as an inviolable norm. Followers have a certain piety for what is, what has been, and what will always be. Stasis is safe, predictable. Rational-legal authority is centered on a system of law and impersonal legal order. Those who have the authority to enact laws likewise are subject to them. On the other hand, charismatic authority describes rule to which the governed submit because of their belief in the extraordinary quality of the specific person. The legitimacy of charismatic rule is based on magical powers, hero worship, and, ultimately, through the welfare of the governed. Its legitimacy is fundamentally unstable, since the worth of the hero must be constantly demonstrated. Weber explains that charismatic leaders do not derive their right to rule through their own will or through some sort of election; rather, it is the duty of those whom the charismatic leader addresses to recognize them as such. Charismatic leadership ebbs and flows with the support or skepticism of ordinary urban dwellers, rather than the ruler or elites themselves.

While leaders of complex societies such as those of the Mayas accessed all three types of authority, Weber's model of achieving political legitimacy through charismatic leadership has become central to archaeologists' understandings of ancient Maya states. For example, proponents of segmentary state models of political organization (Demarest 1992; Fash 1994; Fox et al. 1996; Fitzsimmons 2015) argue that Maya leaders would have been wholly dependent on theater-state ritual and ideology to legitimize their power. The critical element that transformed Maya cities from independent lineage-based factions into coherent wholes was the consistent repetition of mass theatrical events sponsored and organized by the elite (Inomata 2006, 818; Inomata and Coben 2006). The materialization of ceremonial events in the form of public monuments, such as stelae, is an effective, enduring, and unambiguous message of power (Miller and Tilley 1984; DeMarrais et al. 1996; Stuart 1996).

For example, the elaborately carved three-dimensional stelae of Copan, located in the open Great Plaza at city center, would have required expert coordination of time, labor, skill, and sacred knowledge. These stelae are about one meter wide and thick, and nearly four meters tall. Lithic raw material was first removed from a volcanic tuff quarry at the top of the surrounding mountains of the Copan valley. Large blocks were then transported downhill and possibly to a carving workshop. The artisan—with years, if not decades, of training—would have had to work closely with a scribe, priest, or ruler to lay out the design with correct calendrical information and sculptural detail. In Late Classic Copan (600–800 CE), stelae were commissioned by rulers and shaped in their likenesses (Newsome 2001). Although royal people and elites could likely read hieroglyphs, most of Copan's population probably could not (Houston 2000). When completed, perhaps a few months or years later, the intricately carved monolith would have been erected in an astronomically salient, public place (e.g., Pineda de Carias et al. 2017). In total, the elaborate carving of the massive stone block evokes Karl Marx's concept of congealed labor: an astonishment for a product based on the amount of work-time invested to produce it (Miller and Tilley 1984; Miller 2005).

However, aside from its inherent material grandeur, a stela was put into place with much ritual fanfare that aroused the senses (Houston 2006). The smell of ambient odors combined with copal, a tree resin that gives off an aromatic smoke when burned, signaled this special time. Music from instruments—rattles, trumpets, drums, whistles, flutes—heightened the spectacle. Vigorous movement of the body involving the shuffling of feet attracted supernatural onlookers (Houston 2006). A *k'altun* ceremony would have occurred, a ritual that "seated" or "bound" the stela, recalling the terminology of royal office-taking. A stela with a carved royal personage was not a *representation* of the person but an embodiment or extension of them, perpetually enacting this royal ceremony (Stuart 1996). Altogether, the crafting and placement of such monuments literally held the divine essence of rulers, substantiating their royal power.

Here we explore the functional and symbolic roles the moon played in the design of these monuments and mass theatrical events, and how the moon's station and shape were written within the glyphs of the Lunar Series. We ask: What role did the moon play in ancient Maya ceremonial events, especially those taking place in urban contexts? Were such events timed by priests and scribes to occur mainly at night, under a specific moon phase? Perhaps this timing included the practical purpose of providing natural light to see and partake in such ceremonies. Or could moonlight have lent symbolic power as well? Overall, we consider how ancient Maya rulers might have taken advantage of the nighttime, using lunar power to strengthen their authority over city dwellers. There is power in the darkness (chapter 1, this volume) that could be effectively utilized by rulers.

ANCIENT MAYA LUNAR POWER

To answer these questions, we compiled a list of eighty-four ruler accession dates at eleven major Maya cities in the Classic period (Martin and Grube 2008; Stuart and Stuart 2008; Skidmore 2010; Pitts 2011) (table 6.1). These sites were chosen (Calakmul, Caracol, Copan, Dos Pilas, Naranjo, Palenque, Piedras Negras, Quirigua, Tikal, Tonina, Yaxchilan) because their long political history offered a large number of published accession dates, and scholars widely agree on those dates (see Iwaniszewski 2008 and 2018 for more information on the moon at Yaxchilan and Naranjo, respectively). Other areas of the Maya region—for example, the northern lowlands of the Yucatán Peninsula—supported large cities with long political histories, but accession dates are fewer in number, disputed, or unpublished. In analyzing the accession dates, we first converted Long Count dates to the Gregorian calendar using the generally accepted 584,285 correlation constant (pauhatun.org). Then, we used historical lunar data to track the phase of the moon on the dates specified (moonpage.com, which in all cases aligned with Goldstine [1973]). Percent of the moon illuminated (from 0 percent new moon to 100 percent full moon) was converted to lunar day number, or the age of the moon within its 29.5-day cycle (here, Day 1 to Day 29/30). Day 1 is a new moon, Day 14–15 is a full moon, and on Day 29–30 the moon returns to new.

The eleven cities (figure 6.3b) yielded eighty-four different accession dates, the earliest in 378 CE at Piedras Negras, and the latest of 822 CE at Copan. Taken together, the preliminary research we have done establishes an ancient Maya penchant for celebrating ceremonies and royal accessions to power during new and full moons (figure 6.6). For example, on February 10, 822, Ukit Took', the intended seventeenth ruler of Copan, claimed to take power; on this day, the moon was 99.3 percent illuminated, or "full" to the human eye. Results of a Chi-squared test show that the chances of observing this trend, if ruler accessions were equally likely to occur across the lunar cycle, is basically zero ($X^2 = 69.39$, $p < 2.49 \times 10^{-9}$, $df = 14$). Also, if rulers were acceding to the throne on random lunar days, again, the likelihood of accession under a new or full moon is highly statistically significant (full moon z-score = 5.93, $p < 3.10 \times 10^{-9}$; new moon z-score = 4.61, $p < 4.11 \times 10^{-6}$). Within a 95 percent confidence interval, it is twice as likely for a ruler to come to power under a new or full moon than on any other given day. In cross-referencing these dates with solar or lunar eclipse events (Aveni and Hotaling 1994), no ruler came to power on the day of an eclipse. Perhaps they avoided acceding to power during eclipses because they were ominous times for ancient Mesoamericans (Aveni 2018). To understand what this lunar timing could have meant for Maya royalty and

TABLE 6.1. Ruler accession dates at eleven major Maya cities in the Classic period

Ruler	Name	Accession Date		Gregorian Conversion CE	% Illumin.	Phase	
Palenque							
1	K'uk' Bahlam	8.19.15.3.4	1 K'an 2 K'ayab	March 11, 431	89.76	Waxing	Gibbous
2	Ruler II ("Casper")	8.19.19.11.17	2 Kaban 10 Xul	August 10, 435	0	NEW	NEW
3	Butz'aj Sak Chihk	9.2.12.6.18	3 Etz'nab 11 Xul	July 29, 487	47.54	Waning	Crescent
4	Ahkal Mo'Nahb I	9.3.6.7.17	5 Kaban "seating of" Sots'	June 5, 501	13.62	Waxing	Crescent
5	K'an Joy Chitam	9.4.14.10.4	5 K'an 12 K'ayab	February 25, 529	2.08	NEW	NEW
6	Ahkal Mo'Nahb II	9.6.11.5.1	1 Imix 4 Zip	May 4, 565	89.05	Waning	Gibbous
7	Kan Bahlam	9.6.18.5.12	10 Eb Seating of Wo	April 8, 572	72.65	Waxing	Gibbous
8	Ix Yohl Ik'nal	9.7.10.3.8	9 Lamat 1 Muwaan	December 23, 583	12.73	Waxing	Crescent
9	Ajen Yohl Mat	9.8.11.9.10	8 Ok 18 Muwaan	January 4, 605	64.93	Waxing	Gibbous
10	Janab Pakal	Unknown					
11	Muwaan Mat	9.8.19.7.18	9 Etz'nab 6 Keh	October 22, 612	54.18	Waning	Crescent
12	K'inich Janab Pakal	9.9.2.4.8	5 Lamat 1 Mol	July 29, 615	2.93	NEW	NEW
13	K'inich Kan Bahlam	9.12.11.12.10	8 Ok 3 K'ayab	January 10, 684	92.44	Waning	Gibbous
14	K'inich K'an Joy Chitam	9.13.10.6.8	5 Lamat 6 Xul	June 3, 702	10.03	Waxing	Crescent
15	K'inich Ahkal Mo'Nahb	9.14.10.4.2	9 Ik' 5 K'ayab	January 3, 722	88.31	Waxing	Gibbous
16	Upakal K'inich Janab Pakal	Unknown					
17	K'inich Kan Bahlam II	Unknown					
18	K'inich K'uk' Bahlam	9.16.13.0.7	9 Manik 15 Wo	March 8, 764	1.42	Waxing	Crescent

continued on next page

TABLE 6.1—*continued*

Ruler	Name	Accession Date		Gregorian Conversion CE	% Illumin.	Phase	
Piedras Negras							
0	Ruler C	9.3.19.12.12	9 Eb 10 Sek	July 2, 514	35.29	Waning	Crescent
1	K'inich Yo'nal Ahk I	9.8.10.6.16	10 Kib 9 Mak	November 17, 603	61.18	Waxing	Gibbous
2	Ruler 2	9.10.6.5.9	8 Muluk 2 Sip	April 15, 639	39.13	Waxing	Crescent
3	K'inich Yo'nal Ahk II	9.12.14.13.1	7 Imix 19 Pax	January 5, 687	98.67	FULL	FULL
4	Ruler 4	9.14.18.3.13	7 Ben 16 K'ank'in	November 13, 729	91.4	Waning	Gibbous
5	Ha' K'in Xook	9.16.16.0.4	7 K'an 17 Pop	February 18, 767	100	FULL	FULL
6	Yo'nal Ahk III	9.16.6.17.1	7 Imix 19 Wo	March 14, 758	0	NEW	NEW
7	Ruler 7	9.17.10.9.4	1 K'an 7 Yaxk'in	June 4, 781	56.56	Waxing	Gibbous
Yaxchilan							
1	Yopaat Bahlam I	8.16.2.9.1?	7 Imix? 14 Sots'	July 24, 359	94.72	Waxing	Gibbous
2	Itzamnaaj Bahlam I	Unknown					
3	Bird Jaguar I	8.17.1.17.16?	2 Kib 14 Mol	October 7, 378	0	NEW	NEW
4	Yax Deer-Antler Skull	8.17.13.3.8?	4 Lamat 11 Ch'en?	October 21, 389	100	FULL	FULL
5	Ruler 5	8.18.6.5.13?	10 Ben 11 Mol	September 28, 402	98.39	FULL	FULL
6	K'inich Tatbu Skull I	Unknown					
7	Moon Skull	Unknown					
8	Bird Jaguar II	9.1.12.7.8	2 Lamat 1? Keh	October 17, 467	10.6	Waxing	Crescent
9	Knot-eye Jaguar	Unknown					
10	K'inich Tatbu Skull II	Unknown					
11	Knot-eye Jaguar II	Unknown					
12	Itzamnaaj Bahlam II	Unknown					

continued on next page

Table 6.1—*continued*

Ruler	Name	Accession Date		Gregorian Conversion CE	% Illumin.	Phase	
13	K'inich Tatbu Skull II	9.4.11.8.16	2 Kib 19 Pax	February 13, 526	100	FULL	FULL
14	Bird Jaguar III	9.9.16.10.13	9 Ben 16 Yax	September 18, 629	20.76	Waning	Crescent
15	Yopaat Bahlam II	Unknown					
16	Bird Jaguar IV	9.16.1.0.0	11 Ajaw 8 Sek	May 3, 752	100	FULL	FULL
17	Itzamnaaj Bahlam IV	Unknown					
18	K'inich Tatbu Skill IV	Unknown					
Copan							
1	K'inich Yax K'uk' Mo'	8.19.10.10.17	5 Kaban 15 Yaxk'in	September 6, 426	87.9	Waning	Gibbous
2	K'inich Popol Hol	Unknown					
3	K'ahk' ?? Ajaw	Unknown					
4	K'altuun Hix	Unknown					
5	Yu Ku ?? A	Unknown					
6	Muyal Jol ??	Unknown					
7	Bahlam Nehn (Jaguar Mirror, Water lily Jaguar)	9.4.9.17.0	5 Ajaw 8 Yaxk'in	August 6, 524	66.45	Waning	Gibbous
8	Wi'Yohl K'inich	9.4.18.6.12	8 Eb o Mak	November 24, 532	84.15	Waxing	Gibbous
9	Sak Lu	9.5.17.13.7	2 Manik' o Muwan	December 30, 551	96.24	FULL	FULL
10	Moon Jaguar	9.5.19.3.0	8 Ajaw 3 Mak	May 26, 553	2.22	NEW	NEW
11	Butz' Chan	9.7.5.0.8	8 Lamat 6 Mak	November 19, 578	25.97	Waxing	Crescent
12	K'ahk' Uti' Witz' K'awiil (Smoke Imix)	9.9.14.17.5	6 Chikchan 18 K'ayab	February 8, 628	5.83	Waning	Crescent
13	Waxaklajuun Ubaah K'awiil	9.13.3.6.8	7 Lamat 1 Mol	July 9, 695	42.97	Waning	Crescent
14	K'ahk' Joplaj Chan K'awiil	9.15.6.16.5	6 Chikchan 3 Yaxk'in	June 11, 738	72.12	Waning	Gibbous

continued on next page

TABLE 6.1—*continued*

Ruler	Name	Accession Date	Gregorian Conversion CE	% Illumin.	Phase	
15	K'ahk'Yipyaj Chan K'awiil	9.15.17.13.10	11 Ok 13 Pop	February 18, 749	13.48	Waning	Crescent
16	Yax Pasaj Chan Yopaat	9.16.12.5.17	6 Kaban 10 Mol	July 2, 763	93.23	Waning	Gibbous
17	Ukit Took'	9.19.11.14.5	3 Chikchan 3 Wo	February 10, 822	99.3	FULL	FULL
Tikal						
1	Yax Nuun Ahiin I	8.18.8.1.2	2 Ik' 10 Sip	June 18, 404	24.1	Waning	Crescent
2	Sihyaj Chan K'awiil II	8.18.15.11.0	3 Ajaw 13 Sak	November 29, 411	6.12	Waning	Crescent
3	K'an Chitam	9.1.2.17.17	4 Kaban 15 Xul	August 9, 458	97.86	FULL	FULL
4	Chak Tok Ich'aak II	Unknown					
5	Lady of Tikal	9.3.16.8.4	11 K'an 17 Pop	April 21, 511	56.56	Waxing	Gibbous
6	Kaloomte' Bahlam	Unknown					
7	Bird Claw	Unknown					
8	Wak Chan K'awiil	9.5.3.9.15	12 Men 18 K'ank'in	December 31, 537	100	FULL	FULL
9	Animal Skull	Unknown					
10	Ruler 23	Unknown					
11	Ruler 24	Unknown					
12	Nuun Ujol Chaak	Unknown					
13	Jasaw Chan K'awiil I	9.12.9.17.16	5 Kib 14 Sotz'	May 6, 682	39.56	Waning	Crescent
14	Yik'in Chan K'awiil	9.15.3.6.8	3 Lamat 6 Pax	December 12, 734	91.04	Waxing	Gibbous
15	Ruler 28	Unknown					
16	Yax Nuun Ahiin II	9.16.17.16.4	11 K'an 12 K'ayab	December 29, 768	97.17	FULL	FULL
17	Nuun Ujol K'inich	Unknown					
18	Dark Sun	Unknown					

continued on next page

Table 6.1—*continued*

Ruler	Name	Accession Date		Gregorian Conversion CE	% Illumin.	Phase	
19	Jewel K'awiil	Unknown					
20	Jasaw Chan K'awiil II	Unknown					
Dos Pilas							
1	Bajlaj Chan K'awiil	Unknown					
2	Itzamnaaj K'awiil	9.13.6.2.0	11 Ajaw 18 Wo	March 27, 698	80.72	Waxing	Gibbous
3	Ruler 3	9.14.15.5.15	9 Men 13 K'ayab	January 10, 727	96.09	FULL	FULL
4	K'awiil Chan K'inich	9.15.9.17.17	13 Kaban 20 Yaxk'in	June 27, 741	66.54	Waxing	Gibbous
5	Tahn Te' K'inich	9.16.19.0.14	5 Ix 12 Pop	February 2, 770	4.2	NEW	NEW
6	Ajaw Bot	9.17.0.0.0	13 Ajaw 18 Kumk'u	January 24, 771	13.91	Waxing	Crescent
7	Chak Lakamtuun	Unknown					
8	Lachan K'awiil Ajaw Bot	9.18.11.13.4	10 K'an 2 Xul	May 5, 802	0	NEW	NEW
Naranjo							
1	Aj Wosal Chan K'inich	9.5.12.0.4	6 K'an 3 Sip	May 7, 546	64.87	Waning	Gibbous
2	K'uxaj	Unknown					
3	K'ahk' Skull Chan Chaak	Unknown					
4	Lady Six Sky	Unknown					
5	K'ahk Tiliw Chan Chaak	9.13.1.3.19	5 Kawak 2 Yaxk'in	May 21, 693	82.28	Waxing	Gibbous
6	Yax Mayuy Chan Chaak	Unknown					
7	K'ahk' Yipiiy Chan Chaak	9.15.15.3.16	7 Kib 14 Yax	August 19, 746	4.56	NEW	NEW
8	K'ahk Ukalaw Chan Chaak	9.16.4.10.18	9 Etz'nab 11 Muwan	November 22, 755	99.11	FULL	FULL
9	Bat K'awiil	Unknown					
10	Itzamnaaj K'awiil	9.17.13.4.3	5 Ak'bal 11 Pop	February 8, 784	94.53	Waxing	Gibbous

continued on next page

TABLE 6.1—*continued*

Ruler	Name	Accession Date	Gregorian Conversion CE	% Illumin.	Phase	
11	Waxaklajuun Ubaah K'awiil	9.19.4.1.1	1 Imix 19 Mol	June 28, 814			
Caracol						
1	Te' K'ab Chaak	Unknown				
2	K'ahk' Ujol K'inich I	Unknown				
3	Yajaw Te' K'inich	9.2.9.0.16	10 Kib 4 Pop	April 13, 484	6.49	Waxing	Crescent
4	K'an I	9.4.16.13.3	4 Ak'bal 16 Pop	April 15, 531	96.77	FULL	FULL
5	Yajaw Te' K'inich II	9.5.19.1.2	9 Ik' 5 Wo	April 18, 553	76.09	Waning	Gibbous
6	Knot Ajaw	9.8.5.16.12	5 Eb 5 Xul	June 26, 599	2.88	NEW	NEW
7	K'an II	9.9.4.16.2	10 Ik' 0 Pop	March 9, 618	54.76	Waxing	Gibbous
8	K'ahk' Ujol K'inich II	9.11.5.14.0	12 Ajaw 18 Xul	June 25, 658	75.01	Waning	Gibbous
9	Ruler 7	Unknown				
10	Tum Yohl K'inich	Unknown				
11	K'inich Joy K'awiil	9.18.9.5.9	6 Muluk 2 K'ayab	December 12, 799	82.91	Waxing	Gibbous
12	K'inich Toobil Yopaat	9.18.13.10.19?	9 Kawak? 7 Sip	March 10, 804	27.72	Waning	Crescent
13	Kan III	Unknown				
14	Ruler 13	Unknown				
Quirigua						
1	Tok Casper	8.19.10.11.0	8 Ajaw 18 Yax	September 19, 426	6.96	Waxing	Crescent
2	Tutuum Yohl K'inich	Unknown				
3	Ruler 3	Unknown				
4	K'awiil Yopaat	Unknown				
5	K'ahk' Tiliw Chan Yopaat	9.14.13.4.17	12 Kaban 5 K'ayab	January 2, 725	98.89	FULL	FULL

continued on next page

Table 6.1—continued

Ruler	Name	Accession Date		Gregorian Conversion CE	% Illumin.	Phase	
6	Sky Xul	9.17.14.16.18	9 Etz'nab 1 K'ank'in	October 15, 785	47.45	Waxing	Gibbous
7	Jade Sky	Unknown					
Calakmul							
1	Scroll Serpent	9.7.5.14.17	11 Kaban 10 Ch'en	September 4, 579	5.77	Waning	Crescent
2	Yuknoom Ti' Chan	Unknown					
3	Tajoom Uk'ab K'ahk'	9.9.9.0.5	11 Chikchan 3 Wo	March 31, 622	98.55	Waxing	Gibbous
4	Yuknoom Head	Unknown					
5	Yuknoom Ch'een II	9.10.3.5.10	8 Ok 18 Sip	May 1, 636	73.05	Waning	Gibbous
6	Yuknoom Yich'aak K'ahk'	9.12.13.17.7	6 Manik' 5 Sip	April 6, 686	49.07	Waxing	Crescent
7	Yuknoom Took K'awiil	Unknown					
Tonina							
1	Ruler 1	Unknown					
2	Jaguar Bird Tapir	9.6.8.17.2	7 Ik' o Pax	January 16, 563	44.64	Waxing	Crescent
3	Chak Bolon Chaak	Unknown					
4	K'inich Bahlam Chapaat	9.9.1.13.11	10 Chuwen 9 K'ayab	February 2, 615	1.76	NEW	NEW
5	Ruler 2	9.11.16.0.1	1 Imix 9 Mol	July 23, 668	61.7	Waxing	Gibbous
6	K'inich Baaknal Chaak	9.12.16.3.12	5 Eb o Yaxk'in	June 19, 688	100	FULL	FULL
7	Ruler 4	9.13.16.16.18	9 Etz'nab 6 Muwan	November 28, 708	81.86	Waxing	Gibbous
8	K'inich Ich'aak Chapaat	9.14.12.2.7	5 Manik' o Muwan	November 19, 723	91.3	Waning	Gibbous
9	K'inich Tuun Chapaat	Unknown					
10	Ruler 8	Unknown					
11	U Chapaat	Unknown					
12	Ruler 10	Unknown					

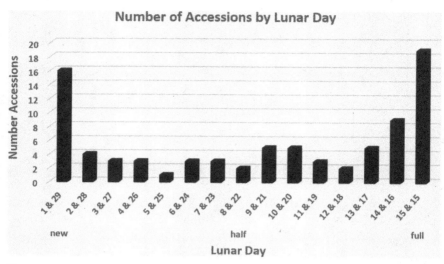

FIGURE 6.6. *Number of accessions of Classic Maya rulers from eleven cities by lunar day. Lunar days range from 1 (new moon), to 8 (half moon, first quarter), to 15 (full moon), to 22 (half moon, third quarter), and back again. Graph: Kristin V. Landau.*

onlookers, we turn to the ethnohistoric and ethnographic records, where connections between the phases of the moon and agriculture abound.

POSTCLASSIC, COLONIAL, ETHNOHISTORIC, AND ETHNOGRAPHIC ACCOUNTS OF LUNAR POWER IN MESOAMERICA

After the Classic period, during the era known as the Postclassic (900–1519 CE), the moon continued to play a prominent role in Mesoamerican culture and ideology. As Fray Bernardino de Sahagún (2009; Taube 1993), a colonial-era chronicler who provided rich documentation of the peoples living in the Valley of Mexico, writes, the moon was born from the ritual sacrifice of two. After five failed attempts at creation, the gods gathered at Teotihuacan, a major metropolis in central Mexico (today a UNESCO World Heritage Site), to select one of their own as a sacrifice to form the new sun. They selected two gods for a potential offering, but at the moment of immolation, one deity faltered and due to his hesitancy eventually became the moon. This act of creation became a driving ideology for Mexica conquest because the sun and moon are said to have required sacrifices to continue traveling across the sky.

KRISTIN V. LANDAU, CHRISTOPHER HERNANDEZ, AND NANCY GONLIN

Thus, warfare was necessary to acquire captives for sacrifice and continue feeding the sun on its journey across the sky and in battles with the forces of darkness (e.g., Taube 1993; Brumfiel and Feinman 2008).

A similar creation story can be found in the Popol Vuh, a K'iche' Maya narrative that provides their history from cosmological origins up to their imperial expansion during the Postclassic. Recorded in this eighteenth-century document is a time before the creation of humans. Male Hero Twins escape their trials in the underworld to eventually become the sun and moon. Although written after Spanish colonization, the Popol Vuh provides insights into aspects of Maya mythology, such as the Hero Twin myth, which can be traced back over 2,000 years (Coe 1973; Saturno et al. 2005; Taube et al. 2010). K'iche' Maya and Mexica stories of creation highlight the fluid gender associations of the moon in Mesoamerica. While the moon was widely treated as a woman and wife of the sun, some Mesoamerican peoples held that it originated as a male aspect (Thompson 1970). Nevertheless, this vital celestial body had a close partnership with the sun since the time of creation, and the moon could be tied to ideology, such as the Mexica justification for warfare as part of maintaining the cosmos.

According to ethnohistoric sources, several Mesoamerican activities were timed according to the lunar cycle. A chronicler from the 1500s, Fray Diego de Landa (Tozzer 1941), noted a relationship between moon phase and rainfall: "The only time it rained during the dry season months of January and February was during a new moon" (Bassie-Sweet 2008, 34). According to Charles Wisdom's (1940) ethnohistoric account, the Chortí Maya in Guatemala associate the waxing moon with growth, both agricultural and for humans (healing wounds, growing adult teeth). Rafael Girard (1949, 192; translation ours) adds that sexual intercourse was governed by strict rules for the Chortí: "It must be practiced during the full moon so that offspring grow, equal to the method followed for the planting of crops." In both Postclassic and later periods, the moon was conceived as a jar for water, with the waxing moon filling up the jar, the full moon representing the full jar, and the waning moon pouring out water (Girard 1949; Iwaniszewski 2006). Jacinto de la Serna, a seventeenth-century chronicler, notes that Mexica women tracked their pregnancies according to the lunar count (Nuttall 1904, 495). In the sixteenth century, Sahagún (2009) recorded that women in the Valley of Mexico feared lunar eclipses because they might lose their baby and give birth to a mouse.

Ethnographic data highlight that among Mesoamerican cultures, various activities—such as planting, harvesting, wood cutting, sex for procreation, and even animal castration—could be timed according to lunar cycles (Thompson

1970, 243–244; Iwaniszewski 2006). K'iche', Chortí, Kaqchiquel and other living Maya peoples time their agricultural seasons—when to plant and when to harvest—by the phases of the moon; they follow these rules ardently. The K'iche' believe that it rains more on a new and full moon. They say the moon is "dangerously tender" when it is new or full, necessitating many prohibitions (Remington 1977). Ethnographic research among the Ch'orti' in Guatemala establishes that farmers know to avoid planting during a new moon, when "the roots of the plant will not be strong"; they may instead wait until a full moon to ensure maximum growth when planting is at its best (Hull 2020, 222–223). Today in Copan, for example, some farmers plant when the crescent moon is waxing around Day 3 or 4, and harvest when the moon is older and waning, around Day 26 or 27 (personal communication to K. Landau, 2009). In the Selva Lacandona region of Chiapas, Mexico, Tzeltal and Lacandon Maya time the planting of various crops—such as beans, plantain, and yucca—during a full moon. Chankin Valenzuela Gómez, an agronomist and Lacandon Maya, has turned our attention to scientific research that suggests the moon influences crop growth (personal communication to C. Hernandez, April 6, 2019). The timing likely reflects the moon's gravitational pull on earth's water; while there are no ocean tides in the Lacandon rainforest, the moon could still play a role in plant uptake of water (Beeson 1946; Brown and Chow 1973; Barlow 2012; Barlow and Fisahn 2012; Torres M. 2012). For example, lunar gravity may affect how water moves in root systems or within cells (Barlow and Fisahn 2012). Although currently debated, this research may complement a truth claimed by generations of Indigenous peoples.

Pervasive ideas about hot and cold, the sun and the moon, and gender have been by documented by Gary H. Gossen (1974) in the community of Chamula, Chiapas, Mexico. Because Gossen spoke with only male interlocutors, thus biasing his study (1974, 394), we recount the more salient aspects of work here. Among the Tzotzil Maya of Chamula, heat and the sun (identified as Jesus Christ) were organizing principles of society. The sun was thought to have brought order to the cosmos, and this same ordering power was expressed among contemporary people as heat. Men were known to gain heat over the course of their lives while women were conceived as becoming colder. Thus, men sat on chairs during evening meals, thereby raising themselves above the cold feminine earth (Gossen 1974, 393). In contrast, women sat on the ground and walked barefoot. The lack of footwear symbolically connected women directly to the earth. The people of Chamula thought of the moon as the Virgin Mary who gave birth to a son. Her child was killed by evil forces, but through death her offspring turned into the sun and brought order to the cosmos. With order established, the moon and sun traveled to the edges of the earth every day, where the celestial bodies plunged into and out of the seas. This cycle explains the daily rise and fall of both heavenly bodies. Although transformed over time, gendered aspects of the ancient Maya Moon Goddess have persisted despite colonial efforts to eliminate pre-Columbian beliefs.

In line with the theme of fertility, John Thompson (1970, 243–244) notes Tzotzil communities once believed that during a full moon, women were most fertile and likely to become pregnant. He relates how the grandfather of one of his Maya colleagues in Belize spoke of the past practice of men and women engaging in sexual intercourse in the period only between the full and new moon. Despite its influence on human activity, the moon could still require assistance to travel across the sky. According to Lacandon elders, the moon needed sustenance and care from humans (McGee and Reilly 1997). Resembling earlier Mexica and K'iche' beliefs, the order of the night sky required offerings given through ceremony, but the Lacandon no longer performed human sacrifice (e.g., McGee 1990). Overall, we surmise that the new and full moon phases are more auspicious for a ruler to come to power since they are associated with bringing rain, fertility, and abundance.

DISCUSSION

Both ancient and modern Mayas associate the moon's sacred cycle with water, planting, fertility, and abundance. How could this symbolism be related to Classic period ruler accessions? In ancient Maya culture, rulers were seen as divine intermediaries between forces of the cosmos and humans. Part of their role was to ensure universal balance for proper rainfall, maize production, and the earth's fecundity. The lunar cycle and its multiple connections to water, growth, and fertility were likely a part of this broader Maya, and indeed pan-Mesoamerican, pattern (Nuttall 1904; Wisdom 1940; Milbrath 1995, 1999; Iwaniszewski 2006; Bassie-Sweet 2008). Like the daily periods of dawn and dusk, accession was a vulnerable, liminal time when leadership and future direction were hazy. Coming to power in an elaborate ceremony during an auspicious moon phase would have reassured the populace, convincing them to lend support to a sprouting new ruler. Lunar phases may have composed a legitimizing element of the accession rite itself (e.g., Schele and Miller 1986). If accession ceremonies occurred at night, as our data suggest, people would have visibly seen and experienced the new ruler's power through spectacle and "conspicuous" performance. As Weber explains, it was up to the people to decide whether a new leader was legitimate, whether they had the god-like charisma of authority. The new and full moon's connection to agricultural growth would have mirrored the ruler's accession—both were maturing to provide sustenance and direction for the larger city.

The ruler's show of power at night would have enhanced royal influence over city dwellers. Moonlight reflecting on white *sacbeob*, or roads, would have visibly led urban residents into their city's core, to witness and partake in accession rituals. In the case of Copan, for example, the Great Plaza covered in white stucco and full of stelae, would have strongly reflected the full moon's light, creating a beacon of sorts for those living on the surrounding hillsides. Sounds from ceremonies and smells from burning copal incense, jocote kindling, and torches would have traveled farther to attract attendees, thanks to changes in humidity associated with nighttime (Shields and Bass 1977). Although few depictions of accession ceremonies exist, the new king would have been accompanied by a group of nobles witnessing and sanctioning the bestowal of royal regalia (Martin 2020, 115). At Copan, perhaps this ritual occurred on top of Structure 4—a radial pyramid on the south edge of the Great Plaza—where the new ruler and attendants would have appeared taller and larger with the reflected moon's up-lighting effect.

A basic conceptual dichotomy in Mesoamerican thought is between day and night (Bassie-Sweet 2008). Whereas the day was safe, the night was potentially dangerous and could contain harmful creatures; snakes, jaguars, and many other predators become more active at night, but it was a powerful time and ideally suited for communing with the ancestors (Taube 1993). We commonly perceive of Classic Maya cities in the daytime as busy places for trade (King 2015), home to social interactions, production of goods (e.g., Widmer 2009), political events, ritual happenings, and quotidian practices (Gonlin 2020a; Robin 2020). Analyses of the remains of households and neighborhoods can reveal power relations within a polity (Landau 2021), among other aspects. However, nighttime experience was an equally persistent aspect of Maya social life (Gonlin and Dixon 2018; Gonlin and Dixon-Hundredmark 2021). The night would have centrally figured in the legitimization of social hierarchy and royal authority in major urban centers.

CONCLUSIONS

This case study provides a prime example of how rulers thrived in the dark urban environment, making the most of the night for themselves, their ancestors, and their subject populations. Accessions could have been a liminal period for the populace, placing the future ruler and urbanites in a state of flux.

Nocturnal rituals and gatherings under the guidance of the ruler might have created an ideal setting for charismatic leaders to calm the masses and reassure them of future productivity while simultaneously reinforcing inequalities and unity. It is little wonder, then, that we have found a correlation between the phases of the moon and a Classic Maya ruler's accession. The ruler's lunar power was essential to the functioning of the polity, day and night.

Acknowledgments. We would like to thank the organizers of the "After Dark" session of the Eighty-Fourth Annual SAA meetings in Albuquerque for inviting us to contribute to this innovative and fun theme. The original idea for this contribution originated in Landau's undergraduate thesis, supervised by Anthony Aveni. Thanks also to the Instituto Hondureño de Antropología e Historia and the Instituto Nacional de Antropología e Historia (Mexico) for permitting Landau's and Hernandez's fieldwork, respectively. We also appreciate our colleagues in Copan and Mensabak for entertaining our questions about the moon, astronomy, and agriculture. Special thanks to Alma professors Brad Westgate and Nhan Le for help with statistics, and Luna the cat for continued inspiration.

REFERENCES

Aveni, Anthony F. 2001. *Skywatchers*. Austin: University of Texas Press.

Aveni, Anthony F. 2018. "Night in Day: Contrasting Maya and Hindu Responses to Total Solar Eclipses." In *Archaeology of the Night: Life after Dark in the Ancient World*, edited by Nancy Gonlin and April Nowell, 139–154. Boulder: University Press of Colorado.

Aveni, Anthony F., and Lorren D. Hotaling. 1994. "Monumental Inscriptions and the Observational Basis of Maya Planetary Astronomy." *Archaeoastronomy*. Supplement to the *Journal for the History of Astronomy* 25 (19): S21–S54.

Barlow, Peter W. 2012. "Moon and Cosmos: Plant Growth and Plant Bioelectricity." In *Plant Electrophysiology*, edited by Alexander G. Volkov, 249–280. Berlin: Springer.

Barlow, Peter W., and Joachim Fisahn. 2012. "Lunisolar Tidal Force and the Growth of Plant Roots, and Some Other of Its Effects on Plant Movements." *Annals of Botany* 110 (2, 1): 301–318.

Baron, Joanne P. 2016. *Patron Gods and Patron Lords: The Semiotics of Classic Maya Community Cults*. Boulder: University Press of Colorado.

Bassie-Sweet, Karen. 2008. *Maya Sacred Geography and the Creator Deities*. Norman: University of Oklahoma Press.

Beeson, C.F.C. 1946. "The Moon and Plant Growth." *Nature* 158 (4017): 572–573.

Brown, Frank A., and Carol S. Chow. 1973. "Lunar-Correlated Variations in Water Uptake by Bean Seeds." *Biology Bulletin* 145 (2): 265–278.

Brumfiel, Elizabeth M., and Gary M. Feinman, eds. 2008. *The Aztec World*. New York: Harry N. Abrams.

Clancy, Flora S. 2015. "The Ancient Maya Moon: Calendar and Character." In *Cosmology, Calendars, and Horizon-Based Astronomy in Ancient Mesoamerica*, edited by Anne S. Dowd and Susan Milbrath, 229–248. Boulder: University Press of Colorado.

Coe, Michael D. 1973. *The Maya Scribe and His World*. New York: Grolier Club.

Coe, Michael D., and Mark Van Stone. 2005. *Reading the Maya Glyphs*. New York: Thames and Hudson.

Demarest, Arthur A. 1992. "Ideology in Ancient Maya Cultural Evolution: The Dynamics of Galactic Polities." In *Ideology and Pre-Columbian Civilizations*, edited by Arthur A. Demarest and George Conrad, 135–157. Santa Fe, NM: School of American Research Press.

DeMarrais, Elizabeth, Luis Jaime Castillo, and Timothy K. Earle. 1996. "Ideology, Materialization, and Power Strategies." *Current Anthropology* 37 (1): 15–31.

Dowd, Marion, and Robert Hensey, eds. 2016. *The Archaeology of Darkness*. Oxford and Philadelphia: Oxbow Books.

Fash, William L. 1994. "Changing Perspectives on Maya Civilization." *Annual Review of Anthropology* 23: 181–208.

Fitzsimmons, James L. 2015. "The Charismatic Polity: Zapote Bobal and the Birth of Authority at Jaguar Hill." In *Classic Maya Polities of the Southern Lowlands: Integration, Interaction, Dissolution*, edited by Damien B. Marken and James L. Fitzsimmons, 225–242. Boulder: University Press of Colorado.

Fox, John W., Garrett W. Cook, Arlen F. Chase, and Diane Z. Chase. 1996. "Questions of Political and Economic Integration: Segmentary versus Centralized States among the Ancient Maya." *Current Anthropology* 37 (5): 795–801.

Girard, Rafael. 1949. *Los Chortis ante el problema maya*. Mexico City: Antigua Librería Robredo.

Goldstine, Herman H. 1973. *New and Full Moons 1001 BC to AD 1651*. Philadelphia: American Philosophical Society.

Gonlin, Nancy. 2020a. "Household Archaeology of the Classic Period Lowland Maya." In *The Maya World*, edited by Scott R. Hutson and Traci Ardren, 389–406. London: Routledge.

Gonlin, Nancy. 2020b. "Urban Nightscapes of the Late Classic Maya of Mesoamerica." In *ICNS Proceedings*, 1st ed., edited by Manuel Garcia-Ruiz and Jordi Nofre, 166–183. Lisbon: ISCTE Instituto Universitário de Lisboa.

Gonlin, Nancy, and Christine C. Dixon. 2018. "Classic Maya Nights at Copan, Honduras, and El Cerén, El Salvador." In *Archaeology of the Night: Life after Dark in the Ancient World*, edited by Nancy Gonlin and April Nowell, 45–76. Boulder: University Press of Colorado.

Gonlin, Nancy, and Christine C. Dixon-Hundredmark. 2021. "Light, Darkness, and Luminosity in the Late Classic Maya World: Illuminating Nocturnal Case Studies from Copan, Honduras and La Joya de Cerén, El Salvador." In *Night and Darkness in Ancient Mesoamerica*, edited by Nancy Gonlin and David M. Reed, 205–241. Louisville: University Press of Colorado.

Gonlin, Nancy, and April Nowell, eds. 2018. *Archaeology of the Night: Life after Dark in the Ancient World*. Boulder: University Press of Colorado.

Gonlin, Nancy, and April Nowell. 2020. "Life after Dark in the Cities of the Ancient World." In *ICNS Proceedings*, 1st ed., ed. Manuel Garcia-Ruiz and Jordi Nofre, 61–74. Lisbon: ISCTE Instituto Universitário de Lisboa.

Gossen, Gary H. 1974. "To Speak with a Heated Heart: Chamula Canons of Style and Good Performance." In *Explorations in the Ethnography of Speaking*, edited by Richard Bauman and Joel Sherzer, 389–413. Cambridge: Cambridge University Press.

Grube, Nikolai. 1992. "Classic Maya Dance: Evidence from Hieroglyphs and Iconography." *Ancient Mesoamerica* 3 (2): 201–218. https://doi.org/10.1017/S095653610000064X.

Houston, Stephen D. 2000. "Into the Minds of the Ancients: Advances in Maya Glyph Studies." *Journal of World Prehistory* 14 (2): 121–201.

Houston, Stephen D. 2006. "Impersonation, Dance, and the Problem of Spectacle among the Classic Maya." In *Archaeology of Performance: Theaters of Power, Community, and Politics*, edited by Takeshi Inomata and Lawrence S. Coben, 135–155. New York: AltaMira Press.

Houston, Stephen D., and Takeshi Inomata. 2009. *The Classic Maya*. New York: Cambridge University Press.

Hull, Kerry. 2020. "A Cosmology of Water: The Universe According to the Ch'orti.'" In *Reshaping the World: Debates on Mesoamerican Cosmologies*, edited by Ana Díaz, 209–247. Louisville: University Press of Colorado.

Inomata, Takeshi. 2006. "Plazas, Performers, and Spectators: Political Theaters of the Classic Maya." *Current Anthropology* 47 (5): 805–842.

Inomata, Takeshi, and Lawrence S. Coben, eds. 2006. *Archaeology of Performance: Theaters of Power, Community, and Politics*. Lanham, MD: Altamira Press.

Iwaniszewski, Stanislaw. 2006. "Lunar Agriculture in Mesoamerica." *Mediterranean Archaeology and Archaeometry* 6 (3): 67–75.

Iwaniszewski, Stanislaw. 2008. "Lunar Cycles and the Ruler's Life at Yaxchilan, Chiapas, Mexico." In *Astronomy of Ancient Societies*, edited by T. M. Potyomkina, 162–171. Moscow: Nauka.

Iwaniszewski, Stanislaw. 2018. "The Observations of the Moon at Naranjo: New Facts and Interpretations." *Mediterranean Archaeology and Archaeometry* 18 (4): 191–198.

Jackson, Sarah E. 2013. *Politics of the Maya Court: Hierarchy and Change in the Late Classic Period*. Norman: University of Oklahoma Press.

Joyce, Rosemary A. 1996. "The Construction of Gender in Classic Maya Monuments." In *Gender and Archaeology: Essays in Research and Practice*, edited by Rita P. Wright, 167–195. Philadelphia: University of Pennsylvania Press.

King, Eleanor M., ed. 2015. *The Ancient Maya Marketplace: The Archaeology of Transient Space*. Tucson: University of Arizona Press.

Landau, Kristin V. 2021. "The Dynamics of Maya State Process: An Integrated Perspective from the San Lucas Neighborhood of Copán, Honduras." *American Anthropologist* 123 (1): 1–20.

Looper, Matthew G. 2002. "Women-Men (and Men-Women): Classic Maya Rulers and the Third Gender." In *Ancient Maya Women*, edited by Traci Ardren, 171–202. Walnut Creek, CA: AltaMira Press.

Looper, Matthew G. 2009. *To Be Like Gods: Dance in Ancient Maya Civilization*. Austin: University of Texas Press.

Martin, Simon. 2020. *Ancient Maya Politics: A Political Anthropology of the Classic Period 150–900 CE*. New York: Cambridge University Press.

Martin, Simon, and Nikolai Grube. 2008. *Chronicle of the Maya Kings and Queens: Deciphering the Dynasties of the Ancient Maya*. New York: Thames and Hudson Ltd.

McGee, R. Jon. 1990. *Life, Ritual, and Religion among the Lacandon Maya*. Belmont, CA: Wadsworth Publishing Company.

McGee, R. Jon, and Kent F. Reilly III. 1997. "Ancient Maya Astronomy and Cosmology in Lacandon Maya Life." *Journal of Latin American Lore* 20 (1): 125–142.

Milbrath, Susan. 1995. "Gender and Roles of Lunar Deities in Postclassic Central Mexico and Their Correlations in the Maya Area." *Estudios de Cultura Nahuatl* 25: 45–93.

Milbrath, Susan. 1999. *Star Gods of the Maya: Astronomy in Art, Folklore, and Calendars*. Austin: University of Texas Press.

Miller, Daniel, ed. 2005. *Materiality*. Durham, NC: Duke University Press.

Miller, Daniel, and Christopher Y. Tilley, eds. 1984. *Ideology, Power, and Prehistory*. New York: Cambridge University Press.

Newsome, Elizabeth A. 2001. *Trees of Paradise and Pillars of the World: The Serial Stela Cycle of "18-Rabbit-God K," King of Copan*. Austin: University of Texas Press.

Nowell, April, and Nancy Gonlin. 2021. "Affordances of the Night: Work after Dark in the Ancient World." In *Rethinking Darkness: Cultures, Histories, Practices*, edited by Nick Dunn and Tim Edensor, 27–37. London: Routledge.

Nuttall, Zelia. 1904. "The Periodical Adjustments of the Ancient Mexican Calendar." *American Anthropologist* 6 (4): 486–500.

Pineda de Carias, María C., Nohemy L. Rivera, and Cristina M. Argueta. 2017. "Stela D: A Sundial at Copan, Honduras." *Ancient Mesoamerica* 28 (2): 543–557.

Pitts, Mark. 2011. "A Brief History of Piedras Negras—As Told by the Ancient Maya." FAMSI. Accessed April 2, 2019. http://www.famsi.org/research/pitts/pitts_piedras_negras_history.pdf.

Remington, Judith A. 1977. "Current Astronomical Practices Among the Maya." In *Native American Astronomy*, edited by Anthony F. Aveni, 75–88. Austin: University of Texas Press.

Robin, Cynthia. 2020. "Archaeology of Everyday Life." *Annual Review of Anthropology* 49: 373–390.

Sahagún, Fray Bernardino de. 2009. *Historia general de las cosas de la Nueva España II*. Barcelona: Linkgua Ediciones S.L.

Saturno, William A., David Stuart, Anthony F. Aveni, and Franco Rossi. 2012. "Ancient Maya Astronomical Tables from Xultun, Guatemala." *Science* 336 (6082): 714–717.

Saturno, William A., Karl Taube, and David Stuart. 2005. *The Murals of San Bartolo, Petén, Guatemala. Part 1: The North Wall*. Ancient America 7. Barnardsville, NC: Boundary End Archaeology Research Center.

Schele, Linda, and Mary Ellen Miller. 1986. *The Blood of Kings: Dynasty and Ritual in Maya Art*. New York: George Braziller.

Sharer, Robert J., and Loa P. Traxler. 2005. *The Ancient Maya*. 6th ed. Stanford, CA: Stanford University Press.

Shields, F. Douglas, and Henry E. Bass. 1977. "Atmospheric Absorption of High Frequency Noise and Application to Fractional-Octave Bands." NASA Contractor Report, 2760. Released June 1977.

Skidmore, Joel. 2010. "The Rulers of Palenque." Mesoweb. www.mesoweb.com/palenque/resources/rulers/PalenqueRulers-05.pdf.

Stone, Andrea, and Marc Zender. 2011. *Reading Maya Art: A Hieroglyphic Guide to Ancient Maya Painting and Sculpture*. New York: Thames and Hudson Ltd.

Stuart, David. 1996. "Kings of Stone: A Consideration of Stelae in Ancient Maya Ritual and Representation." *RES* 29 and 30 (Spring and Autumn): 149–171.

Stuart, David. 2013. "Report: Two Inscribed Bones from Yaxchilan." In *Maya Decipherment: Ideas on Ancient Maya Writing and Iconography.* https://decipherment.wordpress.com/category/yaxchilan/.

Stuart, David. 2020a. "Yesterday's Moon: A Decipherment of the Classic Mayan Adverb *ak'biiy.*" In *Maya Decipherment: Ideas on Ancient Maya Writing and Iconography.* https://mayadecipherment.com/2020/08/01/yesterdays-moon-a-decipherment-of-the-classic-mayan-adverb-akbiiy/.

Stuart, David. 2020b. "Maya Time." In *The Maya World*, edited by Scott R. Hutson and Traci Ardren, 624–647. London: Routledge.

Stuart, David, and George Stuart. 2008. *Palenque: Eternal City of the Maya.* London: Thames and Hudson.

Taube, Karl. 1993. *Aztec and Maya Myths.* Austin: University of Texas Press.

Taube, Karl, William A. Saturno, David Stuart, and Heather Hurst. 2010. *The Murals of San Bartolo, Petén, Guatemala. Part 2: The West Wall.* Ancient America 10. Barnardsville, NC: Boundary End Archaeology Research Center.

Thompson, John Eric Sidney. 1970. *Maya History and Religion.* Norman: University of Oklahoma Press.

Torres M., Alex. 2012. "Determinar la influencia de la luna en la agricultura." BS licenciatura, Facultad de Ciencias Agropecuarias, Universidad de Cuenca.

Tozzer, Alfred M. 1941. *Landa's Relación de las Cosas de Yucatan, Papers of the Peabody Museum of American Archaeology and Ethnology*, Vol. 18. Cambridge, MA: Harvard University Press.

Weber, Max. 1977. *The Theory of Social and Economic Organization.* Translated by Talcott Parsons. New York: Free Press.

Widmer, Randolph J. 2009. "Elite Household Multicrafting Specialization at 9N-8, Patio H, Copan." *Archaeological Papers of the American Anthropological Association* 19 (1): 174–204.

Wilkinson, Darryl. 2019. "Towards an Archaeological Theory of Infrastructure." *Journal of Archaeological Method and Theory* 26: 1216–1241. https://doi.org/10.1007/s10816-018-9410-2.

Wisdom, Charles. 1940. *The Chorti Indians of Guatemala.* Chicago: University of Chicago Press.

7

The archaeology of the night is a new perspective on the ancient world that encourages us to reinterpret archaeological evidence and opens up a wide range of novel research (Gonlin and Nowell 2018a; Gonlin and Reed 2021). This chapter begins to address the dynamic world of ancient nights through an analysis of the Wari empire. First, we focus on the cities of Wari and Conchopata to provide background to this Indigenous South American culture (figure 1.1). Next, we describe the spatial organization of Wari, which was undoubtedly closely related to the position of the stars and that, paradoxically, has not yet received much attention. And finally, we discuss cognitive aspects of Wari nights as they are related to religion, rituals, and beliefs that have persisted until today.

The night is directly infused into many facets of Wari culture. Although not explicitly considered previously, the night was tied into ritual life, religion, and daily life of the inhabitants of the Peruvian highlands. The Wari, like numerous Indigenous civilizations of the Americas, were well known as warriors, architects, artisans, and astronomers. Their cities reflected a consideration of this knowledge, and they built sacred areas unique to this culture. In this chapter, we look at the enigmatic D-shaped structures found throughout the Wari Empire and provide details on their use and how they relate to the nocturnal urban environment. A consideration of Wari astronomical knowledge is necessary to understand their religion, sacred areas of their cities, and the iconographic repertoire.

Every Day Hath a Night

*Nightlife and Religion in
the Wari Empire of Peru*

MARTHA CABRERA ROMERO
AND J. ANTONIO OCHATOMA
CABRERA

https://doi.org/10.5876/9781646422609.c007

Human observation of the celestial vault is probably one of the oldest and most mysterious activities. The movement of the stars, the phases of the moon, and changes in other astronomical bodies invoked a search for meaning and an attempt to understand these phenomena. With knowledge of these observations, ancients could devise a meaningful calendar. This understanding was often reflected in the built environment manifested in architecture and urban planning and incorporated into rituals.

In pre-Columbian societies, rituals were one of the main mechanisms of societal integration, since they generated links between individuals from different social groups and they connected their daily life with that of their ancestors. Roy Rappaport (1999), ecological anthropologist, emphasizes the significance of the environment and the human capacity to adapt to its environment. He explores the role of religion as a useful adaptive catalyst between humans and nature. Thus, Rappaport (1999, 1–2) affirms:

> Given the central place that religious considerations have occupied in the
> thoughts and actions of men and women in all times and places, and given
> the amount of energy, blood, time and wealth that have been spent building
> temples, supporting priests, sacrificing to gods and killing infidels, it is hard to
> imagine that religion, as bizarre as some of its manifestations may seem, is not
> in some way indispensable to the species.

In this sense, rituals are vital in the creation of public spaces and structures. One of the most representative and investigated case studies of this interaction is Teotihuacan, in central Mexico, which was a multiethnic urban center that exhibited an exceptional degree of ordered layout that, for some scholars, was inspired by the observation of the heavens. In fact, a concept deeply rooted in the Mesoamerican worldview is the notion of the four main directions of the world (Cowgill 2008). During its construction, the orthogonal layout of the city reflected the ordered world of the city's rulers, while distinct neighborhoods and residences expressed multiethnicity (Manzanilla 2009, 2017). Commenting on the notion of ritual space, Luis Barba et al. (2007, 56) argue that

> the importance of religion in this city can be assessed in different scales: the
> state religion is evident in the huge plazas (squares) and temples in the city's
> center, in the processions of priests and other officers portrayed in the mural
> paintings, and in the representations of the deities (in sculpture, battlements,
> vases, mural paintings, etc.). There seem to have been barrio temples that inte-
> grated people of particular sectors of the city. And the last scale is the domestic

realm, where altars and temples were set in ritual courtyards and where ceremonies for the ancestors and deities, as well as termination rituals, may be traced.

The significance of this hierarchical division of ritual practice is one of the factors that defines Teotihuacan as a corporate city, with state-controlled and proscriptive building designs, craft production, and control of trade (Manzanilla 2009). Despite the fact that it had a state religion of main gods, there were groups of "barrios," or apartment complexes of foreign communities, that had their own deities and, therefore, different levels and types of rituals. From systematic grid sampling on the floors and chemical residue analysis on the courtyards of one of these apartment complexes, Barba and colleagues (2007, 76) verified that "the hierarchical organization of the households within this apartment compound is also seen in ritual." Thus, the largest ritual courtyard was related to the household bearing the Storm God symbols. This god was considered one of the principal deities of the city, and his iconography is found throughout it, especially on murals, sculptures, and jars (Cowgill 2015, 30). The largest amount of materials foreign to Teotihuacan, such as pottery and stone, was found in this courtyard. Smaller courtyards showed rituals related to other minor gods (Barba et al. 2007) as evidenced through household worship.

In the Peruvian Central Andes, there was an ancient city with similar characteristics to Teotihuacan called Wari. In the period known as the Middle Horizon (500–1100 CE), an empire rose and expanded to control much of what is now Peru (figure 7.1). The capital of this civilization was the city of Wari, a well-organized and complex urban center, whose construction likely demanded the employment of hundreds or thousands of people. Specialists with great knowledge of engineering allowed direction and shaping of architectural spaces with complex and monumental lines, as well as a sophisticated system of underground canals throughout the city for flood control during the rainy season (September to March), a type of infrastructure (see chapter 1, this volume). Craftspeople produced fine vessels with iconographic representations of their cosmography based on a set of deities that, for the most part, were inherited from ancestors distant in time, as old as those of the Chavín civilization (200 BC onward) (Menzel 1964; Cook 1994; Ochatoma and Cabrera 2002, 2010; Cabrera 2007). Wari knowledge was spread throughout most of the Central Andes. For the Wari, everything in their environment was skillfully studied and observed: plants and animals, day and night, floods and droughts. During the day, the Wari people observed the passing of the sun, and at night they looked to the sky to see the movement of the stars and the lunar cycles that were linked to rainfall and plant growth.

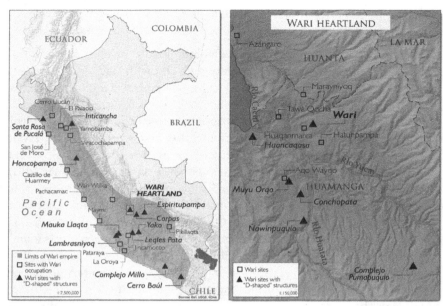

FIGURE 7.1. *Map of the expansion of the Wari empire and its heartland where the sites of Conchopata and Wari are located, Peru. Map: J. Antonio Ochatoma Cabrera.*

One outstanding feature of Wari architecture is the building arrangement known as the "patio group," the arrangement of several structures around a plaza (Isbell 1991). Throughout the empire three formal types of these constructions have been distinguished. The first one is represented by sites with the mark of the "imperial Wari architecture," easily recognizable by its geometry based on rectangular planes, which were in the main provinces of the empire: Pikillacta, Viracochapampa, Azángaro, Inka, Yamobamba, and Pataraya (Anders 1991; Isbell and McEwan 1991; Schreiber 1992, 2013; Isbell 2004; Schreiber and Edwards 2010; McEwan and Williams 2013). Another formal type, located in provincial sites, is one whose technique and style of construction vary, but which follows the patio group construction canon: Conchopata, Honcopampa, Cerro Baúl and Espíritu Pampa (Isbell 1991, 2000, 2008; Ochatoma and Cabrera 2001, 2002, 2010). Unlike the provincial sites in the first category, the distinctive mark of the latter is that they have D-shaped ceremonial structures. Finally, in the third category we have the presence of both building styles, whose construction is exclusive to the capital. Distributed throughout the area of the Wari capital are patio groups with an unplanned layout of structures, those with D-shaped structures, and groups with rectangular structures.

THE ANCIENT ANDEAN NIGHT

The first ethnohistorical reports about the night in ancient Peru date back to the fifteenth century. For the purposes of this research, what Juan de Betanzos ([1551–1557] 1880) has described is relevant because he refers to a paramount creator deity whose emergence dates back to the Tiwanaku culture, many years before the Inkas' presence. This paramount god was called Con Tici Viracocha, and he created the earth and the sky; the light and the day; the moon, the sun, and the stars. Betanzos (2–3) relates:

> In ancient times, it is said that in the province of Peru the earth was dark and
> that there was neither light nor day . . . Of the name of these people and of the
> Lord who commanded them, they do not remember. And in these times that
> this land was all night, they say that it came out of a lake . . . a Lord that they
> called Con Tici Viracocha . . . then, suddenly they say that he made the sun
> and the day, and that he commanded the sun to move along the course that it
> moves; and then they say that he made the stars and the moon.

Betanzos remarks that Con Tici Viracocha emerged accompanied by other people from the Lake Titicaca waters, and they settled in the town of "Tiguanaco" (also known as Tiwanaku). This god held two staffs and transformed people who lived in the times of darkness into stones. This story immediately brings to mind the God of the Staffs of Tiwanaku and Wari (figure 7.2a) represented in a frontal position on the Sun Gate of Tiwanaku (see chapter 5 for material on Tiwanaku) and in the iconography of the Wari pottery. The characters accompanied this god were represented in profile (figures 7.2b and 7.2c), and the people who were turned into stone were the monoliths of Tiwanaku (see chapter 5, this volume) and the Wari.

Another chronicler, Polo de Ondegardo (quoted in Jiménez [1881–1897] 1965), listed the sacred places on one of the roads leading to Cuzco and mentioned a shrine where certain stones were venerated who "were the wives of Ticci Viracocha who had been turned into stone and who walked at night." Finally, Fernando Montesinos ([1642] 1882) compiled a story about a time of darkness when objects came to life and, together with domesticated animals, turned against people. This event was closely related to two astronomical phenomena: the appearance of two comets and two eclipses. Montesinos ([1642] 1882, 48) describes this occurrence:

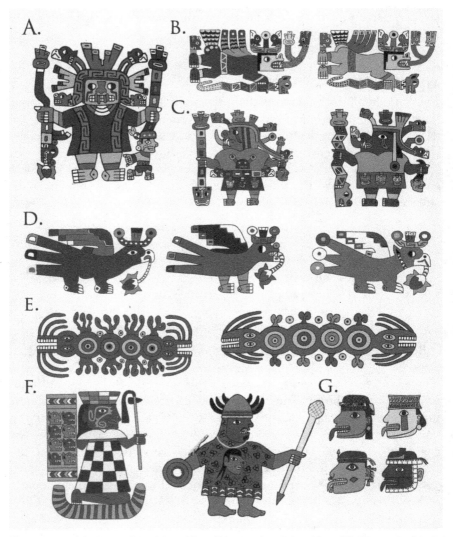

FIGURE 7.2. (a) *The Staff God from Wari.* (b) *"Ccoa" or flying feline.* (c) *Wari gods that escort the Staff God.* (d) *Falconids holding a trachea, heart, and lungs with their beaks.* (e) *Snakes, or "Amarus," with water wells represented on their bodies.* (f) *Warriors on "totora" boats* (left) *and with trophy heads used as a necklace* (right). (g) *Trophy heads of leaders from different regions of the Andes. Drawing: J. Antonio Ochatoma Cabrera.*

After a few years there were two frightful comets that appeared in a lion and snake shape. (Manco Capac) Sent to gather the astrologers and amautas of the king for having happened two eclipses of sun and moon very remarkable, consulted the deities and the Devil made them understand that he wanted to destroy the world for their sins, so he sent a lion and a snake, to destroy the moon. Then, he gathered everyone together, women and children, they cried and forced the dogs to do so as well; because they said that the tears and sighs of the innocent are very dear to the Lord Creator. The people of war set themselves to war and, beating drums, they threw arrows and stones at the moon, making gestures to hurt the lion or serpent, because they said that in this way they would astonish it so that it would destroy the moon. They understood that if the lion and the snake had effect, would be in the dark, and that all the instruments of man and woman would be converted into lions and snakes, and women's spindles into vipers.

A very similar story appears in the "Huarochirí Manuscript" (the stories of myths and beliefs of the Andean world compiled by Francisco de Avila, during his evangelizing campaigns of the Andes in the seventeenth century) and is reported as follows: "They say that in those ancient times the Sun disappeared and the Earth was dark for a period of five days and that the stones met each other, and that the stone mortars rose up against their owners and wanted to swallow them" (Arguedas et al. [1598] 1966, n.p.). These episodes of object and animal rebellion reveal an archaic sense of humanity's loss of power during the reign of shadows and darkness. Night and darkness are attributed a power very close to the divine. Most of these happenings are closely related to the stars.

Although these manuscripts were written after the collapse of the Inka Empire, the accounts reported allude to a society older than the Inkas with a possible origin in Tiwanaku with the God Con Tici Viracocha, variously known as the Staff God. Particularly in Wari, this deity was represented on finely made large urns and *keros*[1] vessels, which were integral to the rituals held in D-shaped structures. They were used, broken, and, in some cases, burned.

KEY CITIES OF THE WARI EMPIRE: WARI AND CONCHOPATA

A background on the two major Wari cities provides the context for some of the nocturnal practices discussed later in this chapter. In the sixth and seventh centuries CE, during the period of intense interaction among a number of cultures located in different parts of the Central Andes region, the Wari

Empire rose (600–1000 CE). It had similar characteristics to the Inka Empire, known as Tawantinsuyo (1450–1532 CE). Both civilizations had political power concentrated in their capital cities, and they had well-organized regions with provincial capitals and administrative centers of different ranks of importance (Lumbreras 2010). To exert control over remote areas, the Wari established provincial centers and developed an extensive road network that served as the basis for the great Inka trail, or Qhapac Ñan. Consequently, the Wari ruled a huge territory and to maintain their sovereignty, they supported their empire through the control of economic production and distribution and by legitimizing their power through a state religion and the symbols associated with that religion (Schreiber 2013).

Specifically, in the south-central highlands of Peru in the Ayacucho basin, two urban centers emerged as the most significant administrative places of the Wari civilization (figure 7.1). The first was the capital city, also known as Wari, and the second was Conchopata, a key center of craft specialists known for depicting rich iconography in their pottery (Menzel 1964; Isbell and McEwan 1991; Ochatoma and Cabrera 2002; Ochatoma 2007; Ochatoma et al. 2015). The basin in which both sites are located is relatively open and is characterized by an average warm temperature during the day, dipping to cold temperatures at night. There are two distinct seasons in this area: the rainy season between December and April, and the dry season between May and November.

The capital city, Wari, is geographically located on a long plateau at 2,750 meters above sea level (9,200 feet), covering around 260 hectares, and was occupied by between 20,000 to 40,000 inhabitants (Isbell 2008). The city of Wari had a complex urban design that lacked a rigid, orthogonal, planned organization, a design seen in its main provincial centers. This configuration was the result of an expanding capital that reflected the growth of the empire. New neighborhoods were continually added (McEwan and Williams 2013). Due to the state of preservation and the dense vegetation, the spatial organization and the evolution of infrastructure during the 500 years of existence are not precisely known. However, with continued excavations, the presence of major buildings is defining the nature of Wari urbanism (Benavides 1991; Isbell and McEwan 1991; Isbell et al. 1991; Ochatoma et al. 2015; Cabrera and Ochatoma 2019). Structures have been uncovered to the east and north of the city of Wari. These sectors, called "palaces," were possibly the only part of the city with orthogonal planning and are notable for the monumentality of their large walls which in several sections are more than eight meters high.

A recently defined "Sacred Area" includes the western sectors of the city: Monqachayoq, Vegachayoq, and Capillapata (Ochatoma et al. 2015). This area was called the "Templo Mayor" (Great Temple) by Enrique Bragayrac and Enrique González Carré, who initially excavated this region. They exposed a pyramidal mound surrounded by high walls with a single entrance on its south side. The main body of the temple is composed of two staggered platforms with the remains of red and white plaster. On the lower wall of one of the pyramids, there were quadrangular structures with evidence of burning. All points of access led to a large trapezoidal square with a D-shaped structure as the main feature, whose access was oriented to the north. This finding led Luis G. Lumbreras (2010) to recognize this area as the "Sacred Area." Research conducted by José Ochatoma Paravicino and Martha Cabrera (one of the authors), uncovered a great variety of funerary structures: simple cists, multiple burial cists, underground galleries, a megalithic mausoleum (built eight meters underground), and seven temples of worship and adoration (known as D-shaped structures) of different sizes and orientations, discussed below (figure 7.3a).

The artisan city of Conchopata is located on a plateau northeast of the modern city of Ayacucho and ten kilometers (six miles) southwest of the Wari capital. It was an extensive city that possibly occupied an entire plateau of 140 hectares. However, due to the construction of the Coronel FAP Alfredo Mendivil Duarte Airport in 1960, along with army barracks and modern houses, the area of the archaeological site was reduced to three hectares. This area was divided into two sectors (A and B) by the construction of the Ejército Avenue, which crosses the area from south to north and leads to the airport facilities (figure 7.2b). The information that we present and analyze below was the result of the excavations in Sector B during 1997 and 1998, carried out by Ochatoma Paravicino and Cabrera (Ochatoma and Cabrera 2001, 2002; Ochatoma 2007).

For a long time, Conchopata was conceived of as a village occupied exclusively by specialist potters (Lumbreras 1974; Pozzi-Escot 1985). As a result, researchers focused their attention on the iconographic representations of the pottery that resembled the icons and symbols on the Sun Gate of Tiwanaku: the Staff God and his companions (Menzel 1964). By comparing the spatial organization of domestic areas proposed by Manzanilla (1990, 2009) for the Mesoamerican city of Teotihuacan, it was determined that Conchopata was not a city with ceramic workshops grouped together. Rather, these domestic spaces corresponded to houses with adjacent workshops that formed part of a household unit. Thus, within a household there were sleeping areas, daily food preparation areas, workshops, and temporary preparation areas (Ochatoma 2007).

Sleeping areas did not have a consistent pattern but varied in their construction. Some walls and floors were plastered and painted and had up to two levels of floor remodeling. All the household units had food preparation/

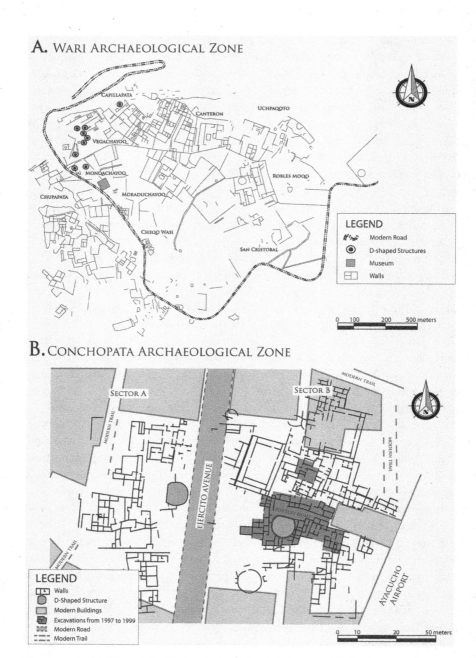

A. Wari Archaeological Zone

CAPILLAPATA

CANTERON

UCHPAQOTO

VEGACHAYOQ

MONQACHAYOQ

ROBLES MOQO

CHUPAPATA

MORADUCHAYOQ

CHEQO WASI

SAN CRISTOBAL

LEGEND

Modern Road

D-shaped Structures

Museum

Walls

0   100   200   500 meters

B. Conchopata Archaeological Zone

MODERN TRAIL

SECTOR A

SECTOR B

MODERN TRAIL

MODERN TRAIL

EJERCITO AVENUE

POTTERY DUMP

MODERN TRAIL

AYACUCHO AIRPORT

LEGEND

Walls

D-Shaped Structure

Modern Buildings

Excavations from 1997 to 1999

Modern Road

Modern Trail

0   10   20   50 meters

Figure 7.3. (a) *Map of the Wari capital and the distribution of the D-shaped structures.* (b) *Map of Conchopata. Maps: Based on site map by Juan Carlos Blacker.*

kitchens, which, in some cases, are where pottery kilns were located. However, the workshops were not necessarily part of a housing unit. In some cases, the workshops were located in courtyards, passageways, or in spaces exclusively for the production of pottery. The temporary preparation areas, represented by patios where many activities took place, had a similar function as the workshops. Such patios were areas where communication with other household units took place and were used for the preparation of the supplies for the production of ceramics, for the drying of these items, for storage, and even as areas for burning. These burnt areas are found mainly in the patios and, more notably, in the D-shaped structures. One of these features, discovered and excavated in 1997 by Ochatoma Paravicino and Cabrera, is possibly the best example for understanding the connection between D-shaped structures and the nature of religious and ritual life.

THE WARI RITUAL AND SACRED PLACES

As in any state or imperial organization, the dominant Wari groups applied power strategies to achieve specific objectives. In some cases, these strategies were based, to a great extent, on the coercive effects of military action; in others, economic action was reflected in the production and distribution of goods; and in other cases, ideology played a basic role in the political and social dynamics (DeMarrais et al. 1996). In the case of the Wari Empire, we can identify a clear iconography of power (Cook 1994), expressed in a specific deity: the Staff God. This deity is typically depicted in frontal view and wears an elaborate headdress and tunic. Both arms extend to the side and each one holds a long vertical staff (figure 7.2a). Secondary or "companion" beings were represented in profile, combining human traits (head, body, arms, legs) with avian and feline traits (figure 7.2c). The best-known example of these representations is seen in the Sun Gate in Tiwanaku. A similar image is found in earlier cultures such as the Chavín, which flourished during the Early Horizon (3000–2200 BCE). The use of these symbols by a dominant society evoked memory of past times and would have left no doubt in the mind of any Andean native that they represented social and political power (Schreiber 2005, 135). Elizabeth DeMarrais and colleagues (1996) identified and defined ways in which ideology can be materialized, two of which are through public monuments and ceremonial events. In the case of the Wari, these two ways have been identified, especially in D-shaped temples.

The D-shaped ceremonial structure is a construction pattern that is quintessentially Wari. It corresponds to the Classical period (Ochatoma 2007), when

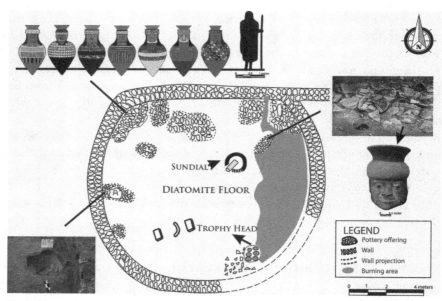

FIGURE 7.4. *Distribution of offerings and the sundial from the Conchopata D-shaped structure. Drawing: J. Antonio Ochatoma Cabrera.*

representations of the altiplanic iconographic repertoire appear (Ochatoma et al. 2015). In the last decade, these structures were discovered scattered throughout the Andean area: Espíritu Pampa, in the jungles of Cuzco; Cerro Baúl, in Moquegua (considered the border area between Wari and Tiwanaku); and Santa Rosa de Pucalá, in Lambayeque (along the Peruvian north coast). However, most of these structures are in the Ayacucho region, two of which are in Conchopata, and to date, ten have been recorded in the Wari capital city.

As the name implies, D-shaped structures have a "D"-shaped configuration (figures 7.4 and 7.5). In the provinces, Conchopata, and the capital, most reached a diameter of approximately ten meters. However, the latest research has identified a larger D-shaped structure, reaching up to twenty-two meters in diameter and with a wall that is 1.70 meters thick. Two small structures, 3.2 meters in diameter, have been recovered (Ochatoma et al. 2015). To date, three sizes (small, medium, and large) of D-shaped structures are recognized. All are oriented to an open plaza or courtyard with access through an opening in the center of the straight wall of the "D."

Inside, the walls were flanked by niches that varied in quantity and distribution according to the size of the structure. The largest structures had 18 niches arranged in two groups of 5 niches on the side, and a group of 4 at the bottom guarded by two groups of 2 on the flanks. The medium D-shaped structures varied in the number of niches, since those found in the provincial sites outside the Ayacucho region had 16 niches distributed in four groups of 4; while in the capital city the number varied between 18 and 22 niches, in both cases forming groups of 5, 4, and 2. The main feature of the medium D-shaped structures is the presence of niches in the straight wall where access was located (figure 7.4). Another attribute of D-shaped structures is a perpendicular tubular stone in the interior known as a sundial, or Intiqawana (figure 7.4). However, this last feature is reported only in Conchopata and the Wari capital. Finally, unlike the medium and large structures, the small variety lacks the architectural attributes described above. They maintain the shape and access on only the straight side of the building.

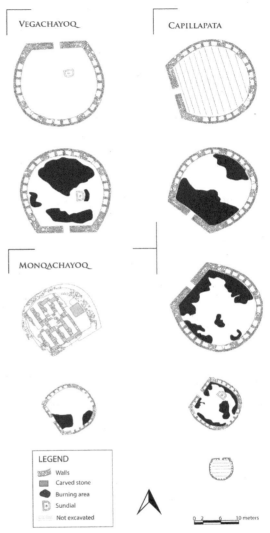

VEGACHAYOQ

CAPILLAPATA

MONQACHAYOQ

LEGEND
- Walls
- Carved stone
- Burning area
- Sundial
- Not excavated

0 2   6   10 meters

FIGURE 7.5. *D-shaped structures of the Wari capital site. Drawing: J. Antonio Ochatoma Cabrera.*

One of the D-shaped structures in Conchopata is surrounded by other rectangular enclosures and passageways with stone walls. Its straight side faces north and provides access to the structure. Its diameter is 10.5 meters and its height varies from 40 to 60 centimeters, from the top of the wall to the floor. The walls on the east, west, and south sides are 72 to 76 centimeters thick, while on the north side they are 50 centimeters thick (Ochatoma and Cabrera 2001, 2002; Ochatoma 2007; Ochatoma et al. 2015). In this D-shaped structure, the following items have been recovered: trophy heads (the skulls of decapitated humans), large burned areas, a sundial, and layers of pottery that were deliberately broken (Ochatoma and Cabrera 2001, 2002; Ochatoma 2007). The numerous pottery sherds contain much information about Wari iconography pertaining to elite people, sacred animals, supernatural beings, and gods (figure 7.4). The offerings were mostly ceramic urns decorated with iconography associated with the Staff God, warriors armed on rafts made from *totora* (figure 7.2f),[2] and dignitaries with sculptural faces in elaborate costumes (apparently members of the ruling elite) (figure 7.2g). This iconographic repertoire was vital for understanding the origins of Wari ideology and religion, as well as appreciating the complicated and little-known relations between Wari and Tiwanaku (Ochatoma and Cabrera 2001).

According to Tiffiny Tung (2012), rituals were closely linked to militarism in the Wari Empire and functioned as legitimizing practices of Wari leaders in managing the expansion and maintenance of their authority throughout their territory. However, some power relation between military leaders and ritual leaders is indicated through the osteological and iconographic evidence. Tung suggests coordination rather than a conflict, since the trophy heads and mutilated body parts belonged to foreign enemies. In this way, the military leaders provided enemy prisoners; the ritual specialists were in charge of dismembering and decapitating them, turning this activity into a ceremony (figures 7.2f and 7.2g).

In the western part of the structure, conical holes of forty centimeters in diameter were uncovered that served as the support for the large urns with conical bases. The bottom of the holes was lined with sherds from ceramic pitchers, and there were traces of brown organic material (figure 7.4). In the central part, the sundial, or Intiqawana, was discovered, which consists of a "small D-shaped structure" of one meter in diameter made with volcanic tuff, associated with a lithic tube sixty centimeters in length and twenty-five centimeters in diameter (Ochatoma and Cabrera 2001). On the northwest side of the D-shaped structure, there was a large concentration of potsherds corresponding to huge face-neck vessels used as containers for liquids that were consumed during rituals (figure 7.4).

In the southern part of the structure, six calcined juvenile human skulls have been buried, separated by small blocks of stone within a diameter of 1.2 meters. A small layer of burned clay covered the skulls (Ochatoma and Cabrera 2001; Ochatoma 2007). Bioarchaeological analyses by Tung (2012) reveals that the cut marks of the trophy heads were made on soft tissue while the heads were being

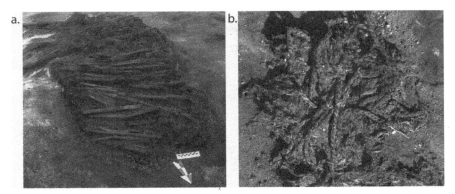

FIGURE 7.6. *Offerings from a D-shaped structure in the Vegachayoq sector of Wari.* (a) *Offering of forty burned lances.* (b) *Offering of burnt ropes of different sizes and thickness.* Photos: Martha Cabrera.

prepared; that is, they were "fresh" bodies and not old bones. One of the most outstanding features of the trophy heads were the holes drilled in the top of the head (or bregma) through which a rope would pass for transport. Also, based on the grayish-white coloration and vitrification of parts of the trophy heads, it was proven that they were subjected to a very high temperature, with an estimated heat of 800 degrees Celsius. Two of these trophy heads had burnt parts, which suggests that some were exhibited with the skin intact to show recognizable features before being subjected to burning. This interpretation is reinforced by the iconography of the Wari pottery, where the trophy heads are part of the deities' attire and are worn as warriors' pendants (Tung 2012, 170) (figures 7.2 and 7.6).

Other D-shaped ceremonial spaces were discovered in the ancient capital city of Wari, in the sectors of Vegachayoq, Monqachayoq, Capillapata and Ocopa. They are characterized by the abundant quantity of contexts that contain burning on the floor. These structures were subjected to an intense fire ritual that reached very high temperatures to the extent that material on the floor became glazed. Unlike Conchopata, the burn marks cover almost the entire interior of these buildings.

Describing each of the D structures would be exhaustive. However, many of them share some common characteristics (figure 7.5). For medium and large D-shaped structures, a sundial (described above in the case of Conchopata) and large areas of burnt floors are common. Similarly, prior to their closure, large holes were dug into the floor surface. Although they all have the same characteristics of closure (filled with debris until completely covered), they differ in orientation and in the offerings left before closure. In some, deer antlers were offered; in others, finely decorated plummets; and in others, prestigious Cajamarca-style pottery from the northern limit of the empire (northern Peru).

In the capital Wari, one of the most representative D-shaped structures is located in the Vegachayoq sector. In its burning contexts, there was a significant amount of straw, totora, thick and thin wood trunks tied with vegetable fiber ropes, camelid wool, cotton, and maize grains. In the northwestern part, charred remains of straw and remains of forty spears made of *chonta* (wood extracted from the jungle) neatly placed, totora, and trunks of thin and thick wood intertwined and tied. Close to this concentration, remains of burnt corn and beans were found. Noteworthy is the discovery of an offering of burnt ropes of different sizes and thicknesses. Possibly these items were quipus, which, as we will see later, were a vital instrument in the storage of knowledge (figure 7.6). The fire reached the walls and caused the detachment of parts of the plaster. This separation allowed us to observe the different layers of burnt plaster in this building and to surmise that the practice of burning and replastering was carried out on different occasions, not only at the time of abandonment. Each time these fire rituals were performed, the internal walls of the building were burned and subsequently renovated with new plaster that covered the burnt walls. Finally, in the last burning event of this building, the structure was systematically closed and filled in with tilled stones and clay.

FIRE RITUALS

It is possible that these fires were purposeful burning events, as fire served as a marker of cosmic and sacred time in Wari tradition. Fire functioned in the main myths and rites of all societies of the ancient world. The relationship between fire and nature was relevant for its role in the main festivities associated with the agricultural cycle. At the social level, the main ceremonies dedicated to fire marked temporal limits and, therefore, indicated the beginnings and closures of different stages and cycles (see chapter 10, this volume, on the Aztec New Fire Ceremony). Thus, fire occupied a central place in the ceremonies of the life cycle. For example, the archaeological evidence of intense burning found in the D-shaped structures of Wari and Conchopata denoted the great significance of fire in the sacred spaces and rituals that marked the end and beginning of the cycle.

This type of activity reminds us of the first sites with monumental architecture in the Andean area during the Final Archaic period (2600 to 1500 BCE) (Kaulicke 2010). Archaeological excavations at the Kotosh archaeological site, led by the Japanese Scientific Expedition of the University of Tokyo in the north-central highlands of Peru, revealed a series of complex superimpositions of quadrangular temples ranging from 5 × 5 meters to 10 × 10 meters. The archaeologists interpreted these remains as a temple renovation preceded by a ritual burning of offerings in the central part of the temple courtyard that was fueled by an underground conduit (Onuki 2014). This practice was not exclusive to Kotosh but was carried out in almost all the temples of the north-central mountain range during the Final Archaic period. For this reason, it was called the "Mito Tradition" (Bonnier 1977).

ASTRONOMICAL OBSERVATORIES

One of the activities that took place during the night was undoubtedly the observation of the moon and constellations. Such sky watching allowed the Wari to form original and innovative norms around space and time to generate their own calendar. The passing of day and night was possibly conceived as a supernatural event linked to the deities. Thus, pre-Hispanic astronomer-priests devised a way of orienting their most emblematic buildings by choosing directions toward the sunrise and sunset on certain auspicious dates (Galindo 2016). One of the possible functions of the D-shaped structures was for tracking time. The shadow generated by the sundial, or Intiqawana, and the distribution and organization of the internal niches could mark the beginning or end of cycles.

One of the most notable examples of the spatial-temporal integration of the Andean worldview is seen in the Inka Empire. Our understanding of this worldview is enriched by the myths and stories told in Spanish chronicles that allow us to outline an element of Andean thinking. After long, detailed, and extensive research, Tom Zuidema (2010, 2015) made the first description of the Inka calendar captured in the quipus, and this interest led him to the roots of the Inkas in the Wari and Tiwanaku cultures (Zuidema 2015, 153). The quipus were an information storage instrument consisting of camelid wool or cotton strings of various colors, provided with knots. For Zuidema, the Inkas had three measuring systems: the solar, the lunar, and the *ceques*. The last one consisted of imaginary lines that oriented toward the four cardinal axes that started from Coricancha, in the center of Cuzco, and went radially toward each *huaca*, forming 328 *huacas* (in Quechua language, huaca refers to a sacred entity that involves things, ancestor mummies, or *mallquis*, and representations of nature: mountains, rivers, caves, natural springs, etc.). With this system of measurement, rituals of adoration were celebrated that indicated the annual passage from the wet season to the dry season. In the Wari case, based on the analysis of a piece of textile, Zuidema defined a system of 360 units: 12 groups of 30 circles in the form of doughnuts, subdivided into 36 columns of 10 circles each (Zuidema 2015, 134). That is, he defined a system of solar measurement.

While this research is a great step toward understanding the Wari measuring system, and thus its worldview, it remains to be deciphered what other measuring systems are possibly found in the D-shaped structures and other architectural elements distributed in the Wari capital. We assumed that the function of these objects was that of an astronomical mirror. So far, we have differentiated three types of observatories: one resembles a large "reflection pool," another is a block of quadrangular stone with holes excavated in the middle, and a third has unworked stone blocks with small holes (figure 7.7).

Two specimens of reflection pools have been recovered in the Vegachayoq sector. The dimensions of one of them is 6.7 meters long and 2.3 meters wide with a variable thickness of 0.16 to 0.18 meters. It was associated with a large obsidian block (0.37 × 0.38 meters) and two intact incense burners with the classic Tiwanaku design that were part of a burning offering. The second specimen is six by two meters with a thickness of 0.5 meters. Its orientation is the same as the first (Ochatoma et al. 2015) (figure 7.7a). These pools reflected certain parts of the celestial vault. In the single specimen of the quadrangular stone, its interior is partially carved. Its base is not flat, but rather has small holes framed in a rectangle (figure 7.7b).

Finally, the third type of observatory is located near the south side of the ancient city of Wari, very close to a cave (known as San Cristóbal) that is a sacred place, even today. There are several blocks of granite stone in which craftspeople carved small holes of various sizes and depths. In this group of stones, we can find stones with only one hole and others aligned in groups of 2, 3, 4, 5, 6, and 7 in each block (figure 7.7c). From this group, there is one stone block that stands out: it has seven aligned holes and has grooves in the shape of a spiral connected to each other. It seems to resemble the constellation Orion while others correlate with sacred animal constellations (figure 7.7c). Presented here is a preliminary sketch of the function of these lithic objects. There are further inquiries that can be made to determine and extend the astronomical measurements to get a better idea of their worth. Undoubtedly, D structures played an astronomical role closely linked to ritual life. Further analysis of their functions for astronomical and calendar purposes is pending. As we shall see, within these structures, key ritual activities were performed.

FIGURE 7.7. *Three types of observatories found among the Wari:* (a) *Reflection pools.* (b) *Reflection pool with holes.* (c) *Granite stone blocks with groups of holes. Photos: Martha Cabrera, José Ochatoma, and J. Antonio Ochatoma Cabrera.*

NOCTURNAL AND UNDERWORLD DEITIES

In the pre-Hispanic societies of the Andean world, the natural forces were considered sacred powers, personified in different deities: geographical features, mountains, snowcapped mountains, and animals with specific faculties and attributes. Andean religion was characterized by its polytheism. In this way, nature was conceived as the manifestation of the different deities.

Dumont and colleagues (2010) interpret iconographic representations as expressing symbolic, religious, and social values. Such symbolic depictions strengthened the religious worldview of pre-Hispanic groups that worshiped certain types of animals, such as felines, snakes, falconids, and other animals expressed in zoomorphic forms within a system of cultural codes. The religious symbol that Wari is based on is the divinity represented in the Staff God in the Sun Gate of Tiwanaku (Menzel 1964; Lumbreras 1974, 1985; Cook 1994; Ochatoma and Cabrera 2001). It is surrounded by a set of mythological characters, among which the falconids, the snake, and the felines stand out, the latter two probably linked to the underworld and the night. Anita Cook (1994) identified the Staff God with the highest mountain in the local landscape, the *wamani*, par excellence. The Wamanis, in the Andean world, are the deities who take the form of a mountain that manifests itself to people in the form of a condor, eagle, or hawk.

During the Middle Horizon the Wari created representations of deities linked to their cosmology. Both diurnal or solar deities and nocturnal deities were linked. In this dichotomy, nocturnal divinities are represented as animals that had an absolute dominion at night, such as the jaguar or the puma. These divinities are portrayed in different materials, such as lithic, fabric, metal, and ceramic.

In Wari iconography it is common to find representations of felines, birds, and snakes. They appear as appendages in the composition of the body and, especially, are incorporated into elements of adornment. Plus, there are abstract representations that bring to mind the "shape of fire." These symbols are usually placed as ornaments on the tufts and on the upper part of the staffs of the Staff God and the deities in vertical position (figure 7.2a, 7.2b, and 7.2c). The details of the representation of the eyes of the deities and the sacred animals that are part of them differ from the eyes of human representations and are divided into two halves: one white and one black. Perhaps they are symbols of the crescent or waning moon that are related to the Andean productive calendar, a system that is still used today by rural populations. Maria del Carmen Valverde (1998) points out that to the extent that lunar energy is fundamental to life, in most Indigenous communities the land must be sown when there is a full moon to guarantee good harvests (see chapter 6, this volume, for a similar observation of Maya agriculturalists).

THE FELINES

The flying feline called Ccoa was and still is pertinent in the Andean world because of its link with fertility. This flying feline was believed to be a puma, throwing lightning through the eyes, urinating rain, spitting hail, and grunting thunder (figure 7.2b and figure 7.8b). It was generally associated with deities and controlled atmospheric phenomena and was subordinate to them but similarly could be perceived as if a deity of the hills had taken such a form. Among the contemporary Quechuas, it is believed that the Ccoa is one of the servants of the tutelary gods and resides in the mountains. This, the most active of the spirits, is closer to the daily work of the people, and it is the most feared because it has lightning and hail. The Ccoa is also an advisor to the sorcerers and is invoked by the less experienced (Mishkin 1940, 237). Another link of the feline is related to death and sacrifice. In Conchopata, a vessel composed of two superimposed heads, that of a feline on a human skull, was recovered from excavations. The sculptural presentation of this vessel alludes directly to the close relationship between felines and death (figure 7.8b).

The Snake or Amaru

The biological structure, shape, and movement of snakes are frequently incorporated into the imagery of ancient civilizations. In some cases, they were highly appreciated and even considered as sacred animals, as in the Andean and Mesoamerican religions. In other cases they were repudiated for symbolizing evil, such as in the Catholic religion.

In the Huarochirí Manuscript (see Arguedas et al. [1598] 1966), the snake or serpent is called Amaru and appears as a powerful being but subordinated to the major gods, capable of fertilizing lands where it was impossible to cultivate. This metaphor is an allusion to the rivers, which, like the snakes, have a wavy form. Therefore, in the Andean world, the Amaru is closely related to agricultural productivity.

In the Wari iconographic repertoire, the snake seems to be part of the paraphernalia of the deities in the form of appendages to the crowns, as belts, replacing the tongues and even on the underside of the staffs (figures 7.2a, 7.2b, 7.2c). These depictions are usually mixed with attributes of other members of the sacred Wari fauna. In some cases, the snake head is replaced by the head of a feline or bird. However, in the earliest Wari period, with the style called Chakipampa, representations of two-headed snakes abound, in whose bodies the Qochas (underground water catchment wells) are represented (figure 7.2e).

The Owl and the Falconids

Perhaps the most remarkable characteristics about owls are that they feed at night and have the ability to adapt to any type of habitat, including trees and steeples. In the Andean world, the owl is related to the night, rains, and storms, and associated with death and sacrifice. A noteworthy precedent for the representation of the owl in the ritual of the pre-Columbian Andean world is found in the Mochica culture (200–700 CE) on the northern coast of Peru. In the Ceremony of Sacrifice, the Owl God, in the company of other gods, gives a cup with blood to the main god, Ai Apaec. In Wari, a vessel was discovered that has the head of an owl with two snakes resting on its shoulders, and on the owl's neck rests a toad looking downward. In its right hand, the owl holds a snake and, in the left hand, a decapitated head (figure 7.8a). The owl has further connections besides the night sky, the stars, and the rain, which symbolize sacrifice and death, that lead us to consider it as the main deity of the night.

Falconids are diurnal hunting birds that are characterized by extended wingspans, acute eyesight, piercing beaks, and short legs with strong claws. In the Andean belief system, they embody the mountain. These characteristics are enough to make them one of the most venerated animals since the origins of Andean civilization. They are linked to ritual and mythical activities. They are even attributed, through myths, to the foundation or origin of the empire of the first lineage of the Inka. In the Wari imagination, the falconids are represented in different ways, in most cases with attributes of other sacred animals or as part of the paraphernalia of supernatural creatures (figures 7.7a, 7.7b, and 7.7c). However, the discovery of these symbols on a Conchopata vessel lead us to believe that these birds, like felines, were closely linked in sacrificial rituals. This representation is a procession of falconids with tufts in profile holding a trachea with a heart and lungs (figure 7.2d). The falconids not only represent the bird itself, but personify the *apus tutelares* of a region, hence the significance of the objects or organs to be offered.

CONCLUSIONS

"Every day hath a night" can be interpreted and understood in several ways. In the present case we relate it to the religious life and beliefs of the Andean people. The conception of night in the Andes was used to interpret the meaning of night in the Wari world. In the same way, as in other societies, the night brings with it the observation of the celestial bodies. Although we approached the night as an astronomical phenomenon with the distribution and spatial orientation of the Wari ceremonial structures, the religious aspect likewise played a dominant role since it is present in the day-to-day life of people, in their fears, beliefs, and relationship with nature. Reconstructing everyday life at night is not an easy task. While daytime and nighttime activities have left their mark on the archaeological record through objects, iconography, and even entire buildings, archaeological reconstructions often privilege daytime ones (Gonlin and Nowell 2018b, 5). However, as we have observed in the archaeological record of the D-shaped structures, we can infer that the activities carried out were even more crucial than the activities performed during the day.

What makes Wari relevant in the history of the Central Andes is that it became the neuralgic center of religion during the Middle Horizon period. Thus, through the iconography inherited from the altiplano, Wari exerted new forms of power and dominion over other societies and, to strengthen this hegemony, propagated the typical Wari ceremonial structure: the D-shaped edifice. There were activities, both mundane and sacred, that were undoubtedly performed during the night. Such sacred activities were restricted to specialists or priests who dedicated themselves to observing the firmament day after day and night after night to understand and interpret the movement

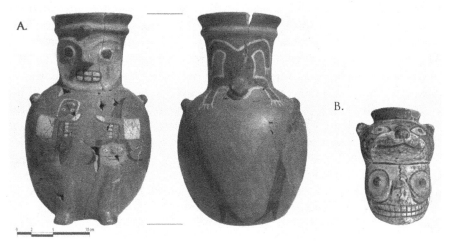

FIGURE 7.8. (a) *A vessel of an owl character holding a trophy head.* (b) *Bottle composed of a feline head* (top) *and a human skull* (bottom). *Photo: Martha Cabrera.*

and phases of the moon and the figures of the constellations that were closely linked to animals in their environment: the felines, the snake, and the falconids. In this sense, astronomical observation reached such a high level of specialization that it formed part of the religious ritual for the sacralization of space. The discovery of small holes carved in blocks of rocks, as well as the rectangular blocks in the form of wells, indicate that these features worked as astronomical mirrors or markers of constellations. We consider the tubular pillars or "sundials" inside the D-shaped ceremonial enclosures and how they worked during the day and at night with the glow of the full moon. Nowadays farming populations use moonlight to harvest corn, an act closely linked to ritual activities.

The recurrent presence of scorched areas as part of the abandonment ritual that took place inside the D-shaped structures leads us to infer that these activities could have taken place during the sunset, as the light of the fire would have been spectacular and unique. Therefore, the nocturnal fire could have marked the end of the prestige of the ceremonial area and its deities, altering the daily life and marking the beginning of a new stage. Finally, we have yet to carry out a detailed study of the orientation in the space of the D-shaped structures, checking their alignment with the stars or deities (geographical features, mountains, etc.). This new direction of inquiry is one in which we will be working to seek answers about the ancient Andean night.

Acknowledgments. The authors wish to thank Nancy Gonlin and Meghan E. Strong for their invitation to participate in the symposium "After Dark: The Nocturnal Urban Landscape and Lightscape of Ancient Cities" (Society for American Archaeology [SAA], 2019) and to be part of this volume. We also thank Nancy for her insightful comments and editorial assistance. Gratitude is extended to Adolfo Domínguez and Jessica Ortiz, as well as José Ochatoma Paravicino, director of the Archaeological Research Project "Uso social de las áreas ceremoniales en 'D' del Complejo Arqueológico de Wari," funded by The National University of San Cristóbal de Huamanga. Last but not least, we thank Martín López for his collaboration in the digitization of Wari and Conchopata maps. In spite of all the help received, there are always errors in writing and lightness in interpretation, the responsibility for which lies solely in our limitations as authors.

NOTES

1. It comes from the Quechua word "qiru" and is used to refer to a ceremonial vessel, usually made of wood, with a truncated cone shape.
2. Totora or *junco*, *Schoenoplectus californicus*, is an aquatic herbaceous plant used as raw material for the manufacture of canoes or boats in pre-Columbian Andes.

REFERENCES

Anders, Martha. 1991. "Structure and Function at the Planned Site of Azángaro: Cautionary Notes for the Model of Huari as a Centralized State." In *Huari Administrative Structure: Prehistoric Monumental Architecture and State Government*, edited by William Isbell and Gordon F. McEwan, 165–197. Washington DC: Dumbarton Oaks Research Library and Collection.

Arguedas, José María, Pierre Duviols, and Francisco de Avila. (1598?) 1966. *Dioses y hombres de Huarochiri: Narración quechua recogida por Francisco de Avila*. Lima: Museo Nacional de Historia.

Barba, Luis, Agustín Ortiz, and Linda Manzanilla. 2007. "Commoner Ritual at Teotihuacan, Central Mexico: Methodological Considerations." In *Commoner Ritual and Ideology in Ancient Mesoamerica*, edited by Nancy Gonlin and Jon C. Lohse, 55–82. Boulder: University Press of Colorado.

Benavides, Mario. 1991. "Cheqo Wasi." In *Huari Administrative Structure: Prehistoric Monumental Architecture and State Government*, edited by William Isbell and Gordon F. McEwan, 55–70. Washington, DC: Dumbarton Oaks Research Library and Collection.

Betanzos, Juan de. (1551–1571) 1880. *Suma y narración de los Yngas*. Madrid: Imprenta de Manuel G. Hernandez.

Bonnier, Elizabeth. 1997. "Preceramic Architecture in the Andes: The Mito Tradition." In *Archaeologica Peruana 2. Arquitectura y civilización en los Andes Prehispánicos*, edited by Elizabeth Bonnier and Henning Bischof, 121–144. Mannheim, Germany: Städtisches Reiss-Museum.

Cabrera, Martha. 2007. "Cosmovisión y simbolismo de los animales en las deidades de Conchopata." In *El desarrollo de las ciencias sociales en Ayacucho: La Universidad Nacional de San Cristóbal de Huamanga*, edited by Luis Millones, Jefrey Gamarra, and José Ochatoma, 61–86. Lima: Fondo Editorial de la Facultad de Ciencias Sociales, Universidad Nacional Mayor de San Marcos.

Cabrera, Martha, and José Ochatoma. 2019. "Funerary Architecture and Ritual in the Monqachayuq Sector, Wari." In *Diversity and Uniformity in the Prehispanic Andes during the Middle Horizon*, edited by Shinya Watanabe. Vol. 8: 46–79. Nanzan, Japan: Research Papers of the Anthropological Institute.

Cook, Anita. 1994. *Wari y Tiwanaku: Entre el estilo y la imagen*. Lima: Pontificia Universidad Católica del Perú.

Cowgill, George L. 2008. "Teotihuacan as an Urban Place." In *El Urbanismo en Mesoamérica/Urbanism in Mesoamerica*. Vol. 2, edited by Alba Guadalupe Mastache, Robert H. Cobean, Ángel Garcia Cook, and Kenneth G. Hirth, 85–112. Mexico City and University Park, PA: Instituto Nacional de Antropología e Historia and The Pennsylvania State University.

Cowgill, George L. 2015. *Ancient Teotihuacan: Early Urbanism in Central México*. Case Studies in Early Societies. New York: Cambridge University Press.

DeMarrais, Elizabeth, Luis Jaime Castillo, and Timothy Earle. 1996. "Ideology, Materialization, and Power Strategies." *Current Anthropology* 37 (1): 15–31.

Galindo, Jesus. 2016. "Calendric-Astronomical Alignment of Architectural Structures in Mesoamerica: An Ancestral Cultural Practice." In *The Role of Archaeoastronomy in the Maya World: The Case Study of the Island of Cozumel*, edited by Nuria Sanz, 21–38. Mexico City: UNESCO.

Gonlin, Nancy, and April Nowell, eds. 2018a. *Archaeology of the Night: Life After Dark in the Ancient World*. Boulder: University Press of Colorado.

Gonlin, Nancy, and David M. Reed, eds. 2021. *Night and Darkness in Ancient Mesoamerica*. Louisville: University Press of Colorado.

Gonlin, Nancy, and April Nowell. 2018b. "Introduction to the Archaeology of the Night." In *Archaeology of the Night: Life After Dark in the Ancient World*, edited by Nancy Gonlin and April Nowell, 5–24. Boulder: University Press of Colorado.

Isbell, William. 1991. "Huari Administration and the Orthogonal Cellular Architecture Horizon." In *Huari Administrative Structure: Prehistoric Monumental Architecture and State Government*, edited by William Isbell and Gordon F. McEwan, 293–315. Washington, DC: Dumbarton Oaks.

Isbell, William. 2000. "Repensando el Horizonte Medio: El caso de Conchopata, Ayacucho. Perú." Boletín de Arqueología PUCP (4), 9-68.

Isbell, William. 2004. "Palaces and Politics in the Andean Middle Horizon." In *Palaces of the Ancient New World*, edited by Susan Toby Evans and Joanne Pillsbury, 191–246. Washington, DC: Dumbarton Oaks.

Isbell, William. 2008. "Wari and Tiwanaku: International Identities in the Central Andean Middle Horizon." In *The Handbook of South American Archaeology*, edited by Helaine Silverman and William Isbell, 731–759. New York: Springer.

Isbell, William, Christine Brewster-Wray, and Lynda Spickard. 1991. "Architecture and Spatial Organization at Huari." In *Huari Administrative Structure: Prehistoric Monumental Architecture and State Government*, edited by William Isbell and Gordon F. McEwan, 19–54. Washington, DC: Dumbarton Oaks.

Isbell, William, and Gordon F. McEwan, eds. 1991. *Huari Administrative Structure: Prehistoric Monumental Architecture and State Government*. Washington, DC: Dumbarton Oaks.

Jiménez de la Espada, Marcos. (1881–1897) 1965. *Relaciones geográficas de Indias: Perú*. Madrid: Ediciones Atlas.

Kaulicke, Peter. 2010. *Las cronologías del Formativo: 50 años de investigaciones japonesas en perspectiva*. Lima: Fondo Editorial de la Pontificia Universidad Católica del Perú.

Lumbreras, Luis. 1974. *The Peoples and Cultures of Ancient Peru*. Washington, DC: Smithsonian Institution Press.

Lumbreras, Luis. 2010. *Plan de manejo del complejo arqueológico Wari*. Ayacucho, Peru: Plan Copesco Nacional.

Manzanilla, Linda R. 1990. "Niveles de análisis en el estudio de unidades habitacionales." *Revista Española de Antropología Americana* 20 (February): 9–18.

Manzanilla, Linda R. 2009. "Corporate Life in Apartment and Barrio Compounds at Teotihuacan, Central Mexico." In *Domestic Life in Prehispanic Capitals: A Study of Specialization, Hierarchy, and Ethnicity*, edited by Linda R. Manzanilla and Claude Chapdelaine, 21–42. Memoirs of the Museum of Anthropology no. 46. Ann Arbor: Museum of Anthropology, University of Michigan.

Manzanilla, Linda R. 2017. "Multietnicidad y diversidad cultural en Teotihuacan, Centro de México." *Claroscuro, Revista del Centro de Estudios sobre Diversidad Cultural: Facultad de Humanidades y Artes* 16 (16): 1–30.

McEwan, Gordon F., and Patrick Ryan Williams. 2013. "The Wari Built Environment: Landscape and Architecture of Empire." In *Wari, Lords of the Ancient Andes*, edited by Susan E. Bergh, 65–81. New York: Thames and Hudson.

Menzel, Dorothy. 1964. "Style and Time in the Middle Horizon." *Ñawpa Pacha* 2: 1–106.

Mishkin, Bernard. 1940. "Cosmological Ideas among the Indians of the Southern Andes." *The Journal of American Folklore* 53 (210): 225–241. https://doi.org/10.2307/535782.

Montesinos, Fernando. (1642) 1882. *Memorias antiguas historiales y políticas del Perú, seguidas de las informaciones acerca del señorío de los Inkas hechas por mandato de D. Francisco de Toledo*. Madrid: n.p.

Ochatoma, José. 2007. *Alfareros del imperio Huari: Vida cotidiana y áreas de actividad en Conchopata*. Ayacucho, Peru: Universidad Nacional de San Cristóbal de Huamanga.

Ochatoma, José, and Martha Cabrera. 2001. "Arquitectura y áreas de actividad en Conchopata." *Boletín de Arqueología PUCP* 4 (4): 449–488.

Ochatoma, José, and Martha Cabrera. 2002. "Religious Ideology and Military Organization in the Iconography of a D-shaped Ceremonial Precinct at Conchopata." In *Andean Archaeology II: Art, Landscape and Society*, edited by Helaine Silverman and William H. Isbell, 225–247. New York: Kluwer Academic/Plenum Publishing.

Ochatoma, José, and Martha Cabrera. 2010. "Los espacios de poder y culto a los ancestros en el Imperio Huari." In *Señores de los imperios del Sol*, edited by Krzysztof Makowski, 129–141. Lima: Banco de Crédito del Perú.

Ochatoma, José, Martha Cabrera, and Carlos Mancilla. 2015. *El área sagrada de Wari: Investigaciones arqueológicas en Vegachayuq Moqo*. Ayacucho, Peru: Universidad Nacional de San Cristóbal de Huamanga.

Onuki, Yoshio. 2014. "Una reconsideración de la fase Kotosh Mito." In *El centro ceremonial andino: Nuevas perspectivas para los periodos Arcaico y Formativo*, edited by Yuji Seki, 105–122. Senri Ethnological Studies 89 (SES 89). Osaka, Japan: National Museum of Ethnology.

Pozzi-Escot B., Denise, 1985. "Conchopata: Un poblado de especialistas durante el horizonte medio." *Boletín del Instituto Francés de Estudios Andinos* 14 (3–4): 115–129.

Rappaport, Roy A. 1999. *Ritual and Religion in the Making of Humanity*. Cambridge: Cambridge University Press.

Schreiber, Katharina. 1992. *Wari Imperialism in Middle Horizon Peru*. Ann Arbor: University of Michigan.

Schreiber, Katharina. 2005. "Sacred Landscapes and Imperial Ideologies: The Wari Empire in Sondondo, Peru." *Archeological Papers of the American Anthropological Association* 14 (1): 131–150.

Schreiber, Katharina. 2013. "The Rise of an Andean Empire." In *Wari: Lords of the Ancient Andes*, edited by Susan E. Bergh, 31–46. New York: Thames and Hudson.

Schreiber, Katharina, and Matthew Edwards. 2010. "Los centros administrativos Huari y las manifestaciones físicas del poder imperial." In *Señores de los Imperios del Sol*, edited by Krzysztof Makowski, 153–162. Lima: Banco de Crédito del Perú.

Tung, Tiffiny. 2012. *Violence, Ritual, and the Wari Empire*. Gainesville: University Press of Florida.

Valverde, Carmen. 1998. "El simbolismo del Jaguar entre los mayas." PhD diss., Facultad de Filosofía y Letras, Universidad Nacional Autónoma de México.

Zuidema, Tom. 2010. *El calendario Inka: Tiempo y espacio en la organización ritual del Cuzco: La idea del pasado*. Lima: Fondo Editorial del Congreso del Perú.

Zuidema, Tom. 2015. *Códigos del tiempo: Espacios rituales en el mundo andino*. Lima: Apus Graph Ediciones.

8

This is the lesson: Great cities are like any other
living things, being born and maturing and weary-
ing and dying in their turn. Duh, right? Everyone
who's visited a real city feels that, one way or another.
All those rural people who hate cities are afraid of
something legit; cities really are different. They make
a weight on the world, a tear in the fabric of reality,
like . . . like black holes, maybe.

   —N. K. Jeminsin, *How Long 'til*
   Black Future Month?, 394–395

Cahokia after Dark

Affect, Water, and the Moon

Susan M. Alt

Cities *feel* different. Urbanism at Cahokia, just as for
any city, was experiential, and as for any city, experiences of the night were a vital aspect of urban affect.
If, as other analysts have noted, cities are bundles or
precise kinds of assemblages (in the sense of DeLanda
2016 or Deleuze and Guattari 1987) or even assemblages
of assemblages (Jervis 2018), then nightly experience
is part of that assemblage (McFarlane 2011; chapters
in Alt and Pauketat 2019 Jervis 2019). Cahokia (figure
1.1) was North America's first Indigenous city north of
Mexico (founded in present-day Illinois around AD
1050). It may not be the first place that comes to mind
when thinking about urbanism, but given new discoveries from a series of major excavations at and around
this unique center (Baires 2017; Pauketat et al. 2017;
Emerson et al. 2018; Alt 2018a; Koldehoff and Pauketat
2018), views about the causes and consequences of
indigenous American urbanism are substantially
changing (figure 8.1). In part, this shift is because we

https://doi.org/10.5876/9781646422609.c008

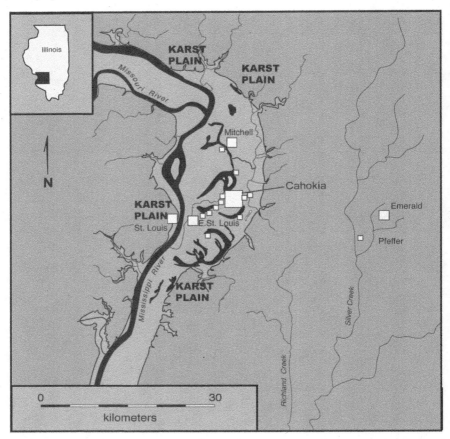

FIGURE 8.1. *Map of Cahokia, location of its major precincts, and places mentioned in the text. Map: Susan M. Alt*

realize that urbanism is not just numbers of people and buildings. Urbanism is an experience emanating from the assembled and rhizomatic connections of sensations, atmospheres, and affects of a time and place. To amplify a quote and points found in Ben Jervis (2018, 111):

> To quote McFarlane 2001b[,] "urbanism does not exist, but occurs." The City therefore becomes "an object which is relentlessly being assembled at sites of urban practice" (Farias 2009:2) and, whilst a city has familiar form, it is also a ruse (Simone 2011:344) that is, it is something which appears stable and definable but is in fact slippery, vibrant, and insecure.

Jervis (2018, 111) is talking about how cities are always becoming, that they are processes, not things (see chapters in Alt and Pauketat 2019). We need to follow the strands of relational webs, or the immanence of cities, to better grasp the urban as Tim Pauketat (2019) notes, following Gilles Deleuze and Felix Guattari (1987). That is to say the urban is not a thing but vibrant assemblages that are simultaneously territorializing and deterritorializing entanglements generating affects. Furthermore, urbanism, particularly Indigenous urbanism, bundles the powers and forces of the unseen world and other than human persons into the urban experience. Cities do not just house human persons but encapsulate many more things that humans recognize as vibrant (Bennett 2010) or living (see chapters in Alt and Pauketat 2019). Cities, in fact, may be places that harbor greater concentrations of otherworldly forces, powers, and other-than-human persons. The night has its own associations with such powers, forces, and beings. In this chapter, I present evidence for why we should not discount the effects and affects of the powers of the unseen world and the nocturnal dimension in understanding Cahokian urbanism.

Experiences related to the night may be even more critical than we might expect when considered as a component of why Cahokia became urban. Urbanization at Cahokia occurred in a short period of time—over the lifetime of one generation, due in good part to an influx of immigrants who helped shape Cahokia as a city (Alt 2006, 2008; Slater et al. 2014). Immigrants came to the American Bottom region and to Cahokia because it was the origin point for a new religion that saw night and the moon as critical powers in the world (Pauketat 2012; Alt 2018b; Alt and Pauketat 2018; Pauketat and Alt 2018; Alt 2019; Alt 2020b).

CAHOKIA'S URBAN ASSEMBLAGE

As an urban place Cahokia would have been extraordinary and alien for most, if not all, visitors and new inhabitants (figure 8.2). A city was a new thing for all America north of Mexico; most people at AD 1050 lived in small communities. There were some larger ones, but those had populations that numbered in the hundreds of people, not in the tens of thousands, as at Cahokia. It has now been demonstrated that at least one-third of the population of Cahokia were immigrants from smaller communities (Slater et al. 2014) who would have found the urban experience to be novel—the packing of persons, buildings, ritual precincts, and monuments would have been surprising, if not overwhelming (in the sense of Thrift 2004). The affects and unseen powers of the night at Cahokia would have been no less strange and awe inspiring, and the

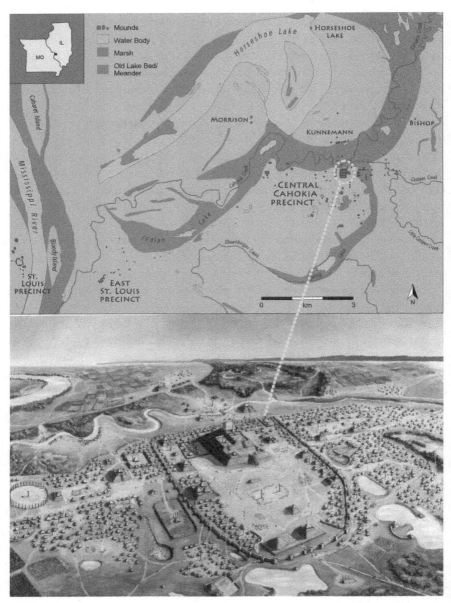

FIGURE 8.2. *(Top) Detail map of Cahokian precincts. Image: Courtesy of Illinois State Archaeological Survey. (Bottom) Central Cahokian Core. Image: William Isminger; provided courtesy of Cahokia Mounds State Historic Site.*

significance of the night may have had a good deal to do with why so many visitors and immigrants came.

Cahokia at AD 1050 was a place with crowded domestic neighborhoods, numerous public facilities, ritual areas, and monumental constructions, such as massive earthen pyramids and plazas (Dalan 1997; Emerson 1997; Fowler et al. 1999; Emerson et al. 2018; Emerson 2002; Pauketat 2009, 2012). Monks Mound, one of the over 200 mounds in and around the various Cahokian precincts, was the largest earthen construction north of Mexico, with a base the size of the Great Pyramid of Giza in Egypt and a height topping 100 feet (Fowler 1997; Pauketat 2004). The Grand Plaza in front of Monks Mound could have contained nearly any other Mississippian center in its entirety so large was its size (Alt et al. 2010). The overbuilt monumental precincts and expansive habitation neighborhoods were surrounded by domesticized landscapes such as farm fields, but its largest precincts were intersected by seemingly less domesticated wetlands, creeks, and the Mississippi River (Baires 2017; Alt 2019). In fact, water appeared in many ways at and around Cahokia—in ponds, sinkholes, and underground rivers and periodically as rain, snow, ice, mist, and fog. Some of the potentially most interesting (yet archaeologically unexamined) interactions with water would have been in a karst field that consisted of over 10,000 sinkholes west and south of downtown Cahokia in upland areas located ten kilometers away from the center (Panno and Luman 2012; Alt 2019, 2020a, 2020b). This karst field is composed of ponds, caves, caverns, and even waterfalls that led to underground cave systems that were periodically washed clean by rain and floods, and inside they were as dark as night (Panno et al. 2009).

At Cahokia's central ceremonial precinct, water was not simply present; it was actually built into the sacred landscape, with ponds made from borrow pits, or with a raised causeway leading through a saturated wetland that directed participants to the south side of the main ceremonial precinct and to burial mounds, such as the well-known Mound 72 mortuary complex and the Rattlesnake Mortuary Mound (Fowler 1997; Baires 2017). Another set of mounds and borrow pits, the Tippets Group, was arranged around a piece of land that juts out between the mounds into the human-made ponds as if to create a stage set in water (Dalan 1997; Baires 2017; Alt 2019). On the other hand, the Grand Plaza was built to control water, constructed with a slight incline to send rainwater to the south of the plaza, with a layer of sand laid beneath its surface to hasten the draining (Dalan 1997; Alt et al. 2010). Even the mounds were built with water control in mind, having layers that acted as drains to prevent water from sitting in the mounds and causing damage

(Collins and Chalfant 1993). The point, then, is that the Cahokians well knew and managed water as part of their urban planning, a pattern that is common to other Indigenous cities (see French et al. [2020] for water construction and management at the Classic Maya site of Palenque, Mexico). But all this water management and watery interactions belie the real significance of this substance, which lay in the powers, forces, and spirits attached to it and its qualities that intersected with the night, the moon, and the stars.

Understanding water and the night at Cahokia requires interpreting Cahokia's archaeological data through a consideration of what mattered to the Cahokians as read in material culture, deposition, and ancient art, as well as in the oral histories of descendant groups, including Siouan speakers (Alt 2020a). In so doing, it becomes very clear that critical Cahokian experiences were marked in landscapes and material objects and often seem tied to water and the moon. These interrelated themes matter, because we now think that the city became urban as a result of a religious movement that drew people into the American Bottom, to Cahokia, and its religious centers (Alt 2018a, 2018c, 2019, 2020b; Pauketat and Alt 2018). Part of what mattered in that new religion related to experiences tied to the night, water, and the moon in both natural and human-made features. Investigations of one hilltop shrine center, the Emerald Acropolis (a religious center with twelve mounds and palimpsests of public and religious buildings, pilgrim housing, and numerous shrines) provided a clear message that water and the moon were critical elements of this new religion and that new religious protocols were developing and drawing in immigrants and pilgrims even before urbanization took hold (Pauketat 2012; Skousen 2016; Pauketat et al. 2017; Alt 2016, 2018a, 2018c, 2019; Pauketat and Alt 2018; Barzilai 2020). The experience of this religion, with a focus on lunar movements, was necessarily tightly tied to nocturnal experiences. Oral histories of probable Cahokian descendants (particularly Siouan speakers) provide suggestions about how the night might have mattered, and how the moon, water, and other materials were inexorably linked.

THE NIGHTLY AND WATERY EVIDENCE OF EMERALD

The significance of the moon and its movements is clear from numerous lines of evidence, both in natural and built features at a Cahokian shrine center, the Emerald Acropolis (figure 8.3). At Emerald, the Cahokians oriented all central structures such that they marked lunar standstill positions. In fact, even the hilltop itself pointed toward such a position (Pauketat 2012; Pauketat et al. 2017). While the hill was naturally shaped and oriented such that it roughly

FIGURE 8.3. *The Emerald Acropolis and alignment with the moon alongside an excavation block with shrines oriented along the same axis. Images: Susan M. Alt.*

pointed toward the lunar standstill, the Cahokians perfected that positioning by removing and adding soils to remodel the sides of the hill to achieve the desired alignment (Pauketat et al. 2017). The use of the hilltop at night is evident in the marked lunar observations and the density of large open fire pits scattered across the top of the acropolis (Barzilai 2020; see Cabrera Romero and Ochatoma Cabrera, chapter 7 in this volume, for discussion of fire among the Wari of Peru).

Emerald, sitting along native built roadways (Skousen 2016), would have glowed with the lights of those fires that would have been visible to people who were many miles away. The vitalness of water was evident in the hill, which sat upon a perched water table such that the hill continued to ooze water well after any rain had fallen, and some of that water released through a spring downslope (Grimley and Phillips 2015). The centrality of the watery qualities of the hill to the Cahokians was made evident in how water was used for the closing ceremonies of principal structures and in events where every burned offering and shrine floor was covered in water-washed soils before being finally buried (Alt 2016, 2018c, 2019). Even a human burial (perhaps a human offering) was covered in water-washed soil before final interment (Alt 2015). And all these water-laden spiritually infused persons, places, and things were oriented in homage to lunar standstill moments. The many lessons at Emerald linking water and the moon are perhaps best contextualized by similar associations made by potential Cahokian descendant groups (Alt 2020a).

ORAL HISTORIES

Siouan speakers are believed by some scholars to be descendants of the Cahokians, though they are probably not the only descendants (Kehoe 2007; Kelly and Brown 2012; Hunter 2013; Diaz-Granados et al. 2015). Given archaeological studies of material culture and human isotopic studies, it seems clear that Cahokia had a multiethnic population (Slater et al. 2015; Alt 2018a; Hedman et al. 2018). More studies are finding Cahokian outposts and connections across the Midwest and Southeast (McNutt and Parish 2020), thus suggesting that other modern Indigenous groups likely had Cahokian ancestors, or indirectly had other Mississippian ancestors who shared basic religious beliefs with the Cahokians. For example, Caddoan speakers claim Spiro Mound Center as an ancestral place, and Spiro's great mortuary mound contained Cahokian-made figurative pipes and other materials with sacred Cahokian imagery (Brown and Kelly 2000; Emerson et al. 2003). Mississippian people, who lived across much of the eastern United States, are defined in part by shared religious beliefs

FIGURE 8.4. *Three Cahokian figurines interpreted as Earth Mother or Old Woman. Image: Courtesy of Illinois State Archaeological Survey.*

thought to have originated at Cahokia. What is clear is the similar association made by many people of different Indigenous language groups that water, the moon, night, and women are bundled or connected concepts.

Water and the moon are linked in the person of "Old Woman Who Never Dies," an Earth Mother figure who is a deity best known from stories of the Dakota and Mandan peoples, both of whom are Siouan speakers (Dorsey 1894; Bowers 1965; Hall 1997; Diaz-Granados and Duncan 2000; Diaz-Granados et al. 2015). The Old Woman is argued by some to be depicted in Cahokian figurative art (figure 8.4), both in stone statuary and parietal art (Hall 1997; Diaz-Granados and Duncan 2000; Diaz-Granados et al. 2015). Stories told by the Mandan and Dakota, among others, tell of how she dwells in the moon and of how her children are stars. She is associated with agricultural fertility, blackbirds, and waterfowl. The waterfowl bring the corn spirits back from the Old Woman every spring when they return. She herself renews and becomes younger by bathing in river water. She is given life and renewal in the water, and she renews and gives life to the crops (Dorsey 1894; Bowers 1965). Many of the Emerald offerings, placed and burned on shrine floors before being covered in water-washed soils, were baskets of corn, seeds, and other agricultural products. Several offerings included heat exploded hoes. The associations of water, the moon, and agriculture as linked to Old Woman were similarly associated in Emerald deposits.

The Lakota see the moon itself as female (Walker 1980), as did the Winnebago (Radin 1990/1923, 286). According to Nancy Lurie (1953, 708), men who took on female characteristics did so after being called by the moon. The Omaha saw the night as female, the direction above as male, and the direction below as female (Fletcher and La Flesche 1992, 134) as did the Skidi Pawnee, who associated corn and rain with the moon and women (Dorsey and Murie 1940, 100). Clark Wissler (1908) reported the Blackfoot as another group who associated the moon with women. The moon and water are related in mappings of the Cosmos by the Osage, as described by Francis La Flesche and reported in Garrick Bailey (1995). The Osage viewed the sky as male and the earth as female. The moon was associated with the west and with death, and the moon was female, as was water. Alice Fletcher (1904, 42) reported the Pawnee association of the moon and the night as female. She (Fletcher 1904, 74) recorded other ritual associations of the night, the moon, and water:

> In this ceremony water is not used except for sacred purposes. We mix the paint that we use upon the sacred objects with running water. When on our journey we come to a stream of running water we cannot step into it to cross it without asking permission of Kawas. Kawas is the mother; she represents the night and the moon, and she can permit us to enter and wade through the stream. So, whenever we come to a river we call upon Kawas to protect us, that our act of passing through the water may not bring punishment, and may not cause the clouds to come between us and the blue dome, the dwelling place of Tira'wa, or break the continuity of life from one generation to another.

Of interest for my purposes is the following Pawnee-Chaui story reported by George Lankford (2008, 32):

> A boy in time of famine is led by the moon (shown as a female of four different ages, presumably representing the lunar phases) to a cave in a spring; a succession of visits produces gifts of games, information on how to construct earthlodges, corn and meat, the buffalo and a sacred bundle, and seeds for planting. The cave then disappears and the spring goes dry (Dorsey 1906:21–28, #3).

Considering these oral histories, and then reflecting upon the lessons learned from the Emerald Acropolis, it seems not unlikely that some similar cosmological principles were being expressed in the offerings and watery interactions at this location. The associations of water, women, the moon, corn, and other agricultural products used as offerings are striking, particularly at a shrine center, where all are oriented to lunar standstill positions, as is the fact that these associations are made by various Indigenous people who are often identified as likely Cahokian descendants (Kehoe 2007; Kelly and Brown 2012; Hunter 2013; Diaz-Granados et al. 2015).

When these associations and interpretations are applied to Cahokia's central ceremonial precincts, they force a rethinking of the urban center (Alt

2019). Cahokia had certain properties whose effects would have emphasized the multiplicity of interactions between water, people, and the moon, and the effects of those things would have given experiences of the night great power.

A DIVERSION INTO NIGHTLY EFFECTS AND AFFECTS

In the dark, human perceptions are altered. Vision, hearing, touch, and even our sense of time are different than that of the daytime, as we tend to sharpen our other senses when we lose the ability to sense through sight (Merabet and Pascual-Leone 2010; Bauer et al. 2017). Obvious to us all experientially but explained by medical science, we cannot see as far or as clearly at night. This is true in part because of how the eye functions—it is not simply that there is less light but that different structures of the eye are engaged under different lighting conditions (Lamb 2016). Human eyes use rods and cones to see, but without adequate light only rods can function. Cones provide color vision and permit more detailed vision. At night, in low light, only the rods are engaged; thus, we have less fine distinction and little to no discernment of color (King 2014). Added to this biological phenomenon, moonlight further alters the perception of color, creating what is known as a "blue shift," a perception that the world has a bluish tint under moonlight (Khan and Pattanaik 2004; Pokorny et al. 2006). Given that moonlight is actually sunlight reflected off the moon, the amount of visible light on Earth's surface at night varies by about three orders of magnitude over the course of a month as a result of the lunar cycle and the precise angles of the Earth, moon, and sun. One recent study attempting to document the amount of light the moon can produce has come up with a maximum value of 0.3 lux and a typical value of 0.05—0.1 lux (Kyba et al. 2017). An example of what this moonlight condition means in practical terms is demonstrated by a report that reviewed numerous studies and concluded that the ability to identify a person at night ranged from thirty meters on moonless nights to ninety meters under a full moon (Nichols and Powers 1964).

Nightly Effects

Interestingly, the dark does not affect just vision, or perhaps limited vision is causal for other physiological and psychological effects. Physiological studies have measured increased startle responses and an increase in blood pressure, heart rate, and subjective distress when subjects are tested in the dark (Grillion 2008). The way people view color and environment in different lighting has been demonstrated to affect mood (Veitch and Newshan 1998; Boyce et al. 2000). People in darkness lack the normal stimulations of the day, and in extreme situations persons left in isolation and in the dark quickly begin to hallucinate, which is why isolation in the dark is considered torture (Tomassoni et al. 2015). Day and night, then, can be expected to evoke different responses in human bodies and minds. These differences might matter when thinking about rituals and other religious engagements (Dillehay 2018). For example, to what degree is a nighttime event more of a "high arousal" occasion (sensu Whitehouse 2004) than one engaged in during the day? Although biology is always experienced through culture, as noted by Mikkel Bille and Tim Flohr Sørensen (2007, 266) "the role of sight within different cultures has also been propelled by acknowledging that sensuous primacy, experiences and linkages between senses may vary tremendously between cultures." It is nonetheless likely that nightly events would be experienced very differently from daytime events.

We know that people living in premodern communities did engage in rituals and ceremonies at night and that, furthermore, they did not stop all other activities just because the sun went down (Dowd and Hensey 2016; Gonlin and Nowell 2018; chapters in this volume). In fact, some tasks were specifically nocturnal tasks, from highly spiritual endeavors such as healing ceremonies, to more mundane endeavors, such as patrolling fields to prevent predation and crop loss. Modern dependence on artificial lighting tends to obscure the fact that many activities are, and were, carried out in low light, and even in the dark (Dowd and Hensey 2016; Gonlin and Nowell 2018; chapters in this volume). Nighttime activities even included farming tasks (e.g., Nathan 2018); planting and harvesting by moonlight are ancient practices and are still promoted today by traditional gardeners and farmers, as well as by the longtime classic *Farmer's Almanac*, which provides calendars describing the correct phase of the moon to start different kinds of plants. And we might remember that the harvest moon, occurring at the fall equinox, was so named as the earlier rise of the full moon aided harvesting after sunset. Harvesting at night can take advantage of the natural rhythms and respirations of plants such that some plants will exhibit different properties when harvested at different times of day or night, as plant moisture level and chemistry will vary with temperature and levels of sunlight (Allwood et al. 2011; Deborde et al. 2017). This practice is likely why there are long traditions of beliefs about the correct times of day to harvest certain herbs, fruits, and vegetables.

In premodern communities, craft production can and did occur at night. Experienced artisans can spin, sew, or carve very productively by firelight, and even in fully dark conditions (Ekirch 2012; Gonlin and Nowell 2018). For example, the common findings of debitage from lithic production in fireplaces as well as other crafting debris have long been suggested (following Binford 1978) to be debris from activities carried out around the fireplace, albeit it was less often assumed to have occurred at night. In cities, arguably, it might be easier to manage activities after dark than in rural areas given the close packing of numerous households with artificial lighting from numerous fires.

Many of the possible activities that can and did occur at night have been reported for historic Indigenous groups including raids and attacks on enemies (Bailey 1995, 85). More important for this discussion, many Indigenous rituals and prayer vigils were known to have occurred at night. In part this timing is because some ceremonies occur principally at night but also because some ceremonies, rituals, and dances were held over many days and continued through the intervening nights. During these events some actions might be specific to the daytime, and others were more appropriate for the night. Some better-known examples of these multiday and -night events are the Busk or Green Corn Ceremony, the Arapaho Sun dance, the Osage Rite of the Wa-Xo'-Be, or the Pawnee Great Cleansing Ceremony (Dorsey 1904; La Flesche 1930; Witthoft 1949; Weltfish 1965; Bowers 1992). The night was a time when messages from the spirit world or from the gods might be passed on to humans through their dreams (Irwin 1994). For example, the infamous Skidi Pawnee Morning Star ceremony could occur only when a dream came to the right person, and it could happen only when the stars were in appropriate alignment (Dorsey 1906; Fletcher 1902; Linton 1926; Weltfish 1965; Murie 1981). At Cahokia at the Emerald Acropolis and in the central ceremonial core, we have evidence on and around the mounds of hearths, some of which were massive and some that had burned so long and hard that the soils under and around them experienced chemical reactions changing the very color of the earth. The effect of the illumination of such fire features would have been all the more impressive in the dark, at night. The remains of rituals like those at Emerald (Skousen 2016; Pauketat et al. 2017; Alt 2018c, 2019; Barzilai 2020) or as seen at downtown Cahokia (Pauketat 1993; Pauketat et al. 2002) suggest that multiday and -night rituals, like those described in ethnohistoric reports for Cahokian descendants, most likely occurred at Cahokia.

NIGHTLY AFFECTS

How different might such events have been in an urban environment and on a plaza that covered fifty acres? A common crowd estimate for parades uses a formula of 2.5 people per square meter (https://www.poynter.org/fact-checking

/2017/this-online-tool-makes-checking-crowd-sizes-easier/). By that calculation the Grand Plaza could have held over 500,000 people! Using another common formula to estimate crowd size for standing room only that allows two square feet per person, the plaza could have held twice that many people. It is therefore not a stretch to suggest that even given the most generous population estimates for the city (no more than 30,000 [Emerson et al. 2020; Pauketat and Lopinot 1997]), all residents and many, many more visitors could have attended any event in the plaza.

During events Cahokia's potentially crowded Grand Plaza not only would have held human persons but would have contained marker posts (Alt et al. 2010), which are argued to have been other-than-human persons in their own right (Pauketat 2012; Skousen 2012) as well as other nonhuman persons, for example, those attached to figurative pipes. All the persons on the plaza would have been flanked by monumental constructions such as the mounds, water features, and public or ritual buildings. Nocturnal events could have been lit by torches and bonfires both on the ground and on the mound tops, where large well-used clay plastered hearths have been found (Moorehead 1929; Smith 1969; Benchley 1975; Pauketat 1993; Fowler 1997). Likely, the event would have been led by religious specialists, dressed in full regalia as depicted in Mississippian art (see Townsend 2004) and positioned on top of mounds so that the crowd could see them (sensu Moore 1996). The city would have resonated with chants, and the music of drumming and flutes, all accompanied by the sounds of bodies and feet that might be executing a ceremonial dance. Add to this ambience the reflections of flames, the moon, and stars in the artificial and natural bodies of water around the city.

Considering the science and experience of sight in low light and moonlight discussed earlier, people on the plaza would have had difficulty seeing the full extent of the crowd in the dark; they would not see colors and details very well, even close at hand. As an interesting aside, the most significant colors for Cahokian ritual endeavors were red and white, as these colors have been found painted on wares from ritual deposits (Pauketat et al. 2002). These colors have been demonstrated by studies of visual physiology and perception as those most often correctly identified in low-light conditions (Ishida 2002; Pokorny et al. 2006). It is interesting to speculate on whether those colors were used in part because their messages could still be read after dark during the nocturnal rituals.

Events held at night during a full moon would have alleviated some visual difficulty, as would the careful placement of hearths, torches, and fires, but such lighting creates its own effects. Moonlight permits vision but limits distance and detail. Colors are washed out, presenting all with a bluish hue. The light from open flame tends to be irregular; it can appear as if it has a life of its own with flickering flames moving in response to every breeze. That flickering can create an illusion of movement in stationary objects and people, enhancing the sense of otherworldly powers and beings amid nightly celebrants. The washed-out colors and blueish hue of the world in moonlight or darkness would further enhance the sense that those on the plaza had entered another dimension—that of the otherworldly powers of the gods and the powers and forces of the unseen world. These effects would at the very least add mystery to an event enclosed in its own bubble of activity, firelight, and smoke within the dark of the night, that dark extending beyond the limits of the plaza and the city, shadowing the great mounds and the watery lands of the dead.

Even on more mundane evenings, changes in the landscapes around Cahokia beyond diminishing vision with the departure of sunlight would be evident. Cahokia was built in the midst of wetlands and swamps such that for much of the year the coming of evening meant the watery realms began to mist, and a misty fog covered the ground with only the mound tops and trees visible above. On any given evening the sounds of the night would have included the thousands of voices of Cahokia's residents talking and telling stories, where some might be chanting or singing, or perhaps people might hear a healing ceremony, or hear the drums and songs of a night dance. People would be engaged in the activities mentioned earlier: spinning, sewing, carving, flintknapping, shelling corn, and even planting or harvesting. Providing background would be the chirping of tree frogs and the calls of bullfrogs in the surrounding wetlands; there would be the buzzing of mosquitos interspersed with the hoots of owls or the screech of a night hawk (Pauketat 2020). Dogs would be barking or growling over the scraps from someone's dinner. But all these sounds might be a comfort, not a cacophony, because those sounds reminded all that Cahokia was a place of safety. Inhabitants felt no need to build protective palisade walls for many generations because at Cahokia, the power of water and the night were built into the city, and the heavens could be brought to the Earth. The poet and philosopher Henry Thoreau (Searls 2009, 54) captures just such an experience in his journal:

There is a certain glory attends on water by night. By it the heavens are related to the earth—Undistinguishable from a sky beneath you. . . . I saw the moon sudden reflected full from a pool—a puddle from which you may see the moon reflected—& the earth dissolved under your feet. The magical moon with attendant stars suddenly looking up with mild lustre from a window in the dark earth.

Such qualities of the night, the moon, and water were, given evidence from the Emerald Acropolis, a critical part of the new Cahokian religion, a balancing of supernatural forces, other-than-human, and human persons at Cahokia. Cahokia's five-degree off-set axis, in fact, is thought by William Romain (2017) to have been a geometric solution that balanced solar and lunar alignments within the city and among its monuments. Moreover, the Emerald lunar complex was connected to the city by a roadway used often enough that it was still visible in early aerial photos (Skousen 2016). The import of the moon and the night can be found in another downtown roadway, one that led south to burial complexes and what Sarah Baires (2017) termed the "watery land of the dead." Given the orientation of the walkway, people processing south on this roadway toward the burial mounds would have experienced a sense that they were passing into the night sky and into the Milky Way (figure 8.5). According to Siouan beliefs (and the beliefs of many other Indigenous groups), south is the direction of the night, and the Milky Way is the path of souls, the stars the hearths of the ancestors (Lankford 2007). To walk south from the Grand Plaza at Cahokia, especially around the time of the all-important Winter Solstice, when the Milky Way forms a band that stretches from the ground up into and across the sky, was to walk through the watery realm and into the night, and into the realm of the ancestors (figure 8.5). To walk along this roadway was to encounter Mound 72, where the bodies of the honored dead and sacrificial burials were placed in carefully constructed burial pits organized into a tableau rich with sacred meanings, and the burial pit of sacrifices was lunar aligned (Fowler 1997; Brown 2003; Pauketat 2012; Emerson et al. 2016). Water, it seems, was the source of both life and death. June-Ann Greeley notes in discussing Indigenous Earth Diver creation stories: "Water thus has been identified as the source of all existence and the deposit of all living things such that once certain forms of life no longer have the capacity to sustain themselves, all will revert back to the primordial pools" (Greeley 2017, 170).

Siouan beliefs connect women to water, the underworld, night, and death (Bailey 1995; Alt 2018c), and these associations can all be found in Cahokia's "watery land of the dead." Just as a female burial was covered by water at Emerald, so were other women, identified as sacrifices, buried in the lower strata of Mound 72, where their remains would be periodically inundated by flood waters after every heavy rain (Fowler et al. 1999; Hargrave and Hedman 2004; Hargrave et al. 2014; Emerson et al. 2016). Some in Mound 72 were male, but most of the internments identified as sacrifices were women. The pattern of female bodies in sacrificial offerings, at Emerald, and at Mound 72, is repeated at East St. Louis, where female bodies were found in decommissioned post

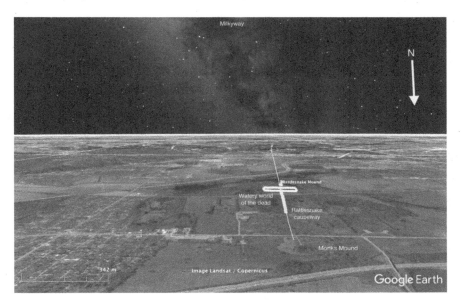

FIGURE 8.5. *Depiction of walkway south through the watery world of the dead and into the Milky Way. Image: Generated with Google Earth.*

pits (Hargrave and Hedman 2004; Hargrave et al. 2014). The preponderance of female bodies in sacrifices suggests attempts to call upon the powers and forces attendant upon women. Perhaps women were preferentially chosen as sacrifices because they were of water, the moon, and the night, and these were powers that mattered in the new Cahokian religiosity (Alt 2018b).

BUILDING ACCESS TO THE NIGHT

The balance of night and day, dark and light, overworld and underworld, is not just visible in the balance of dry land / plazas / north and watery / mortuary / south but is also found in the other construction elements of Cahokia. This cosmological balance is built into the very fabric of the city, with the earthen pyramids and other significant constructions revealing intentionally laid alternating layers of light and dark soils, thus acknowledging overworld, underworld, day and night. The very clays used to construct Monks Mound further cite the watery realms from which they came (Schilling 2010, 308; Pauketat 2012).

Still other Cahokian constructions cite the powers of water and the night. The sweat lodges or steam baths were spaces reminiscent of the night. They were womb-like structures that enclosed a person in darkness as they sweated in the steam created from water and hot rocks (Hall 1997; Alt 2018b). Natural spaces such as caves also re-created night-like spaces, and it is in caves, such as Picture Cave or Gottschall Rock Shelter, places that were in use during the time of Cahokia, that we find images of supernatural beings and creatures related to both the night and day, water, the underworld, and the sky (Salzer and Rajnovich 2000; Diaz-Granados et al. 2015). It is not surprising that such beings were painted in caves, as it is the night that brings the spirit world closer to human beings. At night it is through dreams that visions and messages come from the spirit world to instruct people, to help them understand how to be in the world or when to engage in special rituals (Irwin 1994). Life at Cahokia was surrounded by references to the night replete with reminders that the moon, water, and women were part of the power of the night. Life in the daytime was therefore always informed and reinforced by the messages received in the night.

Cahokians dared place their city not only amidst wetlands and swamps but between and, in part, on top of karst fields. Just southwest of the downtown ceremonial complex was a field of 10,000 sinkholes, another field lay to the north, and another further to the south. To the west, just across the Mississippi River, was the St. Louis Precinct, where the great mound sat on top of the entrance to a karst cave, and miles of caves and caverns ran under what is now modern St. Louis. Another St. Louis mound, this one containing burials, sat atop a cave (Alt 2020a, 2020b). All the sinkholes are in some way related to water—they held water, water rushed through them and in underground tunnels after rain, and caves on the bank of the Mississippi River led to caverns under the St. Louis Mound center. The cave art mentioned above tells us of the connection of caves to the underworld of spirits, to water, and the dark. The burials reveal more about how such were connected, as do the stories from the oral histories previously relayed. These were dangerous powers and forces, and the Cahokians not only lived among them, but sought to access those powers.

CONCLUSIONS: ASSEMBLING THE URBAN ASSEMBLAGE

Cahokia became urban at around AD 1050, in some measure due to an influx of immigrants who came to be part of a new religion that dared to call upon the powers of water, women, and the moon. These powers were tied to the new agricultural pursuits, growing and storing corn (Simon 2014). The evidence from Emerald indicates that immigrants came before Cahokia was urbanized and argues for religious motivations for their presence. Emerald Precinct and other Cahokia precincts provide evidence that foundational elements in that religion were the moon, water, women, agriculture (corn), and the night, which were all entangled on multiple planes. Ethnohistoric reporting of oral histories from descendant communities illustrates numerous relationships between these elements that are echoed in Cahokia art, architecture, rituals, and sacrifices. It was in the assemblages of concepts, things, powers, and persons—some deeply related to the night—that urbanism developed at Cahokia. The nightly experience of this urban center would have affected the people who lived there and those who visited because the night has very real physiological, psychological, and spiritual effects.

Cahokia was a place where night and day, land, water, and sky all reflected back upon one another. To play on the opening quote from N. K. Jeminsin, Cahokia as an urbanism *was* a "tear in the fabric of the reality"; it was something like a black hole. It was a place that dared ask for the powers not just of the sun but of the night sky, the moon, and water. The religious movement that brought together these elements and drew people to this place would have been ever present in the lived experience and sensations related to water and darkness, both natural and recreated. To live at Cahokia would have been a relentless confrontation with the affective qualities of the night, water, and moon; it was to live in and amongst water and the night as the swampy mists covered the ground at night and made the watery realms glow with the light of the moon. The qualities of those things were not just background, not simply part of the atmosphere of Cahokia; rather, they were at the heart of what mattered. They were the powers and forces appealed to with offerings and shrines at Emerald; they were the places of the dead, the spirits of ancestors. They were part of the provocation for Cahokia to become urban.

REFERENCES

Allwood, William J., Ric C. H. De Vos, Annick Moing, Catherine Deborde, Alexander Erban, Joachim Kopka, Royston Goodacre, and Robert D. Hall. 2011. "Plant Metabolomics and Its Potential for Systems Biology Research: Background Concepts, Technology, and Methodology." In *Methods in Enzymology*. Vol. 500, edited by D. Jameson, Malkhey Verma, and Hans V. Westerhoff, 299–336. Burlington, VT: Academic Press.

Alt, Susan M. 2006. "The Power of Diversity: The Roles of Migration and Hybridity in Culture Change." In *Leadership and Polity in Mississippian Society*, edited by

Brian M. Butler and Paul D. Welch, 289–308. Center for Archaeological Investigations, Occasional Paper No. 33. Carbondale: Southern Illinois University.

Alt, Susan M. 2008 "Unwilling Immigrants: Culture, Change, and the 'Other' in Mississippian Societies." In *Invisible Citizens: Slavery in Ancient Pre-state Societies*, edited by Cathy M. Cameron, 205–222. Salt Lake City: University of Utah Press.

Alt, Susan M. 2015. "Human Sacrifice at Cahokia." In *Medieval Mississippians: The Cahokian World*, edited by Timothy R. Pauketat and Susan M. Alt, 27. Santa Fe, NM: School for Advanced Research Press.

Alt, Susan M. 2016. "Building Cahokia: Transformation through Tradition." In *Vernacular Architecture in the Pre-Columbian Americas*, edited by Christina T. Halperin and Lauren Schwartz, 141–157. London: Routledge.

Alt, Susan M. 2018a. *Cahokia's Complexities: Ceremonies and Politics of the First Mississippian Farmers*. Tuscaloosa: University of Alabama Press.

Alt, Susan M. 2018b. "The Emerald Site, Mississippian Women, and the Moon." In *Archaeology of the Night: Life After Dark in the Ancient World*, edited by Nancy Gonlin and April Nowell, 223–248. Boulder: University Press of Colorado.

Alt, Susan M. 2018c. "Putting Religion ahead of Politics: Cahokia Origins Viewed through Emerald Shrines." In *Archaeology and Ancient Religion in the American Midcontinent (Archaeology of the American South: New Directions and Perspectives)*, edited by Brad Koldehoff and Timothy R. Pauketat, 208–233. Tuscaloosa: University of Alabama Press.

Alt, Susan M. 2019. "From Weeping Hills to Lost Caves: A Search for Vibrant Matter in Greater Cahokia." In *New Materialisms Ancient Urbanism*, edited by Susan M. Alt and Timothy R. Pauketat, 19–39. London: Routledge.

Alt, Susan M. 2020a. "Histories of Cahokian Assemblages." In *The Historical Turn in Southeastern Archaeology*, edited by Robbie Ethridge and Eric Bowne, 61–81. Gainesville: University of Florida Press.

Alt, Susan M. 2020b. "The Implications of the Religious Foundations of Cahokia." In *Cahokian Context: Hegemony and Diaspora*, edited by Charles H. McNutt and Ryan M. Parish, 32–48. Gainesville: University Press of Florida.

Alt, Susan M., Jeffery D. Kruchten, and Timothy R. Pauketat. 2010. "The Construction and Use of Cahokia's Grand Plaza." *Journal of Field Archaeology* 35 (2): 131–146.

Alt, Susan M., and Timothy R. Pauketat. 2018. "The Elements of Cahokian Shrine Complexes and the Basis of Mississippian Religion." In *Religion and Politics in the Ancient Americas*, edited by Sarah Barber and Arthur Joyce, 51–74. London: Routledge.

Alt, Susan M., and Timothy R. Pauketat, eds. 2019. *New Materialisms Ancient Urbanism*. London: Routledge.

Bailey, Garrick A. 1995. *The Osage and the Invisible World from the Works of Francis Flesch*. Norman: University of Oklahoma Press.

Baires, Sarah E. 2017. *Land of Water, City of the Dead: Religion and Cahokia's Emergence*. Tuscaloosa: University of Alabama Press.

Barzilai, Rebecca M. 2020. "Material Realities and Novel Ideas: The Vibrancy of Place and Ceramic Practices at the Emerald Acropolis." PhD diss., Department of Anthropology, Indiana University, Bloomington.

Bauer C. M., G. V. Hirsch, L. Zajac, B-B Koo, O. Collignon, and L. B. Merabet. 2017. "Multimodal MR-Imaging Reveals Large-Scale Structural and Functional Connectivity Changes in Profound Early Blindness." *PLoS ONE* 12 (3): e0173064. https://doi.org/10.1371/journal.pone.0173064.

Benchley, Elizabeth D. 1974. "Mississippian Secondary Mound Loci: A Comparative Functional Analysis in a Time-Space Perspective." PhD diss., Department of Anthropology, University of Wisconsin, Milwaukee.

Bennett, Jane. 2010. *Vibrant Matter: A Political Ecology of Things*. Durham, NC: Duke University Press.

Bille, Mikkel, and Tim Flohr Sørensen. 2007. "An Anthropology of Luminosity: The Agency of Light." *Journal of Material Culture* 12 (3): 263–284.

Binford, Lewis R. 1978. *Nunamiut Ethnoarchaeology*. New York: Academic Press.

Bowers, Alfred W. 1965. *Hidatsa Social and Ceremonial Organization*. Bureau of American Ethnology, Bulletin 194. Washington, DC: Smithsonian Institution.

Bowers, Alfred W. 1992. *Hidatsa Social and Ceremonial Organization*. Lincoln: University of Nebraska Press.

Boyce, P. R., N. H. Eklund, and B. J. Hamilton. 2000. "Perceptions of Safety at Night in Different Lighting Conditions." *Lighting Research & Technology* 32 (2): 79–91.

Brown, James B. 2003. "The Cahokia Mound 72-Sub1 Burials as Collective Representation." *Wisconsin Archeologist* 84 (1/2): 81–97.

Brown, James B., and John E. Kelly. 2000. "Cahokia and the Southeastern Ceremonial Complex." In *Mounds, Modoc, and Mesoamerica: Papers in Honor of Melvin L. Fowler*. Vol. 28, edited by Steven R. Ahler, 469–510. Springfield: Illinois State Museum Scientific Papers.

Collins, James M., and Michael L. Chalfant. 1993. "A Second-Terrace Perspective on Monks Mound." *American Antiquity* 58 (2): 319–332.

Dalan, Rinita A. 1997. "The Construction of Mississippian Cahokia." In *Cahokia: Domination and Ideology in the Mississippian World*, edited by Timothy R. Pauketat and Thomas E. Emerson, 89–102. Lincoln: University of Nebraska Press.

Deborde, C., A. Moing, L. Roch, D. Jacob, D. Rolin, and P. Giraudeau. 2017. "Plant Metabolism as Studied by NMR Spectroscopy." *Progress in Nuclear Magnetic Resonance Spectroscopy* 102 (November 1): 61–97. https://doi.org/10.1016/j.pnmrs .2017.05.001.

DeLanda, Manuel. 2016. *Assemblage Theory*. Edinburgh: Edinburgh University Press.

Deleuze, Gilles, and Felix Guattari. 1987. *A Thousand Plateaus: Capitalism and Schizophrenia*. Translated by B. Massumi. Minneapolis: University of Minnesota Press.

Diaz-Granados, Carol M., and James R. Duncan. 2000. *The Petroglyphs and Pictographs of Missouri*. Tuscaloosa: University of Alabama Press.

Diaz-Granados, Carol M., James R. Duncan, and F. Kent Reilly III, eds. 2015. *Picture Cave: Unraveling the Mysteries of the Mississippian Cosmos*. Austin: University of Texas Press.

Dillehay, Tom D. 2018. "Night Moon Rituals: The Effects of Darkness and Prolonged Ritual on Chilean Mapuche Participants." In *Archaeology of the Night: Life After Dark in the Ancient World*, edited by Nancy Gonlin and April Nowell, 179–199. Boulder: University Press of Colorado.

Dorsey, George A. 1904. *Traditions of the Skidi Pawnee*. Boston: Houghton, Mifflin and Company.

Dorsey, George A. 1906. The Skidi Rite of Human Sacrifice. *International Congress of Americanists* 15: 66–70.

Dorsey, George A., and James R. Murie. 1940. *Notes on Skidi Pawnee Society*. Chicago: Chicago Field Museum of Natural History.

Dorsey, James Owen. 1894. "A Study of Siouan Cults." In *Eleventh Annual Report of the Bureau of Ethnology*, 351–554. Washington, DC: Government Printing Office.

Emerson, Thomas E. 1997. *Cahokia and the Archaeology of Power*. Tuscaloosa: University of Alabama Press.

Emerson, Thomas E. 2002. "An Introduction to Cahokia 2002: Diversity, Complexity, and History." *Midcontinental Journal of Archaeology* 27 (2): 127–148.

Emerson, Thomas E., Kristin M. Hedman, Tamira K. Brennan, Alleen Betzenhauser, Susan M. Alt, and Timothy R. Pauketat. 2020. "Interrogating Diaspora and Movement in the Greater Cahokian World." *Journal of Archaeological Method and Theory* 27: 54–71.

Emerson, Thomas E., Kristin M. Hedman, Eve A. Hargrave, Dawn E. Cobb, and Andrew R. Thompson. 2016. "Paradigms Lost: Reconfiguring Cahokia's Mound 72 Beaded Burial." *American Antiquity* 81 (3): 405–425.

Emerson, Thomas E., Randall E. Hughes, Mary R. Hynes, and Sarah U. Wisseman. 2003. "The Sourcing and Interpretation of Cahokia-Style Figurines in the Trans-Mississippi South and Southeast." *American Antiquity* 68 (2): 287–313.

Emerson, Thomas E., Brad H. Koldehoff, and Tamira K. Brennan. 2018. *Revealing Greater Cahokia, North America's First Native City: Rediscovery and Large-Scale Excavations of the East St. Louis Precinct*. Urbana-Champaign: Illinois State Archaeological Survey.

Fletcher, Alice C. 1902. "Star Cult among the Pawnee—A Preliminary Report." *American Anthropologist* 4 (4): 730–736.

Fletcher, Alice C., assisted by James R. Murie. 1904. *The Hako: A Pawnee Ceremony*. Extract from the Twenty-Second Annual Report of the Bureau of American Ethnology. Washington, DC: Washington Government Printing Office.

Fletcher, Alice C., and Francis La Flesche. 1992. *The Omaha Tribe*. Lincoln: University of Nebraska Press.

Fowler, Melvin L. 1997. *The Cahokia Atlas: A Historical Atlas of Cahokia Archaeology*. Illinois Transportation Archaeological Research Program, Studies in Archaeology, Number 2, Urbana: University of Illinois.

Fowler, Melvin L., Jerome C. Rose, Barbara Vander Leest, and Steven R. Ahler. 1999. *The Mound 72 Area: Dedicated and Sacred Space in Early Cahokia*. Springfield: Illinois State Museum, Reports of Investigations, no. 54.

French, Kirk D., Kirk D. Straight, and Elijah J. Hermitt. 2020. "Building the Environment at Palenque: The Sacred Pools of the Picota Group." *Ancient Mesoamerica* 31 (3): 409–430. doi:10.1017/S0956536119000130.

Gonlin, Nancy, and April Nowell, eds. 2018. *Archaeology of the Night: Life After Dark in the Ancient World*. Boulder: University Press of Colorado.

Greeley, June-Ann. 2017. "Water in Native American Spirituality: Liquid Life—Blood of the Earth and Life of the Community." *Green Humanities* 2: 156–179.

Grillion, Christian 2008. "Models and Mechanisms of Anxiety: Evidence from Startle Studies." *Psychopharmacology* 199 (3): 421–437.

Grimley, David A., and Andrew C. Phillips, eds. 2015. *Ridges, Mounds, and Valleys: Glacial-Interglacial History of the Kaskaskia Basin, Southwestern Illinois*. Guidebook 41. Urbana-Champaign: Illinois State Geological Survey, University of Illinois.

Hall, Robert L. 1997. *An Archaeology of the Soul: Native American Indian Belief and Ritual*. Urbana: University of Illinois Press.

Hargrave, Eve A., Dawn E. Cobb, Leanna M. Nash, Julie A. Bukowski, and Sarah Bareis. 2014. "Death and Sacrifice in the American Bottom." Paper presented at the Midwest Archaeological Conference, Illinois State Museum, Springfield.

Hargrave, Eve A., and Kristin Hedman. 2004. "Sacrifice at the East St. Louis Mound Center, St. Louis, Missouri." Paper presented at the 2004 joint Midwest

Archaeological Conference and Southeastern Archaeological Conference, St. Louis, Missouri.

Hedman, Kristin M., Philip A. Slater, Matthew A. Fort, Thomas E. Emerson, and John M. Lambert. 2018. "Expanding the Strontium Isoscape for the American Midcontinent: Identifying Potential Places of Origin for Cahokian and Pre-Columbian Migrants." *Journal of Archaeological Science* 22: 202–213.

Hunter, Andrea A. 2013. "Ancestral Osage Geography." In *Osage Nation NAGPRA Claim for Human Remains Removed from the Clarksville Mound Group (23PI6), Pike County, Missouri*, 1–60. Osage Nation Historic Preservation Office.

Irwin, Lee. 1994. *The Dream Seekers: Native American Visionary Traditions of the Great Plains*. Norman: University of Oklahoma.

Ishida, Taiichiro. 2002. "Color Identification Data Obtained from Photopic to Mesopic Illuminance Levels." *Color Research and Application* 27 (4): 252–259.

Jeminsin, N. K. 2018. *How Long 'til Black Future Month?: Stories*. New York: Hachette Book Group.

Jervis, Ben. 2018. *Assemblage Thought and Archaeology*. London and New York: Routledge.

Kehoe, A. B. 2007. "Osage Texts and Cahokia Data." In *Ancient Objects and Sacred Realms: Interpretations of Mississippian Iconography*, edited by F. Kent Reilly III and James F. Garber, 246–261. Austin: University of Texas Press.

Kelly, John E., and James A Brown. 2012. "Search of Cosmic Power: Contextualizing Spiritual Journeys between Cahokia and the St. Francois Mountains." In *Archaeology of Spiritualities*, edited by Kathryn Rountree, Christine Morris, and Alan A. D. Peatfield, 107–129. New York: Springer.

Khan, Saad Masood, and Sumanta N. Pattanaik. 2004. "Modelling Blue Shift in Moonlit Scenes Using Rod Cone Intercation." *Journal of Vision* 4 (8): 316.

King, Bob. 2014. "What Makes Moonlight Special." Accessed March 23, 2019. www.skyandtelescope.com/astronomyblogs/struckmoonlight12312014.

Koldehoff, Brad H., and Timothy R. Pauketat, eds. 2018. *Archaeology and Ancient Religion in the American Midcontinent*. Tuscaloosa: University of Alabama Press.

Kyba, Christopher, Andrej Mohar, and Thomas Posch. 2017. "How Bright is Moonlight?" *Astronomy and Geophysics* 58 (1): 1.31–31.32.

La Flesche, Francis. 1930. "The Osage Tribe: Rite of the Wa-Xo'-Be." *Forty-Fifth Annual Report of the Bureau of American Ethnology*: 529–833.

Lamb, T. D. 2016. "Why Rods and Cones?" *Eye* 30 (2): 179–185.

Linton, Ralph. 1926. "The Origin of the Skidi Pawnee Sacrifice to the Morning Star." *American Anthropologist* 28 (3): 457–466.

Lankford, George E. 2007. *Reachable Stars: Patterns in the Ethnoastronomy of Eastern North America*. Tuscaloosa: University of Alabama Press.

Lankford, George. 2008. *Looking for Lost Lore*. Tuscaloosa: University of Alabama Press.

Lurie, Nancy O. 1953. "Winnebago Berdache." *American Anthropologist* 55 (5): 708–712.

McFarlane, Colin. 2011. "The City as Assemblage: Dwelling and Urban Space." *Environment and Planning D: Society and Space* 29 (4): 649–671.

McNutt, Charles H., and Ryan M. Parish, eds. 2020. *Cahokian Context: Hegemony and Diaspora*. Gainesville: University Press of Florida.

Merabet, Lotfi B., and Alvaro Pascual-Leone. 2010. "Neural Reorganization Following Sensory Loss: The Opportunity of Change." *Nature Reviews Neuroscience* 11 (1): 44–52.

Moore, Jerry. 1996. "The Archaeology of Plazas and the Proxemics of Ritual: Three Andean Traditions." *American Anthropologist* 98 (December 1): 789–802.

Moorehead, Warren K. 1929. *The Cahokia Mounds*. Vol. 26, No. 4. Urbana: University of Illinois Bulletin.

Murie, James R. 1981. *Ceremonies of the Pawnee*, Part I: *The Skiri*. Smithsonian Contributions to Anthropology, Number 27. Washington, DC: Smithsonian Institution Press.

Nathan, Smiti. 2018. "Midnight at the Oasis: Past and Present Agricultural Activities in Oman." In *Archaeology of the Night: Life After Dark in the Ancient World*, edited by Nancy Gonlin and April Nowell, 333–352. Boulder: University Press of Colorado.

Nichols, Thomas F., and Theodore R. Powers. 1964. *Moonlight and Night Visibility*. Submitted to US Army training center human research unit, presidio of Monterey, California, under the technical supervision of the George Washington University human resources research office operating under contract with the department of the army, AD 438001 Unclassified. Alexandria, VA: Defense Documentation Center or Scientific and Technical Information Cameron Station.

Panno, Samuel V., and Donald E. Luman. 2012. *Sinkhole Distribution and Associated Karst Features of Monroe County, Illinois*. Champaign: Illinois State Geological Survey.

Panno, Samuel V., Donald E. Luman, and Julie C. Angel. 2009. *Sinkhole Density and Distribution of Cahokia Quadrangle, St. Clair County, Illinois*. Champaign: Illinois State Geological Survey.

Pauketat, Timothy R. 1993. *Temples for Cahokia Lords: Preston Holder's 1955–1956 Excavations of Kunnemann Mound*. Memoirs of the University of Michigan Museum of Anthropology, Number 26. Ann Arbor: University of Michigan.

Pauketat, Timothy R. 2004. *Ancient Cahokia and the Mississippians*. Cambridge University Press, Cambridge.

Pauketat, Timothy R. 2009. *Cahokia: Ancient America's Great City on the Mississippi*. New York: Viking-Penguin Press.

Pauketat, Timothy R. 2012. *An Archaeology of the Cosmos: Rethinking Agency and Religion in Ancient America*. London: Routledge.

Pauketat, Timothy R. 2019. "Introducing New Materialisms, Rethinking Ancient Urbanisms." In *New Materialisms Ancient Urbanism*, edited by Susan M. Alt and Timothy R. Pauketat, 1–18. London: Routledge.

Pauketat, Timothy R. 2020. "What Constituted Cahokian Urbanism?" In *Landscapes of Preindustrial Urbanism*, edited by Georges Farhat, 85–107. Washington, DC: Dumbarton Oaks.

Pauketat, Timothy R., and Susan M. Alt. 2018. "Water and Shells in Bodies and Pots: Mississippian Rhizome, Cahokian Poiesis." In *Relational Identities and Other-than-Human Agency in Archaeology*, edited by Eleanor Harrison-Buck and Julia A. Hendon, 72–99. Boulder: University Press of Colorado.

Pauketat, Timothy R., Susan M. Alt, and Jeffery D. Kruchten. 2017. "The Emerald Acropolis: Elevating the Moon and Water in the Rise of Cahokia." *Antiquity* 91 (355): 207–222.

Pauketat, Timothy R., Lucretia S. Kelly, Gayle J. Fritz, Neal H. Lopinot, Scott Elias, and Eve Hargrave. 2002. "The Residues of Feasting and Public Ritual at Early Cahokia." *American Antiquity* 67: 257–279.

Pauketat, Timothy R., and Neal H. Lopinot. 1997. "Cahokian Population Dynamics." In *Cahokia: Domination and Ideology in the Mississippian World*, edited by Timothy R. Pauketat and Thomas E. Emerson, 103–123. Lincoln: University of Nebraska Press.

Pokorny, J., M. Lutze, D. Cao, and A. J. Zele. 2006. "The Color of Night: Surface Color Perception under Dim Illuminations." *Visual Neuroscience* 23 (3–4): 525–530.

Radin, Paul. 1990. *The Winnebago Tribe (originally published 1923)*. Lincoln: University of Nebraska Press.

Romain, William F. 2017. "Monks Mound as Axis Mundi for the Cahokian World." *Illinois Antiquity* 29: 27–52.

Salzer, Robert J., and Grace Rajnovich. 2000. *The Gottschall Rockshelter: An Archaeological Mystery*. St. Paul, Minnesota: Prairie Smoke Press.

Schilling, Timothy. 2010. "An Archaeological Model of the Construction of Monks Mound and Implications for the Development of the Cahokian Society (800–1400 A.D.)." https://openscholarship.wustl.edu/etd/313.

Searls, Damion, ed. 2009. *The Journal 1837–1861: Henry David Thoreau*. New York: New York Review Books.

Simon, Mary L. 2014. "Reevaluating the Introduction of Maize into the American Bottom and Western Illinois." *Reassessing the Timing, Rate, and Adoption Trajectories of Domesticate Use in the Midwest and Great Lakes*, edited by Marie E. Raviele and William A. Lovis, 97–134. Midwest Archaeological Conference, Inc.

Skousen, B. Jacob. 2016. "Pilgrimage and the Construction of Cahokia: A View from the Emerald Site." PhD diss., Department of Anthropology, University of Illinois, Urbana.

Slater, Philip A., Kristin M. Hedman, and Thomas E. Emerson. 2014. "Immigrants at the Mississippian Polity of Cahokia: Strontium Isotope Evidence for Population Movement." *Journal of Archaeological Science* 44 (April 1): 117–127.

Slater, Philip A., Kristin M. Hedman, and Thomas E. Emerson. 2015. "Strontium Isotope Analysis: A Tool for Assessing the Role of Immigration in the Formation of Cahokia, America's First City." *Illinois Antiquity* 30 (3): 26–28.

Smith, Harriet. 1969. "The Murdock Mound, Cahokia Site." In *Explorations into Cahokia Archaeology*, edited by Melvin L. Fowler, 49–88. Urbana: Illinois Archaeological Survey, Bulletin 7.

Thrift, Nigel. 2004. "Intensities of Feeling: Towards a Spatial Politics of Affect." *Geografiska Annaler* 86B (1): 57–78.

Tomassoni, Rosella, Guiseppe Galetta, and Eugenia Treglia. 2015. "Psychology of Light: How Light Influences the Health and Psyche." *Pyschology* 6 (10): 1216–1222.

Townsend, Richard F. 2004. *Hero, Hawk, and Open Hand: American Indian Art of the Ancient Midwest and South*. New Haven, CT: Yale University Press.

Veitch, Jennifer A., and Guy R. Newshan. 1998. "Lighting Quality and Energy-Efficiency Effects on Task Performance, Mood, Health, Satisfaction and Comfort." *Journal of the Illuminating Engineering Society* 27: 107–129.

Walker, James R. 1980. *Lakota Belief and Ritual*, edited by R. J. DeMallie and E. Jahner. Lincoln: University of Nebraska Press.

Weltfish, Gene. 1965. *The Lost Universe: Pawnee Life and Culture*. Lincoln: University of Nebraska Press.

Whitehouse, Harvey. 2004. *Modes of Religiosity: A Cognitive Theory of Religious Transmission*. Lanham, MD: Rowman and Littlefield Publishers.

Wissler, Clark, and D. C Duvall. 1908. *Mythology of the Blackfoot Indians*. New York: The Trustees. https://lccn.loc.gov/11018960.

Witthoft, John. 1949. *Green Corn Ceremonialism in the Eastern Woodlands*. University of Michigan, Museum of Anthropology, Occasional Contributions 13, Ann Arbor.

9

Notes on the Chacoan
Nightscape

Astronomy, Fire, and Gambling

Robert S. Weiner

Of ancient North America's large archaeological sites, none is associated with nighttime as much as Chaco Canyon, a center of monumental architecture that thrived in the San Juan Basin of northwestern New Mexico between circa 850 to 1200 CE (figure 1.1). Chaco's nocturnal associations derive from two sources: first, a superb, Robert Redford–narrated PBS documentary titled *The Mystery of Chaco Canyon* (Sofaer 1999), which brought to the public's attention astronomical knowledge expressed in Chacoan building alignments and rock art; and second, the expansive and clear skies of Chaco Culture National Historical Park, which led to its designation in 2013 as an International Dark Sky Park, "one of the best places in the country to experience and enjoy natural darkness" (Cornucopia 2018). For many of the approximately 55,000 tourists who flock to the canyon every year, the opportunity to behold the sky bejeweled with ceaseless stars—an increasingly rare privilege in the modern age of light pollution—is of equal, if not greater, significance to visiting the ancient buildings. Chaco's vast, clear, dark skies thus continue to captivate today as they did a thousand years ago.

A substantial archaeoastronomical literature details the ways ancient Chaco people engaged with the night sky (e.g., Malville 2004; Sofaer 2007), but there has been little consideration of what practices and dimensions of cultural life were assigned to the hours without light (see Kamp and Whittaker 2018 for a treatment of the affordances night brought to the Sinagua peoples

https://doi.org/10.5876/9781646422609.c009

of Arizona). To enrich Chaco's already strong association with the nocturnal, I explore three dimensions of Chaco's ancient nightscape and lightscape that comprised vital aspects of the "Big Idea" (Stein and Lekson 1992) catalyzing Chaco's monumental developments and influence across the Four Corners region. First, I review work by the Solstice Project that suggests the key role of lunar astronomy and its manifestation in Chaco's built and natural environment as central elements of Chacoan ideology. The construction of Chaco Canyon in dialogue with the cosmos would have provided hierophantic experiences of alignments and linked the authority of Chaco's ruling elite with the order of the cosmos. Second, I consider fire at Chaco, exploring for the first time the role of fireboxes in practices of ritual movement along Chacoan roads that may have related to purification and offering. Finally, I explore the role of nighttime gambling that connected players with the forces of unpredictability and brought together diverse populations of the Chaco world for economic and social exchanges. I focus on the sensory and affective dimensions of these three domains of the Chacoan nightscape to argue that key elements of Chaco's regional influence and sources of power were, indeed, practices and experiences in darkness and of the night. This initial investigation suggests the fruitful potential of further work on the practices, architecture, and ideology of nighttime at Chaco and ancient cities across the globe.

BACKGROUND ON CHACO CANYON

A vast literature describes Chaco's architecture, material culture, and interpretations of its sociopolitical organization, yet researchers fundamentally disagree on basic aspects of the site's history and function. I do not attempt to resolve these debates here, but rather present a brief review of the central issues of Chaco that define the Pueblo II (ca. 900–1100 CE) period in the US Southwest.

Chaco Canyon and its region are best defined by Great Houses, multi-storied buildings constructed with core-and-veneer architecture that contain hundreds of rooms and kivas (circular rooms) enclosed within roomblocks (Lekson 1984). They exhibit a formulaic set of proportions and orientations to astronomical azimuths (Sofaer 2007), which, together with their multistoried construction, demonstrate a high level of architectural design. Undoubtedly, Great Houses were built to impress; the thickness of their walls, massive room sizes, and towering heights are built beyond the scale necessary for daily, domestic needs. Interpretations of Chacoan Great Houses range from large apartment complexes (Vivian 1990) to noble palaces (Lekson 2018), temporary housing for pilgrims (Toll 2006), and ceremonial public buildings (Sofaer 2007; Van Dyke 2007); I prefer "temple" as a descriptor.

Excavations at Pueblo Bonito, the largest Great House in Chaco Canyon, revealed few hearths or room suites that are conclusively domestic in nature (Pepper 1920; Judd 1964; Bustard 2003). Most doors connecting rooms in Pueblo Bonito are small, easily sealed portals with secondary jambs that are not easily walked through, likely indicating storage rooms (Lekson 1984, 25–28). These findings led many researchers to suggest Great House housed only a small number of occupants (Windes 1987; Bernardini 1999), likely a resident elite. Central to discussions of Great Houses and their use is Room 33 in Pueblo Bonito, which contained the remains of two middle-aged men buried with 40,000 pieces of turquoise and conch shell trumpets in a subfloor crypt (Pepper 1909). In the room above, fourteen individuals were interred over the course of 250 years, all of whom were maternally related (Kennett et al. 2017).

In contrast to the monumental Great Houses on the north side of Chaco Canyon, dozens of humble, small residential sites known as Bc sites, or unit pueblos, fill the southern half. Unlike their grandiose counterparts, Bc sites are small room suites with clear evidence of domestic occupation (McKenna and Truell 1986). Skeletal analyses of those interred in Great Houses and small sites revealed that Great House inhabitants were consistently taller and more robust than small house occupants (Akins 1986). The glaring contrast between Great Houses and Bc sites suggests distinct social classes in Chaco Canyon and throughout the Chaco world (Lekson 2015).

The side-by-side occurrence of Great Houses and unit pueblos is found throughout a 100,000-square-kilometer region surrounding Chaco Canyon. Known as Chaco outliers, there are approximately 150 of these settlements stretching throughout and beyond the San Juan Basin, with the most dis-tant sites in Pagosa Springs, Colorado, Blanding, Utah, and south into central New Mexico and Arizona (Kantner and Mahoney 2000; Kantner and Kintigh 2006). Many Chaco outliers exhibit the same iconic architecture found in the canyon: multistoried Great Houses, often ringed by earthen mounds, with multiple monumental roads and a surrounding community of unit pueblos (Stein and Lekson 1992).

The nature of the connection between Chaco Canyon and outliers is poorly understood. Similarities across the region include Great House, earthen mound, and road architecture and shared Dogozshi-style ceramic designs. Some scholars (e.g., Cameron 2009; Lekson 2018) argue for a highly integrated regional system, whereas many others currently posit multiple independent communities emulating Chacoan principles (Van Dyke 2003; Kantner and Kintigh 2006). There is little evidence for ceramic exchange between outliers (see authors in Kantner and Mahoney 2000), and Great Houses across the Chaco world demonstrate microscale distinctions in architectural techniques (Van Dyke 2003). On the other hand, the standardized ground plans of Great Houses suggest centralized influence (Cameron 2008), and Barbara Mills et al.'s (2018) recent network analysis challenges earlier studies that downplay intersite interaction in the Chaco World. Other evidence of regional integration comes from the peacefulness of the Pueblo II period. There is little evidence of intervillage conflict and, instead, momentary expressions of brutalization (Turner and Turner 1999), possibly perpetuated by a Chacoan core.

Unlike the lack of interaction between outliers, there is substantial evidence for regional-scale investment in the monumental center at Chaco Canyon. Chaco depended on a wider world, and the Chuska Slope region particularly, for many goods—for example, over half of the utilitarian ceramics recovered from the Pueblo Alto Great House were made in the Chuskas (Toll 2006). The canyon's inhabitants imported 240,000 timbers from the Chuska and Zuni Mountains (Guiterman et al. 2016). Large corncobs uncovered in Pueblo Bonito display isotopic signatures that suggest they were grown in the Chuska Slope region (Benson et al. 2003). Also, the labor force required to construct Great Houses almost surely drew on populations from beyond the canyon.

Most researchers would agree that religion and ritual played a central role in Chaco's complex developments and regional influence, however strong it may have been. Some emphasize shared cosmologies manifested through astronomical knowledge (Sofaer 2007), concepts of center place (Marshall 1997; Van Dyke 2007), and ritual performances using Mesoamerican exotic goods (Weiner 2015). Others offer specific mechanisms of integration across the region, including pilgrimage (Toll 2006; Van Dyke 2007), political control through an economy of bulk and prestige goods (Lekson 2018), and institutionalized ritual gambling (Weiner 2018).

Chaco's influence extended into the mid-twelfth century, when droughts and social conflict stressed the Chacoan order. By the mid-1100s, major construction ceased in Chaco Canyon, and the subsequent two centuries saw a gradual shift away from monumentality and explicit social hierarchy that culminated in mass depopulation of the Four Corners region around 1280 CE (Ortman 2012).

CHACO AND ALTERNATIVE URBANISMS
OF ANCIENT NORTH AMERICA

The inclusion of Chaco Canyon in a volume on ancient cities at night may strike some readers as puzzling, and a brief discussion of the archaeology of Chaco Canyon in the context of new ways of thinking about ancient North American urbanism is necessary. Recent scholarship emphasizes that trait-list definitions of urbanism reproduce ethnocentric prejudices that obscure premodern forms of cities expressed in ancient North America. Inherited biases of early social-evolutionary anthropology created a legacy of denying complex political formations and urbanism to precontact peoples of North America, though recent works have exposed and critiqued these perspectives (e.g., Pauketat 2007; Lekson 2018). New approaches to the nature of cities in the ancient Americas acknowledge the prevalence of low-density urbanism throughout much of the ancient world, as well as the experiential and affective dimensions of urban built environments.

The concept of low-density, agrarian-based urbanism describes an organization in which widely dispersed settlements represent an alternative type of city. Roland Fletcher (2011, 285), who developed the concept, states: "It is now untenable to define urban as a term restricted to compact and clearly bounded settlements." Indeed, Christian Isendahl and Michael Smith (2013, 133) argue that many cities of the ancient world—those in Mesoamerica, South America, Africa, and Southeast Asia stand out the most—were low-density, challenging a dominant perception of cities as defined principally by population thresholds. Disagreements over Chaco Canyon's population that fluctuate around a rough mean of 2,500 residents (Lekson 2018, 77) may therefore not be central to designating Chaco a city. Instead, Chaco's impact across a 100,000-square-kilometer region and monumental architecture may be more helpful metrics.

In contrast to density thresholds, Stephen Lekson (2015, 2018), following urbanist Amos Rapoport (1993), suggests that Chaco's political influence across a region is a key factor in defining it as a city. Rapoport (1993) lists Chaco among capital cities of the world, which he defines primarily through regional influence that is legitimized through ritual practices and ideological appeals to the past. As discussed above, while some question the notion that Chaco Canyon exerted strong, centralized political influence over outliers (e.g., Van Dyke 2003; Kantner and Kintigh 2006), most would agree that Chaco's belief system was shared by communities throughout the San Juan Basin. Further relating to Rapoport's (1993) conceptualization of capital cities, Ruth Van Dyke (2007) has thoroughly explored how Chacoan leaders appealed to previous eras as an essential aspect of their ideology.

Chaco's monumental built environment and its sensory impact constitute another element suggesting urbanism at Chaco. The authors in Susan M. Alt and Timothy Pauketat (2019; see also Alt, chapter 8 in this volume) offer a contemporary conceptualization of cities within Deleuzian assemblage theory, locating the phenomenon of urbanism in the process of human and nonhuman actors (objects, landforms, celestial bodies, etc.) coalescing and dispersing in interconnected webs of relationships that produce affective and experiential dimensions leading to cultural change. In this view, there is no inherent "cityhood" to be found in Chaco or elsewhere but rather webs of relationships that at times densify and converge as bundles recognized as urban. Van Dyke (2019, 41) utilizes an assemblage framework to characterize Chaco as a "a formal, highly structured landscape—a density of settlement that might be called urban" comprising monumental architecture, water and rainfall, roads, landforms, corn, the movement of celestial bodies, exotic Mesoamerican goods, memories of ancestral populations, and more. Similarly, Rapoport (1993) identifies grandiose architecture as a key component of capital cities. Certainly, downtown Chaco was a highly designed and formalized landscape built to awe and impress, an amalgamation of monumental Great Houses, broad avenues, platform mounds, and earthen rampways sure to dazzle with their theatricality (Stein et al. 2007).

This brief discussion of recent developments in understanding Chaco as urban from disparate theoretical paradigms highlights the necessity of rethinking cities in ancient North America. The monumentality and powerful experiential impact of Great Houses, roads, landforms, and other entities concentrated within Chaco Canyon itself comprise an urban environment, but the influence of this center across communities throughout 100,000 square kilometers, and the various substances, landforms, objects buildings, memories, affects, and persons therein, are of equal importance in defining its cityhood. Thus, my exploration of Chaco at night expands well beyond the canyon walls to encompass Great Houses, roads, landforms, and the skyward motions of the sun and moon.

CHACOAN ASTRONOMY OF THE NIGHT

Commemorating and engaging with astronomical cycles of the night sky appear to have been vital aspects of a centralized Chaco belief system. Twelve of the fourteen largest Chacoan Great Houses are aligned to either the equinoxes, solstices, or lunar standstills (figure 9.1; Sofaer 2007). Furthermore, the layout of buildings within and surrounding the canyon reveals an interconnected, overarching architectonic plan in which Great Houses are positioned

FIGURE 9.1. *Midwinter full moonrise at Chetro Ketl in the year of the minor standstill, January 4, 2015. Photo: Courtesy of Corrina Leatherwood.*

relative to one another on azimuths of astronomical significance (figure 9.2; Sofaer 2007). The interrelationship of Great House alignments suggests a level of integration, rather than overt competition, between Great Houses in Chaco Canyon, built as a reflection and embodiment of the sky—in the words of Pauketat (2014, 438): "Standing in various positions in and around these masonry monuments thus situated oneself at the interstices of an orderly, aligned universe, constituting a 'hierophantic' experience that physically and emotionally linked human beings with the supreme powers of the cosmos." Rather than mirroring the night sky specifically, Chaco's buildings commemorated the rising and setting positions of the sun and moon, and thus the liminal moment of transformation from day to night, and back again.

Jay Williams and colleagues (2006), based on interviews with Diné *hataałii* (medicine people), explore the notion that the layout of floor features in Casa Rinconada (Kin Tł'oo'di Yaanaalkid, "The Building Outside Which Is in Continuous Motion with Time"), a Great Kiva in Chaco Canyon, relates to constellations. They describe the Diné principle of *iikááh*, "mappings of deities," which can be expressed through sand paintings, architecture, astronomy,

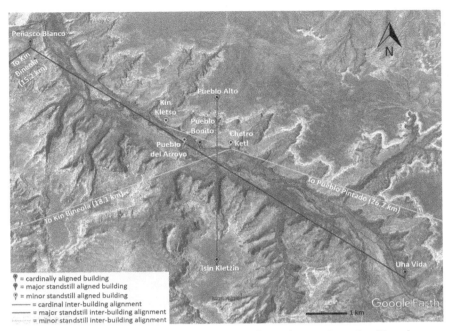

Figure 9.2. *Astronomical organization of Chaco Canyon's central complex. Note the intersite alignment between Peñasco Blanco and Una Vida that emphasizes the canyon's topographic trajectory. Map: Robert S. Weiner.*

and more (Williams et al. 2006, 103). In this conceptualization, the floor vaults, post holes, and fireboxes of Casa Rinconada schematically represent male and female deity forms that are manifest in the constellations of the Big Dipper, Cassiopeia, and Polaris. Thus, the authors suggest that much of Chaco's architecture embodies iikááh and that "the domains of sand paintings, and astronomy are so tightly interwoven that the activation of one domain activates another" (Williams et al. 2006, 112–113), such that to experience Chacoan architecture was to conceptually dwell among the starry, nighttime world above.

The moon and its light played perhaps a preeminent role in the Chacoans' relationship with the night sky. At the Sun Dagger site set high atop Fajada Butte, three sandstone slabs are positioned to produce light and shadow markings on a large spiral petroglyph, marking the solstices, equinoxes, and lunar standstill extremes (Sofaer et al. 1979; Sofaer et al. 1982; figure 9.3). The Sun Dagger site allowed the Chacoans to know the extremes, or endpoints, of the complex 18.6-year lunar cycle, and to track the relative positions between

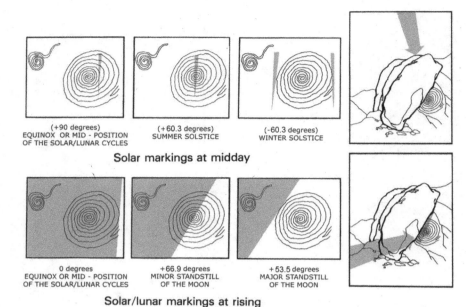

(+90 degrees)
EQUINOX OR MID - POSITION
OF THE SOLAR/LUNAR CYCLES

(+60.3 degrees)
SUMMER SOLSTICE

(-60.3 degrees)
WINTER SOLSTICE

Solar markings at midday

0 degrees
EQUINOX OR MID - POSITION
OF THE SOLAR/LUNAR CYCLES

+66.9 degrees
MINOR STANDSTILL
OF THE MOON

+53.5 degrees
MAJOR STANDSTILL
OF THE MOON

Solar/lunar markings at rising

FIGURE 9.3. *Diagram of solar and lunar markings at the Sun Dagger site on Fajada Butte. Drawings: Courtesy of the Solstice Project.*

the minor and major extremes. The rising midwinter full moon in any given year casts a shadow on the spiral, the location of which reveals the current position within the standstill cycle. Even more dramatically, the Great House at Chimney Rock, 135 kilometers from Chaco Canyon, near Pagosa Springs, Colorado, is positioned on a steep precipice with a view toward two rock pillars that frame the major standstill moonrise once every 18.6 years (Malville 2004). Tree ring cutting dates from the Great House correspond with lunar standstill years (Lekson 2015, 196).

Similar to Chimney Rock, the natural landform of Chaco Canyon itself may have been recognized for a fortuitous topographic alignment to the major lunar standstill (Sofaer et al. 2017). This knowledge appears to have been marked by the Chacoans through intersite alignments of shrines on the high mesas forming the south side of the canyon and by the interbuilding alignment between Peñasco Blanco and Una Vida, both of which are individually aligned to the major standstill (figure 9.2). The landform of Chaco Canyon itself therefore may have been a "hierophany," a place where the earth reflected and perhaps intersected with the night sky.

Why such dedication to tracking the moon's complex 18.6-year standstill cycle, especially, as many researchers are keen to note, knowledge of the standstills serves "no practical function"? For years, and especially in recent decades, archaeologists and anthropologists have come to acknowledge and value the centrality of religion, or what might be better called relating with nonhuman worlds, as a key ingredient in the cultural histories across time and space, especially in premodern contexts (e.g., Alt, chapter 8 in this volume; Pauketat 2013). The moon considered as an animate being differs greatly from a lifeless scientific object studied in modern astronomy. Of course, astronomical knowledge was deeply tied to power in many societies. For example, Mexica and Inka leaders sought to link their authority with the order of the cosmos by constructing astronomically organized landscapes (Broda 2015), and Maya kings timed their ascension dates to the lunar cycle (see Landau, Hernandez, and Gonlin, chapter 6 in this volume). Those with knowledge of, and seemingly control over, heavenly bodies served as mediators between life on earth and the agentive entities of the sky that brought light, gave life to plants, timed the yearly calendar, and shifted across the horizon and throughout the sky.

The moon—often associated with fertility, femininity, and water—is a curious and fascinating entity. Unlike the sun, confined to greet humankind only during the daytime hours, the moon dances betwixt day and night, while simultaneously morphing across its twenty-eight-day month from a sharp, crescentic fingernail paring to a healthy, bright, round face. A cosmic coincidence has led to the sun and full moon appearing the same size in the sky from the perspective of a person on earth, a fact well suited to establishing ideologies of dualism and balance between sun and moon, day and night. Furthermore, the moon illuminated the nocturnal darkness for the Chacoans, brightening the long, cold nights of winter. In the summer, its nighttime brilliance may have enabled travel to and from the canyon in avoidance of the scorching desert sun. In a canyon lacking large quantities of wood to build fires, the moon may have been valued even more dearly by the people of ancient Chaco as a source of nocturnal light.

Finally, the direction north was valued and commemorated by the Chaco culture. North is most accurately determined through a shadow and light compass, the method likely utilized for establishing building and road alignments, especially considering that Polaris was more than five degrees off true celestial north from 900–1200 CE (Lekson 2015, 72). Regardless, north was still likely of great meaning in relation to the nighttime—it is the *axis caelo*, the fixed position around which the constellations whirl in chaotic revelry, called the "heart of the sky" in some Pueblo traditions (Lekson 2015, 72). North may have held significance as the origin place of humans as related in Puebloan and other Indigenous traditions (Sofaer et al. 1989). Williams et al. (2006) suggest that Polaris, though off from due north in the Chaco era, was valued in connection with sacred schematics and incorporated in architecture.

Cardinal alignments were a key feature of Chacoan architecture and settlement design. Numerous Great Houses are cardinally aligned—most notably, the seventy-meter-long wall of Pueblo Bonito—and four major Great Houses in downtown Chaco are organized in a cardinal cross (Fritz 1978; Sofaer 2007). Pueblo Bonito's mid-wall converged with phenomena of both the day and night skies. Every day at solar noon, midpoint of the sun's passage across the sky, the wall would cast no shadow; similarly, at night it would have pointed toward "the heart of the sky," axis point of the starry night heavens.

The Great North Road, among the grandest of Chaco's monumental avenues, stretched at least fifty kilometers due north from the canyon, with a quarter of a degree of accuracy for much of its length and often as parallel routes (Sofaer et al. 1989). The road diverges from north to articulate with the dramatic badlands topography of Kutz Canyon, which may have represented an underworld (and therefore dark) emergence place for the Chaco culture (Sofaer et al. 1989). The North Road then likely continues to link Chaco Canyon with the Great Houses of Salmon and Aztec; in this view, the direction north ordered a multigenerational political ideology in the ancient Southwest (Lekson 2015). Thus, the direction north—most richly experienced by humans as the fixed point around which the night sky spins—was a vital element in Chacoan cosmovision.

Astronomical hierophanies would have been experienced at different scales in the ancient Chacoan world. Only a few select individuals could gather at the Sun Dagger site to witness the lunar shadow markings (as noted by Tewa anthropologist Alfonso Ortiz, quoted in Anna Sofaer [1983]), whereas scores of people could gather in Great House plazas or along their back walls to witness alignments to the rise and set of the sun and moon. A compelling alignment would be present for those gathered at Peñasco Blanco in midwinter of the southern major standstill moonrise, who would have seen the full moon rise in alignment with the topographic trajectory of Chaco Canyon (Sofaer 2007, 245). Beholding the key moments when Chaco's built and natural environment intersected, the movements of the cosmos reinforced notions of Chaco as a center place, or axis mundi (Van Dyke 2007).

The end of the Chaco culture marked a termination of overt architectural expressions of lunar standstill astronomy among descendent populations of Pueblo and Diné cultures. Lekson (2009, 294n136) has proposed an ideological struggle between Chacoan Great Houses with southeast-facing (i.e., lunar[1]) orientations and those with cardinal alignments, with the latter ultimately triumphing around 1100 CE. Shifting alignments "may represent political arguments inscribed on symbolic landscapes" (Lekson 2009, 294n136), or varying cosmological emphases over centuries. The play of alignment schemes over generations may therefore demonstrate fluctuations in the extent of the nighttime's significance in Chacoan religion, with this belief system perpetuated through large-scale architectural alignments and resisted through other constructions. Similarly, alignments to the 18.6-year lunar cycle may have been part of the "knowledge" abused by select groups at Chaco (interviews in Sofaer 1999) and eventually suppressed amidst Chaco's downfall and descendent peoples' readjustment toward more communally-focused social organizations that rejected overt individual expressions of power.

FIREBOXES AND RITUAL MOVEMENT ALONG CHACOAN ROADS

Fire was another key element of the Chacoan nightscape. Rectangular sandstone slab boxes transformed red by intense, hot fires appear throughout the canyon and Chaco's larger region. Termed "fireboxes," these features are often discussed as signaling stations, most recently by Van Dyke and colleagues (2016). Some fireboxes are found on topographic high points—at Pueblo Alto, the highest Great House in the canyon, and at outlier Great Houses on top of buttes including Chimney Rock, Guadalupe, Bis Sa'ani, and El Faro at Pierre's Complex. Pyres lit in these boxes on ancient Chacoan nights would have dotted the open expanses of the Colorado Plateau. Experiments with flares conducted on dark nights by the Chaco Project and an enterprising high school student from Farmington demonstrated the potential for visual unity across 200 kilometers of the far-reaching sagebrush expanses of the San Juan Basin (Lekson 2018, 265n7). Specifically, a fire lit at Pueblo Alto on Chaco Canyon's North Mesa is visible atop Huerfano Peak forty kilometers north, and a fire at the top of Huerfano could be seen 100 km north at Chimney Rock, thus visually connecting Chaco Canyon to the northeastern-most outlier.

One of the best-known firebox features of the Chaco world is El Faro at Pierre's Complex, a dramatic Chaco outlier set along the Great North Road comprised of various ritual structures set atop badlands buttes and pinnacles (Stein 1983). The most striking construction at Pierre's is El Faro, a small Chaco Great House at the base of a steep, cone-shaped pinnacle, which connects with a masonry platform / set of rooms constructed on the slopes of this landform (figure 9.4). Of most relevance for this discussion, "atop this

FIGURE 9.4. *View toward El Faro firebox atop a pinnacle at Pierre's Site, a Chaco outlier located along the Great North Road. Photo: Robert S. Weiner.*

lofty spire is a hearth where many large fires have been built and the visibility in all directions is excellent. Not surprisingly, the tip of this spire with its much-used hearth marks the center of the projected alignment of the North Road" (Stein 1983, 8-1). A fire lit atop could be seen from locations throughout the surrounding sagebrush flats, and those traveling along the North Road—likely as part of a procession, pilgrimage, or other ritualized form of movement—would have perceived the glowing beacon of El Faro appear and disappear in the distance as they crested and descended dunes, communicating the immanence of arrival at Pierre's.

I am skeptical, however, that most Chacoan fireboxes functioned as a signaling communication system. Many are not on elevated positions, and it is unclear if lighting fires across great distances would convey messages more clearly and effectively than dispatching runners. In fact, nearly all the proposed signaling stations across the Chaco world lack evidence of burning (Kincaid et al. 1983, 9.4) and are better interpreted as shrines (Sofaer et al. 2017). Van Dyke et al. (2016) suggest that selenite, a reflective mineral common throughout the San Juan Basin, may have been used to signal from these locations rather than fire, but such a technique would be limited to hours when the sun was properly positioned. Furthermore, a signaling system with fires or selenite would be quite limited in the semantic content it could convey and, I suspect, far less effective for transmitting messages than runners on foot. I do not mean to entirely disregard signaling functions, but I focus on nonsignaling uses of Chaco fireboxes here.

Many fireboxes are found in association with Chacoan roads and likely played a role in practices of ritual movement along them. I follow Sofaer et al.'s (1989, 372) suggestion that "evidence of fire on ramps, burnt structures, elevated fireboxes, and fire pits warrant further investigation for possible ceremonial significance," combined with my own field observations along Chacoan roads. Fireboxes are often found where roads articulate with Great Houses or other monumental architectural features— such as at Pueblo Alto, Pueblo Bonito, Hillside Ruin, Pierre's Site, Coyote Canyon, Kin Hocho'i, Ats'ee Nitsaa, Lowry, and Reservoir Ruin—though this list is not exhaustive. A large mass of fire-reddened sandstone, two meters in diameter and twenty centimeters tall, is present along the highest point of the South Road between Kin Ya'a and its ultimate termination point at the base of the Dutton Plateau (Nials et al. 1987, 35). Burned features are present at other locations along the South Road, such as a section along the Ki-me-ni-oli Wash (Nials et al. 1987, 42–43). Although not a firebox, the constructed ramp by which the Ah-Shi-Sle-Pah Road drops into Ah-Shi-Sle-Pah Wash contains significant quantities of fire-reddened sandstone and witnessed intense burning (Stein 1983, 8-9). Two shrine-like, small buildings associated with the North Road—Halfway House and Burnt Jacal—were burned[2] (Stein and Levine 1983, C-11, C-53), further suggesting the possibility of fire-related rituals practiced along Chacoan roads, perhaps conducted at night, when fire's visual impact is the most impactful.

A striking example of road-associated fireboxes are six features that line the outward face of Hillside Ruin, a massive earthen platform enclosed by masonry retaining walls built against the cliff face northeast of Pueblo Bonito (Judd 1964, 148; Stein et al. 2007, 212–213; figure 9.5a, b). Hillside Ruin is one of the most massive structures in downtown Chaco and the convergence point of numerous monumental roads that ascend the platform via stairways and ramps. Six fireboxes, each approximately one square meter, front Hillside Ruin and "were filled with sand reddened by heat and containing minute particles of charcoal but no discernible wood ash; there was no fusing of mortar and no fragment of pottery or bone in either" (Judd 1964, 148). The prominent position of these fireboxes ensured that those approaching the grand masonry

FIGURE 9.5. (a) *View of fireboxes excavated outside Hillside Ruin. Photo: Judd 1964, pl. X (used with permission of the Department of Anthropology, Smithsonian Institution);* (b) *3-D reconstruction of Hillside Ruin showing its monumentality, road relationships, and fireboxes. Photo: courtesy of Richard Friedman.*

FIGURE 9.6. *View of Fajada Butte and the ramp ascending it* (marked by arrows). *Fireboxes are present at the bottom and top of the ramp. Photo: Robert S. Weiner.*

platform would experience their affordant properties: the sizzling, cracking, and popping of juniper being seared to ash; blast of searing heat; scent of woody smoke; bright, red-orange glow and constant dance of flickering tongues of flame.

Fireboxes marked the lower and upper termini of the massive 210-meter-long ramp that ascends Fajada Butte, a striking sandstone butte that rises 135 meters in isolation above the valley floor of Chaco Canyon and is home to the Sun Dagger site (Ford 1993; figure 9.6). A road segment runs from an isolated Great Kiva in Fajada Gap to "a large concentration of burned rubble and fire-reddened upright slabs," where the road segment articulates with the ramp (Ford 1993, 478). From the firebox at the base, the lower section of the ramp follows a culturally enhanced ridge, ascends a fifteen-meter cliff face, and continues along a constructed ramp defined by massive masonry retaining walls. This middle section of ramp leads to a series of small masonry rooms constructed against the sandstone cliff face (Ford 1993, 479). The alignment continues through natural breaks in the cliff above, passing through a final upper cliff notch to reach the top of soaring Fajada Butte, where, "aligned with the three segments of the ramp is a meter square, fire-reddened slab box" (Ford 1993, 479), celebrating arrival to an upper world with vast, sweeping views across the shadowed desert soil, and into the great, domed blackness above.

Fire is a central aspect of ceremonial practices and mythologies the world round, often as an agent of purification, offering, renewal, or transformation. Insights from the traditions of descendant Indigenous Southwestern cultures offer perspectives for considering the role of fire among the Chacoans and how it may have been engaged with in rituals, though this is not to suggest an unchanging, static continuity between Chaco and ethnographically documented Southwestern practices.

Fire is central in ethnographic descriptions of both Diné and Pueblo ritual practices. The Fire Society is among the most influential medicine societies at Acoma Pueblo, and Big and Little Firebrand Societies are present at Zuni Pueblo (Parsons [1939] 1996, 133). An Acoma ceremony associated with the Corn Clan involves practitioners lighting fires atop sacred mountains and mesas surrounding the village, as well as producing six fires along the routes to these mountains (White 1942, 94–96). During a Zuni pilgrimage to the sacred Lake Kolhu/wala:wa, a participant embodying the Fire God lights fires along the route (Sofaer et al. 1989, 374). Fire is understood in some contexts as transmuting substances to the spirit realm: according to one Zuni story, "whenever one puts anything into the fire, when it burns the ghosts eat it" (Bunzel 1933, 218–219). Zuni and Keresan medicine society initiations sometimes involve fire rites, such as fire eating or walking on hot coals (Parsons [1939] 1996, 441). Finally, New Fire Ceremonies are practiced at numerous Pueblos, including Hopi (Fewkes 1900) and Zuni (Bunzel 1932, 536–537), where kindling a new fire is an aspect of initiating the new year (see Farah and Evans, chapter 10 in this volume, for such ceremonies among the Aztec).

Among the Diné, kǫ' (fire) is a "symbol of annihilation . . . said to burn evil" and "enters into practically every ceremony with many variations" (Reichard 1977, 554). Haashch'éé̜shzhiní (Black God) is the deity of fire and its creation (Reichard 1977, 399) and the god of the night and constellations, and the Pleiades constellation is depicted on some versions of Black God's mask (Griffin-Pierce 1992, 158). One of Black God's principal symbols is the fire drill, which is a key component of Diné medicine bundles (Reichard 1977, 401). Fire is key to a variety of Diné ceremonies, especially the sweat-emetic rite performed to remove evil from the body. Participants process into the *hooghan* (a circular, traditional Navajo home), sunwise as usual, and circle the central fire, pausing at each of the cardinal directions to sing (Reichard 1977,

FIGURE 9.7. *Cedar torches excavated at Pueblo Bonito. Photo: Judd 1954, pl. 79 (used with permission of the Department of Anthropology, Smithsonian Institution).*

724–725). Fire jumping is involved in the sweat-emetic (Reichard 1977, 555–556). Another fire-based practice is the Fire Dance (or the Dark-circle-of-branches or Corral Dance) performed on the ninth and final night of the Mountainway, in which individuals raced around a large fire carrying small torches, which they hit and rub against others and themselves, and, miraculously, emerged unscathed from the flames (Matthews 1887, 441–443; Reichard 1977, 547).

Archaeological finds from Pueblo Bonito give a material dimension to considering fire and fire making in ancient Chaco. Neil Judd (1954, 153) illustrates cottonwood and willow "fire-drill hearths" consisting of ten socket holes in which a drill would be placed and rotated to produce friction. Thirteen cedar-bark bundles uncovered in Pueblo Bonito in Room 226 were "immediately identified . . . as 'torches used in the Fire Ceremony to carry fire from one room to another'" by men from Zuni Pueblo (figure 9.7; Judd 1954, 276, pl. 79). Torch-like sticks burned only at the ends were found in association with a burial in Pueblo Bonito's Room 32 (Pepper 1920, 138). While Judd describes the drill-hearth and torches separately in sections on "household tools" and "objects of religious implication," respectively, these dichotomous categories are no longer tenable.

The principal aim of this section has been to establish an initial association between fireboxes, Chacoan roads, and the magnitude of fire in Indigenous Southwestern ritual practices—I am developing a full exploration of fire-related practices on Chacoan roads as part of my dissertation. A variety of use scenarios are imaginable for Chacoan fireboxes, though analysis of the sediments present therein would be a key next step to understanding their uses. Still, the spatial patterning of fireboxes suggests two main purposes: Those atop high points may have communicated simple messages between distant Chacoan sites and served as beacons to herald travelers, whether corporeal or more numinous, along Chacoan roads (see chapter 3 in this volume, on ancient Mesopotamia for fire beacons). Fireboxes located where monumental roads articulate with Great Houses, platforms, or striking landforms may have alternatively acted as receptacles for offerings or as places of purification, or otherwise marked a conceptual boundary defining the road's termination point (a Great House, butte, or platform) as distinct from the world beyond.

GAMBLING AT CHACO CANYON

Practices of gambling—rich in social functions and affective impact, and often associated with nighttime—were common across pre- and postcontact Indigenous North America (Culin [1907] 1975; Voorhies 2017; Weiner 2018). Diné and Pueblo oral traditions describe gambling's centrality at Chaco, and I have explored these traditions in tandem with archaeological evidence of dice and gaming sticks to propose that gaming and gambling were powerful

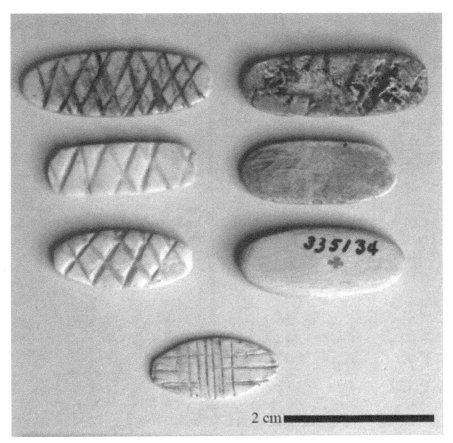

FIGURE 9.8. *Bone dice from Pueblo Bonito. Photo: Used with permission of the Department of Anthropology, Smithsonian Institution (catalog nos. A335126, A335132, A335134).*

undertakings at Chaco (Weiner 2018). Gambling in precontact Indigenous North America and throughout much of the world was not the recreational activity of the contemporary Western world (Voorhies 2017). Games can break the ice for intergroup interaction and trade (e.g., Janetski 2017), divine weather regimes (Culin [1907] 1975, 374), make rain (Stevenson 1903, 480), and provide a setting for social rivalries to manifest and be negotiated (Geertz 1973). Gambling games take place at a variety of scales, from low-stakes wagers played for amusement between friends to state-sponsored contests of chance. Ancient gaming at Chaco Canyon likely related to all these different aspects. Bone dice scattered throughout Pueblo Bonito (figure 9.8) likely represent household-level, low-stake games or divinations, whereas kick sticks, hand game pieces, and shinny sticks, deposited in the oldest portion of the building where other cosmologically charged goods such as macaws and vessels for frothing/drinking cacao were stored, were likely reserved for periodic, high-stakes contests (Weiner 2018, 41–42, table 1).

Ethnographic accounts of Indigenous North American (and, more specifically, Southwestern) gambling make it clear that certain games, especially the hand game, were assigned to nighttime hours (Culin [1907] 1975, 195, 346, 361–362). In the hand game, one player would hide and shift an object (small stone or stick) between their hands, in one of a pair of moccasins, or under a cup, and an opponent would guess where it was hidden. The hidden ball-game (a variety of hand game) was played during winter nights at Santa Clara Pueblo and by the Hopi at night "in the Walpi kivas almost continuously from January 12 to February 3" (Culin [1907] 1975, 36–3621, 368). The Diné moccasin game, another iteration of the hand game, "is only practiced during the dark hours . . . he on whom the sun shines while he is engaged in the game will be struck blind" (Matthews 1889a, 2). This proscription relates to the game's foundational myth, in which nocturnal and diurnal animals, partial to the conditions in which they thrived, play to determine whether the sun would never rise or never set—of course, neither contingent won, and time thus alternates between day and night (Matthews 1889a, 4–6; Mose Jr. et al. 2004). Additionally, a Taos dice game that involved moving a playing piece around a circle of stone markers was played all night on November 3 and thought to be connected to the Day of the Dead celebration (Culin [1907] 1975, 195).

Associations between gambling and darkness are suggested at Zuni, where men played *sholiwe* (a divinatory dice game) in "one of the old interior rooms of the pueblo . . . dimly lighted with a small window of selenite near the ceiling" (Stevenson 1903, 486), especially "during terrific sandstorms or at night" (Cushing 1896, 369). Dim lighting is a conscious design element in modern casinos, thought to facilitate prolonged gambling through a distortion of the perception of time (Schüll 2012). Great Kivas' dimly lit interiors and reverberant acoustics would have provided a compelling atmosphere for gambling accompanied by song and shouting. Similarly, the majority of Great House rooms would have been deeply enclosed within the buildings' monumental lofts and quite dark, conditions conducive to gambling.

Indigenous American gambling events were and are rich auditory experiences. Chanting, drumming, and singing frequently accompanied dice games, and especially forms of the hand game (Culin [1907] 1975, 227–382). In the hand game, one team shouts, screams, sings, shrieks, dances, and makes other sudden movements to distract guessing players (Culin [1907] 1975, 380). Gambling songs with the power to bring great luck and success in matches are common among many North American tribes (Culin [1907] 1975, 306, 325, 347, 350, 362; Matthews 1889a). The excellent acoustic properties of Chacoan Great Kivas and the amphitheater between Pueblo Bonito and Chetro Ketl (Loose 2002) are examples of places within Chaco Canyon where the many lively sounds accompanying gambling matches would have been amplified, distorted, and enhanced. Played at night, the action would need to be illumined by the glow of fire, smoke wafting amidst rhythmic choruses, steady drumbeat, and sudden cries of distraction by those engrossed in the game.

The nighttime association of certain gambling games among Indigenous Southwestern societies relates to larger seasonal and gendered categorizations. At Ohkay Owingeh, for example, games are classified into the dual division system, with both "cold" (marbles, tops, and jacks) and "hot" (shinny) games. In the spring, games associated with winter "are suddenly and dramatically put away, and if anyone is caught playing them he may be flogged by the Towa é [war chiefs]" (Ortiz 1969, 114), emphasizing their powerful ability to influence the natural world. Similarly, men are encouraged to begin playing shinny as a means of invigorating the sun in its return from the south of winter. A review of gambling traditions across Indigenous American groups led Warren DeBoer (2001) to note that dice games were primarily played by women, whereas guessing games were mostly played by men.

Finally, gambling is an emotionally charged practice. Ethnographically in North America, stakes ranged from small wagers to bringing rainfall in the coming year and even being enslaved (Cameron and Johansson 2017). Despair at becoming the slave of one's victorious opponent, or desperately challenging a gambler who appears unable to lose, is conceivable and suggested in Diné oral traditions of the undefeatable Great Gambler at Chaco (summarized in Weiner 2018). Certain individuals can attain immense skill at gambling; for example, Charles Lummis (1930, 185–186) observed at Isleta Pueblo that "an expert pa-tol [stick dice] player will throw the number he desires with almost unfailing certainty by his arrangement of the sticks in his hand and the manner and force with which he strikes them down." Other gamblers exhibit truly uncanny, unexplainable "luck" that gives them an ominous reputation. Facing such an opponent may have been a frustrating, or perhaps even terrifying, element of Chacoan nightlife.

Finally, gambling can be highly addictive, leading to "reduction in the sensitivity of the [brain's] reward system" such that addicts become desensitized to the high of winning and seek increasingly risky stakes (Reuter et al. 2005,

147). Experiences of addiction, compulsion, and the inability to step away from the intoxicating risk of making wagers on "chance" may have been a grim but unavoidable reality of nighttime gambling at Chaco. Indeed, Diné and Pueblo oral narratives express that the excess and addiction caused by gambling was a major part of what led to Chaco's closure and depopulation (e.g., Matthews 1889b; Stirling 1942).

CONCLUSIONS

Night at Chaco—bathed in pale light by the ever-shifting moon, glowing with fires announcing a road's end, and host to buzzing, song-filled games of chance—was very much alive and packed with significance. I have attempted to highlight three salient nighttime domains through which the Chacoan "Big Idea" (Stein and Lekson 1992) was experienced, negotiated, and reproduced through architecture, social practices, and their associated sensory impacts. Astronomical alignments established Chaco as an embodiment of heavenly order on earth, likely linking its leaders to the regularity of the cosmos. The lack of clear, public architectural expressions of lunar astronomy following Chaco's decline suggests that its night-based cosmology may have been rejected in the reorganization of the ancient Southwestern world in the later, Pueblo III and Pueblo IV periods (i.e., post-1280 CE). Some Chacoan fireboxes may have been used for signaling to convey simple messages over great distances at night. But most fireboxes, located where Chacoan roads articulate with architectural structures, appear instead to relate to nocturnal ritual movements and associated practices of purification and offering. Finally, nighttime gambling at Chaco had a variety of valances—from informal games played on long winter nights between friends, to games of religious fervor that forecasted the unknown, and an institutionalized social technology to facilitate trade or even enslavement. While there are many elements of the Chacoan nightscape yet unexplored, this initial investigation underscores the pertinence of thinking deeply about the architecture, practices, religious associations, and experiences of night in ancient sites worldwide.

I close with a short passage evoking the beauty and wonder of nighttime in the vast deserts of the American Southwest, the land in which Chaco rose and fell, by renowned Laguna Pueblo poet Leslie Marmon Silko (2010), who writes:

> Night. Heavenly delicious sweet night of the desert that calls all of us out to love her. The night is our comfort with her coolness and darkness. On wings, on feet, on our bellies, out we all come to glory in the night. (88)

Acknowledgments. I would like to thank Nan Gonlin and Meghan E. Strong for the wonderful opportunity to present in their Society for American Archaeology symposium on ancient cities at night and explore the life of Chaco after dark. I am also grateful to Steve Lekson for passing along their initial invitation. The astronomy section is derived principally from the research of conversations with Anna Sofaer, who has tirelessly instilled in me the importance of the moon and astronomy at Chaco. Rich Friedman and John Stein, as always, were generous with their knowledge of fireboxes and roads in the Chaco world, and the second section owes much to them. Cathy Cameron, Steve Lekson, Scott Ortman, Bob Preucel, Tim Pauketat, and John Cherry also offered important support, guidance, and inspiration throughout this research. Any errors, omissions, and so forth are my responsibility.

NOTES

1. Lekson prefers to identify these southeast-facing alignments as solstitial (Lekson 2009, 294n136). We agree to disagree.
2. Many Chacoan Great House rooms and Great Kivas were burned, likely as a ritual practice of closure (Windes 2003, 30).

REFERENCES

Akins, Nancy. 1986. *A Biocultural Approach to Human Burials from Chaco Canton, New Mexico.* Reports of the Chaco Center 9. Santa Fe, NM: National Park Service.

Alt, Susan M., and Timothy R. Pauketat, eds. 2019. *New Materialisms, Ancient Urbanisms.* New York: Routledge.

Benson, Larry, Linda Cordell, Kirk Vincent, Howard Taylor, John Stein, G. Jang Farmer, and Kiyoto Futa. 2003. "Ancient Maize from Chacoan Great Houses: Where Was It Grown?" *Proceedings of the National Academy of Sciences* 100 (27): 13111–13115.

Bernardini, Wesley. 1999. "Reassessing the Scale of Social Action at Pueblo Bonito, Chaco Canyon, New Mexico." *Kiva* 64 (4): 447–470.

Broda, Johanna. 2015. "Political Expansion and the Creation of Ritual Landscapes: A Comparative Study of Inca and Aztec Cosmovision." *Cambridge Archaeological Journal* 25 (1): 219–238.

Bunzel, Ruth L. 1932. "Introduction to Zuni Ceremonialism." In *Forty-Seventh Annual Report of the Bureau of American Ethnology,* 467–544. Washington, DC: US Government Printing Office.

Bunzel, Ruth L. 1933. *Zuni Texts*. New York: G. E. Stechert and Co.

Bustard, Wendy. 2003. "Pueblo Bonito: When a House Is Not a Home." In *Pueblo Bonito: Center of the Chacoan World*, edited by Jill E. Neitzel, 80–93. Washington, DC: Smithsonian Books.

Cameron, Catherine M. 2008. "Comparing Great House Architecture: Perspectives from the Bluff Great House." In *Chaco's Northern Prodigies: Salmon, Aztec, and the Ascendency of the Middle San Juan Region After AD 1100*, edited by Paul Reed, 251–269. Salt Lake City: University of Utah Press.

Cameron, Catherine M. 2009. *Chaco and After in the Northern San Juan: Excavations at the Bluff Great House*. Tucson: University of Arizona Press.

Cameron, Catherine M., and Lindsay Johansson. 2017. "The Biggest Losers: Gambling and Enslavement in Native North America." In *Prehistoric Games of North American Indians: Subarctic to Mesoamerica*, edited by Barbara Voorhies, 273–285. Salt Lake City: University of Utah Press.

Cornucopia, G. B. 2018. "Night Skies." Online digital resource in *New Perspectives on the Greater Chaco Landscape*, edited by Ruth M. Van Dyke and Carrie C. Heitman. Boulder: University Press of Colorado.

Culin, Stewart. (1907) 1975. *Games of the North American Indians*. New York: Dover Publications.

Cushing, Frank Hamilton. 1896. "Outlines of Zuñi Creation Myths." In *Thirteenth Annual Report of the Bureau of American Ethnology*, 321–447. Washington, DC: United States Government Printing Office.

DeBoer, Warren R. 2001. "Of Dice and Women: Gambling and Exchange in Native North America." *Journal Archaeological Method and Theory* 8 (3): 215–268.

Fewkes, J. Walter. 1900. "The New-Fire Ceremony at Walpi" *American Anthropologist* 2 (1): 80–138.

Fletcher, Roland. 2011. "Low-Density, Agrarian-Based Urbanism." In *The Comparative Archaeology of Complex Societies*, edited by Michael E. Smith, 285–320. Cambridge: Cambridge University Press.

Ford, Dabney. 1993. "Architecture on Fajada Butte." In *The Spadefoot Toad Site: Investigations at 29SJ6.29, Chaco Canyon, New Mexico*, edited by Thomas C. Windes, 471–482. Reports of the Chaco Center No. 12. Santa Fe, NM: National Park Service.

Fritz, John M. 1978. "Paleopsychology Today: Ideation Systems and Human Adaption in Prehistory." In *Social Archeology: Beyond Subsistence and Dating*, edited by Charles L. Redman, Mary Jane Berman, Edward V. Curtin, William T. Langhorne Jr., Nina M. Versaggi, and Jeffrey C. Wansner, 37–59. New York: Academic Press.

Geertz, Clifford. 1973. *The Interpretation of Cultures: Selected Essays.* New York: Basic Books.

Griffin-Pierce, Trudy. 1992. *Earth Is My Mother, Sky Is My Father: Space, Time, and Astronomy in Navajo Sandpainting.* Albuquerque: University of New Mexico Press.

Guiterman, Christopher H., Thomas W. Swetnam, and Jeffrey S. Dean. 2016. "Eleventh-Century Shift in Timber Procurement Areas for the Great Houses of Chaco Canyon." *Proceedings of the National Academy of Sciences* 113: 1186–1190.

Isendahl, Christian, and Michael E. Smith. 2013. "Sustainable Agrarian Urbanism: The Low-Density Cities of the Mayas and Aztecs." *Cities* 31: 132–143.

Janetski, Joel C. 2017. "Gaming in Fremont Society." In *Prehistoric Games of North American Indians: Subarctic to Mesoamerica,* edited by Barbara Voorhies, 119–138. Salt Lake City: University of Utah Press.

Judd, Neil M. 1954. *The Material Culture of Pueblo Bonito.* Smithsonian Miscellaneous Collections 124. Washington, DC: Smithsonian Institution.

Judd, Neil M. 1964. *The Architecture of Pueblo Bonito.* Smithsonian Miscellaneous Collections 147. Washington, DC: Smithsonian Institution.

Kamp, Kathryn, and John Whittaker. 2018. "The Night Is Different: Sensescapes and Affordances in Ancient Arizona." In *Archaeology of the Night: Life After Dark in the Ancient World,* edited by Nancy Gonlin and April Nowell, 77–94. Boulder: University Press of Colorado.

Kantner, John W., and Keith W. Kintigh. 2006. "The Chaco World." In *The Archaeology of Chaco Canyon: An Eleventh-Century Pueblo Regional Center,* edited by Stephen H. Lekson, 153–188. Santa Fe, NM: School for Advanced Research Press.

Kantner, John, and Nancy M. Mahoney. 2000. *Great House Communities across the Chacoan Landscape.* Anthropological Papers of the University of Arizona No. 64. Tucson: University of Arizona Press.

Kennett, Douglas J., Stephen Plog, Richard J. George, Brendan J. Culleton, Adam S. Watson, Pontus Skoglund, Nadin Rohland, et al. 2017. "Archaeogenomic Evidence Reveals Prehistoric Matrilineal Dynasty." *Nature Communications* 8 (14115): 1–9.

Kincaid, Chris, John R. Stein, and Daisy F. Levine. 1983. "Road Verification Summary." In *Chaco Roads Project, Phase 1: A Reappraisal of Prehistoric Roads in the San Juan Basin,* edited by Chris Kincaid, 9.1–9.78. Albuquerque: Bureau of Land Management.

Lekson, Stephen H. 1984. *Great Pueblo Architecture of Chaco Canyon, New Mexico.* Publications in Archaeology 18B. Albuquerque: National Park Service.

Lekson, Stephen H. 2009. *A History of the Ancient Southwest.* Santa Fe, NM: School of Advanced Research Press.

Lekson, Stephen H. 2015. *The Chaco Meridian: One Thousand Years of Political and Religious Power in the Ancient Southwest*. 2nd ed. Lanham, MD: Rowman and Littlefield.

Lekson, Stephen H. 2018. *A Study of Southwest Archaeology*. Salt Lake City: University of Utah Press.

Loose, Richard W. 2002. "Computer Analysis of Sound Recordings from Two Anasazi Sites in Northwestern New Mexico." *Journal of the Acoustical Society of America* 112: 2285.

Lummis, Charles F. 1930. *A New Mexico David and Other Stories and Sketches of the Southwest*. New York: Charles Scribner's Sons.

Malville, J. McKim. 2004. "Ceremony and Astronomy at Chimney Rock." In *Chimney Rock: The Ultimate Outlier*, edited by J. McKim Malville, 131–150. Lanham, MD: Lexington Books.

Marshall, Michael P. 1997. "The Chacoan Roads: A Cosmological Interpretation." In *Anasazi Architecture and American Design*, edited by Baker H. Morrow and V. B. Price, 62–74. Albuquerque: University of New Mexico Press.

Matthews, Washington. 1887. "The Mountain Chant: A Navajo Ceremony." In *Fifth Annual Report to the Bureau of American Ethnology*, 379–468. Washington, DC: United States Government Printing Office.

Matthews, Washington. 1889a. "Navajo Gambling Songs." *American Anthropologist* 2 (1): 1–20.

Matthews, Washington. 1889b. "Noqoílpi, The Gambler: A Navajo Myth." *Journal of American Folklore* 2 (5): 89–94.

McKenna, Peter J., and Marcia L. Truell. 1986. *Small Site Architecture of Chaco Canyon, New Mexico*. Chaco Center Publications in Archaeology 18D. Santa Fe, NM: National Park Service.

Mills, Barbara J., Matthew A. Peeples, Leslie D. Aragon, Benjamin A. Bellorado, Jeffery J. Clark, Evan Giomi, and Thomas C. Windes. 2018. "Evaluating Chaco Migration Scenarios Using Dynamic Social Network Analysis." *Antiquity* 92 (364): 922–939.

Mose, Don, Jr., Baje Whitethrone, Kathryn Hurst, Lucille Hunt, and Clayton Long. 2004. *The Moccasin Game: A Navajo Legend*. Blanding, UT: San Juan School District Media Center.

Nials, Fred L., John R. Stein, and John R. Roney. 1987. *Chacoan Roads in the Southern Periphery: Results of Phase II of the BLM Chaco Roads Project*. Albuquerque: Bureau of Land Management.

Ortiz, Alfonso. 1969. *The Tewa World: Space, Time, Being, and Becoming in Pueblo Society*. Chicago: University of Chicago Press.

Ortman, Scott G. 2012. *Winds from the North: Tewa Origins and Historical Anthropology*. Salt Lake City: University of Utah Press.

Parsons, Elsie Clews (1939) 1996. *Pueblo Indian Religion*. Vols. 1 and 2. Lincoln: University of Nebraska Press.

Pauketat, Timothy R. 2007. *Chiefdoms and Other Archaeological Delusions*. Lanham, MD: Altamira Press.

Pauketat, Timothy R. 2013. *An Archaeology of the Cosmos: Rethinking Agency and Religion in Ancient America*. New York: Routledge.

Pauketat, Timothy R. 2014. "From Memorials to Imaginaries in the Monumentality of Ancient North America." In *Approaching Monumentality in Archaeology*, edited by James F. Osborne, 431–448. Albany: State University Press of New York.

Pepper, George H. 1909. "The Exploration of a Burial-Room in Pueblo Bonito, New Mexico." In *Putnam Anniversary Volume: Anthropological Essays Presented to Frederic Ward Putnam in Honor of His Seventieth Birthday, April 16, 1909, by His Friends and Associates*, 196–252. New York: G. E. Stechert and Co.

Pepper, George H. 1920. *Pueblo Bonito*. Anthropological Papers No. 27. New York: American Museum of Natural History.

Rapoport, Amos. 1993. "On the Nature of Capitals and Their Physical Expression." In *Capital Cities/Les Capitales: Perspective Internationales / International Perspectives*, edited by John Taylor, Jean G. Lengellé, and Caroline Andrew, 31–67. Ottawa: Carleton University Press.

Reichard, Gladys A. 1977. *Navaho Religion: A Study of Symbolism*. Princeton, NJ: Princeton University Press.

Reuter, Jan, Thomas Raedler, Michael Rose, Iver Hand, Jan Gläscher, and Christian Büchel. 2005. "Pathological Gambling Is Linked to Reduced Activation of the Mesolimbic Reward System." *Nature Neuroscience* 8: 147–148.

Schüll, Natasha Dow. 2012. *Addiction by Design: Machine Gambling in Las Vegas*. Princeton, NJ: Princeton University Press.

Silko, Leslie Marmon. 2010. *The Turquoise Ledge: A Memoir*. New York: Viking Press.

Sofaer, Anna. 1983. *The Sun Dagger*. Documentary film. Bullfrog Films: Oley, PA.

Sofaer, Anna. 1999. *The Mystery of Chaco Canyon*. Documentary film. Bullfrog Films: Oley, PA.

Sofaer, Anna. 2007. "The Primary Architecture of The Chacoan Culture: A Cosmological Expression." In *The Architecture of Chaco Canyon, New Mexico*, edited by Stephen H. Lekson, 225–254. Salt Lake City: University of Utah Press.

Sofaer, Anna, Michael P. Marshall, and Rolf M. Sinclair. 1989. "The Great North Road: A Cosmographic Expression of the Chaco Culture of New Mexico." In

World Archaeoastronomy, edited by Anthony F. Aveni, 365–376. Cambridge: Cambridge University Press.

Sofaer Anna, Rolf M. Sinclair, and L. E. Doggett. 1982. "Lunar Markings on Fajada Butte, Chaco Canyon." In *Archaeoastronomy in the New World*, edited by Anthony F. Aveni, 169–181. Cambridge: Cambridge University Press.

Sofaer Anna, Robert S. Weiner, and William Stone. 2017. "Inter-site Alignments of Prehistoric Shrines in Chaco Canyon to the Major Lunar Standstill." In *The Science of Time 2016: Time in Astronomy and Society, Past, Present and Future*, edited by Elisa Felicitas Arias, Ludwig Combrinck, Pavel Gabor, Catherine Hohenkerk, and P. Kenneth Seidelmann, 79–102. Astrophysics and Space Science Proceedings Vol. 50. Cham, Germany: Springer.

Sofaer Anna, Volker Zinser, and Rolf M. Sinclair. 1979. "A Unique Solar Marking Construct." *Science* 206 (4416): 283–291.

Stein, John R. 1983. "Road Corridor Descriptions." In *Chaco Roads Project, Phase 1: A Reappraisal of Prehistoric Roads in the San Juan Basin*, edited by Chris Kincaid, 8-1–8-15. Bureau of Land Management, Albuquerque, New Mexico.

Stein, John, Richard Friedman, Taft Blackhorse, and Richard Loose. 2007. "Revisiting Downtown Chaco." In *The Architecture of Chaco Canyon, New Mexico*, edited by Stephen H. Lekson, 199–224. Salt Lake City: University of Utah Press.

Stein, John R., and Stephen H. Lekson. 1992. "Anasazi Ritual Landscapes." In *Anasazi Regional Organization and the Chaco System*, edited by David Doyel, 87–100. Maxwell Museum of Anthropology Anthropological Papers 5. Albuquerque: University of New Mexico Press.

Stein, John R., and Daisy F. Levine. 1983. "Appendix C: Documentation of Selected Sites Recorded during the Chaco Roads Project." In *Chaco Roads Project, Phase 1: A Reappraisal of Prehistoric Roads in the San Juan Basin*, edited by Chris Kincaid, C.2–C.64. Albuquerque: Bureau of Land Management.

Stevenson, Matilde Coxe. 1903. "Zuñi Games." *American Anthropologist* 5 (3): 468–497.

Stirling, Matthew W. 1942. *Origin Myth of Acoma and Other Records*. Bureau of American Ethnology Bulletin 135. Washington DC: United States Government Printing Office.

Toll, H. Wolcott. 2006. "Organization of Production." In *The Archaeology of Chaco Canyon: An Eleventh-Century Regional* Center, edited by Stephen H. Lekson, 117–151. Santa Fe, NM: School for Advanced Research Press.

Turner, Christy G., II, and Jacqueline A. Turner. 1999. *Man Corn: Cannibalism and Violence in the Prehistoric American Southwest*. Salt Lake City: University of Utah Press.

Van Dyke, Ruth M. 2003. "Bounding Chaco: Great House Variability across Time and Space." *Kiva* 69 (2): 117–139.

Van Dyke, Ruth M. 2007. *The Chaco Experience: Landscape and Ideology at the Center Place*. Santa Fe, NM: School for Advanced Research Press.

Van Dyke, Ruth M. 2019. "Chaco Gathers: Experience and Assemblage in the Ancient Southwest." In *New Materialisms, Ancient Urbanisms*, edited by Susan M. Alt and Timothy R. Pauketat, 40–64. London: Routledge.

Van Dyke, Ruth M., R. Kyle Bocinsky, Tucker Robinson, and Thomas C. Windes. 2016. "Great Houses, Shrines, and High Places: Intervisibility in the Chacoan World." *American Antiquity* 81 (2): 205–230.

Vivian, R. Gwinn. 1990. *The Chacoan Prehistory of the San Juan Basin*. New York: Academic Press.

Voorhies, Barbara, ed. 2017. *Prehistoric Games of North American Indians: Subarctic to Mesoamerica*. Salt Lake City: University of Utah Press.

Weiner, Robert S. 2015. "A Sensory Approach to Exotica, Ritual Practice, and Cosmology at Chaco Canyon." *Kiva* 81 (3–4): 220–246.

Weiner, Robert S. 2018. "Sociopolitical, Ceremonial, and Economic Aspects of Gambling in Ancient North America: A Case Study of Chaco Canyon." *American Antiquity* 83 (1): 34–53.

White, Leslie A. 1942. "The Acoma Indians." In *Forty-Seventh Annual Report to the Bureau of American Ethnology*, 17–102. Washington, DC: United States Government Printing Office.

Williams, Jay S., Taft J. Blackhorse, John R. Stein, and Richard Friedman. 2006. "Iikááh: Chaco Sacred Schematics." In *Religion in the Prehispanic Southwest*, edited by Christine S. VanPool, Todd L. VanPool, and David A. Philips Jr., 103–114. Lanham, MD: Altamira Press.

Windes, Thomas C. 1987. *Investigations at the Pueblo Alto Complex, Chaco Canyon, New Mexico 1975–1979*. Vol. 1, *Summary of Tests and Excavations at the Pueblo Alto Community*. Publications in Archaeology 18F. Santa Fe, NM: National Park Service.

Windes, Thomas C. 2003. "This Old House: Construction and Abandonment at Pueblo Bonito." In *Pueblo Bonito: Center of the Chacoan World*, edited by Jill E. Neitzel, 14–32. Washington, DC: Smithsonian Books.

10

The Aztec New Fire Ceremony and the Illumination of the Night

Kirby Farah and
Susan Toby Evans

Out of the void of nothingness, life was begun in ancient Mesoamerica by creating a fire. New fire ceremonies celebrated new buildings, new sociopolitical entities, and calendric turning points (Boone 2007, 129, 207).[1] Scholars today associate the "New Fire Ceremony" most strongly with the Aztec rituals crucial to the start of the fifty-two-year-long *xiuhmolpilli* (Calendar Round),[2] which represents the convergence of the 260-day ritual calendar and the 365-day solar calendar. The New Fire Ceremony reset the calendars and replayed the original creation of time and light out of the darkness many calendar rounds ago, reawakening their world and assuring its immediate continuance. The last pre-Columbian New Fire Ceremony was celebrated in 1507 CE and the Aztec heartland, the Basin of Mexico (figure 1.1), was a perfect setting for a dramatic, once-in-a-lifetime spectacle of total darkness as every aspect of living fire was extinguished. And then at midnight as the Pleiades passed overhead, on a sacrificial altar atop a hill south of the great urban center Tenochtitlan, flames were coaxed from a bit of smoking tinder, a fire sparked in the chest cavity of a sacrificial victim. This event signaled that life and light had been reborn and would be shared in a magnificent spectacle as lit torches brought the fire to hearths and braziers—and to other torches (figure 10.1). And, thus, fire pulsed through the whole great region around the Aztec capital Tenochtitlan (later known as Mexico City).

https://doi.org/10.5876/9781646422609.c010

FIGURE 10.1. *Page 34 from the* Codex Borgia *(1976) depicting the deities lighting the new fire to create morning light before the world was made.*

The New Fire Ceremony in 1507 CE was a theatrical display unparalleled in Mesoamerica in its time, revealing the impressive demographic strength of Tenochtitlan and the surrounding Basin of Mexico as well as the great success of Aztec culture. This was a variant of Nahua, the Nahuatl-speaking, Toltec-derived set of beliefs and practices that was strongly established in the southwestern Basin even before Tula's fall in circa 1150 CE (see the section "The Fifth Age, Beginning at Teotihuacan"). In the early 1300s the Tenochca formally founded Tenochtitlan. It was then a small fishing camp that would, within 200 years, become the impressive city and imperial capital observed by Hernán Cortés and his entourage.

In the context of the spread of Aztec culture in the later Postclassic period (ca. 1200–1519 CE) (figure 10.2), the New Fire Ceremony was instrumental and influential. It reinforced the power of the Aztec elites, who best understood and thus controlled the complicated calendar and the showy (and ideologically significant) displays of light at night. In addition to providing an appropriately dark backdrop for such displays, the night sky revealed the astronomical bodies, whose cycles indicated the passage of time and informed the scheduling of Aztec rituals. The New Fire Ceremony was also a collective ritual by which "the state articulated its policies and justified the existence of social hierarchies" (García Garagarza 2017, 599). Thus, the New Fire Ceremony, like other state-sanctioned rituals, had implications far beyond the religious

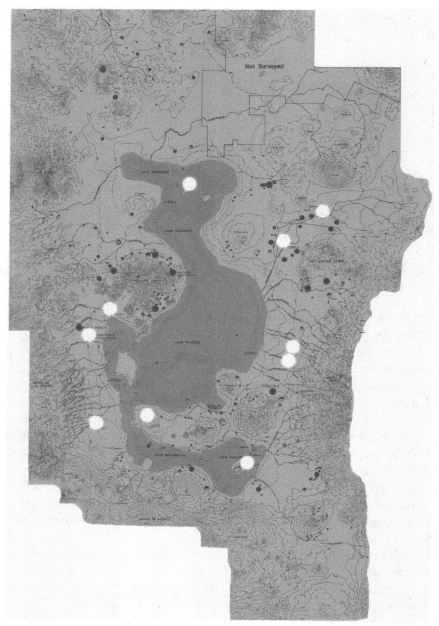

FIGURE 10.2. (a) *Left: Map of the Early Postclassic Basin of Mexico.* (b) *Right: Map of the Late Postclassic (ca. 1519 CE) Basin of Mexico. Images: Adapted from Sanders et al. 1979.*

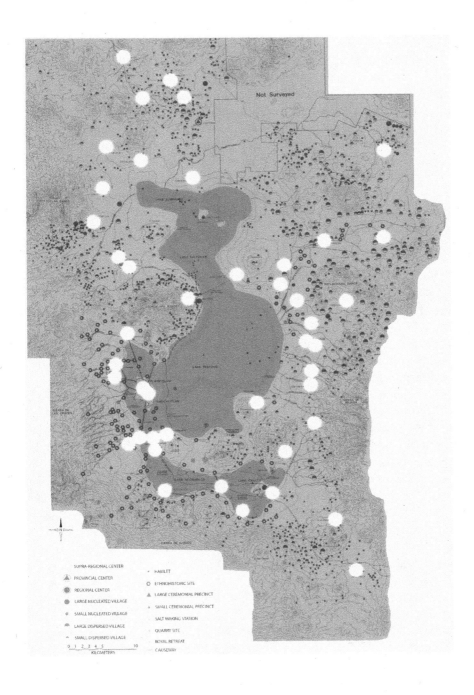

Not Surveyed

SUPRA-REGIONAL CENTER   HAMLET
PROVINCIAL CENTER   ◎ ETHNOHISTORIC SITE
REGIONAL CENTER   ▲ LARGE CEREMONIAL PRECINCT
LARGE NUCLEATED VILLAGE   ▲ SMALL CEREMONIAL PRECINCT
SMALL NUCLEATED VILLAGE   SALT MAKING STATION
LARGE DISPERSED VILLAGE   QUARRY SITE
SMALL DISPERSED VILLAGE   ROYAL RETREAT
                                              CAUSEWAY
0 1 2 3 4 5   10
     KILOMETERS

realm. This ceremony didn't just reset time and light; the synchronization of calendars helped to regulate all kinds of political and economic relations, such as the quarterly payments of tribute (Hassig 2001).

How did the 1507 CE New Fire Ceremony result from the rise of sociopolitical complexity in the context of expansion of the basin's settlement system, its population doubling twice during a few hundred years (1200–1519)? This chapter puts the New Fire Ceremony in its historical and cultural-evolutionary context to examine the ideological roots of this dramatic set of events, and it considers how the setting of night and all the sensations associated with it were intentionally heightened as a part of the ceremony, as well as how the drama of darkness enhanced the impact of the ceremony across the city of Tenochtitlan and beyond.

THE DEEP ROOTS OF THE CALENDAR: AGES OF THE SUN

The Aztecs believed that they lived in a fifth and final "age" of the universe. Like the others, it would begin with the creation of a fire, a new sun, and end in a cataclysm. Each age was distinct, and the sequence reveals an understanding of the coevolution of humans and maize. The Fifth Age was thought to have begun in Teotihuacan, the great city that flourished in the northeastern Basin of Mexico in the Early Classic period (ca. 250–600 CE).[3] There, two minor gods immolated themselves, becoming the sun and moon and initiating time.

The Aztecs knew that the Fifth Age of the Sun had begun many Calendar Rounds before, but no one knew how long it would survive. But the end would probably come at a vulnerable break in time's continuum—the turn of the Calendar Round, a sequence of 18,980 uniquely named days (about fifty-two years) that merged the *tonalpohualli* (260-day divinatory count) of the *tonalamatl* (almanac) with the *xihuitl* (365-day solar year).[4] The completion of each round, called the *toxiuhmolpilia* ("Binding of the Years") must be followed by the successful initiation of the next round, accomplished by a series of rituals that re-created the birth of the sun out of the void of darkness: the greatest of all new fire ceremonies.

The Aztec New Fire Ceremony of 1507 CE took place at night on a hilltop near the great capital Tenochtitlan. Spread out around the great bowl of the Basin of Mexico were nearly a million people, living in half a dozen cities, dozens of sizable towns, and hundreds of farming and fishing villages. Cities and towns were usually located along the edge of the irrigated alluvial plain or the lakes, and villages stretched along the well-developed shoreline of the central lake and surrounded the irrigated alluvial plains, extending along farming terraces that covered the piedmont up to the sierra (figure 10.2).

Ordinarily the nighttime landscape would be lit by torches and braziers burning in the temples and palaces in cities and in the larger towns and villages, especially during the great feasts. But on the eve of the new Calendar Round, the night of the New Fire Ceremony, all was dark, every fire extinguished. The nocturnal setting served to heighten emotion around the ritual and increase its impact. The ritual was believed to be deeply consequential for the well-being of humanity, and it helped generate renewed enthusiasm for political leaders and a sense of unity across an ethnically diverse empire. And while promoting solidarity, the drama of the New Fire Ceremony and the visibility of its collective consequences demonstrated the spread of Toltec-derived Nahua (Aztec) culture. By 1507 CE, Nahua culture was dominant in the Central Highlands, and the New Fire Ceremony was one of several strong associations of light at night with Aztec society's increasingly complex sociopolitical organization, rapidly changing in the context of strong population growth. From immigration and intrinsic growth, the population doubled twice between circa 1200 and 1519 CE (Sanders et al. 1979).

Rapidly growing population and competition between local rulers for resources—like the labor and products of those ever-more-numerous peasants—led to conflicts and the emergence of confederations. The elites indulged in increasingly luxurious and complicated palace practices and religious rituals.[5] Fires burning throughout the night, every night—such as in torches, braziers, and hearths—were costly to maintain but brought great prestige to the palaces and temples.

While all premodern cultures used communal fires in particular situations, perpetual nocturnal illumination is expensive and depends on the ability of an elite powerful enough to extract tribute from the commoners in fuel supplies and maintenance. Those commoners might in their homes nurture the living fire overnight as cooking coals, but lighting up the night was beyond their means or needs.[6] Perpetual illumination of the night is largely limited to societies with urbanized communities centering on civic and ceremonial buildings. For the Aztecs, maintaining fires in palaces and temple compounds was an impressive and showy display of authority, and for that reason, once begun, the practice could not be extinguished without loss of prestige.

If lighting up the night is a correlate of a certain level of urbanization, then it is also associated with civilization, if we understand "civilized" in its essential etymological meaning, pertaining to life in those societies with cities. The Aztec countryside on a normal evening would have grown dark except for towns large enough to maintain local palaces or temple precincts. In the cities, numerous lights would glow in the courtyards of these places.

How much illumination did Tenochtitlan produce in 1519 CE? Imagine a Google Earth view of the world at night in 1500 CE: how would Tenochtitlan's level of luminosity compare with the world's other major cities? Many Old World cities benefitted from technology that captured energy from large domestic animals or simple mechanisms such as gear-driven mills, a technological difference between them and the Aztecs and other New World peoples. However, night-lighting technology was fairly similar across the globe in 1500 CE, so we would expect Tenochtitlan and a few other Aztec capitals to achieve a luminosity similar to other cities of the same size (50,000–100,000[7]) in the Old World. Worldwide, fires burned in lamps, lanterns, candles, torches, hearths, and braziers (see chapter 1, this volume), and except for differences of community size, the intensity of light would have been comparable.[8]

THE FIFTH AGE, BEGINNING AT TEOTIHUACAN

The Aztecs revered Teotihuacan's ruined pyramids and temples as the place where time began, but their immediate cultural forebears, the Toltecs, provided their model for political and social organization. Dominant in the Central Highlands around 1100 CE, the Toltecs ruled from their great capital, Tula, one of the Early Postclassic period's most prominent centers of Nahua cultural traditions, including Nahuatl speech. Tula was just northwest of the Basin of Mexico, which was not thickly settled at this time, and the biggest towns in the western Basin of Mexico—Xaltocan (Otomi/Chichimec culture[9]) and Culhuacan (Nahua culture)—were Tula's main allies. Tula's heyday saw a high tide of migration in Mesoamerica, and Tula provided employment and settled life for groups moving south and east into the Central Highlands, looking for farmland. Migrants represented several ethnicities, most significantly the Chichimec and Nahua. Nahuatl/Aztec culture eventually eclipsed Chichimec in the Basin of Mexico, and modest Chichimec towns with little in the way of civic-ceremonial architecture (their most elaborate shrines were piles of sticks) became Aztec capitals with temple precincts where the Toltec-based belief system was venerated, and with palaces where rulers oversaw their city-states and espoused Nahua calendric and other lore.

Sources on the Aztecs tell us that in these administrative and ritual compounds, fires perpetually burned and signaled the status of the town,[10] because the Aztec palace wasn't simply a much larger and more luxurious house but the visible manifestation of legitimate local political authority. Establishment of a palace was a right that was earned by and conferred upon a chosen family in Toltec-based Aztec culture.

Back in 1100 CE, there were only a few perpetual palace and temple fires lighting the night in the basin (see figure 10.2). Tula's decline had begun by about 1150. By the early 1200s, immigrants had moved into the basin's towns and villages and pioneered marginal lands. Many were Nahua, but some Chichimecs gave up their hunting-camp lifestyle and took over towns. Led by their dynastic founder Xolotl, they made Tenayuca their capital. Its biggest competitor was Azcapotzalco, a nearby Nahua/Tepanec town. As the population grew and rulers became more aggressive, there was a need to secure the hinterland of the city-state, including tributary towns and villages. The ruler of Azcapotzalco in the early 1300s let a group of migrants settle on the edge of its territory, on some boggy islands in the central lake's western lagoon, and thus Tenochtitlan was established. In return the Tenochca served Azcapotzalco's leaders as marauders, harassing other towns into tributary status and building a confederation for Azcapotzalco.

One such town conquered by Azcapotzalco was Tenayuca. In the 1350s Tenayuca's Chichimec dynasty was forced to flee across the lake, making Texcoco its new capital.[11] This conflict was not just political but significant culturally—Xolotl's heirs still spoke a Chichimeca language, but in the course of taking over Tenayuca and other towns, they had been Nahuatlized. And they built extensive palaces, because in premodern agrarian societies, managing well-settled regions required such administrative/residential buildings for the rulers.

As the population of the basin increased, palaces proliferated, built to serve as outposts of administration run by the ruler's *calpixqui* stewards, or to house new dynasties in some towns. For example, in the 1370s the ruler of Azcapotzalco permitted the Mexica (Tenochca and Tlatelolca branches) to establish dynasties and thus allowed them to build palaces.[12] Limited archaeological evidence suggests that calpixqui palaces may have been built in the late 1300s into the early 1400s among the houses on the farming-terrace systems that ringed the basin and accounted for roughly half of its population by the end of the Postclassic. More palaces, more temple precincts, more fires lighting up the night.

Azcapotzalco continued to expand its sway, and in 1418 its army had killed off Texcoco's Xolotl dynasty king, Ixtlilxóchitl, whose dying words to his son Nezahualcoyotl were "Never forget that you are a Chichimec!" Thereupon his mourners cremated him according to Aztec custom (and contrary to Chichimec). Restored to Texcoco by his Tenochca cousins in the early 1430s, Nezahualcoyotl made Texcoco a capital of Aztec culture.[13] By the 1450s, the Texcocan dynasty was thoroughly Nahuatlized—acculturated, enculturated, and

FIGURE 10.3. *Pictorial depiction of the palace of Nezahualcoyotl from the Mapa Quinatzin. Photo: Aubin 1885.*

intermarried—and was becoming famous for its refined version of Aztec culture, including a huge palace with perpetual fires as a major feature (figure 10.3).

Texcoco and Tenochtitlan together shared Azcapotzalco's old confederation and had added to it somewhat, but in the 1450s their expansionist ambitions were thwarted by calamities that brought famine to the basin. The Nahuatl language devised new verbs as synonyms for famine: "the people were Totonac-ed" (selling themselves to Totonac slave traders) and "the people were One-Rabbited" (because famines seemed to coincide with the One Rabbit years that initiated the new Calendar Round). One such year was 1454; the high priests and wise ones agreed that Two Reed/1455 had better portents.

They were right: the year 1455 initiated a Calendar Round of conquests and empire building, boom times that in fact seemed to falter as the new Calendar Round (One Rabbit/1506) approached. There were few new conquests, and disturbing rumors suggested that aliens had landed and were approaching

Tenochtitlan. Folio 41v in the *Codex Telleriano-Remensis* indicates that in 1506 "Motecuhzoma killed a man . . . to placate the gods since for two hundred years there had been hunger in the year one rabbit . . . because it was always a difficult year for them, Motecuhzoma changed it to two reeds [1507]" (Quiñones Keber 1995).[14] The association of One Rabbit with starvation reached back into the 1300s, and we know that as early as 1455 the Aztecs gamed the calendar by delaying the ceremony to Two Reed.[15] By 1507, with four dozen dynasties in power, the Basin of Mexico would have glowed with light at night, except for the night of the New Fire Ceremony.

NEW FIRE CEREMONY OF 1507 CE: FORM AND FUNCTIONS

By the early sixteenth century, the Aztec empire was the largest it had ever been, and it would continue to grow under Tenochtitlan's ninth *tlatoani* (figure 10.4) Motecuzóma Xocoyotzin, also known as Montezuma (1502–1520) (Hassig 1988). State-sponsored rituals, which included the New Fire Ceremony, remained central to Aztec lifeways as they served the dual purposes of honoring the gods and promoting Aztec cultural ideals. State-sponsored rituals during the decades of Motecuhzoma Xocoyotzin's rule may have had heightened meaning as whispers from the east concerning strange visitors reached the Aztec capital. Unbeknownst to Basin of Mexico inhabitants, the 1507 New Fire Ceremony would be the last before the arrival of the Spaniards.

The 1507 New Fire Ceremony is perhaps the best documented pre-Columbian ritual, given both its grandiosity and relative recency. The intricacies of its practice and performance reveal the ideologies and political strategies that underpinned the ritual. They illustrate how the extreme darkness on the night of the New Fire Ceremony was intentionally used to increase the impact of the ceremony for the million or so Basin of Mexico denizens who witnessed it.

Much of what we know about the 1507 New Fire Ceremony has been gleaned from ethnohistorical sources authored during the Early Colonial period (e.g., *Codices Borbonicus, Borgia, Telleriano-Remensis,* and *Florentine*). These accounts describe the preparations made by the residents of Tenochtitlan in the days leading up to the ceremony (see Overholtzer 2017), as well as the most sacred aspects of the ritual conducted by a select group of high-ranking priests.

To prepare for the ceremony, residents of Tenochtitlan and the surrounding regions thoroughly cleaned their houses as well as civic and ceremonial spaces. Sweeping was an especially essential preparatory practice in the days leading up to the New Fire Ceremony as it cleared away dangerous *tlazolli*

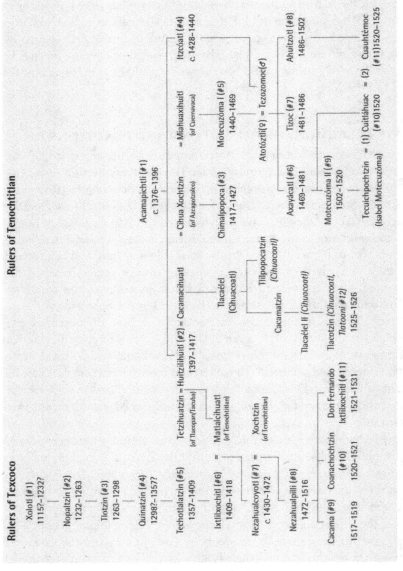

FIGURE 10.4. *Rulers of Texcoco and Tenochtitlan. Diagram: Evans (2013, fig. 17.5).*

(filth), "thus purifying the way to regenerative transformation" (Maffie 2014, 282; see also Sahagún [1950] 1982, book VII, 25). Tenochtitlan's residents swept the floors of their houses, patios, and surrounding streets, whereas priests and priestesses swept the temples.

In the spirit of clearing away accumulated filth to make way for something new, residents disposed of their old or used up household items. These may have included old hearthstones, broken cooking vessels, worn-down utensils, and idols (Sahagún [1950] 1982, book VII, 25–32). New Fire deposits, characterized by a high percentage of reconstructible vessels pertaining to a single stratigraphic layer, have been recovered across the Basin of Mexico and surrounding region (Elson 1999; Elson and Smith 2001). Some of these deposits were created before the formation of the Aztec empire and provide evidence that the New Fire Ceremony was a local ritual that may have predated the arrival of the Mexicas in the Basin of Mexico (e.g., De Lucia 2014; Farah 2017).

While the preparatory activities in the days leading up to the New Fire Ceremony were integral to the ceremony's success, the most central rites were conducted in the hours leading up to and directly following the start of the new Calendar Round. On the evening before the start of the new cycle, a group of high-ranking priests gathered within the city center of Tenochtitlan before setting off on their journey to Huixachtlan (today, Cerro de la Estrella) (Carrasco 1999, 96). Huixachtlan was located on the southern shore of Lake Texcoco—about a nine-mile walk from the center of Tenochtitlan. The priests were dressed in elaborate garb, including intricate masks and feather headdresses to impersonate the gods. A priest dressed as the god Quetzalcoatl led the procession as they walked down Tenochtitlan's southern causeway, before veering east toward Huixachtlan. In addition to the costumed priests, the procession included a single captive, the sacrificial victim at the center of the ceremony. A warrior of high status, the captive was likely selected on the basis of bravery in combat. Some sources suggest that his name included the word *xihuitl* (Maffie 2014, 294).

As the priests embarked on their journey to Huixachtlan, the residents of Tenochtitlan completed last-minute preparations and waited for nightfall. They extinguished *all* fires, including those burning in households and in temples. After the sunset, Tenochtitlan was left in total darkness. Special precautions were taken to ensure that the dangers associated with this cosmologically potent night would not harm anyone. Pregnant women were locked in granaries, and their faces were painted blue to protect them from transforming into monsters during the night. Children were urged to stay awake for fear that they might become mice in their sleep. By nightfall, all work across the region halted. Members of the populace made their way to the roofs of their houses, heads craned toward Huixachtlan, where they waited to learn their fate.

Meanwhile, the procession of priests gathered on the summit of Huixachtlan after their long journey from Tenochtitlan. Standing on a platform high above the cities and villages below, the priests watched the stars, tracking the moment when the Pleiades reached its zenith. At precisely midnight, the highest-ranking priest, who was probably wearing a turquoise mask and dressed as the god of fire, Xiuhtecuhtli, used a large knife to cut the heart out of the captive's chest. A fire was then quickly kindled in the gaping chest of the sacrificial victim using the sacred flint drill. Through the process of feeding the sacrificial victim to the flames, the *teyolia* (life-giving energy, concentrated in the heart) and *tonalli* (animistic force) energies—physically manifested in the forms of the beating heart and blood of the sacrificial victim—were transferred to the cosmos (Maffie 2014, 195). Through this reciprocal act, which mimicked that of the gods in their creation of the Fifth Sun, the Aztecs kickstarted the New Calendar round.

In 1507 the fire successfully lit and burned brightly, as it presumably had with all previous New Fire ceremonies, indicating that the new Calendar Round had begun. Although the populace never had the misfortune of experiencing a failed New Fire Ceremony, legend dictates that if the fire did not light, then *tzitzimime* (monster deities) would emerge and roam in the darkness killing and eating all humanity. Thus, "the essential rationale of the Aztecs of ritually observing the end of a 52-year cycle was not only an apprehension for the termination of a calendar but more importantly for historical time and consequently for human existence" (Carrasco and Pharo 2017, 252).

After the lighting of the New Fire, the initial flame was transferred from the chest of the captive to a huge, highly visible pyre on Huixachtlan. As the flames rose from the pyre, Tenochtitlan's inhabitants were first able to see the New Fire and thus made aware of the success of the ceremony. Using large torches, the New Fire flames were transferred to Tenochtitlan, where they were used to light a fire at the Temple of Huitzilopochtli. Priests were sent from across the region to light their torches and carry the flames back to their local shrines (Sahagún [1950] 1982, book VII, 29; *Codex Borbonicus*, folio 34) (figure 10.5). The final rite of the ceremony involved the burial of a bundle of fifty-two wooden poles, which were bound together by twisted cord. This act represented the literal binding of the previous years, which were buried to symbolize the end of the old calendrical cycle.

Figure 10.5. *Folio 34 from the* Codex Borbonicus *(1974) depicts priests lighting torches in the flames of the New Fire at the Temple of Huitzilopochtli in Tenochtitlan.*

THE DRAMA OF DARKNESS

The New Fire Ceremony has long fascinated scholars across the disciplinary spectrum for its grandeur and the paradox it embodies. Aztec public rituals were conducted to please the capricious gods, to reiterate Aztec cultural beliefs, to foment feelings of solidarity and pride, and even to inspire fear in imperial subjects. These reasons were especially true for the New Fire Ceremony, which necessitated the involvement of not only the sizable population of Tenochtitlan but everyone across the Basin of Mexico.

And yet, the New Fire Ceremony was also very private. While the most sacred aspects of the ritual were conducted on what would have been a highly visible temple platform atop Huixachtlan during the day, under the cover of darkness these practices would have been largely hidden from view. Therefore, the details of some of the most sacred components of the ritual—those involving human sacrifice—while apparently widely known, were directly observed by only a small group of high-ranking priests. Why were seclusion and natural darkness, untainted by the fires that would have normally brightened the nighttime cityscape, necessary for such a widely consequential ceremony? Furthermore, given that so much of the New Fire Ceremony was public, why was the most significant moment of the ritual—that when the fire is kindled in the sacrificial victim's heart—obscured from view?

Certainly, the main reason that the ceremony took place at midnight was because it was the precise time that the old fifty-two-year cycle ended and the new one began. The restarting of a new cycle was not a given, and Aztec priests needed to take special care that the sacrifice was performed at the precise moment that the Pleiades reached their zenith. The night was an appropriate setting for the ceremony because it echoed the dark, primordial time when the gods created the Fifth Age. Moreover, the relative seclusion of the priests, who were dressed as gods, mimicked the seclusion of the creation ritual, which occurred before the current age of humanity. Finally, the timing and darkness of the ritual mimicked the liminality of the creation ritual. As the gods conducted their ritual in a period between suns, between ages, so too did Aztec priests conduct their ritual in a liminal time between the old and new fifty-two-year cycles.

While there is little doubt that cosmology and ideology were key factors in determining when the New Fire Ceremony was conducted, the nocturnal setting would have made the event more impactful and memorable, which in turn might have served a larger political agenda. On the night of the ritual, tensions and fears were almost certainly heightened across the city. Not only was the ending of the fifty-two-year cycle a precarious time for humanity, but the darkness of night, which was intensified by the absence of household fires, was filled with natural and supernatural dangers.

The night would have been characterized by a sense of excitement. Occurring just once every fifty-two years, the New Fire Ceremony was for many a once-in-a-lifetime experience. Children, who otherwise might have fallen asleep hours earlier, stayed awake to bear witness to the rare ceremony. But perhaps the central emotions associated with the New Fire Ceremony would have been jubilation and relief, which were likely felt when the bright light from the New Fire flames was first spotted in the distance, indicating to residents of Tenochtitlan that the sun would rise again.

The range of emotions outlined above, which were probably intensified by the nocturnal setting, helped to strengthen the long-term impact of the New Fire Ceremony. The success of the ceremony did more than just signal the start of a new calendrical cycle; it indicated that the current ruler was capable of earning good favor and protection from the gods. Unsurprisingly, following successful New Fire ceremonies, and bolstered by what was perceived as a divine endorsement of their rule, Aztec leaders often embarked on state building projects. For example, in the year 1455 CE Motecuhzoma I substantially enlarged the Templo Mayor at Tenochtitlan following his successful New Fire Ceremony (Alvarado Tezozómoc [1598] 1944, 119).[16]

The New Fire Ceremony might have helped to foster a sense of unity across an expansive and ethnically diverse region (Farah 2021). One of the most timely aspects of the ritual was the dissemination of the flames of the New Fire, which were rapidly distributed to other cities across the Basin of Mexico and used to relight temples and houses. This process was of great symbolic significance because the fires that illuminated the highest temples in the Aztec capital city were born from the same "mother" flame as the small fires that warmed commoner households in the empire's lowliest villages. Thus, the Aztec empire in its entirety was lit under what was perceived to be a common flame, and the fires that burned across the Basin of Mexico were reminders of the momentous night and the capabilities of Aztec rulers.

CONCLUSIONS

While archaeologists often emphasize the daytime activities of people from the past, the Aztec New Fire Ceremony reminds us that some of the most memorable and consequential events of the past took place during the night. The New Fire Ceremony was among the most vital Aztec ceremonies despite being performed only once every fifty-two years. The ceremony ensured that the sun would rise again but also served to honor the gods and pay tribute to the sacrifices they made to create the fifth sun and the current age of humanity.

Tenochtitlan was a city that ordinarily bustled with activity and glowed with the light of palace and temple fires throughout the night. It follows that the night of the ceremony—when the city, blanketed in the natural nocturnal darkness—would have represented a stark contrast to normal nights. In fact, for city dwellers, as would be the case for those of us who have become accustomed to living in cities today, the darkness might have seemed *un*natural, even unsettling. The preparatory actions leading up to the New Fire Ceremony created an entirely new cityscape—one that was blanketed in darkness—and the halting of normal nightly activities would have created a new sound- and smell-scape. Interrupting everyday sensorial rhythms, the night of the New Fire Ceremony might have felt like a temporal pause to those who experienced it: a collective inhale, while residents waited to learn their fate. The darkening of Tenochtitlan on the night of the New Fire Ceremony transformed the city to something out of place and out of time and, as such, set the stage for a ritual that reenacted a creation born out of a similar temporal-spatial void.

The uncharacteristically dark and distorted city of Tenochtitlan as a backdrop for this once-in-a-lifetime ritual set an apropos stage for such a momentous occasion and created a more visceral connection to the event for those who witnessed it. The drama surrounding the ceremony might have resulted in heightened human emotions—including fear, excitement, and eventually joyous relief. The widespread emotional response to the event would have made the ceremony more impactful and memorable. Creating a lasting impression would have been a key goal for Tenochtitlan's elites, as the broader social and political implications of the ceremony helped solidify their positions and the advantages that came along with them.

So, while the ceremony was grounded in widespread religious beliefs, it served social and political agendas. By inspiring renewed faith in elites, the New Fire ceremony helped to create a sense of unity throughout the city of Tenochtitlan and across a diverse empire. As the empire expanded over the course of two centuries, Aztec leaders necessarily worked to emphasize their own power as well as the power of their capital city. Part of that process involved the dissemination of a shared sense of values, ideology, and history that centered around Aztec beliefs and ideals. The New Fire Ceremony embodied these beliefs and created a framework whereby all citizens of the large city of Tenochtitlan and the surrounding region were necessarily involved. The relationship of interdependence on one another and dependence on the powerful priests who performed the ritual served to reify extant social and political relations. The success of the ritual served as proof that such relationships were just, fair, and ensured the well-being of the broader populace. Thus, the New Fire Ceremony and all the pomp that surrounded it helped to maintain stability across a sprawling political empire.

Acknowledgments. The authors would like to thank Nan Gonlin and Meghan E. Strong for organizing the Society for American Archaeology (SAA) session that inspired this collaboration and Monica Smith for her insights as discussant of the session. Susan Evans appreciates inspiring interchanges with Sarah McClure, Fritz Schwaller, Glenn Storey, and David Webster.

NOTES

1. The "drilling of fire . . . [was] an act that, for the Aztecs and the Mixtecs, established a new cycle of time or a new sociopolitical organization" (Boone 2007, 207).

2. The Calendar Round was the essential Aztec long-term calendar—the Aztecs did not have an eternal "long count" calendar as did the Classic Maya and the modern world.

3. Motifs related to the New Fire Ceremony were found at Teotihuacan (Fash et al. 2009) and in Maya Copan's royal compound (Fash 2011, 156). In the Early Post-classic Central Highlands, a monument at Xochicalco commemorated the New Fire Ceremony (Hirth 2008, 831–832).

4. Scholars disagree about the exact date on which the Aztec solar year began (see Aveni 2017, 109–110.) Schwaller (2019, 173–193) believes that the New Fire Ceremony took place in autumn, in the veintena Panquetzaliztli ("Rasing of Banners"). The 365-day period is a vague year; there is considerable evidence that the Aztecs practiced a "Leap Year" (Evans 2016, 74–78), intercalating a day every four years so that their calendars accounted for the 365.25-day solar year.

5. Palace courtyards saw many rituals, and Spanish proselytizers such as Pedro de Gante used Aztec palace layouts as a model for settings for sermons. The open-air churches of Mexico copied the palaces (McAndrew 1965).

6. There are also urban-rural differences in degree of privacy and activity, as Gonlin and Dixon (2018, 59) suggest for the Maya of the Copan region.

7. Tenochtitlan's estimated population has been wildly overinflated, some values producing a density rivaling that of modern Manhattan (Evans 2013; Márquez Morfín and Storey 2017).

8. In fact, it was not until the late 1600s that Paris pioneered streetlights "after dark on a regular, permanent basis" with a system of lanterns (DeJean 2006, 202).

9. "Chichimec" and "Otomí" cover a range of ethnic identities, most generally "people from the Chichimec arid lands" but more significantly referring to the speakers of a range of related languages. Sources such as *Primeros memoriales* (Sahagún 1993) show Chichimecs wearing skins and carrying bows and arrows, a visual expression of how they were perceived by more urbanized Nahua culture bearers.

10. "Some Indians were deputed to fetch wood, while others had to stand guard and always keep the fire burning. They did almost the same in the houses of the chiefs, where a fire was kept in many places. Even today they build some fires and watch the houses of the chiefs, but not as formerly because today not one-tenth of such houses have a fire" (Motolinía [ca. 1536–1543] 1951, 105).

11. The king driven into exile in Texcoco was Quinatzin, whose Aztec-style palace was still important (see Oxtotipac land maps in Charlton 1991).

12. "Montezuma's Old Palace" faced the Templo Mayor across the ritual precinct and was used as a guesthouse for the Spaniards who lived there from November 1519 to July 1520. It was probably a much-rebuilt version of the first *técpan*-palace, built in the 1370s.

13. His Tenochca cousins looked like crude unlettered bullies. Texcoco "where the teocallis . . . excelled in point of number and size, where the idols were most in evidence, and where they were greatly waited upon by the papas" (Motolinía [ca. 1536–1543] 1951, 99).

14. The sources suggest that it may have been in One Rabbit/1350 that the Aztecs began noticing an association of the year with famine. Tweaking calendar dates was not unprecedented or uncommon. For example, the Aztecs typically shifted a child's ominous birthdate to a nearby promising one for its baptism, so shifting the ceremony to Two Reed/1351 would be in keeping with larger traditions.

15. The Tira de Tepechpan (1596) marks Two Reed years in 1351, 1403, and 1455 as New Fire Ceremony years (Diel 2008, 35, 46, 58).

16. The Templo Mayor is the principal temple in the sacred precinct of the Aztec capital city of Tenochtitlan. It was originally constructed in mid-fourteenth century and reconstructed six times over two centuries.

REFERENCES

Alvarado Tezozómoc, Fernando. (1598) 1944. *Crónica mexicana*. Mexico City: Editorial Leyenda.

Aubin, Joseph Marius Alexis. 1885. *Mémoires sur la peinture didactique et l'écriture figurative des anciens Mexicains*. Paris: Paul Dupont.

Aveni, Anthony F. 2017. "The Measure, Meaning, and Transformation of Aztec Time and Calendars." In *The Oxford Handbook of the Aztecs*, edited by Deborah L. Nichols and Enrique Rodríguez-Alegría, 107–116. New York: Oxford University Press.

Boone, Elizabeth Hill. 2007. *Cycles of Time and Meaning in the Mexican Books of Fate*. Austin: University of Texas Press.

Carrasco, Davíd. 1999. *City of Sacrifice: The Aztec Empire and the Role of Violence in Civilization*. Boston: Beacon Press.

Carrasco, Davíd, and Kirkhusmo L. Pharo. 2017. "The Aztec Temporal Universe." *Groniek* 49 (212): 243–258.

Charlton, Thomas. H 1991. "Land Tenure and Agricultural Production in the Otumba Region, 1785–1803." In *Land and Politics in the Valley of Mexico: A Two Thousand Year Perspective*, edited by Herbert R. Harvey, 223–264. Albuquerque: University of New Mexico Press.

Codex Borbonicus. 1974. *Codex Borbonicus, Codices Selecti, 44*. Graz, Austria: ADEVA.

Codex Borgia. 1976. *Codex Borgia, Codices Selecti, 58*. Graz, Austria: ADEVA.

DeJean, Joan. 2006. *The Essence of Style*. New York: Simon and Schuster.

De Lucia, Kristin. 2014. "Everyday Practice and Ritual Space: The Organization of Domestic Ritual in Pre-Aztec Xaltocan, Mexico," *Cambridge Archaeological Journal* 24 (3): 379–403.

Diel, Lori. 2008. *The Tira de Tepechpan*. Austin: University of Texas Press.

Elson, Christina M. 1999. "An Aztec Palace at Chiconautla, Mexico." *Latin American Antiquity* 10 (2): 151–167.

Elson, Christina M., and Michael E. Smith. 2001. "Archaeological Deposits from the Aztec New Fire Ceremony." *Ancient Mesoamerica* 12 (2): 157–174.

Evans, Susan Toby. 2013. *Ancient Mexico and Central America*. 3rd rev. ed. London: Thames and Hudson.

Evans, Susan Toby. 2016. "Location and Orientation of Teotihuacan, Mexico: Water Worship and Processional Space." In *Processions in the Ancient Americas*, edited by Susan Toby Evans, *Occasional Papers in Anthropology* No. 33: 52–121. University Park: Department of Anthropology, Pennsylvania State University. https://journals.psu.edu/opa/article/view/60114/60001.

Farah, Kirby. 2017. "Leadership and Community Identity in Postclassic Xaltocan, Mexico." PhD diss., University of California, Riverside.

Farah, Kirby. 2021. "The Light Burned Brightly: Postclassic New Fire Ceremonies of the Aztec and at Xaltocan in the Basin of Mexico." In *Night and Darkness in Ancient Mesoamerica*, edited by Nancy Gonlin and David M. Reed. Louisville: University Press of Colorado.

Fash, Barbara W. 2011. *The Copan Sculpture Museum*. Cambridge: Peabody Museum Press.

Fash, William L., Alexandre Tokovinine, and Barbara W. Fash. 2009. "The House of New Fire at Teotihuacan and its Legacy in Mesoamerica." In *The Art of Urbanism*, edited by William L. Fash and Leonardo López Luján, 201–229. Washington, DC: Dumbarton Oaks.

García Garagarza, Léon. 2017. "The Aztec Ritual Landscape." In *The Oxford Handbook of the Aztecs*, edited by Deborah L. Nichols and Enrique Rodríguez-Alegría, 595–604. New York: Oxford University Press.

Gonlin, Nancy, and Christine C. Dixon. 2018. "Classic Maya Nights at Copan, Honduras, and El Cerén, El Salvador." In *Archaeology of the Night: Life after Dark in the Ancient World*, edited by Nancy Gonlin and April Nowell, 45–76. Boulder: University Press of Colorado.

Hassig, Ross. 1988. *Aztec Warfare: Imperial Expansion and Political Control*. Norman: University of Oklahoma Press.

Hassig, Ross. 2001. *Time, History and Belief in Aztec and Colonial Mexico*. Austin: University of Texas Press.

Hirth, Kenneth G. 2008. "Xochicalco." In *Archaeology of Ancient Mexico and Central America*, edited by Susan Toby Evans and David L. Webster, 828–832. New York: Routledge.

Maffie, James. 2014. *Aztec Philosophy: Understanding a World in Motion*. Boulder: University Press of Colorado.

Márquez Morfín, Lourdes, and Rebecca Storey. 2017. "Population History in Precolumbian and Colonial Times." In *The Oxford Handbook of the Aztecs*, edited by Deborah L. Nichols and Enrique Rodríguez-Alegría, 189–200. New York: Oxford University Press.

McAndrew, John. 1965. *The Open-Air Churches of Sixteenth-Century Mexico*. Cambridge, MA: Harvard University Press.

Motolinía, Fray Toribio de Benavente. (ca. 1536–1543)1951. *History of the Indians of New Spain*. Translated by F. B. Steck. Washington, DC: Publications of the Academy of American Franciscan History.

Overholtzer, Lisa. 2017. "Aztec Domestic Ritual." In *The Oxford Handbook of the Aztecs*, edited by Deborah L. Nichols and Enrique Rodríguez-Alegría, 623–639. New York: Oxford University Press.

Quiñones Keber, Eloise. 1995. *Codex Telleriano-Remensis: Ritual, Divination, and History in a Pictorial Aztec Manuscript*. Austin: University of Texas Press.

Sahagún, Bernardino de. (1950) 1982. *General History of the Things of New Spain: Florentine Codex*, edited by Arthur J. O. Anderson and Charles E. Dibble. Salt Lake City: University of Utah Press.

Sahagún, Bernardino de. 1993. *Primeros memoriales: Facsimile Edition*. Norman: University of Oklahoma Press.

Sanders, William T., Jeffrey R. Parsons, and Robert S. Santley. 1979. *The Basin of Mexico: Ecological Processes in the Evolution of a Civilization*. New York City: Academic Press.

Schwaller, John F. 2019. *The Fifteenth Month: Aztec History in the Rituals of Panquetzaliztli*. Norman: University of Oklahoma Press.

11

Cities, both ancient and modern, enable people to engage with nature through an anthropocentric mediation of wind, weather, animals, and vegetation. Even the effects of day and night are reconfigured when structures disrupt lines of sight or create shades that prematurely foreshadow the evening hours. This volume's authors have set forth an exciting new series of questions about the development and meaning of urbanism through one of the most overlooked realities of human life on this planet: day follows night follows day in a pattern that repeats itself hundreds of times a year. The very banality of this observation belies its impact, as humans cannot see in the dark without the aid of some mitigating entity, whether starlight, the moon, or light-giving technology such as lamps, lanterns, and torches. Indeed, it could be said that all our most cherished technological achievements have been about cheating the nightly death of the world by our own Promethean engagements with fire, including its modern incarnation through electricity. These technologies have been used not only to extend the hours of work and play, but on occasion to create wonderful or terrifying spectacles for the crowds that define urbanism as a human phenomenon.

THE EMOTION OF THE NIGHT

In poetry and prose the world over, people have described the night in respectful, even fearful, terms

Nocturnal Urban Landscapes

From the First Cities to the Present

Monica L. Smith

https://doi.org/10.5876/9781646422609.c011

through metaphors akin to blindness and death. Even now we have the feeling that the night is not the time for people to be out and about and that bad things happen in the dark. Work that happens in the middle of the night is called the "graveyard" shift, undertaken in the "wee hours" and in the "dead of night." The unknowables of the human psyche are lodged in those same hours: "In a real dark night of the soul, it is always three o'clock in the morning," as F. Scott Fitzgerald (1936, 35) wrote. But it is not only the quotidian event of nightfall that brings forth philosophical musings; we also take note of other events that bring about unsettling night-like conditions, such as storms, eclipses, volcanic eruptions, and clouds of starlings, locusts, and dust. Our deeply encoded sense of the right "time" for darkness is easily perturbed by both natural events and cultural ones as seen in our much-hated shift to daylight saving time, in which the annoyance of changing the clocks is augmented by a sudden dislocation of our finely tuned physiological and psychological expectations of when the sun ought to be up or down (e.g., Ellis et al. 2018).

The human engagement with the oscillation of night with day took place long before our current technological era, of course. Our species developed responses to the realities of darkness that were manifested in both physical tools and social ritual and whose traces can be seen in the archaeological record of artifacts, architecture, and landscapes. Our earliest ancestors' use of fire came as early as 1.9 million years ago, a development that served to prolong the day and provided the opportunity to cultivate new forms of interaction, such as cooking and commensalism (Wrangham 2009). Being around a shared hearth promoted novel forms of recreation, community interaction, and experimentation. People observed that fire had a unidirectional effect on food, a realization that eventually led to engaging in other pyrotechnical transformations such as fire hardening of stone along with pottery production, smelting, slaking, and glassmaking (Smith n.d.). The resultant interconnections of hearths as places of light and heat, and the subsequent creation of torches and wick lamps as pinpoints of light in the darkness, enabled people to create spaces that were configured according to tasks and seasons (e.g., McGuire 2018; Nowell 2018).

Mediated by technology in both the past and in the present, each turn of the daily solar cycle has become an opportunity to affirm the ties of kith and kin and to engage in the punctuation of social activity as it transitions from the natural light of the day that is dominated by sunshine to the paler cyclical light of the moon and stars that is additionally mediated by human creations of light-giving technologies. The volume's chapters focus on this daily oscillation between day and night, summed up in the reminder by Martha Cabrera

Romero and J. Antonio Ochatoma Cabrera in the conference version of chapter 7 that "cada día tiene una noche" (and to which we might add: "cada noche tiene un día"). Nor is the impact of this oscillation limited to its effects on human vision, because day and night fade into one another with accompanying shifts of heat, humidity, and the rhythmic cycle of diurnal and nocturnal birds and insects. Interwoven with the routine activities of meals and sleep that characterize all mobile life forms, the changes of each daily cycle are individually experienced and affirm the agency of perception and action across the spectrum of species, age, gender, and physical and cognitive ability.

Within the essential change between day and night, the sky provides numerous subtle variations from one day to the next. Elements such as clouds, fog, and smoke hasten or retard the anticipated (dis)appearance of natural light. The waning of the sun is counterbalanced by the luminosity of stars, which appear slowly as the sun fades and vanish long before the dawn; although in our light-polluted age we give little thought to stars, ancient people were likely to have perceived in them a transfixing brightness that prompted more regular attention (as Vranich and Smith 2018 have proposed for the siting and configuration of Tiwanaku, where the thin air of high altitude further accented the visibility of the Milky Way). Every night across the world, there is a waxing or waning moon that adds an incremental measure of light. The regularity of the moon's appearance and disappearance prompted human capacities for calculation and became an essential calibration point for ritual and social calendars, as noted in this volume for Chaco Canyon by Robert S. Weiner and for Cahokia by Susan M. Alt, and the theater of political change described by Kristin V. Landau, Christopher Hernandez, and Nancy Gonlin for the Maya. The sun might be fierce at times, and punitive; by comparison, the moon was a gentler celestial orb that invited scrutiny for as long as one wanted to stare. The pleasure of "moon-gazing" was encoded into poetry and aesthetic appreciation, such as hymns to the ancient Greek goddess Selene and the temple guidebooks of seventeenth-century Edo (Bond 2014).

The human appropriation of the dark lent itself to play, in the deepest sense of manipulation for the purposes of creating an alternative reality. "Play" might consist of designating certain activities to be undertaken only in the bewitching nighttime, or in creating circumstances in which humans succeeded in turning night into day, or day into night. Such unnatural configurations necessitated the development of new technologies, whether through the invention of architecture that enabled humans to dictate the time and place of darkness, or through the invention of light-making technologies that enabled people to selectively illuminate places that were otherwise obscured.

Revolutionary inventions continue to be made that enable ordinary people to magically curate both daylight and darkness, as seen through the deployment of both electricity and photography as the most recent innovations in the long history of light-manipulating technology. In their examination of the concept of the "unseen" rendered visible through camerawork, Christos Lynteris and Rupert Stasch (2019) critically examine what happens when images are captured and fixed in place. One could suggest that in the premodern era as well as in the present, the shocking moments of a sudden plunge of darkness or an explosion of captive light constituted a memory-making event that created the same kinds of "visual epistemologies" that are today experienced vicariously through photography (Lynteris and Stasch 2019, 5).

The comparison of singular night-illuminated events with photography provides further analytical potential for the longitudinal study of the human nighttime experience. First, there were ways that ancient people experienced the brief moment of illumination that is analogous to the effect of flash photography, such as the quick uproar of a bonfire made of highly flammable material, or the intense illumination provided through a bolt of lightning. Second, the concept of a mental image of a moment of frozen time represented by a still frame is not limited to the photographic age but comes from the human capacity to remember events both as sequences and as vignettes (the latter an essential skill in the encapsulation of stories and historical events into a single image whether in rock art, Greek vases, or Renaissance paintings). The capacity to recall singular images, particularly those of intense effect, long predates the advent of film; even in our own times, one can have a memory of a photograph of an event in addition to having a memory of an event in its entirety.

Moments of singularity and movement were woven into the experience of the oscillation of night and day that shifted as humans expanded their settlements to include villages, towns, and cities. Landscape movements in the dark were the kinetic counterpart to the ways in which illuminations were used in settlements themselves. As Maggie L. Popkin describes in chapter 4, the ancient devotees of the Sanctuary at Samothrace marched along lighted paths, bearing torches and lamps whose luminosity was magnified through reflection in the polished marble surface of surrounding buildings. As she further notes, the ephemerality of firelight was a strong contrast to the steadiness of sunshine; at night, the flickering and unsteady flames along the tortuous and rocky pathway would have heightened the feeling of sensory deprivation that accompanied initiation rites. The same curated flames of devotion can be seen in Meghan E. Strong's chapter on Egypt, in which each oil-fueled lamp had a short duration that must have hurried and intensified the ritual to which it was dedicated. Linked to Alt's observations of cities as places of restless becoming (chapter 8), both the act and metaphor of fire provided the opportunity for experiential intensity in crowded places as well as in open spaces. And as Weiner (chapter 9) notes for Chaco Canyon, ritual links of the central canyon installations to their outlying settlement nodes was made through the use of fireboxes along pathways that enabled landscapes to be visually connected. The Chaco experience has parallels with other landscapes in which the transmission of signals by fire (e.g., Swanson 2003; Earley-Spadoni, chapter 3), and the transfer of fire itself (e.g., Elson and Smith 2001) tied together a political landscape and provided a linear, human-created analogue to the tracings imagined among stars.

URBANISM AS A SPECIAL KIND OF DARKNESS

The expectation of a fire in the night long predated urbanism, but the control and management of light sources became increasingly sophisticated in urban settings. Although city dwellers perceive the same daily oscillation of night and day as rural inhabitants, their capacities and responses are different from those in the countryside. As Alt notes in chapter 8, cities "*feel* different" in many ways, and the experience of the natural cycle of light and dark is just one among many sensations that are altered—heightened, diminished, askew—in the urban environment. For densely inhabited settlements, whether or not they were "urban," there were special intensities that encompassed the human experience of nightfall and daybreak.

In the built environments of urban spaces, human topographies supersede natural ones, resulting in new forms of deprivation and access to resources (figure 11.1). Taller buildings create new templates of visibility, and celestial bodies that easily might be visible across the broad expanses of the countryside become difficult to view in urban realms; human-made smoke and haze add to the natural clouds and fog that preempt the moon and the stars. Special architecture provided a literal scaffolding of topography in which larger-than-domestic structures rose into the daytime and nighttime skies alike, as noted in this volume by Alt for Cahokia and Weiner for Chaco. These structures created new frames for the night sky; instead of the outline of distant topography, urban residents instead had their "celestial vault" (sensu Cabrera Romero and Ochatoma Cabrera, chapter 7) trimmed by an anthropogenic angularity of place.

Cities also create new opportunities to capitalize on the efficiencies of captured light. City walls and palisades provided new elevations on which

FIGURE 11.1. Main Street of the Yoshiwara on a Starlight Night *(Utagawa Kunisada, also known as Utagawa Toyokuni III; 1852; Alamy image 2B2D4AT). Image: Public domain.*

watchful nighttime fires could be built to reassure inhabitants that vigil was constant (see Earley-Spadoni, chapter 3). Urban verticalities were platforms for people to place fires and torches, drawing the public eye into the sky in an appropriation of a domain hitherto reserved only for celestial phenomena. There were amplifications of the human effect within structures as well: a fireplace could yield light for a few people in a country home, but the same amount of fuel enabled dozens to see their surroundings in an urban tavern or a factory. For population centers in extreme latitudes, natural darkness was the primary defining characteristic over the long months of winter, accenting the city as a place of camaraderie and liveliness (Christophersen 2015).

The large number of people in cities, and their diverse socioeconomic statuses, made it possible for enterprising individuals to create new and esoteric practices of entertainment that made use of darkness as an enhancing factor. Although rural venues long had the potential for the occasional festival or feast that went on into the night, urban centers were places where distinctive forms of architecture (e.g., theaters) relied on artificial lighting to enable after-dark spectacles to take place on a regular basis. The sense of "play" in an urban setting was not limited to the formal staging of spectacles but could be engaged through routine, everyday activities. Transitions to the night in rural places and in the preurban world tended to be limited to a single threshold: in or out of dwelling, in or out of a cave. But only in a city, with its many different types of buildings, could people go in and out of many different dark and light spaces within the course of a single evening. Chasing their identities through shadows and expanding or contracting their economies through the mitigations of human-provided light, city dwellers created value and playfulness through a world of their own making that transcended natural constraints. For some urban dwellers, movement at night was a second-best option, but for others the city was synonymous with "nightlife" that included distinct opportunities for specific beverages, music, fashion, and sex. The difficulties of seeing and the ease of concealment also played into new forms of desirable risk such as gambling (Weiner, chapter 9).

People can live full and rewarding lives without any artificial light at all, conforming their actions to the oscillation of the sun and the seasons. In rural places, this lifestyle is played out when the end of sunlight brings to an end all but the simplest manual tasks. In urban locales, however, the diversity of employment means a considerable amount of "brain" work compared to "brawn." Intellectual work can continue unabated as the day slips into night, as long as a little light is available by which one can view documents and gauge the reactions of interlocutors. Glenn Storey (2018, 321) reports on scribal practices of nighttime reading and writing in the Roman Empire, where olive-oil lamps permitted the extension of the bureaucratic workday. As Strong notes in her chapter on ancient Egypt (chapter 2), a scribe could write all day but might be expected to read at night. Indeed, one could say that the development of middle-class occupations of accounting, writing, and other forms of record keeping were incumbent on making more hours in the day for the never-ending tasks of bureaucracy (an archaeological observation that places our own nonstop professional lives into perspective; Smith 2018). Factors of wealth, class, and gender further result in differential access to both the night and its positive and negative mitigations and are evident in the class structures of urban design: to thwart the night as a time of thieves, fear, and death, elites can surround their dwellings with walls that turn their residences into protected compounds, as noted for the ancient city of Wari, where palaces had walls up to eight meters high (Cabrera Romero and Ochatoma Cabrera, chapter 7).

As Nancy Gonlin and Meghan Strong point out in their introduction (chapter 1), and as is woven into the other contributions, elites used the seeming privation of darkness to flaunt their wealth in fuel and other resources. Unlike the modern day, when the tradeoff between the electricity bill or the grocery bill abstracts resources through the medium of money, the ancient tradeoff of food and utilities involved a much more direct consideration of resource value, given that fuel for lamps consisted of potentially costly edible substances such as animal fat and vegetal oils (Strong, chapter 2; for a historical perspective on the cost of light, see Brox 2010 and Nordhaus 1996). While lower-status urban dwellers might have extended their workday through a calculation of feeding the flames rather than feeding themselves, those who were well off could make a social statement through lighting up the night with gratuitous, excessive displays of light whether for ritual or secular purposes, in the same way that they could afford to host feasts in which food waste was an expected collateral outcome of hosting. Rulers and other elites could distribute the largesse of light for others to enjoy, both through the public provision of lighted pathways, and through the physical gift of fire as in the case of the Mesoamerican "New Fire" ceremony, in which the flames kindled at the highest ritual levels were then shared throughout the city in poorer and wealthier houses alike (Farah and Evans, chapter 10).

Even for ordinary people, there were many ways to enhance the urban nighttime experience in which fire was used for warmth, light, and purification through the elaboration and decoration of braziers, *incensarios*, and hearths (figure 11.2). The most basic technology of light appears to have been ubiquitous, as judged by the mounds of discarded clay lamps and lanterns found in many urban archaeological sites (see, e.g., Popkin, chapter 4; Elson and Smith 2001).

Like other vessels and tools, the material culture of lighting provided opportunities for cultural encoding through decoration. An excess of fuel might have been accompanied by a special show of wealth in the container

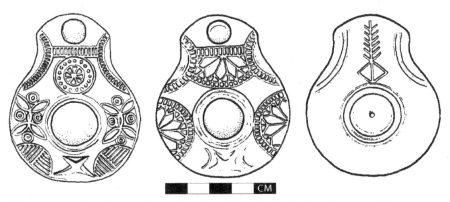

FIGURE 11.2. *Late Roman–Byzantine lamps from Apollonia showing some of the many decorative motifs of these common clay objects. Drawing: Sussman (1983, 79). Permission of Taylor and Francis.*

for that fuel, as Popkin (chapter 4) suggests through the comparison between clay and marble lamps in the Greek period. Some containers for light sat on surfaces, such as Mesoamerican incensarios with fierce faces, or Roman lamps with playful apertures. Others were strung along in the air, such as lanterns of the Japanese Edo period. In a microcosm, each lamp and lantern made a statement about control over the forces of the night and allowed for the full range of decoration and style that archaeologists have readily assessed for vessels used for other practical purposes such as drinking, cooking, and storage.

Urbanism's economies of scale enabled the dovetailing of many different processes simultaneously, such that light (and its corollary, heat), were the result of multivariate resource calculations. In Roman imperial times, Ellen Janssen et al. (2017) have suggested, large public bath complexes must have operated twenty-four hours a day because it took so much fuel to bring the buildings up to the desired temperatures that it was more cost-effective to keep fires burning than to allow them to diminish during the night. We know from other sources that Romans were accustomed to circulating at night, whether for entertainment or for commercial purposes; at Rome itself in the first century BCE, the emperor Julius Caesar ordered that goods transportation by cart should be undertaken only at night to leave the streets open for pedestrians during the day (Favro 2011; Storey 2018).

Nor was the treatment of urban night relegated to illuminating the darkness. Just as cities prolong the day through the placement of artificial lighting, they prolong the night through the creation of unlit spaces. Many urban locales—such as sewers, underground storage places, and the deep interiors of buildings—are obscure even during the daytime, resulting in an atmosphere in which the skills of lighting were not limited to the night. And while human attempts to overcome darkness consist of a struggle to maintain a point-specific source of light that is still always overwhelmed by the surrounding darkness, the inverse is relatively easy to achieve. As Strong and Alt note in their chapters, humans can turn the light into darkness by simply closing the door to an interior room. Dark rooms were certainly possible in the countryside, but the greater size and mass of urban architecture ensured that the deepest recesses of buildings would be night-like at all times. While some of those spaces were practical and secular in their intent, others were imbued with ritual significance in the same way as the subterranean kivas of the Chaco world, the Old Temple of Chavín de Huantar, or the grottoes of the Christian catacombs.

In a city's artificial spaces of darkness-during-day, and lighting-during-night, urban dwellers can cast aside or willfully ignore the natural regulation of day and night. This implied control of the natural world led simultaneously to exalted positions of authority and degraded forms of menial labor (e.g., Wright and Garrett 2018). Places of artificial darkness could render a continuous atmosphere of manipulated lighting conducive to illicit or socially "hidden" pursuits, as Weiner (chapter 9) proposes for the atmosphere of gambling and that we can apply to other activities kept on the social margins of visibility. Other professions were time bound in the sense of capitalizing on the night to have a product ready for daytime use as Gonlin and Strong point out in chapter 1, about bread bakers who made their products ready before dawn and in so doing proved the quotidian viability of the night as a workspace.

The phenomenon of light and dark in an urban environment was enacted on an everyday basis through the markers of otherworldly authority, such as the monoliths of Tiwanaku that could spontaneously be perceived as "alive" during the night (Janusek and Guengerich, chapter 5). The Mesopotamian night belonged to sorcerers, conjurers, and the miscellaneous malevolent individuals who tormented ordinary citizens with sleeplessness and psychological ailments and whose effects were countered by priests skilled in healing the traumas of witchcraft (Earley-Spadoni, chapter 3). Astronomers almost by definition needed the night to be able to make the celestial observations that were essential to ritual and political fortunes. Thieves as well as legitimate traders benefitted from the dark as a mode of concealment for their valuable cargoes. And everyone needed light for night rituals, which were perhaps augmented and amplified in urban environments, where the creation of dense populations of both the living and the dead afforded the space for a nocturnal theater of ritual, as it did in Egypt (Strong, chapter 2).

In cities, there is ample archaeological evidence for the political and celebratory uses of nighttime through the phenomenon of "performative space" (Gonlin and Strong, chapter 1). Calendrical research in the Maya realm by Landau and colleagues (chapter 6) shows that political leaders preferentially selected rituals of accession to coincide with phases of the moon to maximize a celestial seal of approval (but perhaps also, at times of full moons, to let the largest number of people experientially participate in ceremonies in a process that might be akin to the Indian concept of darshan—to see and be seen by a deity). In chapter 10, Kirby Farah and Susan Toby Evans discuss the New Fire Ceremony at Tenochtitlan, in which the city became the focal point and operative center for the beginning of a new calendrical era through the dramatic striking of "new fire" at a sacrificial altar south of the Aztec capital of Tenochtitlan. The dual role of fire as both illuminator and destroyer was part of urban ritual too, as in the use of fire in termination ceremonies that Cabrera Romero and Ochatoma Cabrera describe for the Wari capital in chapter 7.

The phenomenon of light was something common to all ancient cities, but some urban areas were particularly luminous. Simon Ellis (2004), in a telling article about the Roman period titled "The Seedier Side of Antioch," notes that the Eastern Mediterranean city in question was famous for its street lighting and that the author Libanius documented that there were people whose job it was to keep lamps burning in the streets. Although archaeologists have frequently discussed provisioning of food for ancient cities, a study of fuel would yield an equally insightful assessment of the vast networks of rural inputs that would have been necessary to keep cities going. In premodern times, fuel for lighting could come from a variety of sources, including wood, whether culled directly from the forest or repurposed from old furniture, tool handles, and fencing. There was beeswax along with the many different types of oils that emanated from animal fat and from grain crops (flax, linseed, cotton, sunflower, olive) as well as through the renewable resource of secondary products such as butter, sometimes further rendered into ghee.

Against all the backdrops of practical and celebratory light, there is one final aspect of urban lighting that must be addressed: the danger of light that goes out of control. Prior to the development of electricity, every form of nighttime lighting was incendiary: lamps, torches, braziers, and hearths all radiated both heat and light through the mechanism of fire. Any aberrant fire could result in devastating conflagration, such that there was a sense of urban collective responsibility that grew in awareness of the capacity for any tiny agentive flame to create havoc (see also Smith n.d.; Storey 2018). Archaeologists encountering layers of burnt debris often attempt to discern accidental fires from purposeful ones of the type that destroyed settlements such as Aguateca in the New World (Inomata et al. 2001) and Hazor and Megiddo in the Old World (Zuckerman 2007), but from the perspective of their inhabitants any type of widespread fire was catastrophic. In cities made of closely packed flammable dwellings, fires that were out of control could rapidly destroy hundreds of homes and shops, as they did well into historical times (FEMA 1997). While we experience electricity today as a remarkable convenience that brings light at the flip of a switch, we should remember that our illuminations of the night are much safer than those of the past.

A CREPUSCULAR SEGUE BY WAY OF CONCLUSION

In this volume, the authors' focus on light and darkness brings up a wealth of other fruitful potential focal points for the study of urbanism through the exploration of the effects of quotidian phenomena. In addition to light and darkness, there are other compelling ephemera concentrated by the crowding of people and architecture in urban spaces. Several of the authors in this volume have mentioned the smoke, fumes, and aromas that accompanied ancient ritual activities and that can seem highly accented in the darkness (e.g., Popkin for Samothrace, Landau et al. for the Maya region; for more on the archaeology of aroma, see Smith 2019a). In their discussion of Tiwanaku in chapter 5, John Wayne Janusek and Anna Guengerich refer on the one hand to the initial siting of the city relative to the celestial brightness of stars, and on the other hand to factors of topography that resulted in a "mist envelope" and a camelid-dung "smoke envelope" giving the city a distinctive look and feel.

What about the archaeology of urban sound? Not only are cities the places of musical innovation and diverse language communities, but they are noisier overall. In rural settings, the ricochet of human conversations, animal bleats, and household murmurings are dispersed and die away between buildings, whereas in cities the concentration of life results in a constantly generated acoustic palimpsest. Human sounds in the urban realm compensate for factors of loneliness and fear brought about by darkness, but sound is also a way for groups to engage in a "nonspatial way of appropriating space" and declare their legitimacy of presence in an urban environment (see Streicker 1997, 116). Even animals modify their sound regimes in cities: urban birds sing "louder" and with different repertoires than their country cousins (Slabbekoorn and den Boer-Visser 2006). What about the archaeology of urban touch, resulting not only from the greater potential frequency of both sought-after and unwanted sexual encounters, but also from the daily unintended bumping into one another of strangers in crowded corridors and passageways? Finally, there is the potential for the archaeology of transitions, including the physical transitions of locomotion as people adjust to the faster pace of the city at the moment they enter it; transitions of weather experience from moment-to-moment shifts in the intensity of wind and precipitation around urban structures; and transitions in the display of gender, identity, class, and (dis)ability when people cross the boundaries of the urban perimeter (see, e.g., Sneed 2020).

The impact of the night on urban centers is greater than anywhere else on the planet, not only because of urban economies of scale but also because light in the night makes the urban experience distinct. Today, the starkest satellite image of global urban growth is not from the daytime images in which built-up areas grade imperceptibly into brown-green landscapes; rather, it is from the nighttime images of electric lights against a darkened Earth. Further research on the specifics of the night in densely crowded locales, such as the manipulation of architecture to be made toward points of "lunar standstill" (in the words of Alt, chapter 8 in this volume), could be used to compare urban buildings with rural ones. If ancient rulers commanded their realms from the apex moments of the moon's cycles or commissioned their celebratory architecture to align with the stars, we should also consider the extent to which bureaucrats and other planners acquiesced to more mundane realities such as gravity, property ownership, and the ad hoc residues of architectural "dependence" (Till 2009) in their treatment of secular architecture.

In this volume, there has been much written about the loss of light at the end of the day, but somewhat less about the opposite concept of dawn as the counterbalancing, and equally slow, brightening of the sky (but see Weiner on Chaco, Janusek and Guengerich on Tiwanaku). One suggestion for follow-up work would be the archaeological investigation of daybreak, for which there are many sources of both textual and empirical data: poetry and prose about the slow release of the grip of terror-inducing darkness encoded in the hopefulness of the new day, as well as the many instances of houses, places of worship, and plazas having their openings to the east in recognition that it is the incursion of the sun, rather than its loss, that inspires architectural planning. A focus on the uplifting, affirming dawn as a predictable element and moment of optimism in a daily cycle of renewal is an important counterpoise to humanity's unilineal experiences of pregnancy, birth, growth, and demise.

The authors' commentaries about urban darkness provide challenges that can be specifically addressed through archaeological research. Was lighting really too expensive for ordinary people to enjoy, as Strong suggests in her assessment in chapter 2 of ancient Egypt? Our anthropology colleagues often remind us that people make decisions on the basis of personal perceptions and cultural validations of need that may not be "rational" in a minimax economic model (e.g., Wilk 1998; Diner 2001; Fielding-Singh 2017). As archaeologists, we can count the fragments of lamps and incensarios that we find to learn just how much money and other resources people devoted to the lighting of their urban sphere. We also can evaluate the ubiquity of materials such as clay for making lamps as well as landscape-scale calculations of fuelwood, agriculturally derived oils, and animal-produced dung and fats. Are people really alarmed by the dark, as we might conventionally assume? The existence of caves (mentioned by Alt for Cahokia and that existed as a foundational element of other places such as Teotihuacan), and the presence of deep interior rooms in many urban settlements, suggests an ancestral fascination with voluntary sensory deprivation and an acknowledgment that darkness brings much-needed rest to the weary. And given that everyone can easily observe the celestial phenomena of the stars and the moon, what does it mean to suggest that ritual and political elites are in command of calendrical knowledge?

A final, philosophical note: As Gonlin and Strong note in their introduction (chapter 1), we humans always rail against the parts of nature that we cannot control: death, the weather, darkness. Although we have electricity and artificial light today, we are still diurnal creatures, with most of our activities preferentially undertaken in daylight hours (see also Smith 2019b, 232–233). The oscillations of the sun for the creation of night and day constitute one of the most significant transformations that we can experience as human beings: more rapid than most occurrences of sickness and health, more regular than festivals or fairs, and more frequent than nearly any other ecological phenomenon. We have increased the precision with which we measure and chronicle the transitions between light and dark, but these phenomena are still—and will remain—beyond the capacity of human beings to alter. Even as cities grow to house a larger and larger proportion of the world's population, the importance of the shift between night and day will always be with us.

Acknowledgments. I would like to thank Nan Gonlin and Meghan Strong for their invitation to participate in this very interesting symposium and subsequent publication. My own appreciation of the shift between night and day has been heightened by my research time in India, where both the dawn and the dusk are deeply encoded: the collective of Surya Namaskar in the morning; the lighting of incense at sunset; the folk wisdom not to prepare leafy vegetables at night; and the ritual cycles of the moon, planets, and stars.

REFERENCES

Bond, Kevin. 2014. "The 'Famous Places' of Japanese Buddhism: Representations of Urban Temple Life in Early Modern Guidebooks." *Studies in Religion* 43 (2): 228–242.

Brox, Jane. 2010. *Brilliant: The Evolution of Artificial Light*. New York: Houghton Mifflin Harcourt.

Christophersen, Axel. 2015. "Performing Towns: Steps towards an Understanding of Medieval Urban Communities as Social Practice." *Archaeological Dialogues* 22 (2): 109–132.

Diner, Hasia R. 2001. *Hungering for America: Italian, Irish and Jewish Foodways in the Age of Migration*. Cambridge, MA: Harvard University Press.

Ellis, David A., Kirk Luther, and Rob Jenkins. 2018. "Missed Medical Appointments during Shifts to and from Daylight Saving Time." *Chronobiology International* 35 (4): 584–588.

Ellis, Simon. 2004. "The Seedier Side of Antioch." In *Culture and Society in Late Roman Antioch*, edited by Isabella Sandwell and Janet Huskinson, 126–133. Oxford: Oxbow.

Elson, Christina M., and Michael E. Smith. 2001. "Archaeological Deposits from the Aztec New Fire Ceremony." *Ancient Mesoamerica* 12 (2): 157–174.

Favro, Diane. 2011. "Construction Traffic in Imperial Rome: Building the Arch of Septimius Severus." In *Rome, Ostia, Pompeii: Movement and Space*, edited by Ray Laurence and David J. Newsome, 332–360. Oxford: Oxford University Press.

FEMA. 1997. *Fire Death Rate Trends: An International Perspective*. Federal Emergency Management Agency, United States Fire Administration, National Fire Data Center.

Fielding-Singh, Priya. 2017. "A Taste of Inequality: Food's Symbolic Value across the Socioeconomic Spectrum." *Sociological Science* 4: 424–448.

Fitzgerald, F. Scott. 1936. "Pasting It Together." *Esquire* March, 35, 182.

Inomata, Takeshi, Daniela Triadan, Erick Ponciano, Richard Terry, and Harriet F. Beaubien. 2001. "In the Palace of the Fallen King: The Royal Residential Complex at Aguateca, Guatemala." *Journal of Field Archaeology* 28 (3/4): 287–306.

Janssen, Ellen, Jeroen Poblome, Johan Claeys, Vincent Kint, Patrick Degryse, Elena Marinova, and Bart Muys. 2017. "Fuel for Debating Ancient Economies:

Calculating Wood Consumption at Urban Scale in Roman Imperial Times." *Journal of Archaeological Science: Reports* 11: 592–599.

Lynteris, Christos, and Rupert Stasch. 2019. "Photography and the Unseen." *Visual Anthropology Review* 35 (1): 5–9.

McGuire, Erin Halstad. 2018. "Burning the Midnight Oil: Archaeological Experiments with Early Medieval Viking Lamps." In *Archaeology of the Night: Life After Dark in the Ancient World*, edited by Nancy Gonlin and April Nowell, 265–284. Boulder: University Press of Colorado.

Nordhaus, William D. 1996. "Do Real-Output and Real-Wage Measures Capture Reality? The History of Lighting Suggests Not." In *The Economics of New Goods*, edited by Timothy F. Bresnahan and Robert J. Gordon, 29–66. Chicago: University of Chicago Press.

Nowell, April. 2018. "Upper Paleolithic Soundscapes and the Emotional Resonance of Nighttime." In *Archaeology of the Night: Life After Dark in the Ancient World*, edited by Nancy Gonlin and April Nowell, 27–44. Boulder: University Press of Colorado.

Slabbekoorn, Hans, and Ardie den Boer-Visser. 2006. "Cities Change the Songs of Birds." *Current Biology* 16 (23): 2326–2331.

Smith, Monica L. 2018. "Urbanism and the Middle Class: Co-emergent Phenomena in the World's First Cities." *Journal of Anthropological Research* 74 (3): 299–326.

Smith, Monica L. 2019a. "The Terqa Cloves and the Archaeology of Aroma." In *Between Syria and the Highlands*, edited by Stefano Valentini and Guido Guarducci, 373–377. Rome: Arbor Sapientiae.

Smith, Monica L. 2019b. *Cities: The First 6,000 Years*. New York: Viking.

Smith, Monica L. n.d. "Fire as an Agentive Force, from Forest to Hearth to Forest Again." In *The Power of Nature: Agency and the Archaeology of Human-Environmental Dynamics*, edited by Monica L. Smith. In press, University Press of Colorado.

Sneed, Debby. 2020. "The Architecture of Access: Ramps at Ancient Greek Healing Sanctuaries." *Antiquity* 94 (376): 1015–1029.

Storey, Glenn Reed. 2018. "All Rome Is at My Bedside: Nightlife in the Roman Empire." In *Archaeology of the Night: Life After Dark in the Ancient World*, edited by Nancy Gonlin and April Nowell, 307–331. Boulder: University Press of Colorado.

Streicker, Joel. 1997. "Spatial Reconfigurations, Imagined Geographies, and Social Conflicts in Cartagena, Colombia." *Cultural Anthropology* 12 (1): 109–128.

Sussman, Varda. 1983. "The Samaritan Oil Lamps from Apollonia-Arsuf." *Tel Aviv* 10 (1): 71–96.

Swanson, Steve. 2003. "Documenting Prehistoric Communication Networks: A Case Study in the Paquimé Polity." *American Antiquity* 68 (4): 753–767.

Till, Jeremy. 2009. *Architecture Depends*. Cambridge, MA: MIT Press.

Vranich, Alexei and Scott C. Smith. 2018. "Nighttime Sky and Early Urbanism in the High Andes." In *Archaeology of the Night: Life After Dark in the Ancient World*, edited by Nancy Gonlin and April Nowell, 121–138. Boulder: University Press of Colorado.

Wilk, Richard. 1998. "Emulation, Imitation, and Global Consumerism." *Organization and Environment* 11 (3): 314–333.

Wrangham, Richard. 2009. *Catching Fire: How Cooking Made Us Human*. New York: Basic Books.

Wright, Rita P., and Zenobie S. Garrett. 2018. "Engineering Feats and Consequences: Workers in the Night and the Indus Civilization." In *Archaeology of the Night: Life After Dark in the Ancient World*, edited by Nancy Gonlin and April Nowell, 287–306. Boulder: University Press of Colorado.

Zuckerman, Sharon. 2007. "Anatomy of a Destruction: Crisis Architecture, Termination Rituals and the Fall of Canaanite Hazor." *Journal of Mediterranean Archaeology* 20 (1): 3–32.

grave goods, 60, 61
Great Gambler, 229
Great Gods, 14, 58, 71–74, 76–83, 85–91
Great House(s), 18, 209–11, 213, 214, 216, 218, 219, 221, 226, 228
Great Zimbabwe, 11
Greece, ancient, 14, 45, 71, 74. *See also* Eleusis; mystery cults; Samothrace
Gregorian calendar, 131, 134
grH, 34, 35
growth, 143, 144, 145, 146, 155, 160, 243, 271
Guadalupe, 219
Guaquira River, Bolivia, 110

Hadza, 4, 5
Halfway House, 221
Hall of Choral Dancers, *73*, 74, 84–86
hand, 39, 52, 117, 118, 228, 229; left, 76, 116, 173; right, 173
hand game, 228
harbor, 10, 183
harvesting, 39, 143, 192, 195. *See also* agriculture
hataałii, 214
Hazor, 270
head, 53, 78, 102, 113, 118, 141*t*, *158*, 163, 166, 167, 172, 173, *175*, 250
headdress, 163, 249
heart sacrifice, 250, 252
hearth, 14, 50, 98, 107, 112, 193, 194, 196, 210, 220, 238, 243, 244, 260, 266, 269
heavens, 154, 195, 218
Hepdjefa, 36–39
Hero Twins, 143
hierarchy, 146, 211
hieroglyph, *12*, 125, 131, 133. *See also* inscriptions; writing
Hieron, *73*, 74, 78, 79, 80, 84, 85
hierophany, 216
Hillside Ruin, 221, *222*
hinterland, 245. *See also* rural
hominin, 4,
Honcopampa, 156
hooghan, 224
Hopi, 224, 228
horizon, 11, *12*, 125, 217
hot, 39, 128, 130, 144, 198, 219, 224, 229
house, 6, 10, 11, 13, 14, 16, 17, 22, 23, 42, 43, 50, 103, 104, 105, 108, 114, 161, 210, 244, 245, 247, 249, 250, 253, 266, 271. *See also* domestic

building; domestic compound; palace; residence
house cleaning, 247, 249
house lots, 11
house of darkness, 50, 59
household, 10, 11, 20, 41, 42, 50, *111*, 111, 112, 114, 119, 146, 155, 161, 163, 193, 249, 253
household archaeology, 146; nocturnal, 13
household worship, 155
housing, 13, 112, 163, 186, 210
Hrw, 34
huaca, 169
Huarochirí Manuscript, 159, 173
Huerfano Peak, 219
Huitzilopochtli, 250, *251*
Huixachtlan, 249–51
human sacrifice, 145, 251
hunter-gatherer, 4
hunting, 19, 173, 245
Hutson, Scott, 11

identity, 13, 14, 18, 46, 64, 86, 111, 271
ideology, 132, 142, 143, 163, 166, 209, 212, 218, 252, 254
iikááh, 214, 215
Illimani, Bolivia, 102
illness, 21, 61, 62
illuminant, 39, 40, 41, 44
illumination, 13, 14, 42–44, 91, 125, 193, 238, 243, 244, 262, 270. *See also* lighting
immigrant, 183, 185, 186, 198, 245
incensario (incense burner), *113*, 113, 114, 170, 266, 267, 272
incense, 11, 146, 273
Indigenous culture, 193, 218, 224, 226, 228
inequality, 13, 23
infrastructure, 7–10, 11, 14, 22, 23, 58, 89, 97, 102, 131, 155, 160; bounding, 10, 131; circulatory, 10, 131; signaling, 10, 58, 131; static, 10, 131
initiates, 14, 15, 72–74, 76, 77, 82–90
initiation, 72, 73, 74, 76, 80, 81, 84–90, 224, 242; rites, 74, 76, 77, 78, 82, 87, 88, 262
Inka, 100, 116, 156, 157, 159, 160, 169, 174, 217
inscriptions, 18, 38, 77, 81, 86, 87, 88, 89, 90, 91, 130. *See also* hieroglyphs; writing
integration, social/societal, 154, 214; regional, 211; spatial-temporal, 169
intervisibility, 54, 55, *56*, *57*, 57
Intiqawana, 165, 166, 169

camelid, *103*; human, 143, 145, 173, 196, 197, 199, 251, 252, 253

Sahagún, Fray Bernardino de, 16, 142, 143, 249, 250, 255*n9*

sahumador (sahumiero), 112, *113*, 114, 118, 119

Samothrace (Greece), 14, 71–92, 262, 270

San Juan Basin (New Mexico), 208, 210, 212, 219, 221

Sanctuary of Apollo, 71

Sanctuary of Demeter, Eleusis, 76

Sanctuary of the Great Gods (Theoi Megaloi), 14, 72, *73*, 74, 78, *79*, *80*, 81, *82*, 83, 84, *85*, 86, 87, 88, 89, 90, 262. *See also* Central Sanctuary

sandstone, 116, 215, 219, 221, 223

Santa Clara Pueblo (New Mexico), 228

Santa Rosa de Pucalá (Peru), 164

Sargon II, 55

Schoenoplectus californicus, 176*n2*

scribe, 34, 131, 133, 265

sculptures, 76, 84, 85, 86, 98, 100, 103, 105, 116, 130, 154, 155

seasonal/seasonality, 5, 6, 8, 21, 110, 144, 160, 229, 260, 265

secondary center, 99

selenite, 220, 221, 228

Selva Lacandona, 144

semi-fixed feature elements, 8. *See also* Rapoport, Amos

senses, 6, 11, 87, 110, 119, 191, 192

sensory archaeology, 7

sensory experience, 45, 87, 91, 114, 118, 119, 209, 213, 230, 262, 272

serpent, 76, 159, 173. *See also* snake

servant, 172

servant quarters, 9

sewer, 10, 22, 268

sex, 16, 143, 145, 265, 271

shadow, 13, 44, 86, 87, 119, 159, 169, 215, 216, 217, 218, 265

sholiwe, 228. *See also* dice

shrine, 43, 116, 157, 186, 187, 188, 189, 190, 199, 216, 220, 221, 244, 250

signaling, 15, 131, 221, 244; fire beacon, 53, 54, 55, 57, 58; firebox, 220, 263; infrastructure, 10, 58; smoke, 55; station, 219, 220; tower, 58

Silko, Leslie Marmon, 23

Siouan beliefs, 196

Siouan speakers, 186, 188, 189

skyscape, 7

slaughterhouse, *41*

slave, 229, 230, 246

sleep, 4, 5, 7, 10, 15, 21, 51, 65, 105, 112, 161, 249, 252, 261

sleeplessness, 58, 105, 268

smell, 6, 87, 106, 110, 114, 133, 146, 253

Smith, Michael E., 7, 8, 11, 212

Smith, Monica L., 3, 4, 9, 13, 14, 16, 17, 18, 21, 22

smoke, 87, 106, 107, 108, 110, 120, 133, 195, 223, 229, 261, 263, 270

smoke envelope, 106, 107, 110, 270

snake, 78, 80, 146, 158, 159, *162*, 171, 172, 173, 175. *See also* serpent

SnDty, 37

snuff, 116

social memory, 14

social trauma, 59

Sofaer, Anna, 208, 2019, 210, 211, 213, 214, 215, 216, 218, 219, 220, 221, 224

solstice, 6, 115, 119, 196, 213, 231

Solstice Project, 209, 216

Sonaji, Bolivia, 99

sorcerers/sorcery, 5, 15, 23, 172, 268. *See also* witch; witchcraft

soroi, 55

sound, 5, 6, 108, 146, 194, 195, 229, 253, 270

South Road, Chaco Canyon, 221

Southwest (American), 11, 15, 18, 66*n7*, 209, 218, 224, 226, 228, 229, 230

space syntax, 9, 10

Spaniards, 102, 143, 169, 247, 255*n5*, 255*n12*

spiral, 170, 215, 216

spirits, 60, 61, 63, 64, 66*n9*, 172, 186, 189, 198, 199

spirit realm/world, 193, 198, 224

Spiro Mounds (Oklahoma), 188

spring, 189, 190, 229

springs, 110, 169, 188

staff, 157, 163, 172, 173

Staff God, 157, 158, 159, 161, *162*, 163, 166, 171, 172

stars, 20, 87, 106, 120, 125, 153, 154, 155, 157, 159, 173, 175, 189, 193, 194, 195, 196, 208, 215, 218, 250, 259, 260, 261, 263, 264, 270, 271, 272; glyph, 126; starlight, 259, *264*. *See also* constellation

states, 6, 10, 51, 52, 53, 54, 57, 66*n5*, 71, 100, 125, 132, 244, 245

Susan M. Alt is professor of anthropology and the director of Native American and Indigenous Studies at Indiana University, Bloomington, with research interests in the ontological relationships of water, earth, gender, ritual, and human society. Her archaeology focuses on the lower Ohio and central Mississippi valleys, particularly the Indigenous city of Cahokia and its upland shrines and settlement complexes. She is the author of numerous articles and the editor or author of three books, including *Cahokia's Complexities* (Alabama, 2018).

Martha Cabrera Romero earned her MA degree in anthropology and licenciada's degree in archaeology from the National University of San Cristóbal de Huamanga, Peru. She is currently a professor of archaeology at the Department of Social Sciences of the same university. She has led several archaeological research projects at pre-Columbian, historical, and colonial sites. She has published articles and book chapters as the principal author or coauthor that are focused on religion and militarism (*Andean Archaeology II*, Springer), ancestor veneration, symbolism, and funerary architecture (Research Papers of the Anthropological Institute, Japan; CNA of the Peruvian Ministry of Culture). Since 2012 she has been conducting research at the Wari archaeological site, focusing on ceremonial and funerary architecture.

Tiffany Earley-Spadoni is an associate professor of history at the University of Central Florida. She directs the Vayots Dzor Fortress Landscapes Project in Armenia. She is a field archaeologist and historian of the ancient Near East. She received her PhD from the Johns Hopkins University.

Susan Toby Evans is an archaeologist specializing in the Aztecs and Aztec palace life, and in tracing Mesoamerica's cultural evolution. Her book *Ancient Mexico and Central America* (3rd edition, 2013) is the only complete history of a major archaeological culture area to receive the Society for American Archaeology's Book Award.

Kirby Farah is an assistant professor of Anthropology at Gettysburg College. Farah's research and teaching are an intersection of archaeology, ethnohistory, and critical cultural heritage, with emphasis on community identity and social cohesion in the Postclassic Basin of Mexico. In her current book project, *Built to Last: Memory and Solidarity at Past and Present Xaltocan, Mexico*, Farah explores how modern residents of Xaltocan have constructed local identities around a shared past. This work interrogates the role that decades of archaeological research, in tandem with shifting nationalist ideologies and increasingly globalized markets, have played in shaping local conceptions and valuations of pre-Columbian heritage at Xaltocan.

Nancy Gonlin specializes in the archaeology of the night and darkness. This book is her third edited volume on the topic (*Archaeology of the Night* [2018] and *Night and Darkness in Ancient Mesoamerica* [2021]). She has published widely on ancient households and ancient Maya commoners. Gonlin is the co-editor for the journal *Ancient Mesoamerica* and a professor of anthropology at Bellevue College, Washington State.

Anna Guengerich is an assistant professor of Anthropology at Eckerd College. She carries out research in Peru and Bolivia on human-environmental relationships and the social construction of place, including themes of domestic and monumental architecture, political ecology, and anthropogenic landscapes. She is the director of the Tambillo Archaeology Project (Chachapoyas, Peru).

Christopher Hernandez received his PhD in anthropology from Northwestern University in 2017, and was a National Science Foundation Social, Behavioral, and Economic Sciences Postdoctoral Fellow at the University of Illinois–Chicago (UIC). He is an assistant professor at Loyola University Chicago. Hernandez's primary research interests include warfare, inequality, landscape, cultural heritage, and community archaeology. In collaboration with the contemporary Maya community of Mensabak, Chiapas, Mexico, his current project integrates documentary and iconographic analysis with LiDAR (light detection and ranging) mapping and the excavation of fortified settlements to assess trends in Maya war making.

John Wayne Janusek was an associate professor of anthropology at Vanderbilt University. He directed numerous research projects in the Altiplano and the Eastern Valleys of Bolivia over a period of thirty years, including most recently the Jach'a Machaca Project at the Formative period site of Khonkho Wankane. Janusek's research focused on the origins of urbanism in the highland Andes as framed through the lenses of urban and political ecology, animism, and human-landscape relations.

Kristin V. Landau is a Visiting Scholar in the Department of Anthropology at Loyola University Chicago and a SAROI Fellow at the Center for Advanced Spatial Technologies at the University of Arkansas. She directs the Proyecto Arqueológico de los Barrios de Copán and studies citywide political and economic dynamics from the perspective of urban neighborhoods. Landau earned her PhD from Northwestern University in 2016, and BA from Colgate University in 2007. A recent publication includes "The Dynamics of Maya State Process: An Integrated Perspective from the San Lucas Neighborhood of Copán, Honduras" (*American Anthropologist* vol. 123, no. 1 [2021]).

J. Antonio Ochatoma Cabrera earned his BA and licenciatura in archaeology from the Pontificia Universidad Católica del Perú. He has participated in archaeological research projects at the sites of Yamobamba (Cajamarca), Pañamarca (Ancash), Kotosh (Huánuco) and Wari (Ayacucho), as well as in a Nepeña Valley survey (Ancash), all in the Peruvian Andes. He has worked in the survey, mapping, and legal demarcation of archaeological sites in Peru with the use of remote sensing and aerial photogrammetry, as well as in monitoring cultural heritage for the Peruvian Ministry of Culture.

Maggie L. Popkin is the Robson Junior Professor and an associate professor of art history at Case Western Reserve University and a senior member of the American Excavations Samothrace. She is the author of *The Architecture of the Roman Triumph: Monuments, Memory, and Identity* (Cambridge University Press, 2016) and *Souvenirs and the Experience of Empire in Ancient Rome* (Cambridge University Press, 2022). Her research on Greek and Roman art and architecture has appeared in numerous edited volumes and journals, including the *American Journal of Archaeology*, *Hesperia*, the *Journal of the Society of Architectural Historians*, and the *Journal of Late Antiquity*.

Monica L. Smith is a professor in the Department of Anthropology and in the Institute of the Environment and Sustainability at UCLA and holds the Navin and Pratima Doshi Chair in Indian Studies. Over the past fifteen years she has codirected archaeological fieldwork in India with Professor R. K. Mohanty of Deccan College (Pune) at the ancient city of Sisupalgarh and environs in the eastern Indian state of Odisha. She also has directed archaeological fieldwork in Bangladesh and participated in excavation projects in Egypt, Italy, Egypt, Madagascar, Tunisia, and Turkey. Her books include *A Prehistory of Ordinary People*, *The Archaeology of an Early Historic Town in Central India*, and (with R. K. Mohanty) *Excavations at Sisupalgarh*. Her most recent book is *Cities: The First 6,000 Years*, which explores the growth of worldwide urbanism from an archaeological perspective.

Meghan E. Strong is an archaeologist and art historian who specializes in the cultures of ancient Egypt and the Near East. She is an adjunct assistant professor in the Department of Classics at Case Western Reserve University and a research associate at the Cleveland Museum of Natural History. Her research incorporates aspects of sensory archaeology, ritual performance, material cultures studies, and lychnology (the study of ancient lighting devices). Her recent book, *Sacred Flames*, explores the power of artificial lighting in ancient Egypt from the third to the first millennium BC.

Robert S. Weiner is a PhD candidate in anthropology at the University of Colorado Boulder. His dissertation research explores the history, use, and meaning of monumental roads associated with Chaco Canyon and its regional system in the ancient US Southwest. His MA thesis at Brown University, later published in *American Antiquity*, examined evidence for gambling in Chacoan society. More broadly, his research interests include religion, monumentality, cognition and mind, and cross-cultural comparison.